LIBRARY OF SECOND TEMPLE STUDIES

98

Formerly Journal for the Study of the Pseudepigrapha Supplement Series

Editor
Lester L. Grabbe

Editorial Board
Randall D. Chesnutt, Jan Willem van Henten, Judith M. Lieu,
Steven Mason, James R. Mueller, Loren T. Stuckenbruck,
James C. VanderKam

Founding Editor
James H. Charlesworth

THE USE AND FUNCTION OF SCRIPTURE IN 1 MACCABEES

Dongbin Choi

t&tclark
LONDON • NEW YORK • OXFORD • NEW DELHI • SYDNEY

T&T CLARK
Bloomsbury Publishing Plc
50 Bedford Square, London, WC1B 3DP, UK
1385 Broadway, New York, NY 10018, USA
29 Earlsfort Terrace, Dublin 2, Ireland

BLOOMSBURY, T&T CLARK and the T&T Clark logo
are trademarks of Bloomsbury Publishing Plc

First published in Great Britain 2021
This paperback edition published in 2022

Copyright © Dongbin Choi, 2021

Dongbin Choi has asserted his right under the Copyright, Designs and Patents Act, 1988, to be identified as Author of this work.

For legal purposes the Acknowledgements on p. xi constitute an extension of this copyright page.

All rights reserved. No part of this publication may be reproduced or transmitted in any form or by any means, electronic or mechanical, including photocopying, recording, or any information storage or retrieval system, without prior permission in writing from the publishers.

Bloomsbury Publishing Plc does not have any control over, or responsibility for, any third-party websites referred to or in this book. All internet addresses given in this book were correct at the time of going to press. The author and publisher regret any inconvenience caused if addresses have changed or sites have ceased to exist, but can accept no responsibility for any such changes.

A catalogue record for this book is available from the British Library.

Library of Congress Cataloging-in-Publication Data
Names: Choi, Dongbin, author.
Title: The use and function of Scripture in 1 Maccabees / by Dongbin Choi.
Description: New York : T&T Clark, 2020. | Series: Library of Second Temple Studies 98 | Includes bibliographical references and index. | Summary: "Dongbin Choi argues that the book of 1 Maccabees is written with a linguistic technique that utilizes earlier Jewish texts in various ways in order to promote the religiopolitical agendas of its author. Choi offers a philological and thematic analyses on this scriptural language, and engages in the dialogue between the traditional view that tends to simply treat 1 Maccabees as a religious writing, and the radical view that considers it as a political propaganda"-- Provided by publisher.
Identifiers: LCCN 2020026895 (print) | LCCN 2020026896 (ebook) |
ISBN 9780567695420 (hardback) | ISBN 9780567696458 (paperback) |
ISBN 9780567695437 (pdf) | ISBN 9780567695451 (epub)
Subjects: LCSH: Bible. Maccabees, 1st--Criticism, interpretation, etc. |
Jews--History--586 B.C.-70 A.D.
Classification: LCC BS1825.52 .C46 2020 (print) | LCC BS1825.52 (ebook) |
DDC 229/.7306--dc23
LC record available at https://lccn.loc.gov/2020026895
LC ebook record available at https://lccn.loc.gov/2020026896

ISBN:	HB:	978-0-5676-9542-0
	PB:	978-0-5676-9645-8
	ePDF:	978-0-5676-9543-7
	ePUB:	978-0-5676-9545-1

Series: Library of Second Temple Studies, ISSN 2515-866X, volume 98

To find out more about our authors and books visit www.bloomsbury.com
and sign up for our newsletters.

To my dad
For his dedication
To his family and his work

Contents

Acknowledgements	xi
Abbreviations	xiii

Chapter 1
INTRODUCTION — 1
  1.1. General introduction — 1
  1.2. Literature review — 2
    1.2.1. Functionality of Scripture in 1 Maccabees — 2
    1.2.2. Scripture, fulfilment of Israel's hope,
    and the role of the Hasmoneans — 7
    1.2.3. Jewish perception of the past — 15
    1.2.4. Summary — 20
  1.3. Aims and outline of the present study — 21
  1.4. Methodology — 21

Chapter 2
THE CONTRIBUTION OF THE LITERARY, SOCIAL
AND CULTURAL MILIEUS ON THE APPROPRIATION
OF SCRIPTURE IN 1 MACCABEES — 27
  2.1. Textual issues — 27
    2.1.1. Textual variance — 27
    2.1.2. The lost Hebrew original text — 32
    2.1.3. On Greek Scripture — 37
    2.1.4. The Translator's vocabulary — 39
    2.1.5. Summary — 44
  2.2. Authorship and dating of 1 Maccabees — 44
    2.2.1. Authorship — 44
    2.2.2. Dating of 1 Maccabees — 46
  2.3. Availability of Scripture at the time of 1 Maccabees — 55
    2.3.1. 'The Law and the Prophets (and other writings)' — 58
    2.3.2. Conclusion — 64

2.4. Hellenization and the influence of Scripture in 1 Maccabees	64
2.4.1. A conceptual issue	64
2.4.2. Internal features relating to Hellenism	68
2.4.3. External features relating to Hellenism	72
2.4.4. Summary	75
2.5. Jewish perception of the past	76
2.5.1. Biblical and early Jewish literature	76
2.5.2. 1 Maccabees	92
2.5.3. Conclusion	94

Chapter 3
THE USE OF SCRIPTURE IN 1 MACCABEES: PHILOLOGICAL PARALLELS   96

3.1. Introduction	96
3.2. Analysis of Lange and Weigold's biblical references in 1 Maccabees	98
3.3. Results	145
3.3.1. Features of philological parallels	145
3.3.2. Classification of the parallels	146
3.3.3. Result: a revised list of philological parallels	149

Chapter 4
THE USE OF SCRIPTURE IN 1 MACCABEES: CONCEPTUAL PARALLELS   156

4.1. The Deuteronomic covenantal framework	156
4.1.1. Deuteronomy	157
4.1.2. 1 Maccabees	160
4.1.3. Summary	167
4.2. Biblical judges	167
4.2.1. Morphological association	168
4.2.2. Narrative development	172
4.2.3. The leadership of judges and the legitimacy of the Hasmonean leadership	176
4.2.4. Summary	179

Chapter 5
SCRIPTURE AND THE ROLE OF THE HASMONEANS:
A STUDY ON THE EULOGIES OF JUDAS AND SIMON   181

5.1. Judas' Eulogy	182
5.1.1. Restoration of Israel	183
5.1.2. Gathering of the dispersed Israel?	189
5.1.3. Judas as the Davidic messiah?	198
5.1.4. Summary	201

5.2. Simon's Eulogy	201
5.2.1. Restoration of Israel – covenantal blessing	202
5.2.2. The Hasmoneans' territorial expansion and the biblical territorial theme	215
5.2.3. Simon as the Davidic messiah?	220
5.2.4. Summary	224
5.2.5. Conclusion	225

Chapter 6
FINAL CONCLUSION — 226

Bibliography — 233
Index of References — 251
Index of Authors — 265

ACKNOWLEDGEMENTS

The book is a lightly revised version of my doctoral dissertation. As no man makes himself, certainly not me, the book is a fruit of countless supports, co-operations, encouragements, and criticism.

In addition to my dad to whom this book is dedicated, I thank my wife Jeehie, who not only supported me with patience and tolerance, but also managed to continue her own career in the tough financial world, and gave birth to our three adorable children – Ellie, Tony, and Katie. And she still remains as beautiful and graceful as when I first met her. She is my source of inspiration, fuel of joy, and meaning of life.

Special thanks go to Professor Roland Deines who supervised my doctoral research. His meticulous attention to detail and breadth of knowledge in early Judaism helped shape my thesis whenever they were needed most. I am indebted to all his guidance throughout my research.

I would also like to thank the department of Theology and Religious Studies at University of Nottingham, the faculty members and PhD students who gave helpful comments on my papers delivered at seminars.

Dr. Carly Crouch kindly supported me by offering opportunities to present my work in her Biblical Studies Seminar series and providing insightful comments. I am also grateful to the faculty members of Ben Gurion University (Israel) for their discussions during my visit in Israel in 2014, and especially to Professor Cana Werman for her warm hospitality. I would also like to thank Professor Daniel R. Schwartz (HUJI, Israel) for offering insightful conversations and kindly providing me then pre-published copy of his article on textual issues of 1 Maccabees. Special thanks go to Dr. Holger M. Zellentin and Professor Susan Docherty for giving me warm encouragement and helpful comments during the viva.

I am also grateful to Professor Lester L. Grabbe for accepting my work as an addition to the LSTS series. I have always considered his works to be insightful and thoughtful, and am delighted to have my work accepted by him. My friend Mr. Geoffrey R. Dale kindly offered proofreading the whole of the manuscript at short notice, and Dr. Duncan Burns, commissioned by Bloomsbury / T&T Clark took a great care in further editing and polishing the manuscript, and I am very grateful to them.

Abbreviations

AAA	Acta Academiae Aboensis
AASF	Annales Academiae scientiarum Fennicae
AB	Anchor Bible
ABD	*Anchor Bible Dictionary.* Edited by David Noel Freedman. 6 vols. New York: Doubleday, 1992
ABRL	Anchor Bible Reference Library
AJEC	Ancient Judaism and Early Christianity
AM	Anecdota Maredsolana
APOT	*The Apocrypha and Pseudepigrapha of the Old Testament in English: with Introductions and Critical and Explanatory Notes to the Several Books.* 2 vols. Oxford: Clarendon Press, 1913
ASORMon	American Schools of Oriental Research Monograph Series
BA	*Biblical Archaeologist*
BAIAS	*Bulletin of the Anglo-Israel Archeological Society*
BCOTWP	Baker Commentary on the Old Testament Wisdom and Psalms
BEATAJ	Beitrage zur Erforschung des Alten Testaments und des antiken Judentum
BIOSCS	*Bulletin of the International Organization for Septuagint and Cognate Studies*
BJS	Brown Judaic Studies
BZAW	Beihefte zur Zeitschrift fur die alttestamentliche Wissenschaft
CBC	Cambridge Bible Commentary
CBQ	*Catholic Biblical Quarterly*
CBR	*Currents in Biblical Research*
CBSC	The Cambridge Bible for Schools and Colleges
CEJL	Commentaries on Early Jewish Literature
CHJ	*Cambridge History of Judaism.* Edited by William D. Davies and Louis Finkelstein. 4 vols. Cambridge: Cambridge University Press, 1984–2006
CJA	Christianity and Judaism in Antiquity
CJOD	Contraversions: Jews and other Differences
COQG	Christian Origins and the Question of God
CRINT	Compendia Rerum Iudaicarum ad Novum Testamentum
CTM	*Concordia Theological Monthly*
DCLS	Deuterocanonical and Cognate Literature Studies
DJD	Discoveries in the Judaean Desert

DSD	*Dead Sea Discoveries*
EB	Echter Bibel
ECB	Dunn, James D. G., and J. W. Rogerson, eds. *Eerdmans Commentary on the Bible*. Grand Rapids: Eerdmans, 2003
EDDS	*Encyclopedia of the Dead Sea Scrolls*. Edited by Lawrence H. Schiffman and James C. VanderKam. 2 vols. New York: Oxford University Press, 2000
EJT	European Journal of Theology
ESHM	European Seminar in Historical Methodology
FB	Forschung zur Bibel
FOTL	Forms of the Old Testament Literature
HCS	Hellenistic Culture and Society
HO	Handbuch der Orientalistik
HTR	*Harvard Theological Review*
HUCA	*Hebrew Union College Annual*
ICC	International Critical Commentary
IEJ	*Israel Exploration Journal*
INJ	*Israel Numismatic Journal*
ISFCJ	International Studies in Formative Christianity and Judaism
JAJSup	*Journal of Ancient Judaism Supplements*
JAL	Jewish Apocryphal Literature Series
JAOS	*Journal of the American Oriental Society*
JBL	*Journal of Biblical Literature*
JCPS	Jewish and Christian Perspectives Series
JCTCRS	Jewish and Christian Texts in Contexts and Related Studies
JJS	Journal of Jewish Studies
JQR	Jewish Quarterly Review
JSJ	*Journal for the Study of Judaism*
JSJSup	Journal for the Study of Judaism Supplement Series
JSOTSup	Journal for the Study of the Old Testament Supplement Series
JSP	*Journal for the Study of the Pseudepigrapha*
JSPSup	Journal for the Study of the Pseudepigrapha Supplement Series
JTS	*Journal of Theological Studies*
KEHAAT	Kurzgefasstes exegetisches Handbuch zu den Apokryphen des Alten Testaments
LBS	The Library of Biblical Studies
LCL	Loeb Classical Library
LHBOTS	The Library of Hebrew Bible/Old Testament Studies
LNTS	The Library of New Testament Studies
LSTS	The Library of Second Temple Studies
NCB	New Century Bible Commentary
NEA	*Near Eastern Archaeology*
NIB	*The New Interpreter's Bible*. Edited by Leander E. Keck. 12 vols. Nashville: Abingdon, 1994–2004
NICOT	New International Commentary on the Old Testament

NOAB	Coogan, Michael David, Marc Zvi Brettler, Carol A. Newsom, and Pheme Perkins, eds. *The New Oxford Annotated Bible: New Revised Standard Version: with the Apocrypha: An Ecumenical Study Bible.* Oxford: Oxford University Press, 2010
OBC	Barton, John, and John Muddiman, eds. *The Oxford Bible Commentary.* Oxford: Oxford University Press, 2001
OTL	Old Testament Library
OTM	Old Testament Message
OTP	*Old Testament Pseudepigrapha.* Edited by James H. Charlesworth. 2 vols. New York: Doubleday, 1983, 1985
OTS	Old Testament Studies
PS	*Patrologia Syriaca.* Rev. ed. Ignatio Ortiz de Urbina. Rome: Pontifical Biblical Institute, 1965
RB	*Revue biblique*
RevQ	*Revue de Qumran*
RSR	*Recherches de science religieuse*
SBLEJL	Society of Biblical Literature Early Judaism and its literature
SBLSymS	Society of Biblical Literature Symposium Series
SBLTT	Society of Biblical Literature Texts and Translations
SBT	Studies in Biblical Theology
SFSHJ	South Florida Studies in the History of Judaism
SHR	Studies in the History of Religions (supplements to *Numen*)
SJOT	*Scandinavian Journal of the Old Testament*
SNTSMS	Society for New Testament Studies Monograph Series
SPB	Studia post-Biblica
SSEJC	Studies in Scripture in Early Judaism and Christianity
STDJ	Studies on the Texts of the Desert of Judah
TCAAS	Transactions: The Connecticut Academy of Arts and Sciences
TDNT	Kittel, Gerhard, G. W. Bromiley, and Gerhard Friedrich, eds. *Theological Dictionary of the New Testament.* 10 vols. Grand Rapids: Eerdmans, 1964–76
TL	*Theologische Literaturzeitung*
TOTC	Tyndale Old Testament Commentaries
TSAJ	Texte und Studien zum antiken Judentum
VT	*Vetus Testamentum*
VTGASLG	Vetus Testamentum graecum / auctoritate Societatis Litterarum Gottingensis
VTSup	Supplements to Vetus Testamentum
WBC	Word Biblical Commentary
WSAMA	Walberberger Studien der Albertus-Magnus-Akademie
WUNT	Wissenschaftliche Untersuchungen zum Neuen Testament

Chapter 1

INTRODUCTION

1.1. *General introduction*

The book of 1 Maccabees poses some difficulties for Jews and Christians alike due to its place among the so-called Apocrypha (in Protestant terminology) or Deuterocanonical writings (in Catholic and Eastern Orthodox terms) within the Christian Bible(s), and its absence in the Jewish canon despite its obvious 'biblical' character. As scriptural evocation is a prominent feature of the ways in which 1 Maccabees recounts the Hasmonean revolution, the question is raised whether this is an example of a propagandistic subterfuge of a dynasty of usurpers or an honest expression of a religious conviction. The author of 1 Maccabees used these earlier biblical texts in a variety of ways, corresponding to many biblical books. But what is the function of this scriptural language within the author's compositional purpose? Does the scriptural evocation merely serve stylistic ends, acting as nothing more than a formidable, authority-borrowing language? Or, does it simply serve the Hasmonean claim to power, using biblical pretexts to camouflage their worldly ambitions? Or, to the contrary, does it describe the Maccabean revolt and triumph as honestly felt fulfilment of Israel's future hopes expressed in Scripture? And if so, which specific hopes were fulfilled?

Politics and religion cannot be separated from each other, and any attempt at an over-emphasis on one of the two raises a question. It has often been suggested that the author of 1 Maccabees claims that the Davidic messianic hopes have been fulfilled by the Hasmonean family, which raises the question about any further hopes for the future. Other scholars ignore the potential significance of the meaning of the scriptural language largely on the grounds that the book serves an exclusively dynastic purpose which lacks any interest in religious values. In addition, studies on the compositional purpose of the book saw an emerging strand of scholarship putting forward legitimation of the Hasmonean *kingship* in 1 Maccabees as its main aim, leading, however, to disagreements among the experts. Politics, in this scholarly trend, is seen as (re-)shaping religion.

The present study seeks to re-assess these controversies and disagreements with regard to the interpretation of 1 Maccabees by offering a close analysis on the ways in which Scripture is used in the book and its function within the author's compositional purpose. The present study will argue that, through dynamic ways of using Scripture, the author demonstrates the Hasmonean triumph as a proof of continuous divine providence for the covenant people of YHWH. The Hasmonean family's role resembles that of biblical heroes, most prominently biblical judges, who delivered salvation and restoration to Israel. In this way, Israel's future hopes were seen as fulfilled by the Hasmonean family, but not to the extent of eschatological fulfilment. The restoration of the Judean nation under the Hasmonean leadership was seen as part of the on-going Jewish history which extended from scriptural history, and was believed to be guided by the divinely promised future. This also bears implications on ancient Jewish perception of the past as evident in biblical and post-biblical literature, which entails questions of the ways in which the Jews either preserved, manipulated or even ignored their past in writing their history. In a larger context, our study will contribute to on-going studies on the use of Scripture in early Judaism and early Christianity.

1.2. *Literature review*

As a preliminary to this study, a literature review will provide the necessary background to understand the current debates about the use and function of Scripture in 1 Maccabees. Particular attention will be paid to (1) scholars' evaluation of the nature of the biblically styled language in 1 Maccabees, (2) the function of that language within the authorial intention with special regard to the role of the Hasmoneans, (3) and a recent tendency of Hasmonean studies in which use of Scripture has an important bearing on the shaping of Jewish perceptions of the past in antiquity.

1.2.1. *Functionality of Scripture in 1 Maccabees*
Commentaries and introductory and individual thematic studies on 1 Maccabees unanimously observe that its style resembles biblical literature. Furthermore, a majority of scholars claim that individual phrases,

1. Introduction

terms and themes from biblical books were consciously alluded to, either as fulfilment of hopes expressed in Scripture, or as a re-enactment of past events in Israel's history preserved in Scripture.¹ As Robert Doran aptly states:

---

1. For instance, Carl L. W. Grimm already asserted that on almost every page (of 1 Maccabees) one can find speeches and phrases taken from the Hebrew Bible, a phenomenon reflecting the author's conscious and constant use of biblical sources. See Grimm, *Das erste Buch der Maccabäer*, KEHAAT 3 (Leipzig: Hirzel, 1853), xv. An extensive treatment of biblical materials in 1 Maccabees can be found in F.-M. Abel, *Les livres des Maccabées*, EB 38 (Paris: Librairie Lecoffre, 1949). Günter O. Neuhaus carried out a detailed study on the poetic passages in 1 Maccabees, in which he identifies more than one hundred allusions and references to biblical literature. However, he does not discuss whether these references should all be considered as conscious allusions to Scripture rather than simply idiomatic or stylistic without an intention of allusion. See Neuhaus, *Studien zu den poetischen Stücken im 1. Makkabäerbuch*, FB 12 (Würzburg: Echter, 1974). See also John R. Bartlett, *1 Maccabees*, GAP (Sheffield: Sheffield Academic, 1998), especially 30-3 for his comment on use of Scripture. Bartlett's several short commentaries contain numerous biblical cross-references: see Bartlett, *The First and Second Books of the Maccabees*, CBC (Cambridge: Cambridge University Press, 1973); '1 Maccabees', *ECB* 807-30; '1 Maccabees', *NOAB* 1555-98. Uriel Rappaport evaluates the linguistic character of the book in the light of biblical historiography, commenting that 1 Maccabees is 'composed in a style and with a vocabulary similar to biblical historiography', in which several biblical elements, such as 'poetic passages', 'a testament', 'documents' and 'speeches', are incorporated, together with the adoption of biblical names, rightly pointing out that the author's deliberate employment of certain biblical names such as Moab, Ammon, Philistines, Canaan, and his imitation of the phraseology of Joshua's territorial conquest serve 'not only as literary conventions' but also as 'an ideology that compares or assimilates Judas's wars to those of yore' and 'the citation of biblical exempla and precedents'. Uriel Rappaport, 'The First Book of Maccabees', *OBC* 711-34 (712). In contradiction to most commentaries, some introductory studies either do not pay attention to the biblically styled language of the book or only briefly acknowledge it without discussing its precise nature and potentially complex issues related to it. See, for instance, George W. E. Nickelsburg, *Jewish Literature between the Bible and the Mishnah: A Historical and Literary Introduction* (Philadelphia: Fortress, 1987), 114-17. Elsewhere, Nickelsburg claims that the use of biblical images in the eulogy of Simon (1 Macc. 14.4-15) is intended to portray the Hasmoneans as messianic, fulfilling biblical prophecies concerning Israel's future restoration, see Nickelsburg, 'Eschatology (Early Jewish)', *ABD* 579-94 (589). Likewise, Daniel J. Harrington, *The Maccabean Revolt: Anatomy of a Biblical Revolution*, OTS 1 (Wilmington, DE: Glazier, 1988), 57-86; revised Emil Schürer, *HJPAJC* 3:180-5 (181).

[1 Maccabees] is a narrative interspersed with traditional poetic passages and whose syntax imitates that of narrative sections of the Hebrew Scriptures. It is, then, a narrative that consciously aims at incorporating its story into the tradition of the Hebrew Scriptures... 1 Maccabees perceives the events it tells as another reenactment of the events of the Hebrew Scriptures... This view of present-day events reflecting the Scriptures can be compared to the way the Qumran covenanters and the authors of the Gospels interpret the psalms and the prophets as talking about events in their own history. The author has not written a simple presentation of facts, but has woven a highly textured narrative.[2]

However, a few others are either ambivalent about such an intention or even deny any allusions, instead considering the language as merely stylistic. W. Fairweather and J. Sutherland Black state:

The style of the book is that of simple prose narrative, and is modelled on that of the historical books of the O.T. For the most part it is even as unadorned as that of Ezra and Nehemiah. Yet now and then, as in these canonical works, the language rises into impassioned rhetoric (i. 25–28, 38–40, ix. 10, xiv. 8–15) and even into poetry (ii. 7–13, 49–68, iii. 3–9, 18–22, 50–53, iv. 8–11, vi. 10–13).[3]

---

2. Robert Doran, 'The First Book of Maccabees', *NIB* 4:3–178 (51 for the quotation).

3. W. Fairweather and J. Sutherland Black, *The First Book of Maccabees*, CBSC (Cambridge: Cambridge University Press, 1908), 36–7. They observe the sharp difference between 1 Maccabees and Ezra-Nehemiah, such as the quasi-absence of the theocratic view so pervading in biblical historiography, as they claim: 'There is certainly a deep undercurrent of theocratic feeling in the book, but much more reserve in the direct expression of it than we are accustomed to on the part of canonical writers'. A similar viewpoint was already raised by Carl F. Keil, *Die Bücher der Makkabäer*, BCATSup (Leipzig: Döffling & Franke, 1875), 17. In observing the tone and character of 1 Maccabees' historical account in resemblance to Ezra, Nehemiah and Esther, Keil rather hastily moves on to critically evaluate the historical value of the book, without, in my judgement, necessary elaboration on such resemblance to biblical materials. See also Solomon Zeitlin, *The First Book of Maccabees*, trans. Sidney Tedesche, JAL (New York: Harper & Brothers, 1950). Zeitlin discusses the original language of 1 Maccabees and its linguistic affinity with other Jewish literature (33–4 and 50–4, respectively), but hardly makes any mention of the biblical language, although he is clearly aware of it (34), and includes some examples of biblical phraseology and transliteration of Hebrew expressions in Greek in the running commentary. Instead, Zeitlin claims that the Greek translator of 1 Maccabees was 'slavishly' influenced by the Septuagint vocabulary (34).

Their brief, reserved remark on the use of biblical materials in 1 Maccabees is notable when their running commentary already contains numerous biblical references. One wonders how Fairweather and Black regard, for instance, the language of impassioned rhetoric and of poetry: are those rhetorical and poetic expressions merely imitation of style, or are they intended to render a more significant meaning in the text? W. O. E. Oesterley even explicitly states:

> While, as might be expected, there are frequent reminiscences of the language of the Old Testament, the author in no wise imitates this, his writing being marked throughout by his own individual style.[4]

As a result, where paralleled phrases in 1 Maccabees can be found in biblical literature, Oesterley tends to limit them as examples of Hebraism in the book.[5] However, whilst scrutiny is justified, denial is untenable. On the one hand, an individual phrase that can be found in both 1 Maccabees and a biblical material may be an idiomatic expression without an allusion to any specific text, for example, 1 Macc. 5.54 ('until they returned in peace', ἕως τοῦ ἐπιστρέψαι ἐν εἰρήνῃ) in parallel with 1 Kgs 22.27 and 2 Chron. 18.26 ('until I return in peace', עד באי בשלום, ἕως τοῦ ἐπιστρέψαι με ἐν εἰρήνῃ). On the other hand, several dozens of cases show that there are both morphological and thematic resemblances between 1 Maccabees and biblical materials, which clearly indicate something more than reminiscence. One example is 1 Macc. 1.15 ('[the pro-Seleucid Jerusalem authorities] sold themselves to do evil', ἐπράθησαν τοῦ ποιῆσαι τὸ πονηρόν') which is in parallel with 2 Kgs 17.17 (ויתמכרו לעשות הרע), both of which address national catastrophes caused by the defilement of the covenant with God.[6] Moreover, we shall see in due course several long

---

4. W. O. E. Oesterley, 'First Book of Maccabees', *APOT* 1:59–124 (60 for the quotation).

5. One example is the phrase 'they sold themselves to evil' (1 Macc. 1.15), with which the author alluded to Elijah's discourse with Ahab (1 Kgs 21.20) according to many scholars such as Grimm, Keil, and Fairweather and Black to name but a few. Oesterley regards the phrase as an example of Hebraism as in 1 Kgs 21.20 (Oesterley, 'Maccabees', 1:68). This tendency can be observed throughout his commentary with the exception of only a few cases where there are strong reasons to believe the author's conscious use of biblical materials (e.g. 7.16-17, which contains a quotation formula, κατὰ τὸν λόγον, ὃν ἔγραψεν αὐτόν, is commented by Oesterley as 'a shortened form' of Ps. 76.2-3 [1:91]).

6. Discussion on these and other cases is found in §2.1, as well as Chapter 3.

sentences which are identical to specific biblical materials, suggesting intended implicit quotations.⁷

Amongst the majority of scholars who attest to biblical allusion in 1 Maccabees, several scholars further observe the prevalent use of the historical books of the Hebrew Bible and the somewhat ambiguous, implicit attitude of the author toward using prophetic books.⁸ John R. Bartlett points out the ambivalent nature of using prophetic materials in which there is both the conspicuity about echoing biblical prophecies and the lack of explicit use of them, such as mentions of prophets or quotation formulae.⁹ Bartlett suggests:

   7. Thus, the famous verses in Simon's eulogy (14.8, 9, 12), which most commenetators and scholars uniformly point to biblical prophecies such as Zech. 8.12, 4-5 and Mic. 4.4 respectively, and which will be discussed extensively in the present study, are given with these and other biblical references, but without qualification. For a full discussion of this topic see Chapters 3–5.
   8. Thomas Fischer notes that 1 Maccabees contains 'free and literal quotations of, as well as "plays" on, all three parts of the later canon', rightly emphasizing the prominence of the Former and Latter Prophets in comparison to the Torah. See Fischer, 'Maccabees, Books of: First and Second Maccabees', *ABD* 4:438–50. Compare Robert H. Pfeiffer, *History of New Testament Times: With an Introduction to the Apocrypha* (London: Adam & Charles Black, 1949), 461–98. Pfeiffer claims that the author of 1 Maccabees chose Chronicles over Kings as scriptural sources, and intended to write 'a sequel to the Chronicler's work' (486–7). This claim, however, is not sufficiently supported and remains unwarranted. Pfeiffer points out that Joarib, from whose line Mattathias comes (1 Macc. 2.1; 14.29), is the first in the list of priestly lineage in 1 Chron. 24.7-18, but otherwise there is no decisive evidence for the preference of Chronicles over Kings in 1 Maccabees. See Chapter 3 for the list of philological parallels between 1 Maccabees and biblical literature in which materials from Kings appear numerously, if not more than those from Chronicles. Also, J. C. Dancy observes that the book shows 'the usurpation by the Law of many of the functions of Prophecy', but is unclear as to the implication of this preference of the law to prophecy when considering references and allusions to these biblical materials; see Dancy, *1 Maccabees* (Oxford: Blackwell, 1954), 1–3 (2).
   9. Bartlett, *1 Maccabees*, 31–2. Bartlett observes that the return of Jews to Judea under Judas and Simon (5.23, 45, 53-54), which may well have echoed biblical prophecies concerning Israel's return and re-gathering from exile, lacks any allusions to biblical materials. He thus concludes: '[the author] does not give it [prophecy] a major role in either past, present, or future, yet he is undoubtedly aware of it' (32). As for the use of historical books, Bartlett suggests that the author may even intend to 'write a continuation of the Chronicler's history into his own time'. See his commentary (*Books of the Maccabees*) for cross-references to biblical materials throughout 1 Maccabees. The present study will also provide the listing of cross-references to biblical literature in 1 Maccabees in due course.

More interestingly, the author, for all his support of the Maccabees as deliverers of Israel, does not suggest that they fulfil any messianic prophecies or owe anything to the house of David.[10]

Bartlett's solution to that particularly implicit use of biblical prophetic materials is thus a non-messianic claim about the role of the Hasmoneans in 1 Maccabees. We will return to the role of the Hasmoneans in more detail shortly.

In short, concerning the functionality of Scripture in 1 Maccabees, a majority of scholars affirm that the author consciously makes allusions to scriptural materials, although the ambivalence about scriptural allusion expressed by a minority should not be easily dismissed. The question is: *why is the author making such constant allusions to Scripture? What are his aims?*

1.2.2. Scripture, fulfilment of Israel's hope, and the role of the Hasmoneans
The question as to the authorial intention of using scriptural allusions directly encourages consideration of topics such as the authorship and purpose of 1 Maccabees, within which use of Scripture functions. As a starting point, most scholars have affirmed that the book was written with the intention to support the Hasmonean claim of power over the Jewish nation, and that the author either belonged to the Hasmonean court or was at least a pro-Hasmonean Jew.[11] Exceptionally, Robert H. Pfeiffer and Uriel Rappaport viewed the role of the Hasmonean family more neutrally and attributed due weight on other figures such as the Jewish people who participated in the drama of freedom fighting by supporting and cooperating with the family.[12] Doran even suggested the composition as a

---

10. Bartlett, *1 Maccabees*, 30.
11. Most scholars reviewed in this chapter generally affirm the view, and exceptions are discussed below.
12. See, for instance, Pfeiffer (*History*, 493), who puts an emphasis on 'people' as an important character in the book besides the Maccabees. In 3.43-44; 4.59; 5.16; 7.48-49; and 14.28, 'people' take a major role in crucial decision-making. Pfeiffer's discussion on 'people' is rather too brief without showing evidence of accounting political complexity of the Judeans of that time. Nonetheless, his reading of 1 Maccabees offers a case that one ought to be cautious about magnifying the description of the Maccabees in the narrative. One may add that Judas' campaign against Nicanor and his army (7.26-50), during which Jews who came out from nearby cities, played an active role in assisting Judas to chase and destroy Nicanor and his army (7.45-48). A somewhat more emphatic claim about the role of the 'people' in the course of this Judean restoration was made by Uriel Rappaport, 'The

polemic against the Hasmonean dynasty.[13] The majority view in favour of the book's pro-Hasmonean origin, however, better explains some of the quintessentially pro-Hasmonean elements in the book that strongly suggest the author's bias toward the Hasmonean family. Examples include: the author's comment describing the Hasmonean family as 'the seed of those men to whom was given salvation to Israel by their hand';[14] glorification of the Hasmonean heroism as a dominant theme;[15] and as observed by Jan Willem van Henten, the deliberate depictions of a father–son relationship of the Hasmonean family resonating with a royal lineage.[16] Moreover, the legitimacy of the Hasmonean high priesthood is quite plainly alluded to through various elements in the narrative.[17] These examples, to name but a few, indicate a biased view of the author toward the Hasmonean family.

It follows that the majority of scholars generally attest to the salvific role of the Hasmoneans. The question, however, is about the precise nature of that salvific role and its implications on the purpose of 1 Maccabees. From the outset, scholars traditionally attributed a general, non-messianic salvific role to the Hasmoneans, whilst a growing number of scholars attest to the Davidic-messianic role. Both of these views find their support from the scriptural language of the book.

Traditionally, scholars claimed that 1 Maccabees represents a conservative Jewish view, attributing a non-messianic, salvific role to the Hasmoneans,[18] as is aptly restated by Menahem Stern:

Birth of the Hasmonean State', in *Recent Archaeology in the Land of Israel*, ed. Hershel Shanks and Benjamin Mazar, trans. Aryeh Finklestein (Washington, DC: Biblical Archaeological Society; Jerusalem: Israel Exploration Society, 1984), 173–7. Rappaport summarizes the birth of the Hasmonean state in this way: 'the persecution of Antiochus and the pressure to Hellenize may have precipitated the creation of the Hasmonean state, but they did not create it. The true progenitors of the new state were the Jewish nation and its Torah' (176).

13. Doran, 'Maccabees', 4:22.
14. 1 Macc. 5.62.
15. 1 Macc. 13.3; 14.26; 16.2.
16. E.g., J. W. van Henten, 'Royal Ideology: 1 and 2 Maccabees and Egypt', in *Jewish Perspectives on Hellenistic Rulers*, ed. Tessa Rajak, Sarah Pearce, James Aitken, and Jennifer Dines, HCS L (Berkeley, CA: University of California Press, 2007), 265–82 (especially 270–1).
17. E.g. Mattathias calls Phinehas 'our father' who 'received a covenant of everlasting priesthood' (2.54); Alcimus' high priesthood, despite his Aaronite lineage, is proven to be wrong (7.5-50); the Hasmonean high priesthood, through Jonathan, Simon and John Hyrcanus I, is highlighted as legitimate.
18. E.g. Bartlett, *1 Maccabees*, 30–2, and the comment made above; Doran, 'Maccabees', 4:21. Compare Michael Tilly, *1 Makkabäer*, HTKAT (Freiburg im

> [D]espite the eschatological ferment and the yearning for the end of days, no messianic movement arose in Judea at the time of the persecution and no seers or prophets emerged to proclaim the kingdom of the House of David. When the Hasmoneans came to the fore in launching the Jewish rebellion they performed their deeds as a priestly family profoundly loyal to the Jewish religion. Its adherents regarded it as a family to whom the deliverance of Israel had been entrusted at this time of confusion and terror. However, many also felt that the rule of the Hasmoneans would continue only until the reappearance of a prophet.[19]

For Stern, the belief about Israel's ultimate future was common amongst Jews in the Hasmonean era, and expectations of messianic movements, emergences of prophets and restitution of the Davidic kingdom. Nevertheless, the Maccabean revolt was led by 'a priestly family profoundly loyal to the Jewish religion', indicating that the early Hasmonean leaders, for Stern, were primarily interested in religious values and were conservative in preserving older traditions. In this way, Stern made a distinction between the Hasmonean revolt and later messianic movements, claiming that the Hasmoneans 'did not go out to battle either to give dominion to new ideals or to establish the Kingdom of God on earth'.[20] Some scholars additionally either hint or claim the association of the Hasmoneans' role

---

Breisgau: Herder, 2015). Tilly claims that the scriptural language of 1 Maccabees attests to 'konventioneller deuteronomistischer Geschichtstheologie', and specifically, that the particularly implicit style of using biblical prophetic materials is an indication of *Heilsgeschichte* in which the danger of God's people is overcome by the heroic deeds of the Hasmoneans and the support of the God of Israel, defeating the enemy and delivering peace in the land. In this way, Tilly's view of *Heilsgeschichte* echoes the claims of Bartlett and Doran as well as other commentators, and broadly sits within the traditional view on the salvific role of the Hasmoneans. On the other hand, Tilly (48) sets the date of the composition between the death of John Hyrcanus (104 BCE) and the Roman subjugation of Judea under Pompey (64 BCE), which implies a monarchical form of the Hasmonean rulership and the inevitability of monarchical legitimation as part of the pro-Hasmonean author's agendas. And yet, he lacks necessary discussion on the Judean socio-political sensitivity arising from the Hasmonean monarchical institution, let alone the fact that this dating is of a minority view amongst scholars of 1 Maccabees. (Tilly's *terminus ad quem* is based on the author's annalic statement about Hyrcanus I in 1 Macc. 16.23-24, but this statement does not necessitate the end of Hyrcanus' regnal years; see §2.2.2 for a more detailed discussion on dating.)

19. Menahem Stern, 'The Hasmonean Revolt and Its Place in the History of Jewish Society and Religion', in *Jewish Society through the Ages*, ed. H. H. Ben-Sasson and S. Ettinger (London: Vallentine & Mitchell, 1971), 91–106 (99).

20. Stern, 'Hasmonean Revolt', 101.

with biblical judges in this regard.[21] Other scholars have heeded internal details which shed light on the Jewish sensitivity toward kingship in the time when the Davidic throne was absent in Judea.[22]

A notable exception away from this traditional view is John J. Collins who claims that '[t]he Maccabees are repeatedly viewed in the light of Old Testament models and even take on the messianic dimensions',[23] referring here to non-Davidic, salvific figures for the Jewish nation, such as Moses, Joshua, and so forth. Collins' definition of 'messiah' in the Second Temple Jewish context is pluralistic here,[24] but he nevertheless differentiates

---

21. Thus, Doran ('Maccabees', 4:21) identifies three areas of the use of Judges in 1 Maccabees: the attribution of the title 'judge' to Jonathan (9.72) as well as the frequent use of the term 'foreigners' (ἀλλόφυλοι), the resemblance of the narrative structure of Judges in which the crises of Israel are resolved by the acts of judges, and the resemblance of the ideology concerning ethnic-cleansing during the conquest of gentile cities. See also Rappaport, 'Maccabees', 717; 'The Use of the Bible in 1 Maccabees', in *Biblical Perspectives: Early Use & Interpretation of the Bible in Light of the Dead Sea Scrolls. Proceedings of the First International Symposium of the Orion Center, 12–14 May 1996*, ed. M. E. Stone and E. G. Chazon (Leiden: Brill, 1998), 175–9; J. W. van Henten, 'The Hasmonean Period', in *Redemption and Resistance*, ed. Marcus Bockmuehl and James Carleton Paget (London: T&T Clark, 2007), 15–28 (especially 21). For a more detailed comparison between biblical Judges and the Hasmoneans, see Roland Deines, 'Did Matthew Know He was Writing Scripture? Part 2', *EJT* 23 (2014): 3–12 (especially 6).

22. Both Gregg G. Gardner and Joseph Sievers observe that the honorary decree of Simon (1 Macc. 14.25-47), whilst resembling foreign decrees in several ways, conspicuously omits crucial elements relating to kingship, such as the omissions of the pronoun 'saviour' (σωτήρ) and bestowing a diadem upon the honours of the addressee. See Gregg G. Gardner, 'Jewish Leadership and Hellenistic Civic Benefaction in the Second Century B.C.E.', *JBL* 126 (2007): 327–43 (especially 328, 336); Joseph Sievers, *The Hasmoneans and Their Supporters: From Mattathias to the Death of John Hyrcanus I*, SFSHJ 6 (Atlanta, GA: Scholars Press, 1990), 122–4, 126–7. See also, Daniel R. Schwartz, 'On Pharisaic Opposition to the Hasmonean Monarchy', in *Studies in the Jewish Background of Christianity*, WUNT 60 (Tübingen: Mohr Siebeck, 1992), 44–56 (especially 45). To these scholars, the phrase 'Simon should be high priest and ruler of Judea…*until a trustworthy prophet comes*' (1 Macc. 14.41) means a *limited* perpetuity of the Hasmonean dynasty (Gardner, 'Benefaction', 337; Sievers, *Supporters*, 127).

23. John J. Collins, *Daniel, First Maccabees, Second Maccabees: With an Excursus on the Apocalyptic Genre*, OTM 15, 2nd pr. (Wilmington, DE: Glazier, 1989), 147–256 (151 for the quotation).

24. As for the term 'messiah', Collins elsewhere argues that during the Second Temple period there were various figures such as angels, priests and others who were considered as messianic, and these are distinguished from the Davidic heir: John J.

non-Davidic figures and Davidic heirs. Thus, he claims that the reticence about future restitution of the Davidic kingdom in 1 Maccabees does not necessitate a rejection of it; the Hasmoneans could temporarily rule the nation, while the (Davidic) throne was absent.[25]

In contrast to the traditional view, an increasing number of scholars in the last few decades have associated the role of the Hasmoneans with kingship,[26] and the purpose of 1 Maccabees with a Hasmonean kingship propaganda. Diego Arenhoevel had already published a monograph in 1967 in which he proposed that the Hasmoneans in 1 Maccabees are portrayed as Davidic messianic figures who fulfill the messianic promises for Israel's future restoration.[27] Arenhoevel is aware that this view differs

---

Collins, 'Messianism in the Maccabean Period', in *Judaisms and Their Messiahs at the Turn of the Christian Era*, ed. Jacob Neusner et al. (Cambridge: Cambridge University Press, 1987), 97–109. He claims: 'It is quite possible that the author of 1 Maccabees affirmed the traditional hope of the restoration of the Davidic line, but assigned it to the eschatological future' (Collins, 'Messianism', 104). The edited volume, *Judaisms and Their Messiahs*, directly discusses the issue pertaining to the definition of messiah in the Second Temple period.

25. Collins, 'Messianism', 100, 104, 106. Collins rightly notes that the solemn assertion of the Davidic covenant (1 Macc. 2.57) should indicate its permanent validity.

26. This tendency may well be either part of, or in parallel with, the long-standing scholarly dispute over the Jewish belief about Davidic kingship in the Second Temple period, of which the following literature is notable. For a minimalist view on the Jews' acceptance of the hope of Davidic messiah, see W. V. Hague, 'Eschatology of the Apocryphal Scriptures, I, The Messianic Hope', *JTS* 12 (1911): 57–98 (64); Morton Smith, 'What Is Implied by the Variety of Messianic Figures?', in *Studies in the Cult of Yahweh: Vol. 1, Historical Method, Ancient Israel, Ancient Judaism*, ed. Shaye J. D. Cohen (Leiden: Brill, 1996), 161–7; Marinus de Jonge, 'Messiah', *ABD* 4:777–88 (781–6); Kenneth E. Pomykala, *The Davidic Dynasty Tradition in Early Judaism: Its History and Significance for Messianism*, SBLEJL 7 (Atlanta, GA: SBL, 1995), especially 265–71. For a maximalist view, see William Horbury, *Jewish Messianism and the Cult of Christ* (London: SCM, 1998), 52–9; idem, *Messianism Among Jews and Christians* (London: T&T Clark, 2003), 38–50; Antti Laato, *A Star Is Rising: The Historical Development of the Old Testament Royal Ideology and the Rise of the Jewish Messianic Expectations*, ISFCJ (Atlanta, GA: Scholars Press, 1998). For a view somewhat 'in-between', which critically accepts the Jewish belief about Davidic messiah, see Collins, 'Messianism', 97–109; Andrew Chester, *Messiah and Exaltation*, WUNT 207 (Tübingen: Mohr Siebeck, 2007); 205–30; John J. Collins, *Future Hope and Present Reality*. Vol. 1, *Eschatology and Transformation in the Hebrew Bible*, WUNT 293 (Tübingen: Mohr Siebeck, 2012), 237–63.

27. Diego Arenhoevel, *Die Theokratie nach dem 1. und 2. Makkabäerbuch*, WSAMA 3 (Mainz: Matthias-Grünewald, 1967), especially 58–69. In my survey, his

from that of the majority of preceding scholars, who presumed the messianic expectation of the era, and yet reserved such a claim due to the fact that the Hasmoneans are not of Davidic lineage.[28] Nevertheless, Arenhoevel poses the apparent impression from 1 Maccabees that the hope for Israel's future restoration was satisfied under Simon's rule,[29] and sketches the overall narrative development of the book starting from tribulation and finally reaching salvation under Simon,[30] although his argument is rather briefly supported.[31]

---

treatment of 1 Maccabees as a portrayal of the Hasmoneans as a legitimate replacement of the Davidic dynasty, as well as messianic figures, is viewed as a pioneering thesis. This view is put forward and further elaborated upon in the works of Jonathan A. Goldstein, and echoes are also found in the works of Neuhaus (*Makkabäerbuch*, 177, 227–40), Thomas Fischer (*Seleukiden und Makkabäer* [Bochum: Brockmeyer, 1980], 182), Tessa Rajak, and Arie van der Kooij, all of whom are essentially in agreement regarding the Davidic, messianic association of the Hasmoneans in 1 Maccabees. See below for details of their arguments and references.

28. Arenhoevel, *Theokratie*, 58.

29. Arenhoevel, *Theokratie*, 59.

30. In Arenhoevel's terms, the development takes the form of the following process: (1) Die Drangsal – (2) Die Heilszeit – 2.1) Die Rückkehr der Verbannten – 2.2) Die Segenszeit unter Simon – 2.3) Das Ende von Schmach und Knechtschaft (Arenhoevel, *Theokratie*, 59–64).

31. I will give two observations: Arenhoevel does not acknowledge the fact that 1 Maccabees' descriptions of the salvific dimension of the Hasmonean achievements are somewhat ambiguous. For instance, I agree that the concept of 'return from exile' can be found in the book, indicating Jewish migration to Judea as a typically Hasmonean achievement (Arenhoevel [*Theokratie*, 61–2] correctly identifies the following passages: 5.23, 45, 53-54; 9.70, 72; 10.33; in addition, 14.7 can be considered another example; we will discuss these passages as well as the ideas of return from exile and territorial conquest in detail in the present study), but these passages lack any signs of eschatological significance as Arenhoevel suggests. Second, the peaceful state of the Judean nation under Simon and his peaceful regnal years were short-lived, fatally interrupted by a family treachery committed by Ptolemy, his son-in-law (16.11-17). I agree that the book still ends with a positive outlook about the Hasmonean institution, as the tragic incident is quickly resolved by Simon's heir, John Hyrcanus I (16.18-22), and the narrative finally ends by stating Hyrcanus' annals in the biblical manner. However, the narrative of 1 Maccabees as a whole lacks any interest in the final, eschatological salvation of Israel. Instead, in the midst of perpetual antagonistic force, the presence of the Hasmonean leadership always secures the fortune of the Judean nation. The present study will revisit this quasi-inconsistent element of the narrative development of 1 Maccabees (see Chapter 4).

It was Jonathan A. Goldstein who advanced this view further in a number of publications.[32] He argued that the Jews in the pre-Hasmonean era believed themselves to be under the bondage carried on from the Babylonian exile and had hoped for the ultimate future restoration of Israel;[33] the Maccabean revolt and the Jewish triumphs over the Seleucid overloads were then seen as fulfilment of that hope.[34] This cultural atmosphere, said Goldstein, determined the use and function of Scripture in 1 Maccabees in such a way that the Hasmonean family, through their heroic, sacrificial deeds for the Judean nation, fulfilled the promise of future restoration of Israel under a Davidic heir; the Hasmoneans replaced the Davidic throne with their own.[35] The use of various parts of Scripture, many of which allude to fulfilment of messianic prophecies and the imagery of biblical David, was seen by Goldstein as carefully crafted to serve propagandistic ends – a *kingship* propaganda, that is.[36] Notably, Goldstein argues that the author of 1 Maccabees intentionally makes scriptural allusions implicit, rather than explicitly stating that scriptural prophecies concerning future Davidic messianic hope were fulfilled by the Hasmoneans. Taking into account Jewish sensitivity about legitimate kingship, the pro-Hasmonean writer is indirectly alluding to legitimacy of the Hasmonean kingship by overlapping heroic stories and prophecies concerning biblical kingship with the story of the usurpers – the Hasmonean family. This explains, for Goldstein, that the technique of using biblical prophecies is predominantly implicit, without actually stating anything about prophetic fulfilment. This argument was fully integrated into his overall thesis on the composition of 1 Maccabees in which Goldstein suggested that the text was composed as 'propaganda' of the Hasmonean dynasty in an attempt to legitimize the office of Alexander Jannaeus during the domestically turbulent period of his reign

---

32. E.g. Jonathan A. Goldstein, *I Maccabees*, AB 41 (Garden City, NY: Doubleday, 1976); 'How the Authors of 1 and 2 Maccabees Treated the "Messianic Promises"', in Neusner et al., eds., *Judaisms and Their Messiahs*, 69–96; 'The Hasmonean Revolt and the Hasmonean Dynasty', *CHJ* 2:292–351 (especially 329–30, 342).

33. Notably, a group of scholars has advocated that the Jews in the Second Temple era believed themselves to have never truly returned from the Babylonian exile. We will discuss the details of this perception of the past later. Goldstein may share this view to some extent, but differs radically in that the bondage was over through the Maccabean revolt and with the institution of the Hasmonean dynasty.

34. Goldstein, 'Messianic Promises', 69–72.

35. Goldstein, 'Messianic Promises', 75, 80–1.

36. Goldstein, 'Messianic Promises', 75–81.

as high priest and king in Judea (around 91 BCE).[37] More recently, Arie van der Kooij also heeded the ways in which Scripture shapes the role of the Hasmoneans in 1 Maccabees. In particular, he lined up expressions associating the Hasmonean family with Aaronite high priesthood and Davidic kingship, and concluded that the function of Scripture was to legitimize the family's monarchical authority, as well as their high priesthood.[38] Overall, these scholars are in agreement that the monarchical legitimation of the Hasmoneans is the key function of the book.

A similar viewpoint was expressed by Tessa Rajak in her essay on the idea of 'invention of tradition' with the Hasmoneans' usurpation of their kingship.[39] Rajak contended that the Jews perceived human kingship as submissive to high priesthood,[40] and flexible and susceptible to adaptation depending on socio-political needs. The Hasmonean family then adapted the older tradition on kingship, the promise of an eternal throne for the Davidic lineage,[41] and invented a new tradition in which they took up the throne and claimed legitimacy, said Rajak.[42] Like Goldstein, she too observed various expressions in 1 Maccabees which she believed to connote monarchical orientation. We shall return to details shortly. It should be noted that Rajak's thesis bears a minor difference from Goldstein's, namely that the idea of invented tradition and monarchical connotations means Rajak is not dependent on the dating of 1 Maccabees, and advocates an earlier, pre-monarchical period for the composition.

Along the same line of argument in favour of Hasmonean kingship legitimation, Eyal Regev recently proposed that the Hasmonean family consistently developed monarchical power so that the sovereignty of national monarchs was extended to cover religious authority, and Regev

---

37. Goldstein, *1 Maccabees*, 62–4; 'Hasmonean Revolt', 329–30, 342.

38. Details of his argument, the passages in question, and criticism will all be made in Chapters 2 and 5.

39. Tessa Rajak, 'Hasmonean Kingship and the Invention of Tradition', in *The Jewish Dialogue with Greece and Rome: Studies in Cultural and Social Interaction*, ed. Tessa Rajak (Boston: Brill, 2002), 69–96, repr. from *Aspects of Hellenistic Kingship*, ed. Per Bilde et al. (Oakville: Aarhus University Press, 1996), 99–115; 'Hasmonean Dynasty', *ABD* 3:67–76.

40. Deut. 17.14-20; 1 Sam. 8.5. Rajak follows the view of Elias J. Bickerman, who claims, '[a]s the heaven is higher than the earth, so the priesthood of God rises above earthly kingship; except it, because of sin, it is cast off by God and lorded over by earthly kingship'. Bickerman, *The Jews in the Greek Age* (Cambridge, MA: Harvard University Press, 1988), 143.

41. E.g. 2 Sam. 7.8-17; 1 Macc. 2.57.

42. Rajak, 'Invention', 46–7.

extends this ideology to that of the pre-monarchical Hasmonean leaders.[43] The Hasmonean family, from the beginning, said Regev, sought to implement their political agendas by promoting religious motivations and projecting themselves as religious leaders, just as monarchs in Jewish and Greek traditions did.[44]

It emerges from these scholars that the Hasmoneans' monarchical legitimation is increasingly seen as part and parcel of the compositional purpose of 1 Maccabees, and Scripture is used to serve such an aim. On the contrary, I have not come across any studies directly drawing a dialogue between the traditional view and the view of Hasmonean kingship propaganda, and which encourage a thorough engagement across both perspectives. Goldstein's thesis rightly combines, connects and synthesizes literary, socio-historical and cultural contexts, as well as other elements affecting the interpretation of 1 Maccabees in general, and the use of Scripture in particular. In turn, his understanding of the use of Scripture reciprocally sharpens his overall thesis vis-à-vis the purpose of 1 Maccabees. Other scholars such as van der Kooij, Rajak and Regev add important details and perspectives to this enterprise of Hasmonean kingship propaganda. A fresh dialogue is imperative.[45]

1.2.3. *Jewish perception of the past*

Before we move on, there is still one more topic closely related to the function of Scripture in 1 Maccabees, namely providing the cultural milieu in which 1 Maccabees functions. On the use of Scripture in 1 Maccabees, Bartlett remarks that 'the author has used the law, the prophets and the psalms to demonstrate the national and religious importance of the events of the Maccabean revolution. The Maccabees by their actions *continue the history of Israel*, which has not yet reached its end or climax…'[46]

---

43. Regev, *Ideology*, 16–17 and Chapter 4.

44. Regev, *Ideology*, Chapters 3–4. Unlike Goldstein, however, Regev claimed that the domestic conflict threatening the Hasmonean office was not about kingship but only high priesthood. That is, he argues that the Pharisaic oppositions to John Hyrcanus I and his sons were not oppositions to the Hasmonean kingship, but to their high priesthood only (155–60). This is a departure from the argument made by Goldstein in which the controversy among the Judean authorities had a bearing on the sovereign title.

45. The dialogue with these scholars runs throughout the present study. Particularly, see §2.2, and Chapter 5.

46. Bartlett, *1 Maccabees*, 32 (my italics). Bartlett's emphasis on the author's nationalistic tendency to which the scriptural tradition is incorporated to support the agenda is also found elsewhere: '[the author's] attempt to write his history in Old

Use of Scripture in 1 Maccabees is to a degree an application of Jewish ancestral history to the contemporary Hasmonean era, or a lens through which to view the current state of affairs. The question is, how does the author perceive the ancestral past in the first place, or what form of Jewish ancestral history does he acknowledge and present to his audience?

In a series of articles dealing with Jewish perception of the past, Doron Mendels demonstrates that societies in antiquity, specifically those of a Hellenistic heritage, did not possess a precise knowledge of their past. Their understanding of the past was, he claims, fragmented, selective and manipulated by authorities who themselves shaped history.[47]

> Historiography of the Greco-Roman world, that is the formal attempt to write down the events of the past in a given genre, was transmitted poorly in Antiquity. In other words, even those few who were interested in the genre and preserved the awareness of the past in certain societies were thus deprived of much historical knowledge. Furthermore, it is also clear that ordinary citizens were not exposed to a wide range of historiography, which

Testament historical style, and the scope of his narrative all show that he was directly motivated by strong nationalistic feelings' (16). Bartlett places the function of the scriptural tradition within the author's nationalistic, pro-Hasmonean agenda, and yet, such a political stance shows compliance with scriptural tradition without subverting it. That is, the author incorporates his historical knowledge about the Jews' ancestral past, as it is gained from Scripture, into the shaping of the history of the Hasmonean uprising. Similarly, Doran ('Maccabees', 4:19–20) claims that 1 Maccabees is 'a narrative that consciously aims at incorporating its story into the tradition of the Hebrew Scriptures'. The 'ancestral traditions', to which Doran refers, namely the history of Israel as presented in biblical literature, shape the recounting of the history of the Hasmonean uprising. Thus, Doran (4:21) finds Mattathias' deathbed blessing to his sons (2.49-70) analogous to Moses' commission of Joshua (Deut. 31.7-23; Josh. 1.6-9), and David's commission of Solomon (1 Chron. 22.13; 28.20). See also his conclusive statement: 'The Hasmoneans are skillfully portrayed as upholding the traditional ancestral faith while their enemies are destroyers of the social fabric, those who bring in foreign ways' (21).

47. Doron Mendels, 'How Was Antiquity Treated in Societies with a Hellenistic Heritage? And Why Did the Rabbis Avoid Writing History?', in *Why Did Paul Go West? Jewish Historical Narrative and Thought*, JCTCRS (London: Bloomsbury, 2014), 12–30. Mendels' general premise, which runs throughout his other works, and through which he promotes the idea of 'manipulated history', is that historiography is a subjective product and that its subjectivity is determined by the individual, the group or the larger society from which the product is originated. See, for instance, Doron Mendels, 'Phases of Inscribed Memory Concerning the Land of Israel in Palestinian Judaism of the Second Century BCE: The Case of 1 Maccabees', in *Why Did Paul Go West?*, 78–93 (especially 78–84).

was available only to a few highly sophisticated societies at that time. In general, we can say that the broad majority of people still lived in a largely oral society; only the minority elite classes were literate. This fact has significant implications regarding which perceptions of the past could even potentially be acquired… The past in its fragmented and partial form is what dominated the lives of societies in Antiquity and brought about a chaotic and unstable historical perception.[48]

Mendels identifies three types of society: those 'stuck in their past' and constantly referring back to their old memories and ideals, those who constantly manipulated their past, and those who looked forward to a new reality and sought to dispense with the past. He suggests that Jews in antiquity are represented by the latter two groups, predominantly concerned with manipulation of the past to serve present needs. He rightly argues that these modes of manipulating history were caused by social and political innovation as well as revolutions and upheavals through which societies redefined their identities,[49] and that the agents who transmitted historical knowledge to his target audience were authorities and elites/privileged literates[50] in society whose primary concerns were expressing imperialistic viewpoints.[51] Thus, Mendels could say, 'the accurate reporting of past events was not necessarily on the agenda of societies and their authors in Antiquity', and 'societies, groups and individuals were imbued with fragments of their past, but did not respect their histories in their totality'.[52]

Mendels' argument comes from his overall sociological approach which emphasizes changes of human experience and its historicity through changes of society's needs.[53] To view 'history' as a politically biased

---

48. Mendels, 'Antiquity', 12, 24.

49. Mendels' examples include the milestones of Mediterranean history such as Alexander the Great's conquests, the division of his kingdom and subjugation of oriental kingdoms, the rise of Rome and the rise of Christianity as factors that led to manipulation of the past ('Antiquity', 26–7).

50. On the contrary, however, see William M. Schniedewind, 'Orality and Literacy in Ancient Israel', *RSR* 26 (2000): 327–32 (329), who argues that there was a burgeoning writing activity among new social classes such as the military, merchants and craftsmen in Judah in the late Monarchic period which pushes the boundary of literacy out from scribal and aristocratic circles.

51. Mendels, 'Antiquity', 28–30.

52. Mendels, 'Antiquity', 22, 30.

53. Several articles in the following volumes are written in this regard: Doron Mendels, *Memory in Jewish, Pagan, and Christian Societies of the Greco-Roman*

product shaped by imperial ideology is not new, as the work of John Van Seters had already shown previously, in which he famously coined the term 'history writing' in Jewish tradition to specifically denote, following J. Huizinga's definition of history, 'the intellectual form in which a civilization renders account to itself of its past', and which is in turn primarily 'nationalistic' in its intention to serve present needs.[54] What is distinctive about Mendels, nonetheless, are his studies on collective memory in antiquity which set out the background for his view on perception of the past.[55] There, he promoted the idea that a society's public memory of its ancestral antecedents was re-shaped by, what he called, 'sites of memory', such as literature, inscriptions, coins and arts.[56]

How may this Jewish perception of the past be qualified within 1 Maccabees? Mendels proposes as follows:

> The author of the Book of 1 Maccabees is an example [of manipulated history]... [T]he past is mentioned here and there but the overall approach tends towards a *new* beginning... First Maccabees can be seen, then, as an expression of a new beginning in Judaism and this trend is evident in the presentation of the issues that are the most symbolic of the new kingdom.[57]

Indeed, suffice it to say that 1 Maccabees selectively recounts the events concerning the Maccabean revolt with a pro-Hasmonean bias, thus Elias J. Bickerman renders his dictum, 'Makk. I korrigiert also die Geschichte'.[58] Experts on 1 Maccabees have long recognized the politically biased, pro-Hasmonean account of the historical events relating to the Hasmonean revolt,[59] although the recognition has usually been more

---

World, LSTS 45 (London: T&T Clark, 2004); *Why Did Paul Go West?*; *The Land of Israel as a Political Concept in Hasmonean Literature* (Tübingen: Mohr Siebeck, 1987), Chapters 4 and 5.

54. John van Seters, *In Search of History: Historiography in the Ancient World and the Origins of Biblical History* (New Haven: Yale University Press, 1983), 1; J. Huizinga, 'A Definition of the Concept of History', in *Philosophy and History: Essays Presented to Ernst Cassirer*, ed. R. Klibansky and H. J. Paton (Oxford: Clarendon, 1936), 1–10 (9).

55. See Mendels, *Memory*.

56. Mendels, 'Inscribed Memory', 78–93.

57. Mendels, 'Antiquity', 15.

58. Bickerman, *Gott*, 29.

59. Conspicuous examples include: (1) an explicit dichotomy between the law-observing, pro-Hasmonean Judeans on one side and the liberal, pro-Seleucid Judeans and the surrounding gentile nations on the other side, hence, the good and the bad; (2) the narrative's central focus on the achievements of the Hasmonean family,

of ambivalence about the historical value of the book rather than simple dismissal of its value.⁶⁰

However, there seem to be two different types of past in 1 Maccabees, and their distinction might be potentially critical: (1) the recent past from the author's time which refers to the great national turmoil followed by the bravery of the Hasmoneans and the exuberance of the nation, that is, the subject matter of the author's propaganda, which I will call 'the Past^R', and (2) the scriptural past which refers to the Jewish ancestral history through which the author views the meaning and legitimacy of the Past^R, which I will call 'the Past^S'. The selective and, indeed, deliberately manipulative nature of the Past^R is conspicuous as aforementioned. The author's perception of the Past^S, on the other hand, is not immediately apparent. It is clear that the author utilizes his Scripture in order to qualify the course of the Hasmonean acts, i.e. to manipulate the Past^R. But was it also part of his intension to manipulate the Past^S? If so, to what extent does the Past^S get manipulated to serve the Past^R? In other words, how selective and fabricated is the use of Scripture in 1 Maccabees?

This question is particularly worth raising not because we are presuming ancient texts to be free from socio-political and cultural influence, nor because different Jewish communities possessed completely different and independent narratives concerning their ancestral past from others.

---

though there are some exceptions such as the encomiastic description of Rome (ch. 8) and the detailed narrative about the international affairs between Egyptian and Seleucid kingdoms (chs. 10–11). The overall narrative is unambiguously a story of the Hasmonean family, and a pro-Hasmonean one at that.

60. As a result, a majority of commentators on 1 Maccabees and historians underline and defend the historical value of the book, despite some discrepancies and chronological inconsistencies. To name but a few, Fairweather and Black, *Maccabees*, 43–4; Dancy, *Maccabees*, 3–8; Bartlett, *1 Maccabees*, 101–2; Rappaport, 'Maccabees', 712; Schürer, *HJPAJC*, 3:180–3; cf. Keil (*Makkabäer*, 17–18) is rather ambivalent about appreciating the historical value of the book, especially in his comment of several inaccuracies such as the statement that Alexander the Great distributed his empires to his generals in his lifetime (1.6), the description of Rome and its administration (8.1-16), the kinship between the Spartans and the Judeans (12.6-7), and the accounts on the Hasmoneans' travels between regions. Tilly (*Makkabäer*, 43–4) even contends that the letters, alliance and deceits between the Hasmoneans and gentile nations do not reflect historical authenticity but rather the interests and standpoints of the Hasmonean institution, hence his emphasis on the need for a critical acceptance of the conventional notion about the historical value of 1 Maccabees (56–7); cf. Daniel R. Schwartz's review of *1 Makkabäer*, by Michael Tilly, *JSJ* 47 (2016): 442–5.

The question is rather about the extent to which the recent events elaborated the already familiar set of Jewish collective memories.[61] A notable study has been offered by Ehud Ben Zvi, who rightly stresses that different Jewish communities, despite their ideological and political diversity, shared those 'core facts' of Israel's history. Ben Zvi refers to 'Adam and Eve as the common originators of all humanity, the series Abraham–Isaac–Jacob, the exodus, the leadership of Moses and Sinai, David, the building of the Temple by Solomon, the list of kings and the respective length of their reigns, Sennacherib's campaign and Jerusalem's survival, Nebuchadnezzar's destruction of Jerusalem and exile'.[62] The precise listing of these core facts may vary between different sources, but the issue here is about the Jews' attitude towards their ancestral past: did the Jews passively receive from elite/ruling classes what was to be remembered, which was predominantly susceptible to manipulation and distortion? Or, was the set of collective memories shaped around those core facts more concrete and widely shared across different communities? In the present study, we will investigate this potentially more nuanced Jewish perception of their past.

1.2.4. Summary

Many scholars claim that the use of Scripture in 1 Maccabees indicates the author's conscious utilization of abundant scriptural materials in support of his pro-Hasmonean viewpoint, but a few deny that the scriptural language bears any meaning other than a simple, stylistic imitation, irrelevant to the notion of scriptural fulfilment of the hope of Israel's restoration. Amongst those attesting to the use of Scripture in 1 Maccabees in the senses in which certain, specific scriptural materials are quoted, referred or alluded to, a growing number of scholars advocate the view that the use of Scripture is intended to portray the Hasmonean family as messianic figures in replacement of the Davidic dynasty, or fulfilling the messianic hope concerning the restitution of the Davidic dynasty. This notion serves as both a preliminary and corollary argument that the overall purpose of

---

61. The plurality of the accounts of Israel's history presented in Kings and Chronicles is a typical example in this regard. The same can be asked of the different accounts of the Creation narrative or, needless to say, of the four different accounts of Jesus of Nazareth.

62. Ehud Ben Zvi, 'General Observations on Ancient Israelite Histories in Their Ancient Contexts', in *Enquire of the Former Age: Ancient Historiography and Writing the History of Israel*, ed. Lester L. Grabbe, ESHM 9; LHBOTS 554 (New York: Bloomsbury, 2013), 21–39 (especially 36–7 [see also 37 n. 40 for Ben Zvi's other publications discussing this issue]).

1 Maccabees is the legitimation of the Hasmonean kingdom. It is time to offer a fresh dialogue on the use and function of Scripture vis-à-vis the role of the Hasmoneans in 1 Maccabees.

1.3. *Aims and outline of the present study*

In the present study, I seek to answer the following questions. First, in what ways do scriptural expressions appear in 1 Maccabees? In particular, for those implicit and less clear scriptural expressions, do they suggest allusions or simple stylistic imitations? Second, what function does Scripture perform with regard to the purpose of 1 Maccabees? Third, in particular, how do scriptural expressions contribute to the author's portrayal of the Hasmonean family?

In Chapter 2, literary, political, and cultural aspects affecting the study of the use and function of Scripture will be discussed. Chapter 3 will discuss philological parallels between 1 Maccabees and Scripture by critically engaging with the recent work of Armin Lange and Matthias Weigold, with the aim of producing a comprehensive list of biblical cross-references appearing in 1 Maccabees, particularly regarding the identification of ways in which scriptural materials are used. In Chapter 4, I continue to examine parallels between 1 Maccabees and Scripture which I will analyse on conceptual grounds. In particular, I will discuss two concepts, the Deuteronomic covenant and biblical judges, and analyse the extent to which these concepts affect the author's intention. Chapter 5 will extend the consideration of morphological and conceptual parallels by focusing particularly on the eulogies of Judas and Simon wherein dense scriptural evocations have a strong bearing on the roles of the Hasmoneans. Chapter 6 will summarize my final conclusions.

1.4. *Methodology*

The phenomenon of earlier texts appearing in later texts has been one of the most popular subjects within biblical studies, and approaches to understanding such incidences have largely been polarized between author-oriented and reader-oriented approaches.[63] The present study will

---

63. Many biblical scholars have applied the semiotic term and concept of 'intertextuality' coined by Julia Kristeva, 'Word, Dialogue, and Novel', in *Desire in Language: A Semiotic Approach to Literature and Art*, ed. Leon S. Roudiez, trans. Thomas Gora et al. (New York: Columbia University Press, 1980), 64–91 (66). There have been controversies in recent decades as to the term's suitability for traditional biblical studies on use of Scripture which were primarily based on author-oriented

take the form of an author-oriented approach since the questions addressed above are concerned with how the use of Scripture relates to its function within the authorial intention. Furthermore, I take as a premise the notion that the appearance of an anterior text (or texts) in the posterior text is a manifestation of a complex set of various literary, socio-political, and cultural elements, and have subsequently included a chapter (Chapter 2) to clarify these various elements which are important for a fuller

approaches. Critics say, 'intertextuality' meant in Kristevan terms that 'any text is constructed as a mosaic of quotations; any text is the absorption and transformation of another' (66), and this dialogical dynamic is achieved by the reader in his/her appropriation of the text through his/her own experience, knowledge and cultural background. Consequently, as Ellen van Wolde puts it, '[m]eaning…is not so much a product of the writer, as the result of a process of interaction between text and reader'. Van Wolde, 'Trendy Intertextuality?', in *Intertextuality in Biblical Writings: Essays in Honour of Bas van Iersel*, ed. Sipke Draisma (Kampen: Kok, 1989), 43–9 (47). Some scholars therefore encourage keeping the term 'intertextuality' with reader-oriented approaches, whilst labelling author-oriented approaches with terms such as 'inner-biblical exegesis' or 'inner-biblical allusion'. See, for example, Geoffrey D. Miller, 'Intertextuality in Old Testament Research', *CBR* 9 (2010): 283–309 (especially 305); Benjamin D. Sommer, *A Prophet Reads Scripture: Allusion in Isaiah 40–66*, CJOD (Stanford, CA: Stanford University Press, 1998), 6–31. However, other scholars continue to employ the term in studies that take an author-oriented approach, underlining the principle of causality and diachronic relation between the given text and earlier texts. As Michael H. Floyd remarks, intertextual studies become 'unjustifiably arbitrary', if historical questions are excluded (e.g. how the author incorporates earlier texts in his writing), and 'it is possible, and arguably even necessary, to include both the production and reception of texts'. Floyd, 'Deutero-Zechariah and Types of Intertextuality', in *Bringing out the Treasure: Inner Biblical Allusion in Zechariah 9–14*, ed. Mark J. Boda and Michael H. Floyd, JSOTSup 370 (Sheffield: Sheffield Academic, 2003), 225–44 (226). It should also be noted that the poststructural, reader-based association with the term 'intertextuality' is not warranted. Instead, the author-oriented approach can be associated with the term. Jay Clayton and Eric Rothstein outline broadly two types of 'intertextuality' among theorists: one that is more inclined to be author-based and diachronic, whilst the other is reader-based and synchronic, and point out that 'the underlying complex of ideas – some of them venerable and many of them rooted in ongoing academic practice – remained so varied as to make the term [intertextuality] unstable in meaning'. Clayton and Rothstein, 'Figures in the Corpus: Theories of Influence and Intertextuality', in *Influence and Intertextuality in Literary Theory*, ed. Jay Clayton and Eric Rothstein (Madison, WI: University of Wisconsin Press, 1991), 3–36 (3 and 18 for the quotation).

understanding of the phenomenon of using Scripture in 1 Maccabees, rather than limiting the task to source-hunting.⁶⁴

With regards to the approach to the text of 1 Maccabees, despite the general admittance that there may be errors in the process of transmission, as well as elements in multiple foreign documents incorporated in the composition which suggest the author's alteration or interpolation,⁶⁵ I take

---

64. Although my approach does not depend on semiotic conceptions, the understanding of a text as surrounded by various literary, social and cultural elements which influence the writer (or the speaker) is explained by Mikhail M. Bakhtin in many of his works. See, for example, 'The Problem of Speech Genres', in Bakhtin, *Speech Genres and Other Late Essays*, trans. Vern W. McGee, ed. Caryl Emerson and Michael Holquist (Austin, TX: University of Texas Press, 1986), 60–102 (68, 69). Kristeva's proposition about intertextuality is based on the Bakhtinian conception of the interrelation between an utterance and its surrounding various social and cultural elements, like a complex web of 'intertexts', or 'heteroglossia' in Bakhtin's term (Kristeva, 'Word', 66; cf. Bakhtin, 'Speech Genres', 91, 92, 94), but it should be underlined that Bakhtin's notion of 'heteroglossia' does not place an emphasis on the role of the listener (or the reader) quite as radically as does Kristeva. On the contrary, Bakhtin stresses that the author, the listener and the influences upon the speaker (or the author) all have 'inalienable rights to the word' ('The Problem of the Text in Linguistics, Philosophy, and the Human Sciences: An Experiment in Philosophical Analysis', in *Speech Genres*, 103–31 [121–2]). Bakhtin's emphasis on the due roles of the speaker and his *heteroglossia*, as much as that of the listener, upon the determination of the meaning of an utterance is crucial. It ensures the uniqueness of each individual utterance, which is socio-politically and culturally specific, and that its meaning cannot be arbitrary nor absorbed into the listener's appropriation. As a result, language, for Bakhtin, is far from neutral; it is socio-ideological. It speaks of the socio-cultural and ideological contexts it has incorporated through dialogue. Clayton and Rothstein rightly comment that the Kristevan conception of a text was influenced by the Derridean conception of textuality, i.e. a text's 'indeterminacy' and 'dissemination' (Clayton and Rothstein, 'Intertextuality', 18–20), whilst Bakhtin, in contrast, emphasized 'the historical uniqueness of the context of every utterance [which] distanced his terms from the endlessly expanding context of [the Kristevan] intertextuality' (Clayton and Rothstein, 'Intertextuality', 19). Therefore, the approach taken in the present study echoes the Bakhtinian conception of heteroglossia, but is not concerned with the role of the reader, which receives due attention in Bakhtin's works.

65. On the authenticity of 1 Maccabees' presentation of these documents, see the footnote under 'Jewish Perception of the Past' in §1.2. In addition to transmissional errors and the foreign documents, it may also be worth considering the process of the composition of 1 Maccabees in the first place: did the author witness all those events, or did he compile sources preserved orally or as written materials?

the view that the original composition of 1 Maccabees corresponds to our extant text with sixteen chapters, in opposition to recent literary-critical studies proposing a redactional layer or layers in the text, notably those of Nils Martola, David S. Williams and Francis Borchardt.[66] Although their structural analyses are valuable for the interpretation of individual passages in 1 Maccabees, their respective conclusions on the identified redacted parts are not unified and are thus difficult to accept. Borchardt's strict application of the aforementioned criteria has led him to isolate not only such numerous small literary units as secondary to his version of the original composition but also three different redactional layers upon the original one.[67] Furthermore, although Martola and Borchardt agree that 1 Maccabees 8 and 12.1-23 (both of which describe the Romans and the alliance between them and the Judeans) are an abrupt

---

66. Nils Martola paid attention to the structure of 1 Maccabees, starting from the relations between the smallest literary segments up to the overall narrative structure, as well as isolating sections that do not fit, and concluded that chs. 1–7, 9–11, and 12.24–14.15 formed the original composition, whilst ch. 8, 12.1-23, and 14.16–16.24 were added some time after the original. Martola, *Capture and Liberation: A Study in the Composition of the First Book of Maccabees*, AAA A 63/1 (Åbo: Åbo Akademi, 1984), 270–6; D. S. Williams, *The Structure of 1 Maccabees* (Washington, DC: The Catholic Biblical Association of America, 1999). Williams also produced a literary-critical study of 1 Maccabees, similar to that of Martola, but distinctive in that he applied 'the role of repetition', adopted from M. Butterworth's methodology, in which observations of 'repetitions of the same word or root' in each of the smaller literary units serve to determine in/consistencies between the units and eventually lead to identifying the overall narrative structure (see especially Chapter 2 for his identification of repetitive words); also, Williams, 'Recent Research in 1 Maccabees', *CurBS* 9 (2001): 169–84 (172–4). The result of his study identified a chiastic structure of the original composition (1.1–6.17 and 6.18–14.15 chiastically in parallel) and isolated 14.16–16.24 as an addition. Recently, Francis Borchardt also carried out still another literary-critical study on the composition of 1 Maccabees in a similar vein; see Borchardt, *The Torah in 1 Maccabees: A Literary Critical Approach to the Text*, DCLS 19 (Berlin: de Gruyter, 2014) (especially Chapter 1). This time, the literary analysis applied the criteria of 'doublets, parallels, differences in rhetoric and style, abrupt changes in form, context, competing traditions, and irregularities in vocabulary' (43). The marked difference of Borchardt's study from those of his predecessors is his identification of three layers of redaction upon the original composition, each consisting of several small literary units isolated from his version of the original composition: '1 Maccabees Opposition', '1 Maccabees Documentarian', and '1 Maccabees Hasmonean Legend' (159–86).

67. See the footnote above.

insertion into the narrative,⁶⁸ Williams defends their integration into the original composition on the grounds of their chiastic positioning.⁶⁹ What appears to be disruptive about these units, however, does not necessarily prove their disintegration from the rest of the narrative. Indeed, many commentators rightly defend their integration into the narrative,⁷⁰ and this kind of disruption of the narrative was already known as a writing technique in Greek literature, as Menahem Stern has already pointed out.⁷¹ As for authorship, unlike Borchardt's three redactors, each one with different perspectives, Martola stressed the possibility of the same, original authorship on the additions he proposed.⁷²

---

68. Martola, *Capture*, 159–61, 166, 172, 186, 200, 207, 226–36; Borchardt, *Torah*, 95–104.

69. Williams, *Structure*, 131–2. For critiques made on Williams' proposed chiasm, see John R. Bartlett, review of *Structure*, *JTS* 52 (2001): 191–4; Eric R. Gruen, review of *Structure*, *CBQ* 62 (2000): 743–4.

70. Thus, Bartlett (*Books of the Maccabees*, 111) observes that the end of ch. 8 (8.31-32) directly addresses Demetrius I's antagonistic force so that the narrative smoothly flows from ch. 8 to ch. 9, where this Demetrius reappears in the scene (9.1). Goldstein (*1 Maccabees*, 346) also notes that despite the abrupt presence of ch. 8, it is 'an essential part of our author's narrative', because the Hasmoneans' seeking for an alliance with Rome was a natural reaction to the reign of Demetrius I, and the envoy is potentially evidenced by the letter of Gaius Fannius to the people of Cos, in which the former claimed to have received envoys from the Judeans, because the only consul by the name of Gaius Fannius was Gaius Fannius Strabo who was consul in 161 BCE, matching the reign of Demetrius which started at 163 BCE (on the letter of Gaius Fannius, see T. R. S. Broughton, *The Magistrates of the Roman Republic* [New York: American Philological Association, 1951–52], 2:564–5). Rappaport ('Maccabees', 711–13, 731) also defends the literary unity of 1 Maccabees.

71. Menahem Stern, 'Die Urkunden', in *Literatur und Religion des Frühjudentums*, ed. J. Maier and J. Schreiner (Würzburg: Echter, 1973), 181–99 (especially 184–9).

72. Martola (*Capture*, 269) considers 15.1-14; 15.25–16.24 as probably written by the original author, and the rest of the additions as possibly written by him. I accept that the only passage agreed upon by all three scholars, 14.16–16.24, coincidentally matches the argument of the so-called addendum theory, which might provide supporting argument for redaction. The addendum theory basically arose from the observation that Josephus omits chs. 14–16 of 1 Maccabees in their entirety in his close paraphrase of the book in his *Jewish Wars* and *Antiquities of the Jews*, hence arguing that these last three chapters should be seen as an addition to the original composition. For more on this, see, for example, J. Destinon, *Die Quellen des Flavius Josephus in der Jüd. Arch. Buch XII–XVII=Jüd. Krieg Buch* (Kiel: Lipsius & Tischer,

As a remark on employing the terms 'Jew' and 'Judean', the question about a suitable term for Jewish people in antiquity has attracted an increasing number of scholars, instigating enquiries into translating the Greek term Ιουδαιοι with either ethnic/religious (i.e. 'Jews') or geographical/political (i.e. 'Judeans') connotation.[73] What is at stake in this debate is the way these ancient people defined their identity. The term Ιουδαιοι in 1 Maccabees, in contrast to that of 2 Maccabees, has normally been determined as 'Judeans' rather than 'Jews' mainly due to the dynastic nature of the writing and its quasi-lack of religious orientation. The present research will follow this convention and use 'Judeans' for referents in 1 Maccabees, whilst limiting 'Jews' for a broad ethnic group.

1882). Destinon first proposed the theory in his study on Josephus' sources for Jewish history between Alexander the Great to Herod (*Ant.* 12.5–13.7 and *War* Book 1). For a helpful summary of scholarship up to the early twentieth century on the addendum theory, see H. W. Ettelson, 'The Integrity of 1 Maccabees', *TCAAS* 27 (1925): 249–384 (255–64), and for a more up-to-date treatment, see Borchardt, *Torah*, 38–49. Ettelson ('Integrity', 249–384) has made a critique of the theory, and his defence of the literary unity of 1 Maccabees has widely been accepted by subsequent generations of scholars in the field. The recent literary critics' argument for a structural difference of 14.16–16.24 from the rest of the narrative needs to receive more attention than it has up until now. Nevertheless, it should still be pointed out that despite this passage's structural anomaly, Martola and Williams do not make a claim for an existence of a redactor besides the original author; only Borchardt makes that claim.

73. This is a distinction that modern English dictionaries follow: e.g. J. A. Simpson and E. S. C. Weiner, eds., *The Oxford English Dictionary* (Oxford: Clarendon, 1989), 8:291, 228; P. B. Grove, ed., *Webster's Third New International Dictionary of the English Language, Unabridged* (Springfield: Merriam, 1976), 1222–3, 1215. Steve Mason, 'Jews, Judaeans, Judaizing, Judaism: Problems of Categorization in Ancient History', *JSJ* 38 (2007): 457–512, proposed the view that the ethnic/religious connotation of Ιουδαιοι should be avoided, thus entitling his Brill series of Josephus's works as *Judean War* and *Judean Antiquities*. Shaye J. D. Cohen, *The Beginnings of Jewishness: Boundaries, Varieties, Uncertainties*, HCS 31 (Berkeley: University of California Press, 1999), had made a distinction between the pre-Hasmonean era in which Ιουδαιοι meant 'Judeans' only and the era afterward in which religious connotations (i.e. 'Jews') arose. Daniel R. Schwartz, 'Judeans, Jews, and Their Neighbors: Jewish Identity in the Second Temple Period', in *Between Cooperation and Hostility: Multiple Identities in Ancient Judaism and the Interaction with Foreign Powers*, ed. Rainer Albertz and Jacob Wöhrle, JAJSup 11 (Göttingen; Bristol, CT: Vandenhoeck & Ruprecht, 2013), 13–31, recently made a similar claim with the latter, attributing the difference of the term as a difference between priestly Judaism (e.g. 1 Maccabees) and Pharisaic/rabbinic Judaism (e.g. 2 Maccabees).

Chapter 2

THE CONTRIBUTION OF THE LITERARY, SOCIAL AND CULTURAL MILIEUS ON THE APPROPRIATION OF SCRIPTURE IN 1 MACCABEES

2.1. *Textual issues*

The Greek version of 1 Maccabees, which is de facto the main text for any critical study of the book, is widely understood as a translation from a Hebrew original which is completely lost. There is, then, a gap between the original author, whose perspective/intention of composition we seek to access, and the extant translation, and it is a necessary task to identify and resolve issues arising from the gap. The following four sections will deal with these issues. First, we will address textual issues arising from within the Greek of 1 Maccabees to determine the main text for the present study. Second, we will clarify the widely accepted notion that there was an original Hebrew version of 1 Maccabees in order to consider the implication for our study of the Greek version. As of our particular interest in 1 Maccabees' use of Scripture, the fact that one is dealing with the work of a Greek translator necessarily poses a question of whether he consulted Greek Scripture, and if he did, in what ways. In this regard, the third section will clarify our understanding of the nature of Greek Scripture while the last section will consider its influence upon 1 Maccabees.

2.1.1. *Textual variance*
Ideally, we would have access to the Greek text produced by the translator himself. Access, however, is impossible because few of the Greek manuscripts dating close to the time of the Greek translation have survived, and those that have contain textual disagreements. Therefore, in this section I will set out what qualifies as the most reliable text that can be reconstructed from the available textual variants.

In 1936, Werner Kappler carried out a reconstruction of the earliest version of Greek 1 Maccabees with provision of a critical apparatus.[1] He utilized three of the earliest uncials (Sinaiticus, Alexandrinus and Venetus), twenty-six minuscules, grouped as 'q', and those manuscripts witnessing the so-called Lucianic recension grouped as L and l (sub-Lucianic materials).[2] The Lucianic (or Antiochan) recension refers to the fourth-century Christian recension of biblical texts carried out in Antioch.[3] The recension is characterized by smoothing out and improving the text with better Greek, evidence of which is found in patristic citations of biblical texts as well as in some Greek manuscripts and the Old Latin.[4] Kappler's edition of the Greek 1 Maccabees has since been widely accepted in the field and has been taken in preference to the earlier edition by H. B. Swete which basically followed only Codex Alexandrinus.[5]

---

1. I will use the second edition, Werner Kappler, *Maccabaeorum liber I*, VTGASLG IX/1, 2nd edn (Göttingen: Vandenhoeck & Ruprecht, 1967). See especially his introduction (7–47) where he discusses textual issues and his reasons for distinguishing manuscripts in three groups.

2. There are eleven further minuscules which are identical to these three groups, but omitted due to their redundancy. In addition, G. D. Kilpatrick added some more potentially valuable manuscripts omitted by Kappler, see Kilpatrick, 'I–III Maccabees (with Addendum)', in *Studies in the Septuagint: Origins, Recensions and Interpretations: Selected Essays with a Prolegomenon by Sidney Jellicoe*, LBS (New York: Ktav, 1974), 418–33. Relevant to 1 Maccabees is the Durham fragment of a Latin text of the sixth century (Cathedral Library, B. IV. 6 fol. 169), which contains 1 Macc. 6.59-62 and 6.63–7.2. The manuscript is valuable insofar as it is the earliest manuscript witness to the Vulgate. It is also worth mentioning that Syriac and Coptic translations of 1 Maccabees are also available, but are not considered in the present study due to their lesser value compared to Greek and Latin in reconstructing the most likely original reading.

3. Bruce M. Metzger, 'The Lucianic Recension of the Greek Bible', in Jellicoe, ed., *Studies in the Septuagint*, 270–91. For the word 'recension', I mean the sense of 'a self-conscious, systematic, and clearly identifiable revision of an existing text', as defined by Karen H. Jobes and Moisés Silva, *Invitation to the Septuagint* (Grand Rapids, MI: Baker Academic, 2000), 46.

4. Metzger, 'Lucianic Recension', 272–84; Jennifer M. Dines offers three characateristics of the Lucianic recension: (1) replacement of Koine forms with Attic Greek (although, she also noted that this feature already appeared in manuscripts of the first century BCE); (2) the use of synonyms and preference of compound verbs; (3) addition of proper names, personal pronouns and conjunctions for a more precise meaning of the text. Dines, *The Septuagint* (London: T&T Clark, 2004), 103–6.

5. John R. Bartlett is an exception whose commentary on 1 Maccabees does not give an indication of using Kappler's edition, see Bartlett, *Books of the Maccabees*. His mention of Swete's edition as a suggested reading for the text of 1 Maccabees

Especially helpful is Kappler's appreciation and reflection of the Lucianic recension which evidently resulted in marked differences between manuscripts before and after it.

Alongside Kappler's Greek edition of 1 Maccabees, however, the Old Latin edition offered by Dom Donatien de Bruyne is worth consideration.[6] The 'Old Latin' is a collective term for manuscripts available in North Africa, Gaul and parts of Italy (other than Rome) early in the second century CE which are potentially valuable for their witness to Greek manuscripts pre-dating them. As Sidney Jellicoe rightly pointed out, De Bruyne's contention that there is a considerable difference between the Old Latin and the consensus of Greek manuscripts, and that the Old Latin is a witness to the pre-Lucianic Greek texts, should not be ignored.[7] In addition to the Old Latin, the Latin Vulgate is also worth consideration. It is the translation of the Hebrew Bible carried out by Jerome in the late fourth century, and it differs from these Old Latin texts and is considered less reliable. However, unlike other biblical texts which are translated by Jerome, the Vulgate 1 Maccabees is as valuable as the Old Latin version on the grounds that Jerome did not seem to know the Hebrew original of 1 Maccabees and consequently probably used the Old Latin that was available to him.[8]

---

in his introductory book on 1 Maccabees may indicate that Bartlett's ignorance of Kappler's edition may have been deliberate, but without explanation; see Bartlett, *1 Maccabees*, 20. For Swete's text, see H. B. Swete, *The Old Testament in Greek according to the Septuagint*, vols. *I–III* (Cambridge: Cambridge University Press, 1897–1912), especially 3:594–661 for 1 Maccabees.

6. Dom Donatien de Bruyne with Dom Bonaventure Sodar, *Les anciennes traductions latines des Machabées*, AM 4 (Maredsous: Abbaye de Maredsous, 1932). See also Goldstein, *1 Maccabees*, 178; Bartlett, *1 Maccabees*, 14–15, for information on the Old Latin.

7. Sidney Jellicoe, *The Septuagint and Modern Study* (Oxford: Clarendon, 1968), 303–4.

8. Dines, *Septuagint*, 10–11. In a pre-published version of an article on the textual history of 1 Maccabees, which he kindly let me to access, Daniel R. Schwartz also points out that in some cases the Old Latin texts appear to be similar to Cyprian's biblical citations, which again pre-dates the Lucianic recension. Schwartz, 'On the Text of 1 Maccabees', 1–31 (20). For the published version, see Daniel R. Schwartz, 'Textual History of 1 Maccabees', in *Textual History of the Bible*, ed. F. Feder and M. Henze (Leiden: Brill, 2019), 113–17. In the present section, I use his unpublished article instead, because the published version omits several textual examples discussed in the unpublished version and which are very useful for the present section. I am grateful to Daniel Schwartz for granting permission for me to cite the unpublished version. As regards Jerome's statement on 1 Maccabees, see below.

Kappler's critically reconstructed Greek text, however, remains as our main text on the grounds that the variations within the Old Latin texts are so considerable that it seems impossible to determine for certain the most reliable reading. Furthermore, the Latin is a translation garnered from the (Old) Greek, not from the Hebrew original directly. Additionally, Kappler's edition isolates the textual variants of the late, Lucianic recension so that the problem of modifications will not go unnoticed. Instead, the Latin texts will be consulted whenever a textual issue arises which cannot be resolved on the basis of Greek manuscripts alone. Daniel R. Schwartz, for instance, rightly noted that in 1 Macc. 5.66, when Judas is said to go through 'Samaria' after a battle in the land of the Philistines near the south-western coast of Palestine according to Greek manuscripts, the Old Latin texts read 'Marisan' (i.e. Marissa near Philistia) which makes more sense than Samaria.[9]

Lastly, the part of Josephus' *Jewish Antiquities* which corresponds to 1 Maccabees is also potentially worth consulting. He uses chs. 1–13 as his primary source for the relevant period of history, and paraphrases and corrects it where he found necessary. Moreover, scholars have often pointed out that the Greek version of the text was his source.[10] To an extent, then, *Antiquities* is the earliest extant witness to the Greek 1 Maccabees, even though the paraphrased version is not as reliable as the aforementioned Greek and Latin translations.[11] For instance, on the above example of textual variance in 5.66, Josephus agrees with the Old Latin rather than the Greek manuscripts, and rightly selected 'Marissa' over Samaria (*Ant.* 12.353). In this regard, the Loeb edition of *Jewish Antiquities* Books 12–14, includes the comparison between 1 Maccabees and Josephus' account in its commentary[12] and should be added to our list.[13]

---

9. Schwartz, 'Text of 1 Maccabees', 24.

10. E.g. Grimm, *Maccabäer*, xxvii–xxx; Louis H. Feldman, 'Josephus' Portrayal of the Hasmoneans Compared with 1 Maccabees', in *Josephus and the History of the Greco-Roman Period: Essays in Memory of Morton Smith*, ed. F. Parente and J. Sievers, SPB 41 (Leiden: Brill, 1994), 41 n. 3; Bartlett, *1 Maccabees*, 16–17. Some have suggested the possibility of Josephus' access to the Hebrew original as well as the Greek: Williams, *Structure*, 117; Goldstein, *1 Maccabees*, 14, 211, 247, 255, 294–5.

11. See Schwartz ('Text of 1 Maccabees', 23–30) for his observations on the problem of Josephus' rendering of Greek words.

12. Flavius Josephus, *Jewish Antiquities, Books 12–14*, trans. Ralph Marcus, LCL (Cambridge, MA: Harvard University Press; London: William Heinemann, 1986).

13. A helpful comparison between the accounts of 1 Maccabees and Josephus, with many parallel examples, has been made by Isaiah M. Gafni, 'Josephus and 1 Maccabees', in *Josephus, the Bible and History*, ed. Louis H. Feldman and Gohei Hata (Leiden: Brill, 1989), 116–31.

For our Greek text, general rules for determining the best reading among textual variants will be as follows. Just as Kappler cautioned that each case of textual variance should be judged without preference of some manuscripts, scholars such as G. D. Kilpatrick and Schwartz have suggested some basic rules for determining the best reading, and the following three are critically adopted from Kilpatrick. (1) *Hebrew idiom as a sign of the original*: given that other details are equal between two or more manuscripts, one that bears a more Hebraic reading is to be preferred;[14] this is the main rule applied by Kappler. However, we will need to take caution in following this rule because, as Schwartz rightly noted, it is not impossible that later editors, who were familiar with Hebrew, may have revised those less Hebraic readings to look deliberately more Hebraic than they really were.[15] (2) *The more Koine, the more original; the better the Greek, the less original*: as the second rule, G. D. Kilpatrick suggested that if one of two or more readings displays Greek in the *Koine* style rather than in a more developed Greek style with deliberately better phrasing or more precise meaning, this is probably an indication that the *Koine* has not undergone any revision. Again, however, this judgement cannot be taken for granted and other considerations have to be supplied because the difference between 'less' and 'more' developed Greek readings is often unclear. (3) *Atticism as a sign of revision*: Kilpatrick also noted that toward the end of the first century CE, changes occurred not only in the writings of Herodotus and Xenophon but also in the Greek Bible: for instance, the uses of -ττ- and λεώς, instead of -σσ- and λαός, and the preference of η to α (e.g. φήμη instead of φάμα).[16] Accordingly, if any reading is found to possess Attic features, the other, non-Attic reading(s) is to be preferred.

A fourth point Kilpatrick proposed concerns consistency of style as a sign of the original. He suggested that scribes of classical writings, such as Plato and Denosthenes, upon their translating and editing activities, considered integrity and consistency of style as essential. The sign of consistency in style should likewise be considered as evidence of a

14. Kilpatrick, 'Maccabees', 422.
15. Schwartz, 'Text of 1 Maccabees', 21. Such a rationale was upheld by Alfred Rahlfs and led him to choose the opposite case, i.e. a less Hebraic reading as a better reading (21).
16. Kilpatrick, 'Maccabees', 422. Dines, *Septuagint*, 104, 110–15; Jobes and Silva, *Invitation to the Septuagint*, 106–7. For further discussion, see Jaakko Frösén, 'Prolegomena to a Study of the Greek Language in the First Century A.D.: The Problem of Koiné and Atticism' (PhD diss., The University of Helsinki, 1974); Leonard R. Palmer, *The Greek Language* (London: Faber, 1980).

better reading, said Kilpatrick.¹⁷ We will take this suggestion with caution as well, for the following reason: Kilpatrick himself admitted that 1 Maccabees does not have any considerable similarities with classical writings.¹⁸ Nor does Kilpatrick specify what it means to be 'of consistent style'. If he referred to the quasi-inconsistencies of the narrative flow in 1 Maccabees, such as 1.11-15, ch. 8, 12.1-23, as suggested by literary critics, we have contended that these 'interruptions' may well be the author's own literary design.¹⁹ Or, if it refers to the presence of non-Koine, more developed Greek, we have already made note of it above. What is more, where consistency of style is found, it could equally be a sign of revision, just as better Greek appears to be less original. Therefore, the matter of consistency or inconsistency of style will be evaluated in its own context.

2.1.2. *The lost Hebrew original text*

The notion that Greek 1 Maccabees is a translation from a Hebrew original has been widely acccepted among scholars in the field, but it is necessary to delineate the evidence for such a premise. Observing the evidence will also be helpful for understanding the manner and attitude of the translator toward the original text. There is both external and internal evidence in support of the original 1 Maccabees as a Hebrew composition.

Externally, there are two sources. First, Origen, as cited by Eusebius (*Hist. eccl.* 6.25), lists twenty-two books that belong to the Hebrew canon in his commentary on Psalm 1 and comments the following at the end:

> And besides these, there is τα Μακκαβαϊκα which is entitled Σαρβὴθ Σαβαναιέλ...

The last two words have usually been regarded as the Hebrew title for 1 Maccabees, and several propositions for the underlying Hebrew title have been made. Allowing for some corruption to the text (Σαρ originally being Σφαρ), the Hebrew consonants are thus rendered as ספר בית for the first part of the term. For the second part, usually following Robert Estienne's edition of Eusebius' work (which writes the second part of the term as Σαρβαναεέλ), possibilities include שר בני אל ('the Princes of the

---

17. Kilpatrick, 'Maccabees', 422.

18. This claim is supported by the fact that 1 Maccabees' writing style conspicuously follows biblical style. There are, of course, some Hellenistic features found in 1 Maccabees and these will be discussed in §2.4.3.

19. See §1.4.

Sons of God'), שר בני ישראל ('the Princes of the Sons of Israel'),[20] or even סרבני אל ('God's resisters', coined by Goldstein, derogatively referring to those who resist 'against' God, originating from anti-Hasmonean Jews[21]). The problem of identifying Origen's term notwithstanding, it is sufficient to say that the term Σαρβὴθ Σαβαναιέλ clearly points to a Hebrew original, whose title was known to Christian patristic writers.

The second source comes from Jerome's preface to his commentaries on Samuels and Kings in which he says:

> …[in] all the books we have translated…therefore, Wisdom, popularly titled the Wisdom of Solomon, and the book of Jesus ben Sira and Judith and Tobit and the Shepherd are not in the canon, *I have found the First book of Maccabees in Hebrew* (Machabaeorum primum liber Hebraicum reperi); the Second is a Greek book as can also be proved from considerations of style alone.[22]

Like Origen, Jerome states twenty-two books of the Hebrew canon followed by the Apocryphal books including 1 Maccabees. It has often been suggested that the ambiguous verb *reperi*, literally meaning 'found', should mean that Jerome 'inferred' a Hebrew original behind the Greek text, rather than that he 'found' a Hebrew copy of 1 Maccabees.[23] This reading is supported by the fact that Jerome specifically makes this point on 1 Maccabees, whereas the other Jewish writings – Wisdom of Solomon, Ben Sira, Judith, and Tobit – do not receive the same comment.

Internally, there have been various observations for signs of translation from Hebrew to Greek in 1 Maccabees, and the existing Greek translation has accordingly been accredited with careful preservation of the original Hebrew text.[24] As the editor of NETS notes, the Greek shows 'the careful,

---

20. For more options, see Schürer, *HJPAJC*, 3:182–3; Bartlett, *1 Maccabees*, 17–18.

21. Jonathan A. Goldstein, 'The Dynasty of God's Resistors', *HTR* 68 (1975): 53–8; *1 Maccabees*, 14–21.

22. Prologus Galeatus 28.593-604. The English translation is offered by Goldstein (*1 Maccabees*, 16).

23. See Kilpatrick, 'Maccabees', 431–3; Goldstein, *1 Maccabees*, 16; Schwartz, 'Text of 1 Maccabees', 3 n. 3.

24. E.g. Ettelson, 'Integrity', 308–14; Pfeiffer, *History*, 484–6; Goldstein, *1 Maccabees*, 14–16; Bartlett, *1 Maccabees*, 17–19; Doran, 'Maccabees', 4:20. Particularly helpful is Schwartz, 'Text of 1 Maccabees', who deals with overviews of and issues pertaining to (1) the lost Hebrew original, (2) the Greek translation, and (3) the transmission of the Greek text.

extremely literal Jewish-Greek translational style' and 'a deliberate choice on the part of the translator, whose exceptional vocabulary betrays a considerable facility with the Greek language'.[25] We may divide them into three different categories. First, there are idiomatic Hebrew expressions. Pfeiffer pointed out the following: 'many evils have found us' (1.11; 6.13; the combination of רע and מצא, 'to find evil + in someone', in Gen. 44.34; 1 Sam. 25.28; Jer. 23.11), 'they sold themselves to do evil' (1.15; מכר לעשה הרע 'to sell [oneself] to do evil' in 1 Kgs 21.20, 25; 2 Kgs 17.17), and 'two years of days' (1.29; שנתים ימים 'years of days' in Gen. 41.1; 2 Sam. 13.23).[26] Second, the author offers transliteration of names such as Αφαιρεμα, Λυδδα, Ῥαμαθαιμ, and Ιμαλκουε (11.34, 49). Oesterley suggests that Αφαιρεμα is probably either אפרים ('Ephraim', e.g. 2 Sam. 13.23) or עפרון ('Ephron', e.g. 2 Chron. 13.19), Λυδδα from לוד ('Lud', e.g. Isa. 66.19), and Ῥαμαθαιμ from רמתים ('Ramathaim', 1 Sam. 1.1).[27] For Ιμαλκουε, ימלכו is often suggested as the Hebrew rendering.[28] The scope of transliteration also includes Jewish months (e.g. Χασελευ [כסלו] in 1.54; 4.52, 59; e.g. Zech. 7.1; Αδαρ [אדר] in 7.43, 49; e.g. Ezra 6.15; Ελουλ [אלול] in 14.27; e.g. Neh. 6.15; Σαβατ [שבט] in 16.14; e.g. Zech. 1.7). Third, the arrangement of sentences largely follows the order of Hebrew parataxis, with a continuous string of καί + verb + noun + object, rather than the more sophisticated Greek syntactical order which typically contains participles and finite verbs.[29]

---

25. George T. Zervos, '1 Makkabees', in *A New English Translation of the Septuagint: And the Other Greek Translations Traditionally Included Under that Title*, ed. Albert Pietersma and Benjamin G. Wright (Oxford: Oxford University Press, 2007), 478–502.

26. For more examples, see Pfeiffer, *History*, 484–6. Schwartz ('Text of 1 Maccabees', 4) also notes 'lawless sons' (1.11), 'sons of arrogance' (2.47), and 'valiant sons' (3.58) as examples.

27. Oesterley, '1 Maccabees', 1:59–124 (109). The rendering of Ramathaim is not simple because the three major uncials and the group *q* minuscules render it as Ῥαθαμ(ε)ιν; e.g. Rahlfs' rendering. Kappler's rendering, Ῥαμαθαιμ, on the other hand, is found in the sub-Lucianic text. Abel agrees with Kappler (cited by Kappler, 'Maccabaeorum', 119). One could infer that their decision was made on the grounds that despite the three uncials' different renderings, the textual variance on this word is considerable in different manuscripts (Latin, Syriac, and other texts all render differently), and the complication may have occurred from the original Hebrew rendering which is not clear either: רמתים, רמה, etc.

28. E.g. Oesterley, '1 Maccabees', 109; Goldstein, *1 Maccabees*, 436–7.

29. F. C. Conybeare and St. George Stock, *Grammar of Septuagint Greek* (Boston: Ginn & Co., 1905; repr., Peabody, MA: Hendrickson, 1988), 50.

Aside from these three types of evidence for translation from Hebrew to Greek, which suggest the attitude of the Greek translator, the most decisive support for such a translation comes from the fourth type of evidence, namely, translational error.[30] Commentaries on 1 Maccabees discuss numerous such examples and some scholars have dedicated their research solely to collecting them.[31] The following examples sufficiently demonstrate the existence of translational errors. (1) In 1.29, the figure sent by Antiochus IV is called in Greek ἄρχοντα φορολογίας ('chief revenue, or tax, agent'), and שַׂר הַמִּסִּים in Hebrew (e.g. Exod. 1.11),[32] but what he did was unrelated to matters of tax but rather causing a catastrophe in Judea with military force. 2 Maccabees 5.24 identified this figure with a 'Mysarch', a commander of a military unit from Mysia (a region in northwestern Anatolia)[33] which would be rendered in Hebrew as שַׂר הַמֻּסִים, the unvocalized form of the name 'tax official'. (2) In 3.41, the troops who joined the Seleucid army are said to be from 'Syria and the land of the Philistines'. Based on the fact that the army from Syria is obviously already part of the Seleucid army, that the word 'Syria', probably ארם in Hebrew, is visually very similar to אדם, 'Edom', and that Idumea was indeed adjacent to Philistia, scholars have rightly inferred a misreading of אדם as ארם. (3) In 6.34 Seleucid commanders 'showed' (δείκνυμι) their elephants the juice of grapes and mulberries in order to agitate them for battle.[34] This verb, הראו in Hebrew, that is, the *hiphil* form

---

30. Compare Schwartz who further differentiates between failure to understand ambiguous Hebrew words and misreading of clear words ('Text of 1 Maccabees', 7).

31. For discussions of the following examples, see especially commentaries by Abel, Zeitlin, Goldstein, Bartlett. Ettelson ('Integrity', 308 n. 7) also lists previous scholars who discussed translational errors in detail, as well as including his own observation: (1) 'peculiarities of syntax and vocabulary': 1.29, 36; 2.8, 54; 3.3, 9, 15; 4.9, 24; 5.30-33; 6.21; 7.33; 9.44; (2) 'obscurities in and difficulties of text': 6.34; 10.72; and (3) 'other examples of mistranslations': 1.28; 4.19, 24; 9.24. Schwartz devoted himself to explaining several examples in detail, see 'Text of 1 Maccabees', 3–14.

32. Literally, 'taskmaster'. The word 'taskmaster' is often associated with 'tax-gatherer' in the Hebrew Bible, using a more common word נגש (Exod. 5.14; Zech. 9.8; 10.4; Dan. 11.20).

33. Just as the title of Nicanor in 2 Macc. 12.2 is rendered as 'Cypriarch', i.e. governor of Cyprus.

34. P. G. Maxwell-Stuart following Julius Wellhausen's suggestion, preferred הרוו, and rejected the suggestion of A. Geiger who, according to Maxwell-Stuart, suggested ראח as an 'orthographical or dialectical variation' of רוה, which was then confused by the Greek translator who was unfamiliar with that variation.

of ראה ('to see'), could be a misreading of a similar word, הרוו, the *hiphil* form of הרה ('to cause to drink', or 'drench'). (4) In 6.37, manuscripts' renderings are split between 'thirty' and 'thirty-two' for the number of soldiers riding on each Seleucid elephant, and both numbers are obviously absurd. Here, the unvocalized word שלשים might have been erroneously read as שְׁלֹשִׁים ('thirty'), rather than שָׁלִשִׁים ('officers') which makes more sense. If the original rendered 'two officers', this may explain 'thirty-two' in Greek manuscripts.[35] This alternative reading is especially attractive when Exod. 14.8 has all the chariots manned by שָׁלִשָׁם (though, there is no *yod* in Exodus). (5) In 8.29, the document sent by the Romans to the Judeans states the ongoing action of making a treaty between the two nations. The Greek aorist verb ἔστησαν, which should have been either the present or the imperfect form, may be a result of either the mistranslation of a Hebrew perfect or the latter's accidental corruption. (6) In 16.3, Simon addresses his sons about the legacy of the Hasmonean family and the Greek reads: 'my replacement and of *my brother* (τοῦ ἀδελφοῦ μου)'. Schwartz suggested that the singular 'my brother' is obviously misleading since the context refers to all of his brothers who bravely fought and gave up their lives for the law and the nation.[36] However, unlike Greek, in Hebrew the singular and plural terms for 'my brother' are both אחי which could have confused the translator.

Despite these minor errors, which are nevertheless helpful clues for determining the Hebrew original text, it should be re-emphasized that the Greek translator made remarkable efforts in his preservation of the Hebraic character of the text. From the first three types of evidence, it has been unanimously agreed by scholars that the translator carefully and faithfully followed the original Hebrew text. This generally accepted verdict might be the reason that no clear distinction between the Hebrew original and the Greek translation is usually made in exegetical comments on an individual passage, even though this ignorance is not entirely

---

Maxwell-Stuart, however, meant that it was a scribal error made during a dictation of writing the Hebrew text of 1 Maccabees, rather than a translational error. Maxwell-Stuart, '1 Maccabees VI 34 Again', *VT* 25 (1975): 230–3. In contrast, Schwartz ('Text of 1 Maccabees', 7–8) viewed the verse as a translational error. The strategy of agitating elephants to cause them to be blind and become aggressive is found in the Greek world as well as in 3 Macc. 5.2, 10, 45.

35. For different possibilities, see Beezalel Bar-Kochva, *Judas Maccabaeus: The Jewish Struggle against the Seleucids* (Cambridge: Cambridge University Press, 1989), 321–3.

36. Schwartz, 'Text of 1 Maccabees', 5.

justifiable.³⁷ Thus, we may conclude that the Greek 1 Maccabees, despite being a translation of a non-extant Hebrew text, reliably reflects the Hebrew original to a considerable extent.

2.1.3. On Greek Scripture
As for the question about the use of Scripture in 1 Maccabees, the fact that the Greek version remains as our main source necessitates clarification on the nature of the Greek translator's scriptural source. In the following, I will present three aspects of the nature of Greek Scripture as the translator of 1 Maccabees knew it: terminology, plurality of texts, and dating of translated biblical writings.³⁸

First, terminology. The Latin term 'septuaginta', literally meaning 'seventy', is found in the title of Latin manuscripts of biblical writings as 'interpretatio septuaginta virorum' ('the translation by the seventy men'), and is associated with the story of seventy-two scholars from Jerusalem who translated the Pentateuch at Alexandria under Ptolemy II, found mainly in the *Letter of Aristeas*, and partly in the fragments of Hellenistic-Jewish writer Aristobulus (Frag. 3)³⁹ and in Philo's *De Vita Mosis* 2.25-44.⁴⁰ The mentions of Greek translation of biblical writings in patristic literature, as early as the second century CE, were inspired by this story.⁴¹ When used in modern scholarship, however, the designation of the term follows the patristic tradition and surviving manuscripts, all of which point to the more-or-less entire range of biblical writings in Greek, rather than the first five books translated by the seventy-two Jewish scholars.⁴² Also, one cannot take it for granted that the range of individual translated

---

37. See the next section for some examples where Greek 1 Maccabees does not follow the vocabulary of the Septuagint.

38. See Dines, *Septuagint*, 1–24; Tessa Rajak, *Translation and Survival: The Greek Bible and The Ancient Jewish Diaspora* (Oxford: Oxford University Press, 2009), 14–16. For a helpful summary of scholarly debates relating to terminological and textual issues pertaining to studies of the Greek Scripture/Septuagint, see Susan E. Docherty, *The Use of the Old Testament in Hebrews*, WUNT 2/260 (Tübingen: Mohr Siebeck, 2009), 121–30.

39. Eusebius, *Praep. ev.* 13.12.1–2; Clement of Alexandria, *Strom.* 1.22.148.

40. Philo's account of the translation of biblical literature shows some marked differences from the account of the *Letter of Aristeas*. See Dines (*Septuagint*, 65–7), who identifies eight different points between the two accounts.

41. E.g. Irenaeus, *Against Heresies* 3.21.3; Tertullian, *Apology* 18; later in Augustine, *City of God* 18.42.

42. Also, as Jobes and Silva note, the fact that Origen used the term '*Septuagint*' to refer to both the version of Greek biblical writings which he received and

biblical texts available to the Greek translator of 1 Maccabees was the same as that of the Septuagint.⁴³ I follow the widely accepted suggestion of Leonard J. Greenspoon that the earliest form of the Greek translation of a biblical book that can be reconstructed should be designated as 'Old Greek (OG)', whilst the subsequent tradition of textual transmission as 'Septuagint'.⁴⁴

Second, this early Greek translation of biblical texts evidently had multiple versions, such as those well-known textual transmissions attributed to Aquila, Symmachus, and Theodotion from the Jewish tradition, and the Hesychian, Hexaplaric, and Lucianic recensions from the Christian tradition.⁴⁵ This multiplicity of Greek versions raises a question about whether there was ever only one translation. Paul de Lagarde argued that there probably was only one Greek translation – *Urtext* – for each of the biblical texts, and that the textual differences in manuscripts meant the existence of deviating editions of that single translation. Alternatively, Paul Kahle proposed that several translations arose from liturgical needs in synagogues, and that any attempts of unification were made at later stages.⁴⁶ Lagarde's theory has been accepted by the

---

the version which he produced illustrates clearly the difficulty of using the term 'Septuagint' without further qualification (see Jobes and Silva, *Invitation to the Septuagint*, 13–33).

43. Certain scholars are dubious about the available scope of biblical literature in the Hasmonean era. In the following section, however, we will contend that the majority of biblical books were available to the author of 1 Maccabees. See §2.3.

44. Leonard J. Greenspoon, 'The Use and Abuse of the Term "LXX" and Related Terminology in Recent Scholarship', *BIOSCS* 20 (1987): 21–9. This terminology is followed by Dines, *Septuagint*, 3; Jobes and Silva, *Invitation to the Septuagint*, 32; Docherty, *Hebrews*, 123.

45. On the characteristics of the Greek in these Jewish and Christian editions, see Jobes and Silva, *Invitation to the Septuagint*, 45–68; Dines, *Septuagint*, 81–108. For a lengthy discussion with a bibliography on each of the Greek editions see Natalio Fernández Marcos, *Septuagint in Context: Introduction to the Greek Version of the Bible*, trans. Wilfred G. E. Watson (Leiden: Brill, 2000), 109–303. The discovery of the Twelve Prophets scroll from Naḥel Ḥever near the Dead Sea, followed by publications, notably starting with D. Barthélemy (see Jellicoe, *Septuagint*, 62–3), has allowed us to identify the so-called kaige recension, i.e. the consistent use of καί γε as well as other words in translating correspondent Hebrew words, which is found in later revisions.

46. For summaries and discussions on theories about the Greek translation of biblical texts, see Jellicoe, *Septuagint*, 1–24, 59–73; Dines, *Septuagint*, 58–9; Jobes and Silva, *Invitation to the Septuagint*, 274–6; Docherty, *Hebrews*, 122–30. For the critique of Kahle's theory, see Jellicoe, *Septuagint*, 61–3; Marcos, *Septuagint in Context*, 55–7.

majority of scholars,[47] although some have qualified their acceptance with revisions of Lagarde's theory.[48] The implication that there was only one translation with subsequent editions is that those multiple versions of Greek Scripture should rather be regarded as editions developed from previous revisions.

Third, if one accepts that any translation started with the Pentateuch in Egypt during the early Hellenistic period under the rule of Ptolemy II, as the *Letter of Aristeas* claims and most scholars have acknowledged, all other biblical books are thus later.[49] Depending on the date for the translation of 1 Maccabees into Greek, this implies for the present study that the Greek versions of some biblical texts were not yet accessible for the Greek translator of 1 Maccabees. In the next section, I will discuss that some scholars even deny the original composition of some biblical texts by the time of the original composition of 1 Maccabees. Within the field of Septuagint studies, it has been maintained that Joshua, Samuel, Kings, and Chronicles were available in Greek by the early second century BCE, whilst the Prophets, 2 Esdras, and apocryphal works were available by the mid-second century BCE, and the book of Ruth by the early first century CE.[50]

2.1.4. *The translator's vocabulary*

Up to this point, we have made the presumption that the Greek translator of 1 Maccabees was able to consult at least some biblical books in Greek. However, one cannot take it for granted that a reconstruction of the original Hebrew reading of 1 Maccabees can be achieved by consulting the Septuagint only; as we will see in the following, the language of the Greek version, whilst displaying deliberate association

---

47. For the list of scholars in this regard and their bibliography, see Jellicoe, *Septuagint*, 9–25; Marcos, *Septuagint in Context*, 56–7.

48. E.g. J. W. Wevers, 'Barthélemy and Proto-Septuagint Studies', *BIOSCS* 18 (1985): 16–38 (26); Emanuel Tov, *The Text-Critical Use of the Septuagint in Biblical Research* (Jerusalem: Simor, 1997), 11–15; Marcos (*Septuagint in Context*, 43–4, 247) suggests the existence of revisions almost immediately after the translation; Docherty, *Hebrews*, 123–4.

49. This is not to overlook the problem of the letter's authenticity. However, following Marcos (*Septuagint*, 39–40), who points out that the language of the Greek translation of the Pentateuch belongs to the first half of the third century BCE (following A. Deissmann's studies), and that the third-century BCE Hellenistic Jewish writer Demetrius evidently knew Genesis in Greek, I will maintain the letter's authenticity as regards the date of the Greek translation under Ptolemy II in Alexandria in the third century BCE.

50. Dines, *Septuagint*, 41–7.

with the style of the Septuagint in many cases, nevertheless differs from the latter in many occasions.⁵¹ Consequently, when Bezalel Bar-Kochva critiqued Abraham Kahana's reconstruction of the Hebrew *Vorlage* of 1 Maccabees, which is based on the Septuagint only, his comment that the Septuagint vocabulary offers only limited knowledge about the original text is legitimate.⁵²

The influence of Greek Scripture in 1 Maccabees can be observed from several cases. For instance, the translator of 1 Maccabees makes a careful distinction between θυσιαστήριον and βωμός, with the first referring to a Jewish altar and the second to a pagan altar consistently throughout the narrative.⁵³ The same pattern of distinction can be found in Greek Scripture (although there are some exceptions to this rule).⁵⁴ Another case comes from 1 Macc. 5.15, where the mention of 'Tyre, Sidon and all the Galilee of the allophyles' (Τύρου καὶ Σιδῶνος καὶ πᾶσαν Γαλιλαίαν ἀλλοφύλων) potentially echoes Joel 3.4 (4.4 for Hebrew and Greek versions) in which 'Tyre, Sidon and all the regions of the Philistia' (צר וצידון וכל גלילות פלשת) is translated as 'Tyre, Sidon and *all the*

---

51. E.g. Pfeiffer (*History*, 485–6) suggests the influence of Greek Scripture to identify 1 Maccabees with biblical texts such as Ezra, Nehemiah and Chronicles. Similarly, see Bartlett, *Books of Maccabees*, 19; Goldstein, *1 Maccabees*, 1–27; 'Messianic Promises', 74–81.

52. Bar-Kochva, *Judas Maccabaeus*, 168–9. Also see James R. Davila, '(How) Can We Tell if a Greek Apocryphon or Pseudepigraphon has been Translated from Hebrew or Aramaic?', *JSP* 15 (2005): 3–61.

53. θυσιαστήριον: 1 Macc. 1.21, 54, 59; 4.38, 44, 45, 47, 49, 50, 53, 56, 59; 5.1; 6.7; 7.36. βωμός: 1 Macc. 1.47, 54, 59; 2.23, 24, 25, 45; 5.68. Particularly notable is 1.59, where the two words are displayed in close parallel: 'On the twenty-fifth of the month they were sacrificing on *the altar* that was on top of *the altar*' (καὶ τῇ πέμπτῃ καὶ εἰκάδι τοῦ μηνὸς θυσιάζοντες ἐπὶ τὸν βωμόν, ὃς ἦν ἐπὶ τοῦ θυσιαστηρίου). The phrase τοῦ θυσιαστηρίου is supplied with the adjective 'sacrificial' in NETS and with the phrase 'of burnt offering' in NRSV, but in Greek no such words are supplied for these two 'altars'. Their contrasting parallel is solely displayed by the two different words for 'altar'.

54. E.g. Josh.^(Gk) 22.19, '…do not rebel from the Lord by your building an altar (βωμός) other than the altar (θυσιαστήριον) of the Lord our God'. See Emanuel Tov, 'Theologically Motivated Exegesis Embedded in the Septuagint', in *The Greek and Hebrew Bible: Collected Essays on the Septuagint*, VTSup 72 (Leiden: Brill, 1999), 257–70 (263–4). Tov suggested the Greek translators of biblical texts as theological exegetes appropriating and defending Jewish Scripture in the Hellenistic world, thus affecting the translation of passages concerning God, his acts, Messiah, exile and the whole spectrum of religious experience (257–9).

Galilee of allophyles' (Τύρος καὶ Σιδὼν καὶ πᾶσα Γαλιλαία ἀλλοφύλων).[55] The use of 'allophyles' ('foreigners') as a reference to enemies of the Jews is frequently found in 1 Maccabees,[56] and frequently appears (over 200 times) in the Greek Bible – predominantly in Judges, Samuel and Chronicles – as the Greek word for פלשת ('Philistia'), a feature which could suggest both the translator's knowledge of the Greek versions of these specific texts and פלשת as the Hebrew word in the original text of 1 Maccabees.[57] However, the use of 'all the Galilee of allophyles' is even more striking. The probability of Joel 3.4[Gk] having an influence on 1 Macc. 5.15 is high because it mentions the very unique phrase 'Tyre, Sidon and all the Galilee of allophyles'. This phrase in Joel[Gk] is a translational error, occurring from confusing גלילות (stemming from גלל, meaning a 'region', sometimes even rendered as גלילה which is identical with the rendering for 'Galilee')[58] with גליל(ה) ('Galilee').[59] As a result, the Hebrew version of Joel reads 'all the *regions* of Philistia' whereas its Greek text reads 'all the *Galilee* of allophyles'. What is more, the erroneous 'all the Galilee of allophyles' is found nowhere in the Greek Bible but Joel,[60] and the translator of 1 Maccabees is coincidentally repeating the same error. The verse in 1 Maccabees, then, offers a clue to the translational scheme of the Greek version, especially of scriptural expressions in the book: the translator might have accessed Greek Scripture when translating scriptural expressions in the original 1 Maccabees. Schwartz

---

55. See also Chapters 3–4 for details of scholarly discussion concerning the scriptural sources of 1 Macc. 5.15, in which some scriptural sources other than Joel 4.4 are discussed.

56. 1 Macc. 3.41; 4.12, 22, 26, 30; 5.66, 68; 11.68, 74.

57. This suggestion is in contrast to Goldstein, who suggested גוים ('nations') as the Hebrew word for 'allophyles' in 1 Macc. 5.15 as well as in other cases in the book (Goldstein, *1 Maccabees*, 299). However, Goldstein seems to be unaware of the same phrase Joel[Gk].

58. There are five occurrences of this confusing גלילות (or גלילה) in the Septuagint: Josh.[Gk] 13.2; 22.10, 11; Ezek.[Gk] 47.8; Joel[Gk] 3.4. Interestingly, they all display confusion about this word: while the word is correctly translated in Josh.[Gk] 13.2, it is later confused with 'Galgala' (22.10) and even 'Galaad' in the following verse (22.11). Ezekiel[Gk] confuses it with Galilee just like Joel[Gk].

59. Josh. 12.23; 20.7; 21.32; 1 Kgs 9.11; 2 Kgs 15.29; 1 Chron. 6.76; Isa. 9.1 (8.23 for Hebrew and Greek texts).

60. Ezek.[Gk] 47.8 is an exception where the same erroneous reading of גלל occurs (see the footnote above). The combination of three regions, Tyre, Sidon and Philistia, the combination of גלל with Philistia, and the use of 'allophyles' for a reference to Philistia, however, all suggest a strong link between Joel[Gk] 4.4 and 1 Macc. 5.15.

also noted the translator's familiarity with Greek Scripture in 1.24, and his translation as guided by the latter.[61] The Greek word φονοκτονία (1.24, '...carried out φονοκτονία and spoke with great arrogance') is a term only found in the Septuagint, and English translations usually select 'much blood' (NRSV) or 'murder' (RSV, NETS). However, Schwartz noted that murders and bloodshed after the theft of temple vessels (vv. 21-23) are absurd, and Antiochus' return to his land (v. 24) an abrupt ending. Interestingly, φονοκτονία corresponds to חנף in Hebrew which means 'to pollute' (Num. 35.33; Ps. 105[106].38), and it is a possible indication of the translator's knowledge of the Septuagint which guided him to use a word already established as the translation for חנף. Strikingly, Isa. 32.6 reads 'to practice חנף, to utter error concerning the Lord', and it is possible that this prophecy is deliberately alluded to in 1 Maccabees and that the translator consulted Isaiah[Gk].

On the other hand, there are other cases where the translator was independent from, if not ignorant of, the vocabulary of Greek Scripture. Ettelson has already demonstrated that many Greek words in 1 Maccabees are not found in the Septuagint.[62] In addition, I will propose some examples that suggest the translator's ignorance of the Septuagint's vocabulary. In Judas' eulogy, the translator uses γίγας (3.3) for the description of Judas' warrior-like posture, instead of δυνατός, ἰσχυρός or their variants, which are usually used to refer to a 'mighty warrior' in biblical literature (describing God, judges, David, etc.). This is a significant departure from the Septuagint vocabulary in which γίγας refers predominantly to antagonists of Israel, such as Israel's fearful enemies and other evil forces

---

61. Schwartz, 'Text of 1 Maccabees', 8–13. As well as 1.24, which is added to our list, Schwartz also discussed the use of παράνομοι (1.11), which literally means 'law-breakers' or 'renegades', but which, in the context of 1 Maccabees, refers to the Jews politically opposing the Hasmoneans rather than those who fail to adhere to Torah (ibid., 11–13). Schwartz noted that this is also the way the Septuagint renders παράνομοι for the Hebrew word בני־בליעל, which means 'wicked', 'scoundrels' or, literally, 'sons of Belial', but which is not particularly associated with breaking the law (e.g. Deut. 13.13; 1 Sam. 2.12). Whilst Schwartz rightly noted, following Abel, that the Deuteronomic terminology (Deut. 13.13) shaped the whole of 1 Macc. 1, the literary link between the Greek translation of 1 Maccabees and the Greek translation of biblical literature is not as convincing as the other example Schwartz discussed (1.24) because the Hasmoneans are deliberately depicted, with exaggerations, as law-observant Jews, and their political opponents as law-breakers. That the translator's use of the legal term was dependent upon Greek Scripture, thus, seems a weaker argument than the other example.

62. Ettelson, 'Integrity', 322–5; also, Pfeiffer, *History*, 498.

like Nephilim, Anak and their descendants.[63] Had the translator intended his Greek to comply with that of Greek Scripture, he would have made a serious mistake in identifying Judas with the enemies of Israel.[64] It is more likely that in his translation of גבור (the Hebrew word that broadly encompasses both protagonists and antagonists, and most likely the underlying word here), he was unaware of the characteristic of the Greek equivalents, whether δυνατός or γίγας, suggesting the independence of his translation.

Another example is found in the use of prophecies in Simon's eulogy. We will briefly comment on this here and leave the detailed analysis for the next chapter. In the eulogies, there is a reference to an agricultural rejuvenation as a consequence of the Judean restoration under Simon (1 Macc. 14.8). This reference is syntactically identifiable with the prophecy of Zech. 8.12 in such a way that the two verses resemble one another not only in terms and themes but also in their construction. Notable for our discussion is the first part of the sentence in 1 Maccabees which follows the Hebrew version of Zechariah rather than the Greek. The peaceful cultivation in 1 Maccabees ('cultivating their land in peace', γεωργοῦντες τὴν γῆν αὐτῶν μετ' εἰρήνης) is associated with the same, agricultural expression in Hebrew ('sowing of peace', זרע השלום). They are, however, quite distant from Zechariah[Gk] which emphasizes divine initiative in the restoration of the land ('I will demonstrate peace', ἀλλ' ἤ δείξω εἰρήνην), without retaining the agricultural terminology. We may add 1 Macc. 14.12 which bears a syntactical resemblance to Mic. 4.4, but in which the Greek verb, καθίζω, betrays Micah[Gk] which has ἀναπαύω.

Despite the lack of a comprehensive survey on 1 Maccabees' use/non-use of the Septuagint's vocabulary, the aforementioned examples already present us with complexity in determining the relation between 1 Maccabees and Greek Scripture. It is especially difficult to determine whether the translator is deliberately modifying words used in Greek Scripture or whether he is relying on his own knowledge of Greek without consulting an already existing translation of this Scripture.[65] Thus, caution

---

63. There are over 40 references to this usage: e.g. Gen. 6.4; 10.8; 14.5; Num. 13.33; Deut. 1.28; Josh. 12.4; 13.12; 2 Sam. 21.11, 22; 1 Chron. 1.10; 11.15; 14.9; Isa. 3.2; 13.3; 14.9; Ezek. 39.18, 20.

64. Neither is it conceivable to imagine the translator depicting Judas pejoratively in the context where the intention of glorifying and honouring him is conspicuous.

65. See, for instance, a recent article by Jan Joosten, 'Varieties of Greek in the Septuagint and the New Testament', in *The New Cambridge History of the Bible: From the Beginnings to 600*, ed. James Carleton-Paget and Joachim Schaper

has to be taken when interpreting the reason behind the translator's vocabulary choice.

2.1.5. *Summary*

The four sections have reached the following conclusions. (1) The textual variants of the Greek version of 1 Maccabees require not only the use of a critically reconstructed Greek text but also the utilization of the Old Latin and Josephus' paraphrased text, especially where a textual issue arises. (2) Despite the absence of the original Hebrew text, we can say at a syntactical level that the Greek translator reliably preserved the Hebrew. (3) The translator evidently consulted existing Greek Scripture, allowing us to reconstruct Hebrew wordings of certain passages. (4) On the other hand, in other cases, the translator seemed to be free from the influence of his scriptural source, and consulting the Septuagint's vocabulary in our study can be misleading.

2.2. *Authorship and dating of 1 Maccabees*

2.2.1. *Authorship*

Whilst little is known about the author's identity, scholars have unanimously affirmed that he was of Jewish origin, born and brought up in Palestine, probably in Jerusalem, and was acquainted with the geography and topography of Palestine and surrounding regions.[66] Coming from a wealthy family, he was not only well-versed in Hebrew Scripture, but also sufficiently fluent in Greek to incorporate official documents and letters into his writing. His bilinguality (or even trilinguality, granted that he had knowledge of Aramaic too) probably represented the sociolinguistic current of the second-century BCE Judea.[67] From his conspicuously

---

(Cambridge: Cambridge University Press, 2013), 22–45. Here, Joosten showed a generally shared linguistic culture among Jewish communities of the Hellenistic era where Hebraism, as well as use of Koine Greek, was a Jewish characteristic.

66. Most commentators include a short paragraph or two on authorship in the introductory chapter. A helpful, lengthy discussion on authorship is offered by Pfeiffer, *History*, 491–6.

67. Scholars in biblical studies claim that Aramaic was the main spoken language in Judea in most of the Second Temple period, and the use of Hebrew was limited to religious sphere, or even a dead language insofar as the majority population of the Judean society is concerned, a view which was influenced by the works of Abaham Geiger and Gustaf Dalman. Geiger, *Lehr- und Lesebuch zur Sprache der Mischnah: Band 1, Lehrbuch zur Sprache der Mischnah* (Breslau: Leuckart, 1845); Dalman, *Die mit Berücksichtigung des nachkanonischen jüdischen*

pro-Hasmonean attitude, it is clear that the author's interests are considerably in favour of the Hasmonean leadership, even deliberately one-sided when depicting the Hasmoneans in contrast to the pro-Seleucid Judeans and the gentile nations. It is therefore fair to say that he represents a Hasmonean viewpoint.

In general, the author is an adherent of the law of Moses and is patriotic. Scholars have often suggested the author as holding a Sadducean worldview, as opposed to Pharisaic,[68] although not all scholars agree on

---

Schrifttums und der aramäischen Sprache erörtert (Leipzig: J. C. Hinrichs, 1898). Some scholars, such as J. T. Milik and Ben Zion Wacholder, have attested to the so-called revival of Hebrew language during the Maccabean era. Milik, *Ten Years of Discovery in the Wilderness of Judaea*, trans. J. Strugnell, SBT 26 (London: SCM, 1959), 130; Wacholder, 'The Ancient Judaeo-Aramaic Literature (500–164 BCE): A Classification of Pre-Qumranic Texts', in *Archaeology and History in the Dead Sea Scrolls – The New York University Conference in Memory of Yigael Yadin*, ed. Lawrence H. Schiffman, JSPSup 8; JSOT/ASORMon 2 (Sheffield: JSOT, 1990), 257–81 (especially 273–5). However, other scholars have rightly pointed out that the use of Hebrew language was beyond the religious context, reaching various other contexts of daily life of Jews, and used before the Maccabean era as well. See, for instance, James Barr, 'Hebrew, Aramaic and Greek in the Hellenistic Age', *CHJ* 2:79–114 (113); Steve Weitzman, 'Why Did the Qumran Community Write in Hebrew?', *JAOS* 119 (1999): 35–45 (especially 36 n. 11, with his example of Ben Sira manuscripts written in paleo-Hebrew script, which pre-date the Maccabean era). A recent epigraphical survey carried out by Guido Baltes further shows that the sociolinguistic culture of the Jewish society in the second temple period is characterized as a 'trilingual society', using the three languages – Hebrew, Aramaic and Greek – 'side by side' and 'in close connection to each other' in various contexts such as 'military, economic and legal' as well as religious one. Baltes, 'The Use of Hebrew and Aramaic in Epigraphic Sources of the New Testament Era', in *The Language Environment of First Century Judaea: Jerusalem Studies in the Synoptic Gospels, Vol. 2*, ed. Randall Buth and R. Steven Notley, JCPS 26 (Leiden: Brill, 2014), 35–65 (quoted from 53, 64–5). Especially, both Hebrew and Aramaic appear to have been used within a single family or even by one person. An example is the family tomb of the Kallon family in Katamon (Baltes, 'Hebrew and Aramaic', 56–7). That said, the ideological dimension of using Hebrew language by the pro-Hasmonean writer of 1 Maccabees is not to be undermined. Just as the symbolic function of the Jerusalem temple and Torah, as Seth Schwartz rightly puts it, the Hebrew language 'became, not the national language of the Jews, but the language whose representation *symbolized* Jewish nationhood' (my italic). Schwartz, 'Hebrew and Imperialism in Jewish Palestine', in *Ancient Judaism in its Hellenistic Context*, ed. Carol Bakhos, JSJSup 95 (Leiden: Brill, 2005), 53–85 (quoted from 75).

68. E.g. Oesterley, 'Maccabees', 1:59; Dancy, *Maccabees*, 3; Bartlett, *Books of the Maccabees*, 18.

this point.[69] The suggestion was usually based on two observations. First, on two occasions the Hasmoneans are said to have engaged in a war during the Sabbath (2.32-48; 9.43-49). Because Pharisees were probably very unlikely to have broken Sabbath laws and would thus have abstained from partaking in war during the Sabbath, an author with a pro-Pharisaic view would probably have omitted these two references from his text. However, Zeitlin contested that the Sadducees were, to some extent, stricter than the Pharisees in observing the Sabbath, and the principle that 'one might profane one Sabbath in order to keep all the other Sabbaths' was upheld within the rabbinic tradition.[70] Second, there is a lack of evidence for a belief in life after death, which would have been expressed had the author been sharing a Pharisaic worldview.[71] However, borrowing Rappaport's words, it is 'not necessary to assume that the expression of every idea should be defined on sectarian lines'.[72]

2.2.2. Dating of 1 Maccabees
Scholars generally date 1 Maccabees during one of the following three periods: (1) the early period of John Hyrcanus I's reign (ca. 135–129 BCE); (2) the late period of, and the period shortly after, Hyrcanus I's reign (ca. 115–104 BCE); and (3) the domestically conflicting period during Alexander Jannaeus' reign (particularly close to, but not later than, 91 BCE).

The early period of John Hyrcanus I: proponents of this view offer three supporting arguments. First, in the very last two verses of 1 Maccabees (16.23-24), the narrative ends with the author's brief mention of John Hyrcanus I's achievements that were apparently recorded and stored. According to supporters of this date, this passage does not indicate any significant achievements, conquests, or territorial expansions. Instead, it only mentions Hyrcanus' fortification of Jerusalem's walls, an act which took place at the time of Antiochus VII's invasion of Judea, ca. 129 BCE. The date of the composition should thus be close to 129 BCE

---

69. Pfeiffer, *History*, 492–3; Zeitlin, *Maccabees*, 25–6; Rappaport, 'Maccabees', 711.

70. Zeitlin, *Maccabees*, 25–6. See *b. Yom.* 85b; *b. Shab.* 19a (cf. *t. 'Erub.* 3.7).

71. Oesterley ('Maccabees', 1:59) suggests Mattathias' deathbed blessing in which scriptural heroes are described (2.52-60), including Elijah who was 'taken up into heaven' (2.58). Dancy (*Maccabees*, 3) adds 3.59 and 9.9-10 in which Judas exhorts his soldiers to choose death in war over fleeing in cowardice.

72. Rappaport, 'Maccabees', 711.

(Bar-Kochva, Regev).[73] Second, it was argued by Schwartz in particular, in his study of Hyrcanus' and Aristobulus I's expansions of the Judean territory, that the nationalistic, anti-gentile tendency of 1 Maccabees seems contradictory to the regime of Hyrcanus who had formed a foreign troop as part of his army during the latter part of his reign. To avoid the contradiction, the composition is then placed prior to 130 BCE when such diplomacy originated.[74] Third, Momigliano suggested that the description of Rome in 1 Macc. 8.1-16, which shows no indication of any significant events such as the incident at Pergamum or Rome's establishment of their province in Asia, dates the composition to no later than 129 BCE.[75]

The late period of, and the period shortly after, Hyrcanus I's reign: this view is dominant and is supported in five ways. First, some scholars have observed that the book does not indicate any domestic conflict but implies only a harmonious national state, suggesting that the date should be earlier than the time when Alexander Jannaeus faced such conflict (Bickerman, Fischer, Babota).[76] Second, the final two verses of 1 Maccabees indicate, contrary to the former group's reading, that the date should reflect the latter part of Hyrcanus' reign, or the time shortly after his death (Rappaport, Attridge, Oesterley).[77] In particular, Grimm claims that the date should be *just before* Hyrcanus' death in 104 BCE because the alleged annals of Hyrcanus are unusually stated and incomplete when compared to other examples found in biblical literature (e.g. Kings); it does not include the number of Hyrcanus' regnal years, nor does it state

---

73. Bar-Kochva, *Judas Maccabaeus*, 152–70; Eyal Regev, *The Hasmoneans: Ideology, Archaeology, Identity*, JAJSup 10 (Göttingen: Vandenhoeck & Ruprecht, 2013), 26.

74. Seth Schwartz, 'Israel and the Nations Roundabout: I Maccabees and the Hasmonean Expansion', *JJS* 42 (1991): 16–38 (especially 17, 36–8).

75. Arnaldo Momigliano, 'The Date of the First Book of the Maccabees', in *Sesto Contributo Alla Storia Degli Studi Classici e Del Mondo Antico, vol. 2*, ed. A. Momigliano (Rome: Storia e Letteratura, 1980), 561–6; *Alien Wisdom: The Limits of Hellenization* (Cambridge: Cambridge University Press, 1975), 103.

76. Elias J. Bickerman, *Der Gott der Makkabäer: Untersuchungen über Sinn und Ursprung der makkabäischen Erhebung* (Berlin: Schocken, 1937), 29; Fischer, 'Maccabees', 4:441; Vasile Babota, *The Institution of the Hasmonean High Priesthood*, JSJSup 165 (Leiden: Brill, 2014), 11–12.

77. Uriel Rappaport, 'Maccabees', 711–34 (711); *The First Book of Maccabees: Introduction, Hebrew Translations, and Commentary* (Jerusalem: Yad ben-Zvi, 2004) (Hebrew), 61; H. Attridge, 'Historiography', in *Jewish Writings of the Second Temple Period*, ed. M. E. Stone, CRINT 2 (Assen: van Gorcum; Philadelphia: Fortress, 1984), 171; Oesterley, 'Maccabees', 1:60.

his successor.⁷⁸ Third, the statement in 13.30, 'this tomb, which he [Simon] made in Modein, remains to this day', indicates that we should allow at least a one-generation gap between the burial and the composition of the book for this statement to make sense. Since the erection of the tomb and monuments around it occurred between ca. 142–134 BCE, the date cannot be earlier than ca. 120–112 BCE (Fairweather and Black, Sievers, Babota).⁷⁹ Fourth, the derogative description of coveting kingship – 'and in all this not even one of them has put on a crown nor have they wrapped themselves in purple so as to show their power by it' (8.14) – suggests that such 'sensitivity'⁸⁰ towards monarchy should place the date at any time before the Hasmonean enthronement, thus, pre-104 BCE (Stern, Sievers, Babota).⁸¹ Finally, Babota mentions that the term 'his wars' (τῶν πολέμων αὐτοῦ) at the end of the book (16.23) may include Hyrcanus' expeditions in Samaria and Idumea (*War* 1.57-66; *Ant.* 13.249-81). Using Barag and Finkielsztein's excavations which date those expeditions to ca. 108 BCE,⁸² Babota suggests that the date should not be earlier than that.⁸³

78. Grimm, *Maccabäer*, xxiv; also, Rappaport, 'Maccabees', 711; cf. 1 Kgs 14.19, 29; 16.14, 27; 22.40; 2 Kgs 1.18; 10.34.

79. Fairweather and Black, *Maccabees*, 42; Sievers, *The Hasmoneans and Their Supporters*, 3; Babota, *Institution*, 11–12.

80. It is generally accepted in scholarship that this verse represents Jewish sensitivity at the time when the Davidic throne remained destroyed and, owing to the Davidic covenant concerning his everlasting kingdom (e.g. 2 Sam. 7), it may have been the case that the average Jews refrained from allowing anyone of non-Davidic lineage to sit on the throne. See, for instance, Pss. Sol. 17, where the writer condemns the Hasmonean monarch and revives the hope of restitution of the Davidic kingdom.

81. Menahem Stern, *Studies in Jewish History: The Second Temple Period* (Jerusalem: Yad ben-Zvi, 1991) (Hebrew), 348–9; Sievers, *Supporters*, 3; Babota, *Institution*, 11–12.

82. D. Barag, 'New Evidence on the Foreign Policy of John Hyrcanus I', *INJ* 12 (1992/93): 1–12; G. Finkielsztein, 'More Evidence on John Hyrcanus I's Conquests: Lead Weights and Rhodian Amphora Stamps', *BAIAS* 16 (1998): 33–63.

83. Babota, *Institution*, 11–12. An unusual argument for this dating was offered by Doran, see 'Maccabees', 4:22. Three internal elements – the unnecessary episode of the glorious Simon's rather tragic death (16.11-17), the contrast between the ideal model of the Roman government and Simon's one-man rule (14.41-45), and the hostile attitude toward the foreigners (the same point raised by Schwartz) – may point to a critique made to Hyrcanus shortly after his death. Doran's view on the author's standpoint is contradictory to that of most scholars who presume the author's pro-Hasmonean standpoint. It is legitimate to maintain that there are elements the author aims to highlight other than legitimizing the Hasmonean leadership, but not to the extent that undermines his deliberately pro-Hasmonean viewpoint. See §1.2.

Alexander Jannaeus (close to, but no later than, 91/90 BCE): this view was proposed by Goldstein (followed by the revised Schürer, van der Kooij[84]) based on the following reasons.[85] First, he views that the final passage concerning the annals of Hyrcanus should date the composition to a time after his death. Second, he utilizes his theory of 'Epistle 2' in the introductory sections of 2 Maccabees (2 Macc. 1.10b–2.18) in his dating of 1 Maccabees. Epistle 2, which he dates to 103 BCE, mentions that copies of some books of importance to the Jews would soon be sent to the recipient of the letter (2 Macc. 2.13-15), and Goldstein points out that there is no mention of 1 Maccabees in the list of important books. One might infer that the composition had not yet been formed (hence, again, a date after Hyrcanus' death).[86] Third, with regard to the harmonious relationship with Rome, the composition should be earlier than 91/90 BCE since Rome suffered from its social war in 91 BCE and the description of Rome in 8.1-16 is completely ignorant of that event. How, then, does Goldstein cope with the author's derogative statement about kingship in v. 14? Goldstein suggests that since there were growing domestic conflicts against the Hasmoneans in Judea near the proposed date, Alexander Jannaeus, in his attempt to secure his throne, 'temporarily' left it to settle the conflict, based on some overstruck coins attributed to Jannaeus that omit the sovereign title.[87]

Let us turn to evaluation of these claims by setting out a *terminus ad quem* and a *terminus ante quem*, whereby I will demonstrate that the most likely date of the composition is around the late period of Hyrcanus I's reign which predates the Hasmonean monarchy.

---

84. Schürer, *HJPAJC*, 3:181; Arie van der Kooij, 'The Claim of Maccabean Leadership and the Use of Scripture', in *Jewish Identity and Politics between the Maccabees to Bar Kokhba: Groups, Normativity, and Rituals*, ed. Benedikt Eckhardt, JSJSup 155 (Leiden: Brill, 2011), 29–49.

85. Goldstein, *1 Maccabees*, 62–4.

86. Goldstein's theory of Epistle 2 in 2 Maccabees cannot be the evidence for the late date of 1 Maccabees either, since the passage in question, 2 Macc. 2.13-15, has no clear indication about 1 Maccabees. In v. 14, the passage merely comments on those scriptures that were lost as a result of Antiochus Epiphanes' persecution in Judea but were later re-discovered and collected (as narrated in 1 Macc. 1.56-57, 3.48 and 12.9). The statement is not intended to list all literature available in Judea, but to highlight the fact that, just as in Nehemiah's time, re-collection and preservation of literatures regarded as sacred and authoritative were achieved by Judas, and they were available to the Egyptian Jews in order that they may preserve and devote themselves to Jewish ancestral religion through reading them.

87. Goldstein, *1 Maccabees*, 355–6.

2.2.2.1. *Terminus ad quem*

Two passages will be considered: 1 Macc. 13.27-30 and 16.23-34.

First, in the author's comment on the Hasmonean tombs in 13.27-30, the sentence 'this tomb...remains to this day' has been suggested as an indication of the passing of at least one generation after the event took place, but we cannot be more precise than saying this approximate 'long time' or 'at least a generation'. Indeed, the passage might refer to several generations passing. Perhaps one can suggest that the stress in the statement is that *the tomb has not so far been violated.* This may underline either length of time or safeguarding. For length of time, one may need to allow not only one generation but perhaps several generations to leave such a statement. However, in terms of safeguarding, passing a few domestic and international conflicts may be sufficient for one to make the aforementioned statement. This means, we can by no means rule out the time of John Hyrcanus I as a strong candidate. After his father Simon, Hyrcanus defended his nation from the Seleucids, even successfully carrying out military campaigns to neighbouring regions. That is, although the period of Hyrcanus' reign may be somewhat too early (approximately 40 years too early, between Jonathan's burial in 143/2 BCE[88] and Hyrcanus' death in 104 BCE), the many wars he fought for his nation, as well as his protection and fortification of the Judean cities for the next 40 years, may allow his time to be an eligible candidate for the date of the composition.[89]

The second passage for discussion is 16.23-24, which is a much-disputed part of 1 Maccabees:

> And the rest of the story about John and his wars and his heroic deeds which he did and the building of the walls which he built and his actions, look, these have been written in the book of days of his high priesthood from the time when he became high priest after his father.[90]

---

88. Although the actual date for the burial is not given in the text, it can be estimated fairly precisely from looking at surrounding episodes which occurred within a couple of years, for example Trypho's execution of Jonathan, Simon's receipt of his bones and burial, and the Jewish authorities' recognition of Simon's high priesthood and rulership followed by Demetrius' (Goldstein, *1 Maccabees*, 170–1; Schürer, *HJPAJC*, 1:190).

89. For the same view, Grimm, *Maccabäer*, xxiv; Abel, *Maccabées*, xxviii–xxix; Fairweather and Black, *Maccabees*, 42.

90. Kappler's apparatus does not contain any notable textual variance on these two verses.

These verses do not need to postdate Hyrcanus' death, as some scholars have presumed, because whilst similar to the biblical phrases, they do not include Hyrcanus' regnal years.[91] But do these verses support the first view, dating the text to the early Hyrcanus I? Bar-Kochva paid attention to 'the building of the walls which he built' (τῆς οἰκοδομῆς τῶν τειχῶν, ὧν ᾠκοδόμησεν), identifying the phrase with Hyrcanus' fortification of the Jerusalem walls in the time of Antiochus VII's invasion. Babota focused upon 'his wars' (τῶν πολέμων αὐτοῦ), identifying this with Hyrcanus' military campaigns to Samaria and Idumea, leading respectively to the dates of the early Hyrcanus I and the latter part of Hyrcanus' reign with the period shortly after his death. Both scholars were probably right in identifying those key achievements during Hyrcanus' regnal years, but I will contend that the central term in this passage seems to be τὰ λοιπὰ τῶν λόγων Ιωαννου ('the rest of the story of John').[92] If we view καὶ as a heading of each phrase, what emerges as a structure is as follows:

Καὶ τὰ λοιπὰ τῶν λόγων Ιωαννου
καὶ τῶν πολέμων αὐτοῦ
καὶ τῶν ἀνδραγαθιῶν αὐτοῦ, ὧν ἠνδραγάθησεν,
καὶ τῆς οἰκοδομῆς τῶν τειχῶν, ὧν ᾠκοδόμησεν,
καὶ τῶν πράξεων αὐτοῦ,
ἰδοὺ ταῦτα γέγραπται ἐπὶ βιβλίῳ ἡμερῶν ἀρχιερωσύνης αὐτοῦ, ἀφ' οὗ ἐγενήθη ἀρχιερεὺς μετὰ τὸν πατέρα αὐτοῦ.

In addition, πόλεμος καὶ ἀνδραγαθία is a unique term in 1 Maccabees occurring four times to summarize the heroic character of the Hasmoneans: 5.56; 9.22; 10.15; 16.23 (cf. its attribution to the Romans in 8.2).[93] We join the second and third lines as follows:

---

91. One can even suggest that in the phrase, ἐπὶ βιβλίῳ ἡμερῶν ἀρχιερωσύνης αὐτοῦ, ἀφ' οὗ ἐγενήθη ('[written] on the book of days of his high priesthood from when he became...'), the use of ἡμερῶν...ἀφ' οὗ ἐγενήθη, rather than πάσας τὰς ἡμέρας αὐτοῦ ('all his days') as in other occasions to describe a person's overall reigning period (3.12; 10.47; 14.4), may indicate that the composition was made before Hyrcanus' reign was complete.

92. The word λόγων is translated here as 'story' (e.g. Bartlett, *Books of Maccabees*, 212; cf. NETS with 'stories'). Other translators and commentators deviate from this by translating as 'acts' (e.g. NRSV; Oesterley, '1 Maccabees', 124; Fairweather and Black, *Maccabees*, 263) or 'history' (e.g. Goldstein, *1 Maccabees*, 523).

93. This is an exception but takes a similar direction in terms of describing war heroes. Surprisingly none of the surveyed commentators note this potentially important phrase and I have not come across any other studies on 1 Maccabees which mention this pattern. I noted this while carrying out previous research, see Dongbin

A: Καὶ τὰ λοιπὰ τῶν λόγων Ιωαννου
a: καὶ τῶν πολέμων αὐτοῦ καὶ τῶν ἀνδραγαθιῶν αὐτοῦ, ὧν ἠνδραγάθησεν,
a: καὶ τῆς οἰκοδομῆς τῶν τειχῶν, ὧν ᾠκοδόμησεν,
a: καὶ τῶν πράξεων αὐτοῦ,
B: ἰδοὺ ταῦτα γέγραπται ἐπὶ βιβλίῳ ἡμερῶν ἀρχιερωσύνης αὐτοῦ, ἀφ' οὗ ἐγενήθη ἀρχιερεὺς μετὰ τὸν πατέρα αὐτοῦ.

The phrase 'the rest of Hyrcanus' stories' comprises three types of achievement, namely, 'his wars and brave deeds', 'the building of the walls that he built', and 'his other achievements', and they are written in 'the annals of his high priesthood'. The author was well aware of Hyrcanus' other episodes and achievements, then, and for some reason was only reticent about recounting them in his writing, just as the incident of Antiochus VII's invasion of Jerusalem was unmentioned.

2.2.2.2. Terminus ante quem

The positive description of the Romans in 1 Macc. 8.1-16 gives a strong case that a *terminus ante quem* has to be no later than Pompey's siege of Jerusalem in 63 BCE which marked the beginning of the Roman subjugation of the Judeans.[94]

Choi, 'Are the Hasmoneans Legitimised in 1 Maccabees?' (MRes diss., University of Nottingham, 2014), 33–5. I would say this phrase is, in fact, formulaic in such a way that the same term is applied repeatedly to the Hasmoneans. The use of the term to describe the Romans (8.2) is not inconsistent since the author's attitude towards them is deliberately favourable and optimistic.

94. E.g. Goldstein, *Maccabees*, 62–3. He further suggests 91 BCE to be *a terminus ante quem*, because such was the year in which the so-called Allied War began and the inglorious history of the Romans during that time is unknown to the author of 1 Maccabees. Momigliano argues that the *terminus ante quem* should be 129 BCE, based on the manner in which the Romans are described in the passage (Momigliano, 'Date', 561–6). The kernel of his argument is that the transformation of the kingdom of Pergamum into a Roman province, which occurred around 129 BCE, is not indicated in our passage. Instead, the author still calls Pergamum a kingdom in v. 8. With this date, Momigliano is convinced that the rest of the passage is in harmony with the events preceding 129 BCE, such as vv. 9–10 concerning the Romans' defeat of the Greek revolts as a reference to the Romans' defeat of Achaean League and the destruction of Corinth in 146 BCE (564). However, some of Momigliano's observations are unconvincing. The end of v. 8 gives a reference to Eumenes as King of Pergamum, but it tells the reader nothing more than a recounting of a past event, and it does not necessitate the author's knowledge of Pergamum's history to be limited to the latter's monarchical period. As Antiochus III in v. 6 is a figure of the past, so is Eumenes. His identification of vv. 9–10 with the event in 146

2. The Contribution of the Literary, Social and Cultural Milieus 53

The most decisive clue for a *terminus ante quem* comes from 8.14:

> And in all this not even one of them has put on a crown nor have they wrapped themselves in purple so as to show their power by it.
>
> καὶ ἐν πᾶσιν τούτοις οὐκ ἐπέθεντο αὐτῶν οὐδὲ εἷς διάδημα, οὐδὲ περιεβάλοντο πορφύραν ὥστε ἁδρυνθῆναι ἐν αὐτῇ·

As several scholars have already noted,[95] this verse references Jewish sensitivity towards a monarchical institution and, particularly, to one's self-enthronement. The repeated negative conjunctions (οὐκ... οὐδὲ... οὐδὲ) unmistakably stress the author's derogative view. Notably, whilst 'kings' and 'kingdoms' are frequently used within the passage (8.4, 5, 6, 8, 11, 12, 13) to express the Romans' superiority, the Romans themselves refused self-enthronement, highlighting their modest virtue. This trait of the Romans recalls the same virtue of the Hasmoneans expressed in the book,[96] just as their πόλεμος καὶ ἀνδραγαθία is a virtue in connection with the Jewish heroes, as mentioned earlier.

BCE may be correct, but the descriptions in vv. 11–13 may well include the event of the Roman subjugation of Pergamum, hence 129 BCE as a past date. Momigliano himself admits that the statements about the Hasmonean family's burial site (13.27-30) and Hyrcanus I's regnal years (16.23-24) weaken his argument for the early date, but his response that these were written 'with future readers in mind' and are thus considered as 'a vague prophetic element' is insufficient. Momigliano, 'Date', 565–6.

95. In addition to Stern, Sievers, and Babota, see Doron Mendels, *The Rise and Fall of Jewish Nationalism*, ABRL (New York: Doubleday, 1992), 60. Uriel Rappaport ('Maccabees', 723) regards the passage as 'simply a factual description of the Roman constitution, with admiration and a focus on what was extraordinary in it, in the eyes of one who was used to the Hellenistic monarchies of his day'. His comment may be taken as a caution against eisegesis. On the other hand, such a negative remark on self-enthronement may not be read by the audience without an attitude attached to it when their state of affairs was both kingless and king-awaited. In any case, we have seen that Rappaport's date of 1 Maccabees is also the date of the later reign of Hyrcanus. See Doran ('Maccabees', 4:105), who suggests that 'only victorious generals were allowed to wear a diadem and purple-coloured clothing, which were royal prerogatives, during triumphal celebrations'. Against Rappaport's comment, one could say that the author's insertion of the diadem remark may really be seen as a positive expression on the Romans, who only wore a diadem on certain specific occasions. In other words, the implied message is strongly against self-enthronement.

96. E.g. 1 Macc. 2.51-60; 13.3-6; 16.2-3; also compare the contrasting portrayals of Seleucid kings who coveted a throne (e.g. 1.1-10; 7.4; 10.52-53; 11.13, 52, 54; 12.39; 13.32).

There are three possible explanations for the author's negative comment about self-enthronement: (1) a criticism of the self-enthroned Hasmonean king; (2) as proposed by Goldstein, Alexander Jannaeus, in order to calm down the domestic animosity toward him, temporarily abandoned his throne, issued overstruck coins omitting any sovereign title, and wrote propaganda which criticizes kingship; (3) the pre-monarchical Hasmonean leader, whose gradual accumulation of wealth and growth of power might have been seen negatively by conservative Jewish groups, diplomatically claiming the derogative view on self-enthronement and expressing his family's limit of authority and perpetuity.

Of these three, the first option is inconceivable insofar as the author's pro-Hasmonean agenda is concerned. As for the second option, it should be stated above all that the scenario of Jannaeus' temporary abandonment of his throne lacks any evidence, and is only suggested based on some overstruck coins of Jannaeus that omit the sovereign title.[97] This scenario, however, does not recognize the fact that the primary cause of the Jewish opposition was the Hasmonean high priesthood, and abandonment of his throne could not have resolved the issue. The last option, namely the pre-monarchical period, seems to be the most reasonable, given the absence of monarchy in the Judean nation. The pro-Hasmonean writer's need for an anti-monarchical agenda, or, more precisely, an agenda of anti-self-enthronement, is not immediately obvious. Josephus lacks any explanation for the Pharisees' sudden opposition to the Hasmoneans. However, the Hasmonean family's gradual increase of power and wealth, which involved potentially controversial methods like opening David's tomb and hiring foreign troops, may have precipitated their relationship with conservative Judeans who had already been ambivalent about the legitimacy of the Hasmonean high priesthood, a point which will be explained further in the following section.

2.2.2.3. Summary

This section has discussed and narrowed down the date of composition of 1 Maccabees. For a *terminus ad quem*, the καί structure of the final verses of the book (16.23-24) demonstrates the author's awareness of Hyrcanus' numerous deeds which require a considerable span of time. The passage does not necessarily indicate Hyrcanus' death, and the omission of his successor and other literary ambiguities, as suggested by Rappaport, may be an indication that Hyrcanus was still alive at the time of the composition. Nevertheless, these absences do not offer decisive evidence. The author's

---

97. See §1.2.2 for a more detailed discussion.

comment concerning Hasmonean tombs (13.27-30) also suggests that a long period of time had to have passed before the composition, and the beginning of Hyrcanus' reign should probably be considered as too early in time. As for *terminus ante quem*, Momigliano's suggestion of 129 BCE based on his interpretation of the optimistic description of Rome (8.1-16) is unconvincing due to the ambiguous language of the passage, and a later date is certainly conceivable. The derogative comment about self-enthronement (8.14) places the date before the Hasmonean self-enthronement. Contrary to Goldstein, it has been argued that the text dates most plausibly to the later period of Hyrcanus' reign, whose authority as high priest and ruler in Judea was under growing threat, and a diplomatic assertion to his conservative audience was much needed. In short, the best possible date for the composition was around the last phases of Hyrcanus' life.

2.3. *Availability of Scripture at the time of 1 Maccabees*

In order to clarify what is meant by 'Scripture' as it was known to the author of 1 Maccabees, we have discussed some of the issues surrounding the complex textual variants and traditions of biblical literature both in Hebrew and Greek, the awareness of which is required when we discern individual scriptural sources influencing the text. In this section, a question is raised concerning the scope of biblical literature that was potentially available to the author. On the surface, it may seem obvious that scriptural expressions in the book are self-evident for the existence of written scriptural sources.[98]

Recently, however, Francis Borchardt challenged this by claiming that biblical references and allusions in the book do not necessarily prove written texts as their source, and that these may be derived from what he calls 'oral transmission of prophecy and nationalistic legends'.[99]

---

98. Most major commentators on 1 Maccabees include references to biblical literature in their commentaries. Goldstein's in particular contains numerous references to biblical sources, perhaps due to his proposition that the author, a Hasmonean propagandist, intends to portray the Hasmonean dynasty as messianic, fulfilling the promised restitution of the Davidic dynasty. Outside of commentaries, see Martha Himmelfarb, '"He Was Renowned to the Ends of the Earth" (1 Maccabees 3:9): Judaism and Hellenism in 1 Maccabees', in *Jewish Literatures and Cultures: Context and Intertext*, ed. Anita Norich and Yaron Z. Eliav, BJS 349 (Providence, RI: Brown University Press, 2008), 77–97.

99. Francis Borchardt, 'Concepts of Scripture in 1 Maccabees', in *Early Christian Literature and Intertextuality: Vol. 1, Thematic Studies*, ed. Craig A. Evans and Daniel Zecharias, LNTS 391, SSEJC 14 (London: Continuum, 2009), 24–41 (especially

Borchardt does not completely deny the availability of written biblical texts by the Hasmonean era, but only accepts the availability of the Torah, and considers that other biblical writings should be placed under scrutiny.[100] The background of this minimalist position may be partly Borchardt's general contention that oral tradition, as opposed to scribal activity, played a major role by the time of the Hasmonean era. Hence his thesis on 1 Maccabees argues that the present form of 1 Maccabees is itself a redacted product whose original form developed through additions of orally preserved legends of the Hasmoneans.[101] In the same way, Borchardt contends that the Jews' ancestral traditions were orally preserved, and that this oral form of media was their primary source for scriptural expressions. There is no doubt oral tradition coexisted by the time of 1 Maccabees' composition: but is it a valid claim to minimize the available scope of the written form of Hebrew Scripture to the Pentateuch and some other books as fringes?

29, 33, 35; quotation from 41). His view is recapitulated in a more recent article, 'Influence and Power: The Types of Authority in the Process of Scripturalization', *SJOT* 29 (2015): 182–96, '[a]llusions to texts are a poor proof of authority because they neither identify their source nor often do they provide any overt indication of status. It thus falls to the biblical scholar to decide whether something is a textual allusion (and to which text!) and what intent the author had in making this reference' (185). Also see Borchardt's 'Deuteronomic Legacy in 1 Maccabees', in *Changes in Scripture: Rewriting and Interpreting Authoritative Traditions in the Second Temple Period*, ed. Marko Marttila, Juha Pakkala and Hanne von Weissenberg, BZAW 419 (Berlin: de Gruyter, 2011), 297–319.

100. In fact, he points out that in a few passages of 1 Maccabees, use of written scriptural sources seems probable. In his critical assessment of Thomas Hieke's article about the use of Scripture in Mattathias' deathbed blessing, Borchardt claims that there are at least some examples strongly suggesting use of biblical texts other than the Pentateuch (Borchardt, 'Scripture', 34–6). See Hieke, 'The Role of "Scripture" in the Last Words of Mattathias (1 Macc. 2:49-70)', in *The Books of the Maccabees: History, Theology, Ideology – Papers of the Second International Conference on the Deuterocanonical Books, Pápa, Hungary, 9–11 June 2005*, ed. Géza Xeravits and József Zsengellér, JSJSup 118 (Boston: Brill, 2007), 61–74 (66–7, 69). Thus, for instance, the author's descriptions of Phinehas and David in Mattathias' blessings seem to be aware of Num. 26.6-15 and 2 Sam. 7.16 respectively, says Borchardt (Borchardt, 'Scripture', 34, 35). His emphasis, however, is repeatedly made on his preference of the Pentateuch as scriptural (whilst degrading the other biblical writings from that status), and along with it, taking a minimalist view on scriptural references as a proof of the existence of written source.

101. See §1.4 for my critique of literary-critical studies on 1 Maccabees, and the conclusion that there is no firm evidence for redactional layers in the book.

There is an ongoing dispute on the date of the production of biblical texts amongst scholars. Niels Peter Lemche dates most biblical writings to the Hellenistic period or later, hence referring to the Bible as 'a Hellenistic book'.[102] He first argues that biblical literature has little bearing on representing real history of ancient Israelites, and that a large part of it focuses on narratives of the Patriarchs, the exodus and the conquest of the land which, for Lemche, is mainly concerned with the creation of the Jewish diaspora. Lemche believes that the type of history written in the biblical literature bears considerable resemblances to that found in Greek literature. He therefore dates the composition of the biblical literature as Hellenistic.[103] Similarly, Peter Ackroyd questions the Maccabean dating (or earlier) of biblical literature by critically assessing the convenient criteria often assumed for the dating, namely linguistic, theological and historical elements of evidence.[104] He instead argues that some biblical texts show redactional layers reflecting pro-Hasmonean agendas.[105] In contrast, however, Lester L. Grabbe produced a helpful table of a detailed list of biblical references in the so-called the Praise of the Fathers in Ben Sira (chs. 44–49) which demonstrated a striking feature, namely that not only a large range of biblical literature is presented there, but also in the same order as the modern Hebrew Bible, many of which are very similar in wording.[106] As he put it, 'he [Ben Sira] has chosen to use primarily

---

102. Niels Peter Lemche, 'The Old Testament – A Hellenistic Book?', *SJOT* 7 (1993): 163–93.

103. Lemche, 'Hellenistic Book?', 182–4. See also Lemche, 'Herodotus and the Persians', *Transeuphratène* 23 (2002): 129–51. A critical review of Lemche's thesis on the Hebrew Bible as a Hellenistic product has notably been made by a number of contributors in Lester L. Grabbe, ed., *Did Moses Speak Attic? Jewish Historiography and Scripture in the Hellenistic Period*, JSOTSup 317 (Sheffield: Sheffield Academic, 2001).

104. Peter R. Ackroyd, 'Criteria for the Maccabean Dating of Old Testament Literature', *VT* 3 (1953): 113–32. For scholars who argued that Ben Sira quoted written scriptural source, see 'Criteria', 115 n. 3.

105. Ackroyd ('Criteria', 126) points out that altering the order of priests by placing Joarib as the first in the list in Chronicles (1 Chron. 24.7-19) may reflect the manipulation of the Hasmoneans who belong to that family (1 Macc. 2.1). This is possible, but Ackroyd is unconvincing when he rejects Ben Sira's reference to numerous biblical figures and events especially in the Praise of the Fathers (Sir. 44–49) as the evidence for the author's access to written biblical sources.

106. Lester L. Grabbe, 'The Law, the Prophets, and the Rest: The State of the Bible in Pre-Maccabean Times', *DSD* 13 (2006): 319–38 (323–7). He in fact pushes this formation of Scripture as early as the end of the Persian period ('State of the Bible', 322–3).

the order of their mention in the text as his organizing principle... [He] has listed, paraphrased, and quoted material too parallel to our present canonical text to be coincidental.'[107]

In this section, we will look into a set of Jewish texts often discussed in relation to this debate, particularly focusing on the formulaic term, 'the Law and the Prophets (and other writings)'. Although this term has often been discussed in the quest for the canonization of biblical texts, this enquiry of canon is useful to our discussion insofar as it brings us to the question of the availability of individual biblical books by the Hasmonean era. The often discussed Jewish texts are: the prologue to the Greek translation of Ben Sira in which the term appears, and the second of the two epistles incorporated into the beginning of 2 Maccabees and the Halakhic letter from the Dead Sea Scrolls known as 4QMMT, both of which contain similar terms.[108] Through our discussion, I will contend that the scope of available biblical books already encompassed the Torah, the Former/Latter Prophets and even some of the Writings.

2.3.1. *'The Law and the Prophets (and other writings)'*
2.3.1.1. *Prologue to the Greek version of Ben Sira*

The grandson of Ben Sira, who translated the work of his grandfather from Greek to Hebrew, attached a prologue to his translation, reminiscent in form and style to classical and Hellenistic literature.[109] Written during the early Hasmonean era, that is, during the reign of King Euergetes in Egypt (132–117 BCE),[110] the work was either contemporary or written prior to the composition of 1 Maccabees, and is thus chronologically significant for our enquiry.

The author of the Greek version of Ben Sira, who claims to be Ben Sira's grandson, writes to his Jewish audience in Egypt by exhorting them to adhere to the law of Moses.[111] There he deploys a term 'the Law and the Prophets (and other writings)' several times. The identification of the first

---

107. Grabbe, 'State of the Bible', 327.

108. Also, Josephus (*Ag. Ap.* 1.38–40) uses a very similar term but is excluded from our headings due to its late dating (the early second century CE).

109. Patrick W. Skehan and Alexander A. Di Lella, *The Wisdom of Ben Sira: A New Translation with Notes by Patrick W. Skehan; Introduction and Commentary by Alexander A. Di Lella*, AB 39 (New York: Doubleday, 1987), 133.

110. Skehan and Di Lella, *Ben Sira*, 134–5.

111. The style of Greek in the Prologue conforms to ordinary Greek syntax in stark contrast to the Hebraic style of Greek which the grandson uses for the translation. See Benjamin G. Wright, 'Sirach: To the Reader', in Pietersma and Wright, eds., *A New English Translation of the Septuagint*, 715–19 (719); 'Translation Greek in Sirach in

two components, 'the Law and the Prophets' (ὁ νόμος καὶ αἱ προφητεῖαι), with the Torah and the Former/Latter Prophets is less debated among scholars in comparison to the third component of the term. For instance, it has often been argued that 'the Prophets' could include Chronicles, Samuel, and Kings, as these writings were evidently used by Ben Sira in the 'Praise of the Fathers' (chs. 44–49).[112] For the Latter Prophets, we may infer that biblical prophecies were already in the form of 'literary prophecy', using Armin Lange's term,[113] in which a prophet's oracles were presumably collected, preserved and edited by his followers, a widespread phenomenon across the Ancient Near East, ancient Israel and Greece before the Maccabean period.

The third component reads either 'the others that followed them' (τῶν ἄλλων τῶν κατ' αὐτοὺς ἠκολουθηκότων), 'the others of ancestral books' (τῶν ἄλλων πατρίων βιβλίων), or 'the rest of the books' (τὰ λοιπὰ τῶν βιβλίων), and its identification with the Writings in the modern canon of the Hebrew Bible has often been suggested,[114] though some have argued that the term is vague and non-specific.[115] Others have contended that the

---

Light of the Grandson's Prologue', in *The Texts and Versions of the Book of Ben Sira: Transmission and Interpretation*, ed. Jean-Sébastien Rey and Jan Joosten, JSJSup 150 (Leiden: Brill, 2011), 75–94 (75).

112. J. L. Koole, 'Die Bibel des Ben-Sira', *OTS* 14 (1965): 374–96 (385); Arie van der Kooij, 'The Canonization of Ancient Books Kept in the Temple of Jerusalem', in *Canonization and Decanonization*, ed. Arie van der Kooij and K. van der Toorn, SHR 82 (Leiden: Brill, 1998), 17–40 (24); Grabbe, 'State of the Bible', 324–6.

113. Armin Lange, 'Literary Prophecy and Oracle Collection: A Comparison between Judah and Greece in Persian Times', in *Prophets, Prophecy and Prophetic Texts in Second Temple Judaism*, ed. Michael H. Floyd and Robert D. Haak, LHBOTS 427 (New York: T&T Clark, 2006), 248–75. See also, Michael H. Floyd, 'The Production of Prophetic Books in the Early Second Temple Period', in the same volume (276–97). Floyd reaches a conclusion that 'prophetic books emerged in a matrix defined by particular aspects of the Persian restoration' (292).

114. R. T. Beckwith, *The Old Testament Canon of the New Testament Church and Its Background in Early Judaism* (London: SPCK, 1985), 111, 164. Van der Kooij ('Canonization', 24, 30) further notes that Josephus' mention of a similar phrase, 'the remaining books (αἱ δὲ λοιπαὶ τέσσαρες)' (*Ag. Ap.* 1.40), points to a defined set of writings. Interestingly, Josephus also seems to follow Ben Sira's probable inclusion of Job among the prophets, placed between the major and minor prophets (Sir. 49.9; *Ag. Ap.* 1.40). Also, Skehan and Di Lella, *Ben Sira*, 544.

115. For instance, H. P. Rüger, as cited in van der Kooij, 'Canonization', 23. Harry M. Orlinsky, 'Some Terms in the Prologue to Ben Sira and the Hebrew Canon', *JBL* 110 (1991): 483–90. Contrary to Patrick W. Skehan's translation of the τῶν ἄλλων as 'the other *authors*', Orlinsky contends that it should be translated as 'the

definite article in each of the three variations may suggest a specific designation. Despite the uncertainty about the precise list of 'the writings', the scope of available biblical writings by the time of Ben Sira's grandson at the latest, that is, the second half of the second century BCE, seems considerably large.

That Ben Sira already knew most written biblical texts is also evident from his use of them in the 'Praise of the Fathers' (chs. 44–49). As noted above, the table organized by Grabbe reveals a considerable number of references to biblical figures and events in an order very similar to that of the Hebrew Bible, and there are considerable literary connections between Ben Sira and its biblical source. Worth noting in this regard is that the Minor Prophets are referred to as one unit, 'the Bone of the Twelve Prophets' (Sir. 49.10), and the unit is placed after Ezekiel.[116]

Thus, this conjoined reference to the Pentateuch and historical and prophetic writings, as well as other writings, makes a strong case for their availability prior to the Hasmonean era. The internal evidence that Ben Sira was acquainted with the texts and had access to them further supports this conclusion. They were available for imparting education and wisdom in the Jewish community.[117] The fact that his grandson required for his translation precision of finding the right terms in Greek could indicate the insufficiency of oral tradition and the existence of written texts.

2.3.1.2. *4QMMT*

The large collection of literature found at the Qumran site includes not only the majority of biblical literature, but also extra-biblical writings such as the book of Jubilees, as well as sectarian documents such as the Pesharim, Midrash, liturgical texts, and so forth.[118] Notable are the Pesharim which offer interpretations of the prophetic corpus (for example,

---

other *writings*' (based on the other two phrases which explicitly render βιβλίοι, i.e. 'books'). He also argues that the term 'the Law and the Prophets' is an indication of a bipartite canon, and the writings within Ketuvim were only partly available.

116. Skehan and Di Lella, *Ben Sira*, 544, note that the strange connection of the Book of Twelve with the message of comfort and hope of Jacob may be related to the very last two verses which contain the promise of Elijah redivivus (Mal. 3.23-24 in Heb.).

117. For the same viewpoint on biblical literature in Ben Sira, see Wright, 'Translation Greek', 75–94.

118. The list of sectarian documents containing several biblical materials includes, Florilegium (4Q174), Catena^a (4Q177), Mechizedek (11Q13), Pesher Isaiah^c (4Q163), to name but a few. For an overview, see Moshe J. Bernstein, 'Scriptures: Quotation and Use', *EDDS* 2:839–42 (839–40).

of the Minor Prophets such as Habakkuk and Nahum, as well as Isaiah) and Psalms, just as the Pentateuch is interpreted.[119] In addition, the Halakhic letter, or 4QMMT, contains numerous examples of scriptural expressions and exegetical comments on several biblical writings.[120] In particular, just as we have seen in the Greek version of Ben Sira's prologue, it states a similar formulaic phrase relating to a body of biblical literature:

> [10] to you we have [written] that you must understand the book of Moses [and] the book[s of the pr]ophets and Davi[d...] [11] [the annals of] each generation. And in the book is written [...] ... not
>
> [10] [כתב]נו אליכה שתבין בספר מושה [ו]בספר[י הנ]ביאים ובדוי[ד ...]
> [11] [במעשי] דור ודור ובספר כתוב [...]... לוא
> (4Q397 *frag.* 14–21 column 10, ed. Martínez and Tigchelaar)

Here too, the rationale of emphasizing the need/benefit of acquiring understanding through reading a similar set of literature is underlined. The reference to 'the book of Moses and the books of the prophets' is synonymous to 'the Law and the Prophets', although the reference to David is less clear. The presumption that this is a designation of a tripartite canon is disputed. For instance, Eugene Ulrich suggested that a critical examination into the plate, transcription and translation of the column would lead rather to uncertainty about a tripartite canon.[121] However, he does not deny that the column still refers to a large body of biblical literature under a bipartite canon, 'the Law and the Prophets'.[122] In fact, a considerable

---

119. Devorah Dimant, 'Pesharim, Qumran', *ABD* 5:244–51; 'Qumran: Written Material', *EDDS* 2:739–46; Shani L. Berrin, 'Pesharim', *EDDS* 2:644–7.

120. On 4QMMT's extensive use of biblical literature, see Moshe J. Bernstein, 'The Employment and Interpretation of Scripture in 4QMMT: Preliminary Observations', in *Reading 4QMMT: New Perspectives on Qumran Law and History*, ed. John Kampen and M. J. Bernstein, SBLSymS 2 (Atlanta: Scholars Press, 1996), 29–51; George J. Brooke, 'The Explicit Presentation of Scripture in 4QMMT', in *Legal Texts and Legal Issues: Proceedings of the Second Meeting of the International Organization for Qumran Studies, Cambridge, 1995: Published in Honour of Joseph M. Baumgarten*, ed. M. J. Bernstein, F. García Martínez and J. Kampen, STDJ 23 (Leiden: Brill, 1997), 67–88.

121. Eugene Ulrich, 'The Non-Attestation of a Tripartite Canon in 4QMMT', *CBQ* 65 (2002): 202–14. A similar argument against reading a tripartite canon in 4QMMT is offered by Timothy H. Lim, 'The Alleged Reference to the Tripartite Division of the Hebrew Bible', *RevQ* 20 (2001): 23–37.

122. Ulrich, 'Non-Attestation', 211–14. For the early date for a bipartite canon in light of Qumran texts, see also Cana Werman, 'The Canonization of the Hebrew

number of scholars have read this column as evidence for a substantial body of biblical literature being already available in the Hasmonean era.¹²³

2.3.1.3. *2 Maccabees 2.13-15*

Another source of a formulaic term for biblical literature comes from a letter allegedly composed under Judas Maccabee (2 Macc. 1.10b–2.18),¹²⁴ sent from Judea to the Jews in Egypt to share the annual celebration of Hanukkah – the purification of the Jerusalem Temple.¹²⁵ In 2 Macc. 2.13-15, the author of the letter mentions various kinds of literature preserved and now available in the Temple. It states as follows:

> ¹³ The same things are reported in the records and in the memoirs of Nehemiah, and also that *he founded a library* (καταβαλλόμενος βιβλιοθήκην) and *collected the books about the kings and prophets, and the writings of David, and letters of kings about votive offerings* (ἐπισυνήγαγεν τὰ περὶ τῶν βασιλέων βιβλία καὶ προφητῶν καὶ τὰ τοῦ Δαυιδ καὶ ἐπιστολὰς βασιλέων περὶ ἀναθεμάτων). ¹⁴ In the same way Judas also collected all the books that had been lost on account of the war that had come upon us, and they are in our possession. ¹⁵ So if you have need of them, send people to get them for you. (2 Macc. 2.13-15)

In this passage, a similar phrase relating to a substantial body of literature can be found. The writer of the epistle mentions a wide range of writings which allegedly formed Nehemiah's temple library, and stresses

---

Bible in Light of Second Temple Literature', in *From Author to Copyist: Essays on the Composition, Redaction, and Transmission of the Hebrew Bible in Honor of Zipi Talshir*, ed. Cana Werman (Winona Lake: Eisenbrauns, 2015), 337–65.

123. E.g. Elisha Qimron and John Strugnell, *Qumran Cave 4.V: Miqsat Ma'aśe Ha-Torah*, DJD 10 (Oxford: Clarendon, 1994), 58–9; van der Kooij, 'Canonization', 37–8; Hanan Eshel, '4QMMT and the History of the Hasmonean Period', in Kampen and Bernstein, eds., *Reading 4QMMT*, 53–65 (59); Lawrence H. Schiffman, 'The Place of 4QMMT in the Corpus of Qumran Manuscripts', in Kampen and Bernstein, eds., *Reading 4QMMT*, 81–98 (95).

124. The date of this letter (2 Macc. 1.10b–2.18) is uncertain due to signs of interpolations and chronological inconsistencies about events. For the authorship of Judas Macccabee, see Jonathan A. Goldstein, *2 Maccabees*, AB 41A (New York: Doubleday, 1983), 157–9. After a detailed analysis, Ben Zion Wacholder concludes that the letter is 'with great probability a document written soon after the stunning news of the death of Antiochus IV in Persia reached the holy city', see Wacholder, 'The Letter from Judah Maccabee to Aristobulus: Is 2 Maccabees 1:10b–2:18 Authentic?', *HUCA* 49 (1978): 89–133 (132).

125. Wacholder, 'The Letter', 129–32. Daniel R. Schwartz, *2 Maccabees*, CEJL (Berlin: de Gruyter, 2008), 133–4.

that the library in Judas' time had a similar collection. Several scholars have understood the phrase referring to kings, prophets and David as a reference to biblical writings such as historical/prophetic writings and psalms,[126] whilst others were rather ambivalent about whether the phrase definitely points to canonical writings.[127] Stefan Schorch has recently claimed that this phrase had little to do with biblical writings, and rather referred to official documents privately kept in archives.[128] However, his argument seems to lead to a rather radical interpretation of the phrase. For instance, Schorch claimed that τὰ περὶ τῶν βασιλέων βιβλία καὶ προφητῶν cannot be a reference to biblical writings, especially in the case of τὰ περὶ…προφητῶν, because the phrase lacks explicit mention of 'words of prophets', nor does it have a definite article, unlike Ben Sira's prologue.[129] However, his conclusion that this phrase meant 'stories or accounts *about* prophets'[130] does not seem to fully reach his initial claim: if 'stories about prophets' were kept alongside 'writings about kings' (which he does not discuss), does that mean he admits that there were at least biblical writings equivalent to the Former Prophets?[131] He went on to argue that the phrase τὰ τοῦ Δαυιδ does not refer to the Psalms, but to '"books written by David" in general'.[132] Again, it seems unclear why these writings cannot be referencing the Psalms. From 11QPs[a], for instance, it is evident that David was regarded by Jews as the author of several psalms.[133] Schorch

---

126. Sid Z. Leiman, *The Canonization of Hebrew Scripture: The Talmudic and Midrashic Evidence*, TCAAS 47 (Hamden, CT: Archon, 1976), 29–30; Beckwith, *Canon*, 152; Schwartz, *2 Maccabees*, 166; Lim, 'The Alleged Reference', 23–37; van der Kooij, 'Canonization', 17–40.

127. Jonathan G. Campbell, 'Josephus' Twenty-Two Book Canon and the Qumran Scrolls', in *The Scrolls and Biblical Traditions: Proceedings of the Seventh Meeting of the IOQS in Helsinki*, ed. George J. Brooke, Daniel K. Falk, Eibert J. C. Tigchelaar and Molly M. Zahn, STDJ 103 (Leiden: Brill, 2012), 19–46 (20–1); Armin Lange, '2 Maccabees 2:13-15: Library or Canon?', in Xeravits and Zsengellér, eds., *The Books of the Maccabees: History, Theology, Ideology*, 155–67 (160–1).

128. Stefan Schorch, 'The Libraries in 2 Macc 2:13-15, and the Torah as a Public Document in Second Century BC Judaism', in Zeravits and Zsengellér, eds., *The Books of the Maccabees*, 169–80.

129. Schorch, 'Libraries', 171.

130. Schorch, 'Libraries', 171 (his italics).

131. A suggestion already made by van der Kooij, 'Canonization', 30.

132. Schorch, 'Libraries', 171.

133. For interpretation and discussion on 11QPs[a], other biblical materials, and the Dead Sea Scrolls with regards to David's composition of psalms, see Roland Deines, *Die Gerechtigkeit der Tora im Reich des Messias: Mt 5,13–20: als Schlüsseltext der matthäischen Theologie*, WUNT 177 (Tübingen: Mohr Siebeck, 2004), 618–34.

claims that understanding ἐπιστολὰς βασιλέων περὶ ἀναθεμάτων as 'royal documents' is legitimate, but he has not convincingly explained why royal documents cannot be placed alongside sacred writings and other texts. Armin Lange, in his comparative study on the libraries of the ancient Near East, the Greeks, and the Jews of Palestine and Qumran, convincingly showed common characters shared across these libraries, namely that they were often located within a local temple and that they contained a wide range of writings, such as archival documents, omen texts, and other documents, as well as liturgical texts.[134] It is reasonable to assume that the library of Judas, which allegedly took after the shape of the collection in Nehemiah's time, was similar.[135]

The passage appears to give fewer explicit clues about the value of these writings than the prologue of Ben Sira and 4QMMT, but v. 15 still hints at the Judean community's encouragement for the Egyptian Jews' reading of these writings, which resembles a similar attitude to that of Ben Sira's grandson towards his Jewish audience in Egypt. Overall, then, this passage does promote a similar Jewish viewpoint about the scope of Scripture in the Hasmonean era.

2.3.2. Conclusion

We have seen that the term 'the Law, the Prophets (and other writings)' repeatedly found in the Greek version of Ben Sira, 2 Maccabees, and 4QMMT was a designation of a large body of Jewish Scripture, preserved and read amongst Jewish communities. Attached to this term is an attitude of encouragement to the Jewish communities residing outside Judea to read and learn from those books, suggesting they were perceived as playing a part in the forming of Jewish collective identity. The dispute as to the precise scope of this set of literature notwithstanding, it seems clear that the term denotes not just the Pentateuch and a limited range of other books, but rather the more-or-less full range of the Former and Latter Prophets, Psalms, and some other writings as well.

2.4. Hellenization and the influence of Scripture in 1 Maccabees

2.4.1. A conceptual issue

The relation between Hellenism and Judaism in Palestine during the Hellenistic period is one of the most discussed topics in Jewish studies. Martin Hengel argued that the assimilation of the two cultures occurred

---

134. Lange, 'Library', 160–1.
135. Lange, 'Library', 155–61, 66.

early on, that the catalyst of their conflicting state was Antiochus IV Epiphanes, and that Hellenistic Judaism in Judea disappeared until it was reclaimed in the era of the early Christians' gentile mission. Hengel's thesis has accelerated active responses from scholars in the field with various opinions on this topic emerging as a result.[136] Scholars have offered a spectrum of opinions on the extent of Hellenization in Judea around the Hasmonean era, from a minimal influence of Hellenism proposed by Arnaldo Momigliano on one side to the substantial Hellenized form of Judaism by Victor Tcherikover on the other.[137] Not only are opinions persistently in disagreement with one another, but some scholars are increasingly calling for a shift of enquiry away from simply discussing what is and what is not Hellenistic to defining the form of Judaism that existed in the Hellenistic period.[138] Recently, Michael L. Satlow even

---

136. As Lester L. Grabbe puts it, 'one can no longer talk of Judaism *versus* Hellenism nor of Palestinian *versus* Hellenistic Judaism', regardless of one's acceptance or rejection of Hengel's thesis; see Grabbe, 'The Jews and Hellenization: Hengel and His Critics', in *Second Temple Studies III: Studies in Politics, Class and Material Culture*, ed. Philip R. Davies and John M. Halligan, JSOTSup 340 (London: Sheffield Academic, 2002), 52–66 (64); Martin Hengel, *Judaism and Hellenism: Studies in Their Encounter in Palestine during the Early Hellenistic Period*, 2 vols., trans. John Bowden (Philadelphia: Fortress, 1974). Critiques have been made notably by Louis H. Feldman, 'Hengel's *Judaism and Hellenism* in Retrospect', *JBL* 96 (1977): 371–82; 'How Much Hellenism in Jewish Palestine?', *HUCA* 57 (1986): 83–111; Fergus Millar, 'The Background of the Maccabean Revolution: Reflections on Martin Hengel's "Judaism and Hellenism"', *JJS* 29 (1978): 1–21; Lee I. Levine, *Judaism and Hellenism in Antiquity: Conflict or Confluence?* (Seattle: University of Washington Press, 1998). Amongst many, helpful reviews with balanced viewpoints are offered by Grabbe, 'Hellenism', 52–66; Kevin G. O'Connell and James K. Aitken, review of *Judaism and Hellenism*, by Martin Hengel, *JBL* 123 (2004): 329–41. Also, see Hengel's response to his critiques in Hengel, 'Judaism and Hellenism Revisited', in *Hellenism in the Land of Israel*, ed. John J. Collins and G. E. Sterling, CJA 13 (Notre Dame: University of Notre Dame Press, 2001), 6–37.

137. Momigliano, *Alien Wisdom*, especially Chapters 4–5; Victor Tcherikover, *Hellenistic Civilization and the Jews*, trans. S. Applebaum, repr. (New York: Atheneum, 1977).

138. As Doron Mendels cautiously remarked: '[t]he question should anyhow shift from how rigorous Hellenization was to what was the nature of native Palestinian 'paganization' in Jewish society. A common error among scholars is to choose one single text of this era to trace 'Hellenistic' influences (whilst lacking a deep and essential understanding of the wider context critical for judging what is Hellenistic and what is but a vague echo of Hellenistic traits) and then to pronounce on the extent of Hellenization in Jewish society'; see Mendels, 'Memory and Memories: The Attitude of 1–2 Maccabees toward Hellenization and Hellenism', in *Jewish Identities*

questioned the dichotomy between Judaism and Hellenism, and instead called for a complete confluence of the two cultures resulting in a new culture from the beginning as one underlying the culture of the Palestinian Jews in the Hellenistic era.[139]

In this section, the task will be confined to examining the use/rejection of Hellenism by the Hasmoneans and in 1 Maccabees in order to directly serve the present study. From the outset, it should perhaps be said that in response to Hengel's thesis, there is now a growing body of scholarship promoting two points: that the seemingly resistant movements of the Jews in Judea were not against Hellenism but against paganism; and that Hellenism is infused in the Jewish culture, particularly that of the Hasmonean ideology.[140] But in what terms does this Hellenism-related trait appear in the Hasmonean ideology and particularly in 1 Maccabees? Where do Hellenistic features appear and where do they not? Is the culture promoted by the Hasmoneans characteristically Hellenistic or Jewish, or completely assimilated without partial emphasis?

in Antiquity: Studies in Memory of Menahem Stern, ed. Lee I. Levine and Daniel R. Schwartz, TSAJ 130 (Tübingen: Mohr Siebeck, 2009), 41–54 (54 n. 23).

139. Michael L. Satlow, 'Beyond Influence: Toward a New Historiographical Paradigm', in Norich and Eliav, eds., *Jewish Literatures and Cultures*, 37–53. By going further than using phrases such as 'Jewish ideas in Greek forms' like Erich S. Gruen (*Heritage and Hellenism: The Reinvention of Jewish Tradition*, HCS 30 [Berkeley: University of California Press, 1998]) or 'combination of strict Judaism and Hellenistic form' like John J. Collins ('The Epic of Theodotus and the Hellenism of the Hasmoneans', *HTR* 73 [1980]: 91–104 [103]), Satlow claimed that the interactions between Hellenistic and Jewish cultures are a process of creating what may be called 'the Hellenistic Jewish culture' (though he even rejected the noun form of 'culture' which renders the sense of being a static category, and preferred to use it as a verb which captures the sense of subtlety and fluidity of the interactions). In essence, he would even regard the word, 'influence' as anachronistic, see Satlow, 'Beyond Influence', 38.

140. Caution has to be taken in viewing the ideology of the family whose regimes were rather inconsistent. The gradually shifted focus of the revolt from an exclusively religious motivation kindled by Mattathias to a regaining of political power, the national independence and territorial expansion under the Maccabean brothers and Simon's descendants, and Aristobulus' transformation of the government into a kingdom as per Josephus, to name but a few, illustrate to some extent a process of ideology-shift of the Maccabean-Hasmonean family. The recognition of this differentiation is of paramount importance in the study of 1 Maccabees where, contrary to the advocates of the Hasmonean-kingship propaganda, the Hasmonean monarchs' ideology of kingship may be less relevant than has often been put forward. Also, see Tcherikover (*Hellenistic Civilization*, 251), who noted the inconsistency of the Maccabean-Hasmonean regime(s).

2. *The Contribution of the Literary, Social and Cultural Milieus*   67

Our task is to evaluate scholarly opinions and observations on the topic, which can sometimes create confusion. The diagrams below may be useful in clarifying the currently available scholarly positions:

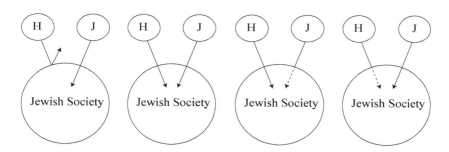

Starting from the left, the first model represents the view that Hellenism was either irrelevant to Jewish societies or left no significant features in Jewish literature of that time, such as 1–2 Maccabees. Mendels and Goldstein respectively claimed that there is nothing distinctively Hellenistic in these Jewish writings, with the particular implication that any conflict between Hellenism and Judaism is, for them, dubious.[141] The second model represents Satlow's view in which a complete confluence between the two cultures is put forward.[142] A divisive understanding between the two cultures is, in this model, artificial, and a complete hybrid culture is a preferred term for the Palestinian Jewish society. The third model, put forward by Tcherikover, suggests not only the diffusion of Hellenistic ideas in the Jewish society, but also the presence of a fully Hellenized form of Jewish culture.[143] The fourth model, advocated by a growing number of scholars, suggests that whilst Hellenization is evident in those aforementioned Jewish writings, these writings demonstrably put forward Jewish values so that their characteristics remain more Jewish than Hellenistic.[144] In the remainder of the section, we will see that the

---

141. Jonathan A. Goldstein, 'Jewish Acceptance and Rejection of Hellenism', in *Jewish and Christian Self-Definition*. Vol. 2, *Aspects of Judaism in the Greco-Roman Period*, ed. E. P. Sanders, A. I. Baumgarten, and A. Mendelson (London: SCM; Philadelphia: Fortress, 1981), 64–87; Mendels, 'Hellenism', 41–54.

142. Satlow, 'Beyond Influence', 37–53; Himmelfarb, 'He Was Renowned', 77–97.

143. Tcherikover, *Civilization*, especially 235–65.

144. Tessa Rajak, 'The Hasmoneans and the Uses of Hellenism', in *A Tribute to Geza Vermes: Essays on Jewish and Christian Literature and History*, ed. Philip R. Davies and Richard T. White, JSOTSup 100 (Sheffield: Sheffield Academic, 1990), 261–80; repr., in Rajak, ed., *The Jewish Dialogue with Greece and Rome*,

fourth model best represents the viewpoint of 1 Maccabees, by evaluating the book's internal and external features relating to Hellenism.

2.4.2. *Internal features relating to Hellenism*

Various comments have been made on the Greek vocabulary of 1 Maccabees concerning its presentation/ignorance of Greek concepts and its resemblance of Greek linguistic styles. However, it will be highlighted that the arguments deriving from these observations are sometimes simplistic, requiring a more sophisticated conclusion.

First, a few scholars have observed that 1 Maccabees does not really contain any distinctively Hellenistic terms, and clearly prefers other more general terms.[145] According to Judith Lieu who provided a survey of various terms referring to the antagonists in the book, terms relating to Ἑλλήν are notably rare, compared to other terms generally referring to 'others', 'gentiles', 'foreigners', or 'nations'.[146] In addition to this lack of ethnic terms denoting Hellenists, Mendels observed the lack of any mentions about an established 'Hellenistic party' in Judea or Greek habits/deities during Mattathias' purification process (2.15-27, 45-48),[147] as well as the fact that the cause of the ensuing calamities in Judea (1.51-64) is seen as, what he called, 'the standard transgressions' (the abandonment of the law), not Hellenization.[148] Instead, it is often claimed that in 1 Maccabees, the antagonists are gentiles and the opposition is made to paganism, rather than Hellenists/Hellenism.[149] This lack of opposition to Hellenism raises a question about whether 1 Maccabees supports any resistance against Hellenism.

61–80; Gardner, 'Jewish Leadership', 327–43. Gardner included Himmelfarb in this group, but Gardner's sharp observation, which he rightly made, on an *interactive* state between the two cultures as found in the Hasmoneans' incorporation of Greek honorary decrees, as well as his point that the Jewish decrees are to a certain extent distinctively different from their Greek counterparts, seems distant from Himmelfarb's argument that the Jews used Hellenistic ideas 'unself-consciously' (Himmelfarb, 'He Was Renowned', 96).

145. Goldstein ('Jewish Acceptance', 78–9) pointed out that Qumran texts also share this similar tendency of the lack of any references to a Hellenist/Hellenism. See also Rajak, 'Hellenism', 62–3; Judith Lieu, 'Not Hellenes but Philistines? The Maccabees and Josephus Defining the "Other"', *JJS* 53 (2002): 246–63 (248–55).

146. See a brief but concise table in Lieu, 'Not Hellenes', 249–50.

147. Mendels, 'Hellenism', 51–2.

148. Mendels, 'Hellenism', 51.

149. This is well attested by Millar, 'Background', 2. Also, Mendels, 'Hellenism', 45–6.

Second, a few scholars have observed Greek ideas and concepts in 1 Maccabees. Roger Tomes, for instance, identified three types of heroism in 1–2 Maccabees that closely follow Greek ideas: the warrior, the martyr, and the suicide (the first two of these are applied in 1 Maccabees).[150] To name a few, the Hasmoneans' brave deeds[151] echo the deeds of heroes in Diodorus Siculus,[152] fighting 'manfully' (ἀνδρωδῶς, 1 Macc. 6.31) just as in Polybius (1.31.8), and facing death with courage (9.10), which is, as Tomes said, 'one of the four cardinal virtues of the Greeks'.[153] Martha Himmelfarb also argued that the use of δόξα/δοξάζω departs from the biblical, Jewish concept of כבוד, and resembles more the Greek idea; unlike biblical accounts where attribution of 'glory' is quintessentially made to God, 1 Maccabees consistently avoids it, and rather attributes it to heroic human individuals which, as Himmelfarb suggested, resembles the work of the Athenian orator Isocrates to some extent.[154]

Third, the Hasmoneans' titles and honours received from the Seleucids and Romans have often been suggested as bearing Hellenistic connotations. Tcherikover, for instance, suggested implications of their titles as Seleucid civil servants.[155] Jonathan was bestowed by Alexander Balas the title, among others, μεριδάρχης of Judea (10.65), which Tcherikover suggested as an official position, a 'governor'[156] in the Seleucid state, governing a large territory with power. Likewise, Simon received the title of στρατηγός from Tryphon (11.59) with military authority over a large part of the land, which was later extended to the title ἐπιστράτηγος (15.38), additionally covering coastal areas. Gregg Gardner showed that the honorary decrees of Onias III (2 Macc. 4.1-2), Simon (1 Macc. 14.25-49), and John Hyrcanus I (Josephus, *Ant.* 14.149-155) considerably resemble conventional Greek honorary decrees, suggesting the integration of the idea of Hellenistic civic benefaction.[157] These figures were bestowed

---

150. Roger Tomes, 'Heroism in 1 and 2 Maccabees', *BI* 15 (2007): 171–99.
151. 1 Macc. 5.56; 9.22; 10.15, and 16.23 all described using ἀνδραγαθίοι.
152. E.g. Diodorus 10.6; 11.5; 17.6.2.
153. E.g. Plato, *Republic* 427D–435A. See Tomes ('Heroism', 178–9, 181, 184) for more examples in this regard.
154. Isocrates, *Philippus* 134–135. Himmelfarb, 'He Was Renowned', 83–90. Notable is her suggestion of similar examples in Ben Sira's description of ancestors as well as High Priest Simon son of Onias in chs. 44–50 (90–4).
155. Tcherikover, *Hellenistic Civilization*, 236–8.
156. E.g. Apollonius, μεριδάρχης of Samaria, governed a large political unit (Josephus, *Ant.* 12.261). Also, see Rajak, 'Hellenism', 68–9.
157. Gardner, 'Benefaction', 327–43. The close linguistic association between Simon's decree and Greek honorary decrees has already been studied by Jan Willem

by Hellenistic authorities the title of εὐεργέτης which carried with it gifts, honour and authority. The decrees of Simon and Hyrcanus in particular are closely associated with Greek counterparts insofar as their structures and contents are considerably similar.[158]

Fourth, we may add the description of the mysterious, sudden death of Alcimus when he attempted to defile the Jerusalem Temple (1 Macc. 9.54-56), an incident which shares the theme of divine protection of a local temple in the Greek tradition.[159] Examples include Herodotus' account of the divine protection of the temple at Delphi,[160] the Lindian account of the divine protection of their temple,[161] and Pausanias' recounting of Herodotus' temple epiphany.[162] These incidents all share the Greek idea of divine defence of sacred temples. 2 Maccabees illustrates this idea more explicitly as Robert Doran has comprehensively shown in his monograph on the book.[163] 1 Maccabees is less explicit than 2 Maccabees and it is

---

van Henten, 'The Honorary Decree for Simon the Maccabee (1 Macc 14:25-49) in Its Hellenistic Context', in Collins and Sterling, eds., *Hellenism in the Land of Israel*, 116–45; 'Royal Ideology', 265–82; Edgar Krentz, 'The Honorary Decree for Simon the Maccabee', in Collins and Sterling, eds., *Hellenism in the Land of Israel*, 146–53. Gardner's contribution, however, is the integration of other Jewish decrees. His conclusion is also distinctive in that he rightly observed some remarkable differences between Jewish and Greek decrees, which may suggest the Jews' conscious interaction with Hellenism.

158. Gardner, 'Benefaction', 332–9.

159. I have not come across classicists who specifically explore this temple epiphany in Greek literature. See, however, Kendrick W. Pritchett, *The Greek State at War.* Part 3, *Religion* (Berkeley, CA: University of California Press, 1979), 19–39, 92–153. Pritchett offers a comprehensive list of epiphanic phenomena occurring at battles in Greek literature.

160. Herodotus, *History* 8.35-39 (LCL).

161. Column D of the Chronicles. For a critical edition of the text, see Carolyn Higbie, *The Lindian Chronicle and the Greek Creation of their Past* (Oxford: Oxford University Press, 2003), 42–9.

162. Pausanias' *History* 10.23.1-10 (LCL).

163. Robert Doran, *Temple Propaganda: The Purpose and Character of 2 Maccabees*, CBQMS 12 (Washington, DC: The Catholic Biblical Association of America, 1981), especially 47–52, 98–104. For a similar view, see Goldstein, *2 Maccabees*, 198–9; E. J. Bickerman, *Studies in Jewish and Christian History: A New Edition in English Including the God of the Maccabees*, AJEC 68/1 (Leiden: Brill, 2007), 432–64. The Jewish epitomizer's use of Greek epiphanies as his source, however, seems a little over-stated in Doran's work. The epiphanic tradition, particularly that of temple protection, can be traced within the Hebraic-Jewish tradition. For instance, the epiphanic motif in the story of Sennacherib's invasion

characteristically reticent concerning theological expression (for example, its silence on using the word 'God' and replacing it with words such as 'heavens'). Thus, Alcimus' death is not explained in theological terms, and the mystery of the incident rather matches the whole drama of the Maccabean revolt in retrospect.

These four points suggest that Hellenism was far from being rejected by the pro-Hasmonean author of 1 Maccabees, but rather diffused into his writing style and ideas. However, this should not necessarily indicate a complete confluence between Hellenism and Judaism. Regarding Simon's decree, Gardner rightly emphasized that whilst it resembles Greek decrees in its structure and content, there are some significant differences[164] which are worth detailing: the Jewish decree uniquely highlights Simon's defence of the Jerusalem Temple and the law (1 Macc. 14.29, 31, 36); there are conspicuous absences of crowns among various symbols of authority, a statue of the benefactor, any references to games and competitions, or the conventional title 'saviour of people';[165] the decree includes phrases quintessentially biblical, such as 'Jonathan…was gathered to his people',[166] or '…until a trustworthy prophet should arise'.[167] Thus, whilst modelled after Hellenistic ones, the Jewish decree is demonstratively Jewish. This suggests, in Gardner's words, 'an active and dynamic encounter between traditional Israelite interests and those of the second-century Hellenistic world… a transformation of the otherwise standardized form of euergetism in order to account for aims and interests that were characteristically Jewish'.[168] This conclusion seems subtly different from that

---

of the Jerusalem Temple and the massive killing that followed (2 Chron. 32.1-22; 2 Kgs 18.17–19.36; Isa. 36–37) is not only prevalently re-used by later Jewish authors (e.g. 3 Macc. 6.5; Sir. 48.21; Josephus, *War* 5.388), but also an emphatic theme within the narrative of 2 Maccabees. Thus, 2 Macc. 8.19, as well as 15.22-24, provides this Hebrew epiphany as a governing motif of the victories of Judas' battles. See, for instance, Schwartz, *2 Maccabees*, 337, 506; Andrew Y. Lau, *Manifest in Flesh: The Epiphany Christology of the Pastoral Epistles*, WUNT 2/86 (Tübingen: Mohr Siebeck, 1996), 182–9. One could state that both the Hebraic-Jewish and Greek traditions on temple epiphany may have grown within the larger cultural pool of the Mediterranean world.

164. Gardner, 'Benefaction', 336–7.

165. For a conventional set of common features in Greek honorary decrees, see Hubert Cancik and Helmuth Schneider, eds., *Brill's New Pauly: Encyclopedia of the Ancient World* (Leiden: Brill, 2002), 1:356–57.

166. 1 Macc. 14.30 echoing Gen. 25.17; 35.29; 49.33; Num. 20.24, 26.

167. 1 Macc. 14.41, potentially echoing Deut. 18.15; Mal. 4.5-6 (Heb. 3.23-24).

168. Gardner, 'Benefaction', 340.

of Himmelfarb who concluded that Greek conceptions are synthesized with Jewish ones 'unself-consciously', and 1 Maccabees 'gives no hint of anxiety that its embrace of the categories of glory and honor represents a departure from the traditions of Israel's past or even that it recognizes these categories as a foreign import'.[169] Where Himmelfarb saw 'cultural synthesis' processed unconsciously,[170] Gardner saw dynamics and interaction through which conscious judgement was made by the Jews upon their incorporation of Hellenism. This is even more distant from Mendels who claimed not only rejection of Hellenism but also an absence of any presence of Hellenistic ideas in 1 Maccabees: 'there is very little evidence for an extensive penetration of Hellenistic values, knowledge, tradition, etc.'.[171]

2.4.3. *External features relating to Hellenism*

Like the aforementioned internal features of Hellenism, external features are also shown to have played a role in the maintenance of the Hasmoneans' Jewish identity. Hellenistic material features were indeed part and parcel of the Jews' expression in architecture and numismatics, yet this cultural expression often sharply retains an awareness of their religious identity. In this way, we may argue that the Jews' embrace of Hellenism was not an unconscious process, but a process undertaken through conscious evaluation of what was acceptable and what was not. Three examples will be discussed: Hasmonean names, tombs, and coins.

First, the Hasmoneans have frequently used Greek names alongside their Hebrew names. Tal Ilan states that Greek names such as Hyrcanus,[172] Aristobulus, Antigonus, Alexander, Alexandra and Agrippa have frequently been used by Hasmoneans,[173] although the Hasmonean individuals preceding John Hyrcanus I only had Hebrew names. Tcherikover noted

---

169. Himmelfarb, 'He Was Renowned', 96–7.
170. Himmelfarb, 'He Was Renowned', 97.
171. Mendels, 'Hellenism', 81.
172. Note that the name was already in use prior to the Hasmonean usage: 'Hyrcanus son of Joseph son of Tobias' (Josephus, *Ant.* 12.4, 6-11, 186-236). Complications have occurred surrounding the name's origin, with propositions such as Greek, Verkânian and Egyptian origins, but it is clear that the name was in any circumstance most probably promulgated by Hellenistic rulers prior to the Hasmonean era. For a summary of scholarly debates, see Daniel A. Machiela, 'A Brief History of the Second Temple Period Name "Hyrcanus"', *JJS* 61 (2010): 117–38. Machiela argues for an Egyptian etymology as the name's origin.
173. Tal Ilan, 'The Greek Names of the Hasmoneans', *JQR* 78 (1987): 1–20.

that Judas Aristobulus I was even called *Philhellen* (Josephus, *Ant.* 13.318).[174] As well as the Hasmonean family, pro-Hasmonean Jews evidently used Greek names: Numenius son of Antiochus, for example, and Antipater son of Jason (1 Macc. 12.16).[175]

Second, the Hasmonean tomb complex, described in detail in 1 Maccabees, shows close architectural parallels with Hellenistic tombs found throughout the Mediterranean world before and around the same era. Simon, after the death of his brother and predecessor Jonathan, erected family tombs which the author of 1 Maccabees details in this way:

> [27] And Simon built upon the grave of his father and of his brothers and made it highly visible with hewn stone on the back and on the front. [28] He also set up seven pyramids, each one opposite another, for his father and his mother and his four brothers. [29] For them he devised mechanisms, setting large pillars around them, and he placed suits of armour on the pillars for an everlasting name and beside the suits of armour carved ships to be seen by all those who sail the sea. [30] This tomb, which he made in Modein, remains to this day.

The particular architectural design – a tomb raised by a stone basement, topped by a pyramid, surrounded by free-standing pillars, and decorated with military objects and sculpture of ships – is a quintessentially Hellenistic feature.[176] Examples include the monumental tombs at Hermel and Kalat Fakra in Lebanon, the famous Mausoleum at Halacarnassus, as well as the Belvi Monument in Asia Minor, and the tomb of Hamrath in Syria which, beside the basement, pyramid and pillars, contains

---

174. Josephus, *Ant.* 13.3, 11, 318. Tcherikover, *Hellenistic Civilization*, 248, 252–3. Schürer (*HJPAJC*, 1:217 n. 6) states that Parthian kings and Nabatean king Aretas acquired the same designation.

175. Also, see Tcherikover, *Hellenistic Civilization*, 248, 252–3; Collins, 'Theodotus', 103.

176. Steven Fine, *Art and Judaism in the Greco-Roman World: Toward a New Jewish Archaeology* (Cambridge: Cambridge University Press, 2005), 61; Andrea M. Berlin, 'Power and Its Afterlife: Tombs in the Hellenistic Palestine', *NEA* 65, no. 2 (2002): 138–48; 'Jewish Life before the Revolt: The Archaeological Evidence', *JSJ* 36 (2005): 417–70 (453–66). See also a detailed description of Hellenistic tombs by Theodore Fyfe, *Hellenistic Architecture: An Introductory Study* (Cambridge: Cambridge University Press, 1936), especially Chapter 3; Lee I. Levine, *Jerusalem: Portrait of the City in the Second Temple Period (538 B.C.E.–70 C.E.)* (Philadelphia: The Jewish Publication Society, 2002), 98–9.

shields and other military objects in its decoration.¹⁷⁷ Similar tombs were also found in Jerusalem. The tomb of Jason, notable with its conical pyramid on the top, contains the image of a warship pursuing two other ships.¹⁷⁸ Likewise, the tombs of Zechariah and Absalom, both of which are located on the Kidron Valley, consistently show the cultural embrace in the Hellenistic period, as identifiable from their conical pyramids and surrounding pillars.¹⁷⁹

Third, the Hasmonean coinage further represents a close cultural association between the Hasmonean ideology and Hellenism.¹⁸⁰ The purposes of issuing coins were, as Arie Kindler remarked, not only 'to render means of payment easily [*sic*] to handle', but also for 'the expression of independence and sovereignty' and 'the profit gained from the issue'.¹⁸¹ Various features derivable from Hasmonean coins and their comparisons to Seleucid coinage confirm the cultural relationship between Judaism and Hellenism as sophisticated and interactive, rather than as non-existent, with Hellenism playing no significant role in Jewish culture. Several scholars have already expressed the continuation of Seleucid numismatic features in the Hasmonean coinage,¹⁸² such as the adopted symbol of

---

177. One may add the Macedonian tomb of Lyson and Kallikles which contains the image of a Macedonian shield, helmets and a sword.

178. See L. Y. Rahmani who suggests the date of the tomb to some time between the reign of Alexander Jannaeus and the fall of the dynasty, and by a wealthy Jewish family, see Rahmani, 'Jason's Tomb', *IEJ* 17 (1967): 61–100.

179. One may add in this regard the tombs of the Kings in East Jerusalem, now identified with the burial site of Queen Helene of Adiabene, which, according to Josephus (*Ant.* 20.95), had a conical pyramid above each of the three tombs. See a reconstruction model suggested by N. Avigad, 'The Architecture of Jerusalem in the Second Temple Period', in *Jerusalem Revealed: Archaeology in the Holy City, 1968–1974*, ed. Yigael Yadin (New Haven: Yale University Press, 1976), 14–20 (17).

180. For a brief survey of scholarship on the Hasmonean coinage in the last half century or so, see David Hendin, 'Current Viewpoints on Ancient Jewish Coinage: A Bibliographic Essay', *CBR* 11 (2013): 246–301. Also, see Eyal Regev's monograph on Hasmonean ideology which is also devoted to an extensive, focused discussion on Hasmonean coinage (Regev, *Hasmoneans*, 175–213).

181. Arie Kindler, 'The Hellenistic Influence on the Hasmonean Coins', in *XII. Internationaler Numismatischer Kongress, Berlin 1997: Akten – Proceedings – Actes, vol. I*, ed. Bernd Kluge and Bernhard Weisser (Berlin: Preußischer Kulturbesitz – Staatlichen Museen zu Berlin, 2000), 316–23.

182. Kindler, 'Hellenistic Influence', 316–23; Y. Meshorer, *AJC*, 1:60–8; Fine, *Art and Judaism*, 63; Regev, *Hasmoneans*, 180–223.

the anchor,[183] flower,[184] and wreath[185] to name but a few, which typically illustrate Hellenistic political and military expressions. However, some Hellenistic features are conspicuously absent from Jewish coins. The most notable is the avoidance of human/deity images on the coins, a feature prevalent throughout Greek and Roman coins.[186] Some have also observed the Hasmonean coins' distinctive emphasis on religious authority, especially Hyrcanus I, unlike Hellenistic coins whose purpose is primarily concerned with political authority.[187] To this, we may add Regev's observation that the Hasmonean monarchs, such as Alexander Jannaeus and Mattathias Antigonus, avoided any honorary titles to their monarchical authority, contrary to Hellenistic kings.[188]

2.4.4. *Summary*

The various internal/external features suggest, first of all, that Hellenistic ideas penetrated deep inside Palestinian Jewish culture in the Hasmonean era, and they are manifest in various forms of the Jews' cultural expression. More accurately, however, their presentations are demonstrably Jewish rather than Hellenistic. Whenever elements incompatible with Jewish traditions were found, the Jews either omitted or altered them to fit their customs and beliefs. Integration of Hellenistic influences

---

183. Meshorer, *AJC*, 1:61; Fine, *Art and Judaism*, 63; Kindler, 'Hellenistic Influence', 320.

184. Alongside the emblem of lily present on some coins, it has often been suggested that there is another floral type of emblem and it should be identified as a rose rather than lily, resembling some Hellenistic coins, especially those from the island state of Rhodes, and issued by the Hasmoneans probably in accordance with their schemes of attracting foreign mercenaries: P. Romanoff, *Jewish Symbols on Ancient Jewish Coins* (Philadelphia: Dropsie College for Hebrew and Cognate Learning, 1944), 50; Kindler, 'Hellenistic Influence', 318–20; David M. Jacobson, 'The Lily and the Rose: A Review on Some Hasmonean Coin Types', *NEA* 76, no. 1 (2013): 16–27.

185. For the wreath as a symbol of kingship, authority and used for the purpose of coronation, see Meshorer, *AJC*, 1:62.

186. Regev, *Hasmoneans*, 182, 200–201; Rajak, 'Hellenism', 71; Kindler, 'Hellenistic Influence', 317–18; Fine, *Art*, 69–73.

187. Kindler, 'Hellenistic Influence', 318; Regev, *Hasmoneans*, 183. Regev added Judas Aristobulus I's coins in this regard.

188. Regev, *Hasmoneans*, 184; for the honorary titles expressed in Hellenistic coins, see 184 n. 26. Regev further suggested that it is Paleo-Hebrew that was used for the Hasmoneans' high priestly title, whereas the monarchical titles were written in either Aramaic or Greek (185).

into the Jewish worldview occurs in a similar way to that of previous centuries: Yahwism was able to integrate elements of Canaanite religions or influences of Persian religion without losing its own integrity. In the same way, Judaism in the Hellenistic period appropriated ideas and topics but in such a way that they became Jewish ideas, compatible with their Hellenistic surroundings but, nevertheless, identifiably Jewish.

2.5. *Jewish perception of the past*

In the Introduction, we raised a question concerning 1 Maccabees' view on the ancestral past, that is, Past^S. Whilst the Past^R was perceived and shaped with an invariably pro-Hasmonean bias, the perception of Past^S was not immediately apparent. In this section, we will first explore some characteristics of how Jewish tradition appreciated their ancestral history by looking at biblical literature as well as other Jewish literature written in the periods leading to the Hasmonean era. The second part will examine the case of 1 Maccabees.

2.5.1. *Biblical and early Jewish literature*
2.5.1.1. *Constant re-telling of the same history*

In Jewish tradition, first of all, there is a constant re-telling of the well-known narrative of Israel's history.[189] As we discussed in the Introduction, Ben Zvi's observation on what he calls 'core facts' agrees with it.[190] In these re-tellings, the narrative, often combined with biblical accounts of creation, the Patriarchs, Moses and the exodus, the monarchical period, and the Babylonian exile, constantly recurs in various forms of speech such as entreaty, lament, ritual, encomium, rhetoric, and so on, and in various forms of literature such as historiography, prophecy, apocalypse,

---

189. N. T. Wright (*Paul and the Faithfulness of God*, COQG 4 [London: SPCK, 2013], 114–39) demonstrated that there is a constant retelling of Israel's salvific history in Jewish literature, and it is this same story, however many multiple forms there may be, that is remembered across different Jewish communities. As he aptly puts it: '[t]he main point about narratives in the Second-Temple Jewish world, and in that of Paul, is not simply that people liked telling stories as illustrations of, or scriptural proofs for, this or that experience or doctrine, but rather that Second-Temple Jews believed themselves to be *actors within* a real-life narrative... [T]he main function of their stories was to remind them of earlier and (they hoped) characteristic moments *within the single, larger story* which stretched from the creation of the world and the call of Abraham right forwards to their own day, and (they hoped) in to the future' (114, his italics).

190. See §1.2.3.

and wisdom.[191] The subtle differences in these accounts notwithstanding, this repertoire of Israel's history provides motives, justification and role models for later generations.

We may take the classical example of Chronicles. Its subtly different theological and ideological perspective compared to other biblical books covering either wholly or partly the same material is well-known, but Ben Zvi shows that there is compelling evidence of 'lack of deviation' of historical information in the book, characterized by the ways in which certain 'core facts' are preserved without change.[192] Despite the ideologically independent and different standpoint, the Chronicler preserves the genealogy of the Patriarchs and the sequence of kings of Judah, as well as the recognition of the Northern Kingdom's monarchs just as they are found in Samuel and Kings. He also preserves major events in Judahite monarchic history, as well as frequent references to Moses[193] and the mention of the Babylonian exile.[194]

2.5.1.2. *Repetitive patterns in the course of history*

This general observation on the repertoire of 'core facts' leads to another point, namely that Jewish history is perceived as a repetition of what is basically the same cycle of sequential events. Carol A. Newsom has recently proposed what she calls a 'rhyming pattern' in the basic structure of Jewish history.[195] It is worth noting that in his classic *Time*

---

191. Examples are numerous and widely spread throughout extra-biblical Jewish literature: Ezek. 20.4-44; Neh. 9.6-37; Pss. 78; 105; 106; 135; 136; Jdt 5.5-21; Wis. 10.1–12.27; 1 Macc. 2.49-60; the Apocalypse of Weeks and the Animal Apocalypse in *1 Enoch*; the Cloud Vision in the Syriac Baruch; Acts 7.2-53; Jas 5.10-11; Heb. 11.2-39; Josephus' speech before the walls of Jerusalem in *Jewish Wars* 5.375-93.

192. Ehud Ben Zvi, 'Shifting the Gaze: Historiographic Constraints in Chronicles and Their Implications', in *The Land That I Will Show You: Essays on the History and Archaeology of the Ancient Near East in Honor of J. Maxwell Miller*, ed. J. Andrew Dearman and M. Patrick Graham, JSOTSup 343 (Sheffield: Sheffield Academic, 2001), 38–60. In contrast, see S. Japhet, *The Ideology of the Book of Chronicles and Its Place in Biblical Thought*, BEATAJ 9, 2nd edn (Bern: Peter Lang, 1997).

193. E.g. 1 Chron. 6.34; 15.15; 21.29; 22.13; 23.15; 26.24; 2 Chron. 1.3; 5.10; 8.13; 23.18; 24.6, 9; 25.4; 30.16; 33.8; 34.14; 35.6, 12.

194. 1 Chron. 9.1; 2 Chron. 36.11-20.

195. Carol A. Newsom, 'Rhyme and Reason: The Historical Résumé in Israelite and Early Jewish Thought', in *Israel's Prophets and Israel's Past: Essays on the Relationships of Prophet Texts and Israelite History in Honor of John H. Hayes*, ed. Brad E. Kelle and Megan Bishop Moore, LHBOTS 446 (New York: T&T Clark, 2006), 293–310 (293).

and Narrative, Paul Ricoeur made a distinction between two types of temporality through which historical cognition is to be made: the 'chronological temporality' in which one event simply happens after another, and the 'configured temporality' in which the configuration of events, or 'emplotment', as he calls it, allows the temporality to curve and form a structure.[196] This configured temporality thus has a beginning and an end. What Newsom adds to these two modes of temporality is 'the temporality of rhythm' which 'serves both to enhance the configuration by repeating it but also to undermine its effect of closure by this same repetition'.[197] Thus, the focus of Jewish historiographical practice shifts from creating anything new in the course of history to re-affirming what should continue to happen. In other words, the multiple accounts of history in Jewish tradition do not necessarily convey new information, but underline the significance of the recurring events.

2.5.1.3. *Theological perspective as a moulder of history*

The Jewish perception of the past is fundamentally shaped by a theological perspective. In numerous cases the recitation of the basic form of Israel's history is aimed at remembering what God has done for his people and, often as a flip side of it, reminding of the people's disobedience to him. As I will discuss at length in Chapter 4, the Deuteronomic covenantal framework provides the causality of the course of Israel's history, as it is delineated in Deuteronomy 28–30 and inherited in the Former/Latter Prophets, as well as later Jewish literature, including 1 Maccabees. Dependent upon commitment on the part of God and on the necessary obligation on the part of Israel, the narrative of Israel's history unfolds systematically.

---

196. Paul Ricoeur, *Time and Narrative* (Chicago: University of Chicago Press, 1984–88), 1:66–7. Mendels is rightly aware of the relevance of the question about biblical notion of *time* in the study of ancient perceptions of their past, but his conception of the matter is too simplistic. In reference to Polybius' two concepts of time, cyclic and linear, he contends, 'the past as a full linear process that receives an inscribed expression remains the domain of annalistic historians, whereas the past in its fragmented and partial form is what dominated the lives of societies in Antiquity and brought about a chaotic and unstable historical perception' (Mendels, 'Antiquity', 24). The issue pertaining to the notion of time in biblical literature requires more detailed dialogues with the large body of scholarship on the subject, and his short critique on Arnaldo Momigliano (24) does not seem sufficient.

197. Newsom, 'Rhyme', 297.

In the so-called historical Psalms, the same attitude toward history can be found. In Psalm 78, the opening stanza runs through the first eight verses, highlighting in a didactic manner the vitality of acknowledging God as the main actor in the drama of their history and the gravity of the need for preserving such a theologically shaped history through generations.[198] God 'established a testimony in Jacob', 'appointed the law in Israel', and 'commanded them to teach their children' (v. 5) in order for his people to 'set their hope in God and not forget the works of God but keep his commandments' (v. 7). This theological perspective determines the structure and the sequence of the historical narrative in the rest of the psalm. The causality of the sequence between the heydays of Israel and the catastrophes is explained by Israel's disobedience of, and lack of compliance with, the covenantal responsibility on the part of Israel (vv. 10-11, 17, 30-32, 36-37, 56-58). Such a divine causality in the sequence of Israel's history is also found in Psalms 105–106. Like Psalm 78, vv. 1-5 of Psalm 105 open the psalm with a theological reflection of past events. The hortatory speech of the Psalmist addressed to the audience (vv. 5-6) connects them (the present) with their ancestors (the past), making the God of their ancestors relevant to the people here and now. He opens the narrative of historical events by reaffirming the covenant made between God and their ancestors, with Abraham being the first in the line (vv. 7-11).[199] After recapitulating miraculous events of ancestral history through which God demonstrated his care for his covenant

---

198. Artur Weiser suggests that the psalm is in connection with 'the tradition of the Covenant Festival', the liturgical procedure of which may have been similar to the feast of the renewal of the covenant of the Qumran sectarian group; see Weiser, *The Psalms* (London: SCM, 1962), 538–9 (539 n. 1). The absence of any reference to the destruction of the Jerusalem Temple makes Weiser conclude that the psalm predates the event (540). For other opinions on the dating of the psalm, see John Goldingay, *Psalms: Vol. 2, Psalms 42–89*, BCOTWP (Grand Rapids, MI: Baker Academic, 2007), 481.

199. Weiser (*Psalms*, 673–83) contextualizes the paired psalms in Israel's cultic practice at the 'Covenant Festival' through which renewal of the covenant between God and his people was affected (674). In view of the ending verses of Ps. 106, however, a question remains as to the Psalmist's climaxing, solemn entreaty for restoration of his community, saying, 'Save us, O Lord our God, and gather us from among the nations, that we may give thanks to your holy name and glory in your praise' (v. 47). This cry resonates with the devastated and exilic state of the whole community, an impossible state for holding a festival at the Jerusalem Temple. Compare Weiser's comments on this verse: 'It cannot conclusively be proved that here the whole people is thought to be in exile; the verse can just as well be understood to

people, the ending verse of the psalm concludes that all these things happened because God remembered his covenant (replacing 'covenant' in the beginning of the psalm with '*holy* promise' perhaps to add the sense that the promise belonged to God and it was his responsibility to keep the promise he made). Thus, the Psalmist's historical knowledge, which is profoundly shaped by theological perspective, is particularly characterized by covenantal terms. In the pairing psalm (Ps. 106), where the Psalmist contrasts the same account by highlighting Israel's sins, the description coheres with covenantal defilement and the following curse. In the last verses (106.44-48) the psalmist draws a conclusion by recalling the covenant, and God's faithfulness to it, as a rationale behind Israel's overcoming of, and triumph over, their misfortune. Israel's act of repentance (v. 44) causes God to relent from cursing to re-blessing (vv. 45-46). In other words, the causality of the audience's ancestral history is essentially and explicitly covenantal. The curse precipitated by defilement of covenant was overturned to blessing through the act of repentance.

The same pattern of inscribing the past in a theological outlook continues in Psalm 135, another historiographical Psalm,[200] and is further extended to other texts such as Nehemiah 9 and 3 Maccabees 6.[201] Thus, theological perspective is deeply implicated in the causality of historical sequence in biblical and later Jewish literature. It is the people's acknowledgement of God and his relationship with them through the covenant that determines the meaning of the past, sustains their consciousness of history, and locates the present and the future within it.

---

refer to a calamity that has come upon the people, for instance after the destruction of the Northern Kingdom' (682). Alternatively, Mitchell Dahood considers the phrase, 'from among the nations', in v. 47 as a 'clear indication of the *Sitz im Leben*' of the psalm; this is the prayer of the Israelite community in the diaspora or dispersion after the destruction of Jerusalem in 587 B. C.'; see Dahood, *Psalms III: 101–150*, AB 17A (Garden City, NY: Doubleday, 1984), 76.

200. E.g. Dahood, *Psalms*, 135.

201. Jacques Vermeylen sees the theological understanding of the pattern of Israel's history in which God's mercy/blessing and Israel's rebellion/repentance repeat, see Vermeylen, 'The Gracious God, Sinners and Foreigners: How Nehemiah 9 Interprets the History of Israel', in *Deuterocanonical and Cognate Literature Yearbook 2006: How Israel's Later Authors Viewed Its Earlier History*, ed. N. Calduch-Benages and J. Liesen (Berlin: de Gruyter, 2006), 77–112 (esp. 100–104). For 3 Macc. 6's theological presentation of Israel's history, followed by confession of trust, lament and praise, which resembles the structure of lament psalms, see Jeremy Corley, 'The Review of History in Eleazar's Prayer in 1 Macc 6:1-15', in Calduch-Benages and Liesen, eds., *Deuterocanonical and Cognate Literature*, 201–29.

2.5.1.4. *Chronological listing of ancestral heroes*

Another point which relates to ways of rendering accounts of the past is that there is a tendency to compose a chronological list of ancestral heroes. This tendency may share some characteristics with the repetitive and rhythmic pattern of Israel's history. Thus, there is repetitive highlighting of pious acts of the ancestors and their rewards in a chronological process, implying rewarding of the pious to be paradigmatic. In addition, chronological listing explicitly illustrates selectivity, thus preserving certain historical figures whilst deliberately removing others from memories. This is explained in Ben Sira's introduction (Sir. 44.1-15) to the long passage on Praise of Fathers in chs. 44–49, or 44–50.[202] In this introduction, especially vv. 8-15, it is evident that whilst the name of the pious continues to be remembered and be a part of history, the name of the impious (e.g. 44.9) is forgotten and no longer remembered.[203] This is Ben Sira's rationale behind understanding history, and functions rhetorically in his writing. The point is that the criteria of selectivity are to do with reassurance of theologically shaped history through remembering the conduct and conventions that correspond with covenantal obligations.

---

202. For the passage as introduction to the following chs. 44–49, see Skehan and Di Lella, *Ben Sira*, 499. Similarly, Jeremy Corley, 'Sirach 44:1-15 As Introduction to the Praise of the Ancestors', in *Studies in the Book of Ben Sira: Papers of the Third International Conference on the Deuterocanonical Books, Shime'on Centre, Pápa, Hungary, 18–20 May, 2006*, ed. Géza G. Xeravits and József Zsengellér, JSJSup 127 (Leiden: Brill, 2008), 151–81. Corley suggests the whole of chs. 44–50 as being used in a 'ceremony remembering the past national leaders' and 'a ceremony held in the temple precincts', just as the Greek encomium, which shares a number of similarities with the Jewish one, originated from 'epic deictic oratory' rather than from a written text (154). He suggests the doxology in Sir. 45.26 and 50.23 as the evidence. Further, Corley suggests the feast of Rosh Hashanah, celebrated ten days prior to the Day of Atonement, as a possible occasion for the ceremony because of the feast's strong association with the theme of remembrance and Sir. 50.5-21 in which the imagery of trumpet-blowing and remembrance resembles the liturgy of Rosh Hashanah (155). As to Corley's inclusion of ch. 50, compare Di Lella's comment that the chapter, which describes the family of contemporary high priest Simon II of Oniad, should be separated from the Praise of the Fathers because the chapter praises the high priest 'who as a contemporary of Ben Sira can hardly be reckoned as one of the Ancestors of Old' (Skehan and Di Lella, *Ben Sira*, 499).

203. See Corley, 'Introduction', 168–72. In contrast, however, Di Lella (*Ben Sira*, 499) claims, following Ceslas Spicq, that these forgotten people meant to be the same pious people were 'simply not remembered by future generations' (with a reference to Isa. 57.1-2).

2.5.1.5. *Changes of historical details and their complex motives*

The next three points relate to fragmentary Hellenistic Jewish writings preserved through Eusebius and Clement of Alexandria.[204] These writings, many of which were composed in a diaspora setting, provide a significant understanding about Jewish perceptions of the past in the Hellenistic world. The provenance of many of these writings has been identified as Egypt, which means they arose from mutual interest in co-existing cultures such as Jewish, Greek and Egyptian. What is more, the subjugation of oriental nations under the imperial power of Greece meant that preservation of the subject groups' identities was often made in an apologetic and exaggerated manner in order to claim the superiority of their own cultures over Greek imperial arrogance, which forced them to subsume their cultures into the imperialistic agenda. In this way, for the Jews, writing history or writing about the past was inevitably propagandist. Yet, there is subtlety in this type of historiography. As we will see, manipulation of details was a typical mode of interacting with the past. The ancestral past of the Jews was deeply fused with the Greek mythology. Or, more precisely, it is Greek tradition that was integrated into Jewish tradition to encomiastically portray Jewish ancestors. However, such an adapted account of history was not aimed at implanting new memory, but rather

---

204. I mainly consult the following works in this regard: *FHJA*, especially vol. 1: *Historians*; various writers in *OTP*, especially 3:775–918; revised Emil Schürer, *HJPAJC*, 3:180–6, 3:509–58; Attridge, 'Historiography', 157–84 (esp. 160–71); also *DEJ*, especially the articles on the Hellenistic Jewish writers. As a general remark, these Jewish writings are preserved only fragmentarily and third-hand. That is, the works and their authors are allegedly mentioned and cited mainly by Greek historian Alexander Polyhistor, which are then preserved by Eusebius in his *Preparatio Evangelica* (Books 9, 10, 13). Outside of Eusebius' work, there are other ancient writers, such as Josephus, Clement of Alexandria, and Jerome, who partly preserve those fragments and the authors (e.g. Holladay, *FHJA*, 1:1–21). The English translation of the following quotations reflects a combination of the editions in *Pseudepigrapha* and the work of Holladay. Where they disagree, my own judgement will be made on translation. It is also worth appreciating the blurring edges with regard to which writings consist of Jewish historiography as opposed to other genres. Charlesworth's *OTP* offers distinctions between 'history' and others such as 'romance', 'poetry', 'chronography'. However, the level of difference between history and chronography is very different from, say, the level of difference between history and poetry or oracles. In fact, the similarity between history and chronography should be emphasized. We will thus include works that potentially contribute to the Jewish historiographical milieu of the Hellenistic era. Lastly, although we say these writers are Jewish, some of them are of disputed ethnicity, and proposed as Samaritan (e.g. Thallus).

aimed at adding new perspectives and contents to the already established sequence of events, 'core facts'. It is this apologetic aspect that requires due weight and appreciation in discussing Jewish perceptions of the past.

Thus, whilst there are deliberate changes of historical details, the motives for these changes are sophisticated and not primarily intended to undermine the already existing account of history. For instance, the writings that were composed in Egypt often depict key ancestral figures, such as the Patriarchs and Moses, as founders of culture in Egypt. In the fragments of Artapanus,[205] a Jewish writer who probably resided in Egypt during the mid-second century BCE,[206] the histories of Abraham, Joseph and, in greater length, of Moses, are recounted. Artapanus writes that Abraham apparently came to Egypt to teach astrology to the Egyptian king (*Praep. ev.* 9.18.1). Likewise, Joseph is portrayed as having established an efficient and egalitarian system of land division and organization (*Praep. ev.* 9.23.2). Moses in this writing is even more influential. First

---

205. Frags. 1–3 in Eusebius, *Praep. ev.* 9.18.1; 9.23.1-4; 9.27.1-37, and Frag. 3, par. 23–25 also in Clement, *Strom.* 1.23.154.2-3. Its title is called 'Concerning the Jews' by both Eusebius and Clement. Its genre, despite its broadly historical style, is less decisive and *OTP* categorizes it as 'romance' (John J. Collins, 'Artapanus', *OTP* 2:889–903).

206. Holladay (*FHJA*, 1:189–91) provides three reasons for Egyptian provenance: (1) Artapanus' name bears a Persian origin, (2) his preoccupation with and glorification of Jewish tradition and figures indicates his Jewishness, and (3) the citations of Egyptian local traditions, as well as providing names for Egyptian places and figures such as Pharaoh and his daughter, are not known in the biblical accounts. The dating is less certain. Collins ('Artapanus', 2:890–1) suggests Ptolemy IV Philopator (ca. 221–204 BCE) as a possibility based on some of Artapanus' statements that have correspondences to the historical context of this Egyptian king (e.g. organization of Dionysus cult, permission of the Egyptian peasantry). Cf. Holladay (*FHJA*, 1:190, 230 n. 28), who prefers Ptolemy VI Philometor (ca. 180–145 BCE) based on Artapanus' mention of the Jewish Temple in Leontopolis built by Onias IV (ca. 167–164 BCE) (Frag. 2, par. 23.4). A more recent analysis on the authorship and provenance of Artapanus has been provided by Holger M. Zellentin, 'The End of Jewish Egypt: Artapanus and the Second Exodus', in Gardner and Osterloh, eds., *Antiquity in Antiquity*, 131–51. Zellentin argues that Artapanus was written by a Jewish writer residing in Egypt during the end of the second reign of Ptolemy VIII and his two wives (145–116 BCE), and written in response to Ptolemy's *philantropa* decree (118 BCE) which sought to relieve agricultural burdens of small farmers including the Egyptian veterans of the army. His use of Jewish patriarchs, says Zellentin, was aimed at persuading the Jewish military aristocracy of Ptolemaic Egypt to 'leave Egypt for "Syria" [i.e. Palestine in Ptolemaic geography]', as though calling for the second Exodus (30).

of all, he is identified with Musaeus of Athens who is a legendary figure in Greek tradition. The description of his many contributions, such as inventing ships, machines, weapons, and land division systems, as well as playing a leading role in establishing polytheistic worship in Egypt, all reflect various Greek sources and indicate Artapanus' active incorporation of them, thus accordingly shaping the image of Jewish ancestors (*Praep. ev.* 9.27.3-6). A similar tendency is found in the fragments attributed to Pseudo-Eupolemus.[207] The pseudonymity of these fragments is generally determined by its tendency to syncretism, unlike the other five fragments attributed to Eupolemus in which this tendency is minimal. The Patriarchs in these fragments show a close association with pagan culture. Abraham, born in a Babylonian city, acquired knowledge of astrology and Chaldean science, and travelled around Phoenicia and Heliopolis teaching the locals astrology (*Praep. ev.* 9.17.2-4, 8-9). In both of these writings, whilst various options have been proposed as to the intention behind such departure from the Hebrew Scripture and the target audience, it is generally agreed that the change of historical details primarily served apologetic ends.

There are also changes of the past that reflect political influence. Eupolemus, who has often been identified as a Jewish writer residing in Judea in the mid-second century BCE, apparently composed writings of which only five fragments survive.[208] The fragments contain a summary

---

207. For a brief history of scholarship on identification of this work with someone other than Eupolemus, see Holladay, *FHJA*, 1:158–9 and the corresponding footnotes. Holladay follows J. Freudenthal on the Samaritan origin. In contrast, Robert Doran ('Pseudo-Eupolemus', *OTP* 2:873–82 [874–6]) argues for identification of the first of the two fragments with Eupolemus (leaving the question for the second fragment open). On the provenance of these fragments, Samaria has often been suggested. With Holladay's assertion that the writer's conspicuous bias toward the temple at Mount Gerizim is a strong indicator for Samaritan origin, the date was no later than 132 BCE when John Hyrcanus ushered in campaigns to Samaria and Idumea. With Doran, the date falls within the Hasmonean period when Eupolemus was alive. The remarkable polarity between the two views arises with regard to provenance – Samaria or Judea – which has critical impacts on the purpose of the work. Some scholars have identified the purpose of the writing as a pro-Babylonian bias, e.g. Ben Zion Wacholder, 'Pseudo-Eupolemus' Two Greek Fragments on the Life of Abraham', *HUCA* 34 (1963): 83–113 (especially 105).

208. Frags. 1–4 in *Praep. ev.* 9.26.1; 9.30.1–34.18; 9.34.20; 9.39.2–5, and Frag. 5 in Clement, *Strom.* 1.141.4. Clement preserves Fragment 5, which is missing in Eusebius' work, and this last fragment appears to be in a form of summary whereas the other four fragments survive in quotation by Eusebius. Its title, 'Concerning the Kings of Judea', is given by Clement, although there is a possibility that these

of history between the times of Moses and David, particularly the account of Solomon, his building of the Jerusalem Temple, the exchange of letters between Solomon and pagan kings, Hiram and Vaphres, and an encomiastic description of Solomon. The fragments further contain the prophecy of Jeremiah during the reign of Jehoiakim and a comprehensive Jewish history from Adam to Eupolemus' time. In these fragments, Eupolemus was apparently ignorant of some basic facts about Israel's history. He states that Eli was high priest at the time of Solomon's coronation, which appears to be anachronistic because Eli lived in the time of Samuel according to 1 Samuel 1–4 (*Praep. ev.* 9.30.8). Eupolemus might have intentionally removed Zadok who was present at Solomon's coronation according to the biblical account (1 Chron. 29.22) and inserted Eli, because the Zadokite priests were pro-Seleucid at the Hasmonean era and therefore opponents of the Hasmoneans. Furthermore, he changes the starting date of the Jerusalem Temple building project from the fourth year of Solomon's reign, as in 1 Kings and 2 Chronicles, to the second year of his reign.[209] For the measurement of the sanctuary in Solomon's Temple, Eupolemus records both the length and width of it as sixty cubits each, which contradicts these two texts where the width is twenty cubits.[210] One could say that these changes seem to be an exaggeration intended to highly praise Solomon and the Jerusalem Temple.

fragments come from more than one source. For a brief overview of the discussion, see Holladay, *FHJA*, 1:100 n. 7; F. Fallon, 'Eupolemus', *OTP* 2:861–82 (esp. 861–3). Both suggest unity of Fragment 5 with the rest. Scholars generally assert that the author was a Greek-speaking Jewish historian, residing in Palestine during the mid-second century BCE (e.g. Holladay, *FHJA*, 1:93; Fallon, 'Eupolemus', 2:861–3). Holladay derives the author's Jewishness from the writing's Hebraism, dependence on the Septuagint, heroic depiction of Jewish figures (Moses and Solomon in particular), and cultic interest (knowledge of/devotion to the Jerusalem Temple) (1:93–7 and the corresponding footnotes). That its provenance is Palestine is derived from its use of the Hebrew measuring unit, *cors* (Frag. 2, par. 33; κόρος), use of the MT tradition, and its chronological calculation corresponding with the Seleucid calendar (Frag. 5). It is generally consensual that this Eupolemus is the same figure who appears in 1 Maccabees as one of Judas' two ambassadors sent to Rome to establish an alliance (1 Macc. 8.17-20; 2 Macc. 4.11; Josephus, *Ant.* 12.415; *Ag. Ap.* 1.218). For further references to this, to Eupolemus in the Church Fathers, and the history of discussion on authorship/date/provenance, see Holladay, *FHJA*, 1:93, 98–100 n. 1–6.

209. *Praep. ev.* 9.34.4; cf. 1 Kgs 6.1; 2 Chron. 3.2.

210. *Praep. ev.* 9.34.4; cf. 1 Kings[Gk] where the length is forty cubits. Holladay suggested that the width of sixty cubits might have been derived from Ezra 6.3, which means that Eupolemus was referring to the Second Temple (Holladay, *FHJA*, 1:148 n. 70).

In some other cases, distortion of biblical information occurs, but with ambiguous motives. In the works of Artapanus, for instance, Joseph was not sent in slavery to Egypt by his brothers, as in the account of Genesis, but went voluntarily after he anticipated their conspiracy against him.[211] Likewise, Moses' murder of the Egyptian was committed not in defence of his kinsman as in the account of Exodus, but in self-defence.[212] In addition to Artapanus, the author of Pseudo-Eupolemus reversed the chronological order between Gen. 12.10-20 and Genesis 14 (*Praep. ev.* 9.17.4–9). He is reticent about Abraham's rescue of Lot, women, and people in Gen. 14.16, and instead emphasizes Abraham's capture of the enemy's women and children (*Praep. ev.* 9.17.4-5). These examples show that motives and intentions of historical manipulation can sometimes be rather unclear.

Changes of the past are further complicated in cases where these changes were shared and spread across different Jewish communities. In the fragment attributed to Theodotus,[213] the eight fragments that have survived focus on the biblical account of the rape of Dinah in Genesis 34. Theodotus narrates that after Dinah was violated, the necessity of the Shechemites' circumcision was raised as an issue among the Israelites, but there is no mention of their actual circumcision in these fragments and not even in the summative account of the rape in Fragment 4.[214] Due to the fragmentary nature of Theodotus' work, it cannot be proven whether the Shechemites' circumcision was deliberately omitted by the author. However, as Fallon suggests, the Shechemites' circumcision was possibly omitted deliberately by Theodotus with an intention to cover the embarrassment the Jews felt about the Patriarchs' slaughtering act upon the Shechemites who were already circumcised.[215] What is more, as rightly pointed out by Fallon, the circumcision of the Shechemites is again removed from the narrative of the rape in Jubilees 30. In the Testament of Levi, the author even deliberately points out the Jews' embarrassment

---

211. *Praep. ev.* 9.23.1; cf. Gen. 37.18-24.
212. *Praep. ev.* 9.27.18; cf. Exod. 2.11-15.
213. F. Fallon, 'Theodotus', *OTP* 2:785–93. The author's association with Samaritan origin has been a dominant view, though there are minor voices asserting him as Jewish (see Fallon's summary, 'Theodotus', 2:785–89). Whether Samaritan or Jewish, it has generally been accepted that the composition was made between the late third and the mid-second century BCE.
214. The Shechemites are repeatedly portrayed as evil (*Praep. ev.* 9.22.4-6, 9), whilst at the same time Theodotus emphatically underlines the importance of circumcision (*Praep. ev.* 9.22.7); cf. Gen. 34.24.
215. Fallon, 'Theodotus', 2:786.

of the Shechemites' circumcision by adding Jacob's mourning after the deaths of the Shechemites who were already circumcised. The author explicitly mentions Levi's detestation of the Shechemites and his claim to his father that they should not be circumcised (T. Lev. 6.3). In the following verse, his father becomes sorrowful and sick due to the death of those who were circumcised (the Shechemites) by the hands of Levi and other brothers (6.6-7). The story then ends by Levi's self-justification that 'they had wanted to do the same thing to Sarah and Rebecca that they did to Dinah… But the Lord prevented them' (6.8). These three accounts of the rape of Dinah illustrate that manipulation of historical details is likely to involve a complex process of reasoning and, notably, the sharing and spreading of the manipulated account across different Jewish communities.

In summary, what we gain from the changing of various types of historical details in Jewish writings across Egypt, Judea and Samaria, is as follows. The motives for amendment are far more complex than a simple intention of implanting new memories upon the Greek-speaking Jews in order to distort their old memories. The changes are expressions of the creativity of Jewish identity formation in reflection of, and in reaction to, their cultural surrounding, exhibiting both the Jews' fluidity in perceiving their past within their Hellenistic cultural setting and their deep appreciation of their own ancestral tradition. The motives for manipulation and fabrication of biblical and historical details are diverse, and it seems too simplistic to assume the Jewish authorities' political aims as a singular motive. It is worth noting that these Hellenistic traditions of the Jewish patriarchs have not stood the test of time; only the canonical account of the Patriarchs survived in Jewish traditions.

2.5.1.6. *Desire for accurate history*

The sixth characteristic for discussion is the strong desire to present accurate history in some Jewish writings. The six fragments of Demetrius, who was probably a Jewish writer residing in Alexandria during the last quarter of the third century BCE,[216] reveal an example of 'scientific

---

216. Frags. 1–5 in Eusebius, *Praep. ev.* 9.19.4; 9.21.1–19; 9.29.1–3; 9.29.15; 9.29.16, and Frag. 6 in Clement, *Strom.* 1.141.1-2. Unity of the six fragments is not warranted since the title, 'Concerning the Kings in Judea', as it is rendered by Clement, does not match the contents of the first five fragments where some of the stories of Genesis and Exodus are recounted. However, J. Hanson comments that it is 'not necessary to posit disunity…[because, for instance,] Justus of Tiberius wrote a history of Judean kings in which he covered Moses to Agrippa II. Philo, too, can call Moses a "king" (*vit Moses* 2.292)' (Hanson, 'Demetrius the Chronographer',

chronography',[217] to use Hanson's term. The fragments contain narratives about the Patriarchs, Moses, and the exodus that demonstrate clear interests in rendering chronological calculation, recording historical events with fairness and objectivity, and wrestling with inconsistencies of historical details in the biblical account. Thus, concerning the apparently logical problem of Jacob having twelve children born to him within seven years, Demetrius' solution is to calculate the birth of each of the twelve children by one of four women: Leah, Rachel, and their female servants (*Praep. ev.* 9.21.3-5). Likewise, he points out a moral inconsistency of Joseph not contacting his father during the first nine years of his governorship in Egypt, and explains it by saying that a shepherd (Joseph's fathers' vocation) was considered among the Egyptians as an embarrassing job and so Jacob told his brothers to pretend to be cow-herds instead, when asked by the Egyptian king (*Praep. ev.* 9.21.13). Demetrius explains the inconsistency between the Israelites crossing the Red Sea without weapons, as described in Exodus, and the same Israelites who later engaged in armed fighting against the Egyptian army (*Praep. ev.* 9.29.16). Maren R. Niehoff recently described the attitude of the opponents of the Hellenistic Jewish writers in Egypt as 'Homeric scholarship' which contested the veracity of the Hebrew Scripture.[218] Whether this is true or not, the passage shows

---

OTP 2:843–54 [843]). Also, Clement's summative style should be understood within the context of his work in which he gives his own version of a comprehensive chronology of world history by adding summaries of his Jewish, Greek and Roman sources. His intention is far from citing actual words but is rather the integration of the viewpoints of ancient historians into his own account of history. The accounts from these other sources are also written in his own summary, so that Demetrius may seem perfectly congruous. It is generally asserted that the author was Jewish, residing in Alexandria during the last quarter of the third century BCE. The work appears to know the Septuagint only, using its vocabulary and phraseology, a feature which makes Palestinian residence difficult, and the mention of Ptolemy IV Philopater (ca. 222–205 BCE) in Fragment 6 may confirm this as well as narrowing down the date of composition (Holladay, *FHJA*, 1:51; Hanson, 'Demetrius', 2:844).

217. Hanson, 'Demetrius', 2:844. A similar type of writing was already a well-known phenomenon in the wider Hellenistic world: *Chronographiai* by a Greek author called Eratosthenes (ca. 275–194 BCE), *Aigyptiaka* by Egyptian Manetho (ca. 280 BCE) and *Babyloniaka* by Berossus of Babylon (ca. 290 BCE) are examples given by Hanson (2:845). The intellectual horizon of ancient chronography may include other Jewish works that include chronography such as Jubilees, Genesis Apocryphon and Seder Olam Rabbah, although Demetrius' work differentiates the style of chronography from that of other Jewish works (e.g. Holladay, *FHJA*, 1:52).

218. Maren R. Niehoff, *Jewish Exegesis and Homeric Scholarship in Alexandria* (Cambridge: Cambridge University Press, 2011), 38–57.

evidence of the opponents by insertion of phrases such as 'but someone asked' and 'for they said', which imply some interrogation and criticism about the biblical account of history. The inconsistency of the Israelites' action allowed the opponents of Demetrius to claim that they were leaving Egypt only for a few days in order to offer a sacrifice in wilderness before returning, implying that they never truly desired to leave Egypt. Here, Demetrius defends the biblical account by explaining that some were unarmed when crossing the Red Sea whilst others were carrying weapons for them. In this way, the Israelites could still cross the Red Sea and later engage in armed battle.

There are more examples of this kind, but these three clearly show Demetrius' desire for accuracy as his motivation for historiography. Chronographical elements can also be found in the works of other writers, such as Eupolemus and Thallus.[219] Demetrius' style, however, is uniquely characterized by his seeking of accuracy and logical reasoning to resolve not only chronological difficulties but also apparent logical and moral inconsistencies in the causality of history. Moreover, writing this type of historiography was apologetically motivated.[220]

2.5.1.7. *Pursuit of a comprehensive history*

Last but not least, there is, in Hellenistic Jewish writings, a tendency to try and pursue a comprehensive history. In Demetrius' sixth fragment, preserved through Clement of Alexandria, we find evidence that his work continues through the monarchical and exilic periods up to his present day, that is, the reign of Ptolemy IV, around the last quarter of the third century BCE:

> But Demetrius says, in his [work] 'On the Kings of Judaea', that the tribe of Judah and [those of] Benjamin and Levi were not taken captive by Sennacherib, but from this captivity to the last [captivity], which Nebuchadnezzar effected out of Jerusalem, [there were] 128 years and 6 months. But from the time when the ten tribes of Samaria were taken captive to that of Ptolemy the 4th, there were 573 years and 9 months. But from the time [of the captivity] of Jerusalem [to Ptolemy IV], there were 338 years [and] 3 months. (*Strom.* 1.141.1-2)[221]

---

219. On Thallus, see Holladay, *FHJA*, 1:343–69. On Eupolemus, see the following section.
220. Compare, however, P. M. Fraser, *Ptolemaic Alexandria* (Oxford: Oxford University Press, 1972), 1:173. Fraser remarked that Demetrius was 'an academic writer with little interest in apologetic or propaganda'.
221. The English translation here and others are taken from *OTP*.

Demetrius here offers a summary of calculations of the years from Northern Israel's and Southern Judah's captivity up to his present day, showing an effort to stretch the awareness of the past and connect it with the present for a comprehensive history.[222] Moreover, in the middle of Fragment 2, we have evidence that the lost parts of his work included the time of Adam, thus suggesting that his chronographical interest covered a large span of time, spanning the beginning of humanity up to his present:

> From Adam until the time when the brothers of Joseph came into Egypt there were 3,624 years; from the flood until Jacob's arrival in Egypt there were 1,360 years; and from the time when Abraham was chosen from among the nations and came from Haran into Canaan until the time when those with him came into Egypt there were 215 years. (*Praep. ev.* 9.21.18)

Furthermore, his use of the Ptolemaic calendar in the sixth fragment to indicate the present time may also suggest interlocking between Jewish history and the imperial, pagan history. Thus, this comprehensive scope of history, both in time and space, suggests an example of Jewish writing in which there is no intention of political manipulation or distortion of the previous account of history. The emphasis is rather on preservation of what is already known, and promoting a full and precise knowledge of it.

This pursuit of a comprehensive history is also found in the fifth fragment of Eupolemus:

> Further, Eupolemus also says in a similar treatise that all the years from Adam to the fifth year of the reign of Demetrius (while Ptolemy[223] was in his twelfth year as king of Egypt) are five thousand, one hundred and forty-nine, and from the time when Moses led the Jews out of Egypt to the

---

222. The period between the fall of Samaria and that of Jerusalem is 128 years and six months according to Demetrius. But if one supplies seven years between Shalmaneser's taking of the ten tribes and the fall of Samaria (2 Kgs 17.2-6; 18.9) as Demetrius is also aware, the years become 135 years and six months. This latter figure may explain what appears to be inconsistent in Demetrius' calculations of the total 573 years and nine months between the exile of the ten tribes and the time of Demetrius IV, and the total 338 years and three months between the fall of Jerusalem and the time of Demetrius IV, the difference of which is 235 years and six months. Hanson ('Demetrius', 2:854) suggests some corruption in the process of transmission, altering the number 473 to 573, or 438 to 338, or that Demetrius might have allowed 235 years before the Persian period.

223. That is, Ptolemy VII Euergetes II Physcon (ca. 170–116 BCE).

aforementioned date there are two thousand, five hundred and eighty years. (From this time until the Roman consuls Gnaius Dometianus and [G.] Asinius[224] one hundred and twenty years are summed up.) (*Strom.* 1.141.4)

Here, again, Eupolemus covers the period from the time of Adam up to his own present, that is, the fifth year of the reign of the Seleucid king Demetrius I Soter (162–150 BCE).[225] His use of the Seleucid calendar, as well as that of Ptolemy, seems to further suggest the interconnection of Jewish history with the imperial histories, just as Demetrius did for his account of Jewish history.

Exploration of these Hellenistic Jewish writings has identified three ways in which the Jews engaged with their past. The Jews were clearly interested in composing a comprehensive history. They were also interested in resolving apparent chronological, logical, and moral inconsistencies of their history. They were equally devoted to developing a creative account of historical knowledge by adding, altering or removing some details of it. However, within these creative historiographical practices, it should be underlined that such changes often served apologetic ends. This means that changes such as the Patriarchs' association with Greek legend, numerical alteration and exaggeration of Jewish architecture are targeted at either pagan or paganized Jewish audiences. The consequences are not to impose a new Jewish history in place of the old, but preservation and strengthening of the old, ancestral history. Some other changes such as silencing the Shechemites' circumcision show that a new or different historical knowledge could become widespread. In this case, however, it is difficult to assume that there was any dominating agenda of party politics; more likely is that it reflected the general opinion of average Jews who highly valued the practice of circumcision through which one entered a covenant with God.

2.5.1.8. *Summary*

We have so far explored seven traits of how Jews perceived their past in antiquity. The seven points arise from a study of fragmentary Hellenistic Jewish writings and the wider Hebrew and Jewish corpora, and reveal the Jews as having a deep sense of appreciation of their ancestral past. The

---

224. The date in this case is 40 BCE, and this additional material to the original work of Eupolemus is either from Alexander Polyhistor or other sources (Fallon, 'Eupolemus', 2:872).

225. On the problem of the correlation between the fifth year of Demetrius I and the twelfth year of Ptolemy VII, i.e. 158/7 BCE, see Fallon, 'Eupolemus', *OTP* 2:863.

ancestral past provided a lens through which the present state of affairs was to be understood. It provided a paradigm in that the Jews expected the course of history to be repeated in the same pattern as it occurred in their ancestral past. Their ancestral history was like a site of memory about their God. To remember it was to remember him and what he did and would continue to do for them. Recognition of the value and authority of this ancestral past was especially reinforced in the midst of the Hellenistic environment, not only by creatively incorporating traditions outside of their own with apologetic motives, but also by pursuing the comprehensiveness, accuracy, and reliability of it. The Jewish perception of the past in Antiquity, therefore, provides multi-faceted and dynamic characteristics and yet demonstrates Jews' deep appreciation of their ancestral history.

2.5.2. *1 Maccabees*

Turning now to 1 Maccabees, we will continue to see that whilst certain events and characters in Scripture are mentioned, emphasized, or omitted, these cannot simply be regarded as a manipulation or distortion of accepted history. The pro-Hasmonean writer does not seem to impose markedly different historical knowledge on his reader. Instead, he reminds his audience of what they already know in order to solidify his legitimizing portrayal of the Hasmonean leadership.

2.5.2.1. *Chronological, repetitive and theological view of history*

In Mattathias' deathbed blessing (1 Macc. 2.49-70),[226] there are traits echoing some of the seven points about Jewish perception of the past in antiquity discussed earlier. This passage, which lays out a legacy for the Maccabean revolt, lists ancestral heroes and their rewards in chronological order: Abraham, Joseph, Phinehas, Joshua, Caleb, David, Daniel's friends, and Daniel (2.49-60).[227] Despite its brevity, this passage echoes

---

226. The passage is generally considered as a deathbed blessing similar to the ones attributed to Jacob (Gen. 49), Moses (Deut. 33), and Samuel (1 Sam. 12). Abel (*Maccabées*, 45) adds two more biblical materials: (1) Josh. 23, where Joshua summaries his deeds and commands the leaders of Israel not to covet idolatry, but to remain faithful and keep the covenant of God; (2) 1 Kgs 2, where David, before his death, calls Solomon and instructs him in a similar manner. Bartlett (*Books of the Maccabees*, 42) adds similar blessings to Jacob's sons in Testaments of the Twelve Patriarchs.

227. Goldstein (*1 Maccabees*, 7–8), suggests that these ten biblical figures are carefully selected to correspond to each of the Hasmonean family members, especially Mattathias, his five sons, and John Hyrcanus. This kind of correspondence may be possible, but it is difficult to prove that such selection was intended by the author.

Ben Sira's praise of the fathers (Sir. 44–50).[228] The repetitive mentions of heroic individuals, their pious acts, and their subsequent rewards build up a pattern that would continue in the lives of Mattathias' five sons, and rhetorically encourages the implied reader to imitate the pious acts in order to receive rewards paradigmatically. Moreover, in his introduction (2.49-51), Mattathias stresses the ancestral covenant as the cause of historical sequence. In other words, within the covenantal framework, Jewish history is seen as running its course, continuing in the present as well as in the future.[229] The rest of the narrative of 1 Maccabees then depicts the process of the Hasmonean revolt with language borrowed from historiographical writings such as Joshua, Judges, Samuel and Kings. By using these materials in a variety of ways, such as quotations, allusions and imitations, the story of the second-century Jewish restoration becomes a continuation of essentially the same story repeating throughout Jewish history.

2.5.2.2. *Covenantal theme as a moulder of the Hasmonean story*

Second, the author of 1 Maccabees takes up the idea of a Deuteronomic covenantal framework in which there are four stages building up a cycle – Covenantal Defilement, Curse, Repentance, and Blessing – and he shapes his narrative accordingly. I will only make summative statements here, and will elaborate in Chapter 4. The 'covenant' made between the pro-Seleucid Jerusalem authorities and Antiochus IV Epiphanes and the following introduction and exercise of Greek customs are described by the author as 'apostatizing from the holy covenant' and 'selling themselves to do evil' (1 Macc. 1.15). The rest of ch. 1 subsequently describes the catastrophes that befell Jerusalem and then Judea, just as the wages of covenantal defilement were anticipated in Deuteronomy 28 and 29. Mattathias' arrival on the scene, his lament, his murder of a renegade Jew and a Seleucid officer who attempted to defile the Jewish altar,[230] and especially his exhortation to his fellow Jews emphasizing zeal for the

---

228. The resemblance of the passage with Sir. 44–50 is also noted by Fairweather and Black, *Maccabees*, 84; Oesterley, 'Maccabees', 1:74.

229. Cf. Bartlett (*Books of the Maccabees*, 42), who claims 'the *law* in particular is constantly referred to throughout the speech' (his italics). I would contend that there seems to be no divisive understanding between the law and the covenant in 1 Maccabees, as they are frequently paired as a reference to a single idea (e.g. 1.11, 57; 2.27, 50). The similar passage in Ben Sira (chs. 44–50) also seems to use these two words interchangeably in the descriptions of Jewish ancestral heroes (e.g. Sir. 44.20; 45.5, 17).

230. Probably in fulfilment of Deut. 13.9, and in imitation of Phinehas' similar act in Num. 25.7-8. See also Oesterley, 'Maccabees', 1:72.

covenant (2.20, 27), as well as his legacy to his sons to whom he emphasized the paramount importance of keeping the covenant (2.20, 50), all demonstrate an outburst of the covenant people's repentance, in close resemblance to the Deuteronomic model.[231] Throughout the rest of the narrative, which entails constant repetition of crisis and resolution, the Judean nation gradually experiences triumph, restoration and rejuvenation, or, in other words, covenantal blessing (see Chapter 4 for a detailed discussion). Thus, this narrative scheme illustrates a repetitive pattern in the course of history and theological perspective as the lens through which to view the historical events relating to the Hasmonean revolt.

2.5.2.3. Summary

1 Maccabees presents evidence favouring a coherent, accurate, authoritative and unified Jewish historical consciousness as part of its cultural environment. This kind of historical knowledge served as a means through which the Hasmonean family was glorified and legitimized. Their collective memory of the history in which God's providence dwelt among his covenant people becomes the present living reality. The writing style is pro-Hasmonean insofar as it aims to legitimize the current Hasmonean high-priestly institution, but this affirmation was achieved through re-stating the old, well-known history of their ancestors. In this way, 1 Maccabees displays an example of politically intended writing which seeks support and acceptance through religious claims based on the already available and generally accepted sacred history of God's people. What emerges from this observation is that the best description of the perception of the ancestral past in the case of 1 Maccabees may have to do with widespread and shared collective memories with which the author apologetically connects the recent past events that occurred around him and his audience.

2.5.3. Conclusion

In our time, the recognition of the diversity of Jewish tradition has become a norm, and incorporation of it into biblical studies has become a necessary corollary. However, this tendency often undermines the sense of unity among the variety of traditions, and portrays ancient Jewish society as fragmented, sub-divided, and pluriform with its segments incompatible with one another. Whilst the recognition of diversity provides a necessary platform for understanding the complex setting in which people lived, and encourages scholars to sharpen and broaden their methodologies to

---

231. E.g. Deut. 13.9; 30.1-2.

understand the complex society, it is my contention that there has to be appreciation of something consistent throughout the course of Jewish history and widespread across socio-political and geographical boundaries. Our investigation shows that despite the evidence of a pluriform perception of the ancestral past in Scripture and beyond, in the Jewish tradition there is a persistent sense across diverse communities of sharing one unified, sacred history of Israel, manifested through a variety of characteristics. Furthermore, the course of the Hasmonean revolt, from the catastrophes through the vigorous uprising to the national rejuvenation, fully conforms with the pattern of Israel's history as configured in accordance with their theological worldview. The Hasmonean story is yet another sub-cycle within the spiral shape of Israel's history, highlighting God's everlasting providence for his covenant people. 1 Maccabees' use of Scripture, through which collective memories associated with historical figures and events revive, should be contextualized in this particular mode of Jewish perception of the past.

Chapter 3

THE USE OF SCRIPTURE IN 1 MACCABEES: PHILOLOGICAL PARALLELS

3.1. *Introduction*

This chapter will provide a comprehensive list of scriptural references and allusions in 1 Maccabees, critically adopted from the listing of Armin Lange and Matthias Weigold.[1] Although most major commentaries contain numerous relevant biblical references, there is, to the best of my knowledge, a surprising absence of tables, complete lists, or focused discussions on criteria of the use of Scripture in 1 Maccabees within these commentaries.[2] Furthermore, many of them, as we shall see, do not differentiate between what is intentionally referenced/alluded to by the author of 1 Maccabees and what is only detected by the commentator as a biblical phrase (whereby it is unclear whether this was an intended allusion to the biblical passage or simply a stylistic borrowing). This differentiation is necessary for the purpose of the present study, namely to explore the connection between the use of Scripture and its function within the authorial intention of 1 Maccabees. Lange and Weigold, however, recently produced what they claim to be a comprehensive list of 'explicit/

---

1. For discussion on cross-references between 1 Maccabees and biblical/other Jewish literature, see Armin Lange and Matthias Weigold, *Biblical Quotations and Allusions in Second Temple Jewish Literature*, JAJSup 5 (Göttingen: Vandenhoeck & Ruprecht, 2011), 239–41.

2. I have consulted several commentators, but here I will only state their surnames and the year of their publication, and only their surnames and page number for the rest of the chapter. Full bibliographical references can be found in Chapter 1's 'Literature Review' (§1.2) and the bibliography. Commentaries consulted are: Grimm (1853); Keil (1875); Fairweather and Black (1908); Oesterley (1913); Abel (1948); Zeitlin (1950); Dancy (1954); Bartlett (1973 and 2010, marked as Bartlett[1] and Bartlett[2], respectively); Goldstein (1976); Collins (1981); Doran (1996); Rappaport (2001); Tilly (2015).

implicit quotations' of, and 'explicit/implicit allusions' to, the Hebrew Bible in Second-Temple Jewish literature (including the Apocrypha, Pseudepigrapha and the Dead Sea Scrolls).[3] They identified these references by a combined use of Accordance 8 and James Charlesworth's concordance, which made it possible to search every case where the anterior and posterior texts contain at least two or three words in parallel. Lange and Weigold's seventy-plus cross-references to biblical literature in 1 Maccabees, however, require critical adaption due to their omissions and unwarranted inclusions of biblical references that are critical for understanding the use of Scripture in the book.[4] This evaluation will be carried out by incorporating commentaries into discussion and displaying results in a table. Discussion will also incorporate other relevant studies, including articles dealing with aspects of scriptural use in 1 Maccabees,[5] and introductions to the book.[6]

---

3. See especially their introductory chapter (Lange and Weigold, *Quotations and Allusions*, 15–48), where their definitions of 'explicit/implicit quotation/allusion', as well as other methodological grounds, are discussed. See below (§3.3.2) for my critique of their terminology.

4. We will see that Lange and Weigold's list of biblical cross-references to 1 Maccabees omits some important cases and includes either irrelevant, incompatible cases or cases not mentioned at all by commentators. These problems may partly arise from methodological grounds: the Greek text of 1 Maccabees is most probably a translation from Hebrew, and the comparison between the vocabulary of 1 Maccabees[Gk] and that of the Septuagint can cause misunderstanding about how the actual author of 1 Maccabees used his scriptural sources which were probably in Hebrew form. Lange and Weigold's tool only deals with morphological comparison between 1 Maccabees[Gk] and the Septuagint.

5. Goldstein, 'Messianic Promises'; Devorah Dimant, 'Use and Interpretation of Mikra in the Apocrypha and Pseudepigrapha', in *Mikra: Text, Translation, Reading and Interpretation of the Hebrew Bible in Ancient Judaism and Early Christianity*, ed. Martin Jan Mulder, CRINT 2/1 (Assen: Van Gorcum; Philadelphia: Fortress, 1988), 379–419; Hieke, 'The Role of "Scripture"'; Himmelfarb, 'He Was Renowned'; van der Kooij, 'Maccabean Leadership', 29–49. These studies identify only a handful of biblical cross-references in 1 Maccabees and are thus excluded from the list of scholars on the table given in §3.2. Nevertheless, they are still valuable sources to assist the analysis in this chapter, and are especially important dialogue partners with regard to conceptual parallels between Scripture and 1 Maccabees, a topic which will be covered in the next chapter.

6. There are only two relevant introductions to 1 Maccabees in this regard: Pfeiffer, *History*, 461–98; Bartlett, *1 Maccabees*, esp. 31–3. For other introductions which discuss scriptural language in 1 Maccabees, see §1.2.1.

3.2. Analysis of Lange and Weigold's biblical references in 1 Maccabees

Biblical Sources	1 Maccabees	Grimm	Keil	F. & B.	Oesterley	Abel	Zeitlin	Dancy	Bartlett	Goldstein	Collins	Doran	Rappaport	Tilly
2 Kgs 17.17	1.15									+				

1 Maccabees 1.15, '[the pro-Seleucid Jerusalem authorities] *sold themselves to do evil*' (ἐπράθησαν τοῦ ποιῆσαι τὸ πονήρον): here, the pro-Seleucid Judeans amongst the Jerusalem authorities introduce Hellenistic customs to the citizens, build a gymnasium in the city, and cause the Judeans to hide the mark of their circumcision, which is in turn described by the author as 'selling themselves to do evil', which Lange and Weigold identify with 2 Kgs 17.17 (יתמכרו לעשות הרע בעיני יהוה).[7] Just as in 1 Macc. 1.15, the immediate context, 2 Kgs 17.7-18, highlights the acts of the Israelites in which they 'despised the covenant…and followed other nations' and 'abandoned the commandment of the Lord' (2 Kgs 17.15, 16). Reference to 2 Kgs 17.17, however, is surprisingly sparse amongst commentators. Only Goldstein includes the verse in addition to Deut. 28.68 and 1 Kgs 21.20.[8] Alternatively, 1 Kgs 21.20 is, in fact, the reference favoured by several scholars. Ahab's act of selling himself to do evil in 1 Kgs 21.20 shares the morphological arrangement of the phrase in 2 Kgs 17.17, except that the former has a third person singular suffix for מכר to describe Ahab. It can be inferred that 2 Kgs 17.17 can be preferred as the scriptural source on the grounds that its third person plural form of מכר is identical to the one in 1 Macc. 1.15, and that the act of selling oneself to do evil here is committed at a corporate level, the price of which was an unprecedented and fatal national catastrophe upon Northern Israel, just like in 1 Maccabees.

Biblical Sources	1 Maccabees	Grimm	Keil	F. & B.	Oesterley	Abel	Zeitlin	Dancy	Bartlett	Goldstein	Collins	Doran	Rappaport	Tilly
Amos 8.10	1.39-40	+	+	+	+	+			+	+		+		+

7. The absence of בעיני יהוה ('in the eyes of the Lord') in 1 Macc. 1.15 is probably due to its characteristic reticence about any direct references to God; the Greek rendering is identical with 1 Macc. 1.15.
8. Goldstein, 201.

1 Maccabees 1.39, '*Her* [Jerusalem] *feasts were turned to mourning*' (αἱ ἑορταὶ αὐτῆς ἐστράφησαν εἰς πένθος): the combination of four words, ἑορτή + στρέφω + εἰς + πένθος, appears in Amos 8.10 (אבל + ל + חג + הפך)[9], and most commentators agree with Lange and Weigold. The latter add the next verse, 1 Macc. 1.40, probably because part of the phrase, στρέφω + εἰς + πένθος, appears again. But this shorter phrase alone is nothing more than idiomatic, and the combination with the plural form of ἑορτή ('feast') more decisively creates an association with the Amos prophecy. Notable is Doran,[10] who adds Lam. 5.15-18 which also contains the phrase אבל + ל + הפך, describing the cessation of dancing (Lam. 5.15), and the whole passage visualizes the terror falling upon Mount Zion just like in 1 Maccabees. The possibility of an allusion to Amos 8.10, however, can be found again in 1 Macc. 9.41 (see my comment under the verse). When put together with 9.41, our verse in 1 Macc. 1.39 may be an allusion to Amos 8.10, although the possibility of an allusion to Lamentations is also plausible (see also my comment on 1 Macc. 2.9).

Biblical Sources	1 Maccabees	Grimm	Keil	F. & B.	Oesterley	Abel	Zeitlin	Dancy	Bartlett	Goldstein	Collins	Doran	Rappaport	Tilly
Lev. 11.43	1.48		+	+		+	+			+		+		+

1 Maccabees 1.48, '[Antiochus IV Epiphanes commanded the Judeans] *to make their souls abominable in every unclean* and profane thing' (… βδελύξαι τὰς ψυχὰς αὐτῶν ἐν παντὶ ἀκαθάρτῳ…). Lange and Weigold find the combination of words, βδελύσσω + ψυχή + πᾶς + ἀκάθαρτος, in Lev. 11.43,[11] 'You shall not make yourselves (נפש; ψυχή in Greek) detestable (שקץ; βδελύσσω) with any swarming thing that swarms, and you shall not defile yourselves with them, and become unclean (טמא; βεβήλωσις) through them'. The circumstance of the Judeans under the Seleucid king's command alludes to Leviticus' prohibition from making one's soul abominable/detestable by all the unclean things. Many commentators agree with these two cross-references.[12] By using the imagery

---

9. The term also appears in Tob. 2.6.
10. Doran, 4:37.
11. Also, Lev. 20.25.
12. Cf. Goldstein (223) further adds Lev. 21.4, but it has less relevance than the other two.

of covenantal defilement prohibited by the Mosaic law, the author of 1 Maccabees conveys a message that the Hellenizing project of Antiochus IV Epiphanes was fundamentally contradictory to the law of Moses.

Biblical Sources	1 Maccabees	Grimm	Keil	F. & B.	Oesterley	Abel	Zeitlin	Dancy	Bartlett	Goldstein	Collins	Doran	Rappaport	Tilly
Lev. 20.25	1.48		+	+		+				+		+		+

See the footnote under Lev. 11.43.

Biblical Sources	1 Maccabees	Grimm	Keil	F. & B.	Oesterley	Abel	Zeitlin	Dancy	Bartlett	Goldstein	Collins	Doran	Rappaport	Tilly
Dan. 9.27	1.54	+	+	+		+	+	+		+	+	+		+

See the footnote under Dan. 11.31.

Biblical Sources	1 Maccabees	Grimm	Keil	F. & B.	Oesterley	Abel	Zeitlin	Dancy	Bartlett	Goldstein	Collins	Doran	Rappaport	Tilly
Dan. 11.31	1.54	+	+	+	+	+	+	+	+	+	+	+	+	+

1 Maccabees 1.54, 'he [Antiochus IV Epiphanes] constructed an *abomination of desolation* (βδέλυγμα ἐρημώσεως) on the altar': the 'abomination of desolation', which probably refers to a gentile altar erected on the altar of burnt offering (1.59), is a well-known term uniquely found, and three times repeated, in the Septuagint of Daniel 7–12 (9.27; 11.31; 12.11). The association with Dan. 11.31 is unanimous amongst commentators, although some of them ignore either 9.27 or 12.11. Only Grimm points out that the translator of 1 Maccabees consulted the Greek text of Daniel.[13]

13. Grimm, 31.

For the term's association with Ba'al Shamim, as a pun, as well as with Zeus Olympus,[14] Dancy gives a detailed discussion compared to other commentators.[15]

Biblical Sources	1 Maccabees	Grimm	Keil	F. & B.	Oesterley	Abel	Zeitlin	Dancy	Bartlett	Goldstein	Collins	Doran	Rappaport	Tilly
Dan. 12.11	1.54	+	+	+	+	+		+	+	+	+			+

See the footnote under Dan. 11.31.

Biblical Sources	1 Maccabees	Grimm	Keil	F. & B.	Oesterley	Abel	Zeitlin	Dancy	Bartlett	Goldstein	Collins	Doran	Rappaport	Tilly
Jer. 49.26	2.9													

1 Maccabees 2.9, 'Her infants were killed *in her city squares*, *her young people* by the sword of an enemy (…ἐν ταῖς πλατείαις αὐτῆς, οἱ νεανίσκοι αὐτῆς…)': Lange and Weigold's identification of this verse with Jer. 49.26 and 50.30 is, at a glance, somewhat dubious because 1 Maccabees has infants killed in ταῖς πλατείαις and νεανίσκοι by swords of an enemy, whilst both Jer. 49.26 and 50.30 have νεανίσκοι ('fell') in ταῖς πλατείαις with no mention of infants. Moreover, the contexts of the Jeremiah prophecies speak of divine punishment upon Damascus and Babylon, respectively, not Israel, and are thus messages of hope for the Jews. It should not be surprising that none of commentators make the connection with the Jeremianic prophecies. Several scholars' suggestion of Lam. 2.11 for 'infants…in the squares', and 2.21 for 'young men by the sword', in fact makes better association of the verse. Lange and Weigold may have ignored these verses because, on their methodical grounds, only two words in each verse are in parallel with 1 Macc. 2.9, and do not thus qualify as 'implicit allusion' in their terms). Abel points out Lam. 2.11, 21.[16] Goldstein even observes

---

14. See 2 Macc. 6.2.
15. Dancy, 78–82.
16. Abel, 33.

within 1 Maccabees' descriptions of the calamities in Judea (especially chs. 1–2) several echoes of Lamentations.[17] Also, Bartlett suggests that the whole lament of Mattathias in 1 Macc. 2.7-13 echoes Lamentations 1.[18] It can also be inferred that the motif of Lamentations has every reason to be a model for the author's lamentable description of the calamities in Judea. Tilly further suggests for the image of infants dying Jer. 4.31, Ezra 7.23, and Lam. 2.11, 21; 4.7-10.[19]

Biblical Sources	1 Maccabees	Grimm	Keil	F. & B.	Oesterley	Abel	Zeitlin	Dancy	Bartlett	Goldstein	Collins	Doran	Rappaport	Tilly
Jer. 50.30	2.9													

See the footnote under Jer. 49.26.

Biblical Sources	1 Maccabees	Grimm	Keil	F. & B.	Oesterley	Abel	Zeitlin	Dancy	Bartlett	Goldstein	Collins	Doran	Rappaport	Tilly
Num. 25.6-15	2.24, 26	+	+	+	+	+	+	+	+	+	+	+	+	+

1 Maccabees 2.24–26 narrates Mattathias' killing of a renegade Jew and a Seleucid official, which kindles the outbreak of the Hasmonean revolt, and the author adds a comment in v. 26, 'he [Mattathias] became zealous in the law as Phinehas had done against Zambri son of Salom'. This statement, together with the description of Mattathias' act of killing a Jewish renegade out of his zeal for the law, clearly identifies the similar story of Phinehas in Num. 25.6-15 as a scriptural source. However, several commentators make some important addition to this. In v. 24, it says, ἀνήνεγκεν θυμὸν κατὰ τὸ κρίμα, of which the term, κατὰ τὸ κρίμα (כמשפט in Hebrew), requires attention. NETS translates the phrase as 'his anger arose *in judgement*', RSV/NRSV as 'he gave vent in righteous anger'. Contrary to

---

17. E.g. 1 Macc. 1.38-39 echoing Lam. 5.1, 2, 18; 1 Macc. 2.9 echoing Lam. 2.11, 21; 1 Macc. 2.11, 12 echoing Lam. 5.16, 1.10 respectively; 1 Macc. 3.51 echoing Lam. 1.4.

18. Bartlett[2], 1561.

19. Tilly, 93.

this translation, the phrase can be read as 'he rose in anger *in accord with*, or, *in keeping with the law/rule/precept*', in which case the term κατὰ τὸ κρίμα could, in fact, become a quotation formula. Most of the twelve references to the term in the Hebrew Bible[20] are understood in the latter way.[21] Thus, several commentators rightly point out this term.[22] The question of which specific law is referred to in 1 Maccabees 24–26 remains less clear. Many of these aforementioned commentators suggest Deuteronomy 13, which commands that anyone swaying people to defile the covenant with YHWH must be put to death, and which Mattathias certainly fulfills in his act. This is also plausible since the whole Deuteronomic chapter plays a crucial role in the theological shaping of the story in 1 Maccabees 1, namely the renegade Jews' defilement of the covenant of YHWH and the calamities which ensued in Judea. One must add, in my judgement, Deut. 7.5 which commands that any defiled altars should be broken. This is what Mattathias does after killing the two individuals (2.25, '…and tore down the altar'). In fact, this act repeatedly appears in 1 Maccabees.[23] See more details in my comments on 1 Macc. 2.25-26, 45; 5.68.

Biblical Sources	1 Maccabees	Grimm	Keil	F. & B.	Oesterley	Abel	Zeitlin	Dancy	Bartlett	Goldstein	Collins	Doran	Rappaport	Tilly
Exod. 34.13-14	2.25-26			+		+								+

1 Maccabees 2.25-26, '…and [Mattathias] tore down the altar': As already discussed in the footnote under 1 Macc. 2.24, 26 (Num. 25.6-15), the act of tearing down the altar complies with the law of Moses in Deut. 7.5. It reads: 'you shall break down their altars and dash in pieces their pillars and chop down their Asherim and burn their carved images with fire'. Lange and Weigold, on the other hand, suggest Exod. 34.13-14, where the same commandment appears. One has to acknowledge the fact

---

20. Also in Pss. Sol. 2.13.
21. E.g. Num. 35.24; 2 Kgs 11.14; 4.20; Neh. 8.18; when the term should be translated as 'in judgement', it is always supplied with an additional possessive noun to clarify the meaning; otherwise, the term with the singular τὸ κρίμα in fact always means the law of Moses.
22. Grimm, 39; Keil, 61; Fairweather and Black, 78; Oesterley, 1:72; Abel, 38; Dancy, 85; Goldstein, 232; and Tilly, 97.
23. 1 Macc. 2.45; 5.68; cf. 2 Macc. 10.2.

that the commandment of slaying any defiled altars frequently appears in the Hebrew Bible with the combination of נתץ + מזבח [24] and this motif is also frequently taken in the reforming acts of Israel,[25] all of which echo the act of Mattathias. In fact, 1 Maccabees contains several occasions of defiled altars destroyed by the Hasmoneans.[26] Most commentators ignore the Exodus material for 1 Macc. 2.25, but prefer to mention the Deuteronomic motif instead as it plays a central role in the account of the Hasmonean revolt (we will see the Deuteronomic covenantal motif in more detail in the next chapter). Those who spot the Exodus material include: Fairweather and Black in addition to Deut. 12.3 and Judg. 6.25;[27] Dancy in reference to κατὰ τὸ κρίμα in 2.24;[28] Tilly in addition to Deut. 12.2-3 and 2 Chron. 14.4.[29] We will see in this chapter, however, that the Exodus materials repeatedly appear as scriptural sources, which increases the possibility that the commandment in Exod. 34.13-14 should be added to our list.

Biblical Sources	1 Maccabees	Grimm	Keil	F. & B.	Oesterley	Abel	Zeitlin	Dancy	Bartlett	Goldstein	Collins	Doran	Rappaport	Tilly
Gen. 22.1-19	2.52	+	+	+	+	+	+	+	+	+	+	+	+	+

1 Maccabees 2.52a, 'Was not Abraham found faithful in temptation?': the first of ten biblical characters mentioned in Mattathias' deathbed blessing is Abraham, and Abraham's being 'faithful in temptation' (πίστος ἐν πειρασμός) most likely refers to his attempt to sacrifice Isaac in Gen. 22.1-19, as identified by Lange and Weigold (also, note the word πειράζω in Gen. 22.1 which further confirms the connection). The same combination of three words, Αβρααμ, πίστις, and πειρασμός also appears in Jewish tradition in the Hellenistic period,[30] and later in early Christian

---

24. Exod. 34.13; Deut. 7.5; 12.3; Judg. 2.2.
25. Judg. 6.28, 30; 2 Kgs 11.18; 23.12, 15, 17; 31.1; 34.4, 7; cf. 2 Kgs 33.3 which has Manasseh re-erecting the altars of Baal which Hezekiah had torn down.
26. 1 Macc. 2.25, 45; 5.68 (cf. 10.84); also 2 Macc. 10.2.
27. Fairweather and Black, 78.
28. Dancy, 85.
29. Tilly, 97.
30. Sir. 44.20; Jdt 5.25-26.

tradition,[31] and rabbinic tradition.[32] Note, however, Bartlett who suggests that the reference is either to the sacrifice of Isaac or his trust in God's unbelievable promise of heirs.[33] Likewise, Doran suggests that Abraham's faithfulness is credited through many tests according to Jewish traditions.[34]

Biblical Sources	1 Maccabees	Grimm	Keil	F. & B.	Oesterley	Abel	Zeitlin	Dancy	Bartlett	Goldstein	Collins	Doran	Rappaport	Tilly
Gen. 15.6	2.52	+	+	+	+			+	+		+		+

1 Maccabees 2.52b, 'it was accounted to him as righteousness (ἐλογίσθη αὐτῷ εἰς δικαιοσύνην)': the identification with Gen. 15.6b should not be disputed since the Septuagint rendering of Gen. 15.6b is identical. The Masoretic text's rendering of Gen. 15.6b has a *qal* verb instead, taking God in 15.6a as the subject, compared to the passive ἐλογίσθη in 1 Macc. 2.52b, as well as the Septuagint of Gen. 15.6b. This difference may be a result of either the Greek biblical literature's influence upon the translator of 1 Maccabees or 1 Maccabees' characteristic avoidance of references to God, although the latter is unnecessary here.[35]

Biblical Sources	1 Maccabees	Grimm	Keil	F. & B.	Oesterley	Abel	Zeitlin	Dancy	Bartlett	Goldstein	Collins	Doran	Rappaport	Tilly
Gen. 39.7-12	2.53	+		+	+		+			+		+		+

1 Maccabees 2.53a, 'Joseph in the time of his affliction observed the commandment': the second biblical character mentioned by Mattathias is Joseph, but the phrases 'the time of his affliction' and 'observing the commandment' require attention. Lange and Weigold identify them with

---

31. Jas 2.21-24; Heb. 11.17.
32. *m. 'Abot.* 5.3.
33. Bartlett[1], 42.
34. Doran, 4:50, including Jub. 17.17-18; Pseudo-Philo, *LAB* 6.
35. Cf. in Rom. 4.3, Gal. 3.6 and Jas 2.23, the identical phrase appears, indicating the preference of the Septuagint rendering amongst the authors of the New Testament epistles; also, Irenaeus, *Haer.* 4.32.2.

the temptation caused by Potiphar's wife,[36] and a majority of commentators agree. However, Keil, Abel, and Bartlett alternatively suggest that 'the affliction' refers to Joseph's overall experience of slavery.[37] This suggestion is valid insofar as the nature of 'the affliction' is concerned, but in my judgement, it does not quite explain in what ways Joseph 'observed the commandment' in this case. Jubilees' retelling of Joseph's story seems to make the connection between Joseph's endurance of the temptation of Potiphar's wife and observing the commandment: 'And he [Joseph] did not surrender himself but he remembered the Lord and the words which Jacob, his father, used to read, which were from the words of Abraham, that there is no man who (may) fornicate with a woman who has a husband (and) that there is a judgement of death which is decreed for him in heaven before the Lord Most High… And Joseph remembered these words and he did not want to lie with her.'[38]

Biblical Sources	1 Maccabees	Grimm	Keil	F. & B.	Oesterley	Abel	Zeitlin	Dancy	Bartlett	Goldstein	Collins	Doran	Rappaport	Tilly
Gen. 41.39-45	2.53											+		+

1 Maccabees 2.53b, 'became lord of Egypt': Lange and Weigold rightly chose Gen. 41.39-45 as a cross-reference, presumably on the grounds that the passage narrates the process of Joseph's appointment as lord of Egypt. Amongst commentators, only Doran and Tilly specify this cross-reference.[39]

Biblical Sources	1 Maccabees	Grimm	Keil	F. & B.	Oesterley	Abel	Zeitlin	Dancy	Bartlett	Goldstein	Collins	Doran	Rappaport	Tilly
Num. 25.11-13	2.54	+	+	+	+	+	+	+	+		+			

36. Gen. 39.7-12; retold in Jub. 39.6.
37. Keil, 66; Abel, 47; and Bartlett[2], 1562.
38. Jub. 39.6-7; trans. from *OTP*.
39. Doran, 4:50; Tilly, 106.

1 Maccabees 2.54, 'Phinehas our father, by becoming zealous with zeal, received a covenant of everlasting priesthood' (Φινεες ὁ πατὴρ ἡμῶν ἐν τῷ ζηλῶσαι ζῆλον ἔλαβεν διαθήκην ἱερωσύνης αἰωνίας): this verse is not divided into two in Lange and Weigold's list because the whole verse and its morphological association can be found from the passage of Num. 25.11-13, 'Phinehas the son of Eleazar, son of Aaron the priest, has turned back my wrath from the people of Israel, *in that he was jealous with my jealousy* (בקנאו את־קנאתי; ἐν τῷ ζηλῶσαί μου τὸν ζῆλον) among them... Behold, I give to him my *covenant of peace* (ברית שלום; διαθήκην εἰρήνης), and it shall be to him and to this descendants after him *the covenant of a perpetual priesthood* (ברית כהנת עולם; διαθήκη ἱερατείας αἰωνία).' Most commentators who directly identify the passage in Numbers are aware of this morphological association.

Biblical Sources	1 Maccabees	Grimm	Keil	F. & B.	Oesterley	Abel	Zeitlin	Dancy	Bartlett	Goldstein	Collins	Doran	Rappaport	Tilly
Num. 32.12	2.55									+				

1 Maccabees 2.55a, 'Joshua, by fulfilling the command' (ἐν τῷ πληρῶσαι λόγον): Lange and Weigold identify this act of 'fulfilling the command' with Num. 32.12, where it says 'Joshua...wholly followed the Lord (מלאו אחרי יהוה; συνεπηκολούθησεν ὀπίσω κυρίου), presumably because there is otherwise no identical phrase in the Hebrew Bible, and because the phrase 'fulfilling the command' can be interpreted as 'following the Lord'. However, most commentators identify Joshua's commission by Moses in Num. 27.16-23 and by God in Josh. 1.2-10 as scriptural sources alluded to in the phrase in 1 Macc. 2.55.[40] Only Goldstein identifies the phrase in 1 Macc. 2.55a with Num. 32.12, stating that '[o]ur author may have added 'the Word' to supply an object for the transitive verb "fulfill"'.[41] They refer to 1 Kgs 2.27 and 2 Chron. 36.21 as examples. The issue is whether the emphasis should be placed on the act of fulfilling or the object that is fulfilled by the act. On the grounds that there is no morphological association between 1 Macc. 2.55 and Num. 32.12, there is no good reason to make the connection between the two here. Instead, the object is

---

40. Grimm, 47; Fairweather and Black, 85; Doran, 4:50; Tilly, 106; cf. for Num. 27.16-23 only, Keil, 67; Abel, 48; Dancy, 87.
41. Goldstein, 240.

clarified in the commission passages in Num. 27.16-23 and Josh. 1.2-10, and the act of fulfilling is narrated throughout Numbers and Joshua which Mattathias and the author of 1 Maccabees are evidentially familiar with (several other materials are drawn from these biblical books).

Biblical Sources	1 Maccabees	Grimm	Keil	F. & B.	Oesterley	Abel	Zeitlin	Dancy	Bartlett	Goldstein	Collins	Doran	Rappaport	Tilly
Josh. 24.25	2.55											+		

1 Maccabees 2.55b, '[Joshua] became a judge (κριτής) in Israel': this phrase does not immediately echo any biblical materials, because, as Goldstein notes, Joshua is never called a judge in biblical and extra-biblical Jewish literature.[42] Although most commentators do not suggest any biblical sources for this phrase, Lange and Weigold identify it with Josh. 24.25, 'So Joshua made a covenant with the people that day, and put in place statutes and rules for them at Shechem'. Their decision is probably based on the Septuagint rendering which slightly deviates from that of the Hebrew, and identifies slightly more with the wording in 1 Maccabees: 'And Joshua made a covenant with the people that day and gave them law and judgement at Shiloh before the tent of the God of Israel'. In this latter case, the three words Ἰησοῦς, κρισίς, and Ἰσραηλ may create a linguistic connection between the two texts to some extent. Doran also notes this biblical material, and further claims that Joshua is mentioned as leader of Israel at the beginning of Judges, implying his role as a judge.[43] We will see in the next chapter that there are many echoes of Judges in 1 Maccabees, and that may explain why Mattathias called Joshua a judge. The theme of Joshua's conquest of the land, however, is not explicitly mentioned in Mattathias' statement. This may appear to be absurd since one of the Hasmoneans' major achievements is the conquest of Seleucid cities which once belonged to Israel under the Davidic dynasty, and scholars traditionally viewed the biblical motif as consciously taken up by the Hasmoneans. This reticence about the biblical territorial theme caused scholarly dispute, and we will discuss this in more detail in Chapter 5.

42. Goldstein, 240.
43. Doran, 4:50.

3. *Philological Parallels*

Biblical Sources	1 Maccabees	Grimm	Keil	F. & B.	Oesterley	Abel	Zeitlin	Dancy	Bartlett	Goldstein	Collins	Doran	Rappaport	Tilly
Num. 13.30; 14.6-9	2.56	+	+	+	+		+	+	+		+			+

1 Maccabees 2.56a, 'Caleb, by bearing witness in the assembly': Caleb's act can be found in Numbers 13–14, where Caleb, together with Joshua, confidently reports to the congregation of Israel about the land of Canaan and encourages them to conquer it. Lange and Weigold identify the phrase in 1 Macc. 2.56a with Caleb's speech in Num. 13.30 and 14.6-9, presumably on the grounds of conceptual association rather than word-for-word connection between the texts. Commentators also note these biblical references without any addition.

Biblical Sources	1 Maccabees	Grimm	Keil	F. & B.	Oesterley	Abel	Zeitlin	Dancy	Bartlett	Goldstein	Collins	Doran	Rappaport	Tilly
Num. 14.24, 30	2.56	+	+	+	+		+	+	+		+			+

1 Maccabees 2.56b, '[Caleb] received an inheritance of land': Lange and Weigold refer to Num. 14.24 and 14.30, where God speaks to Moses of his promise of a portion of the land to Caleb. It is Num. 14.24 in particular which contains at the end of the verse the word κληρονομέω in the Septuagint, just as κληρονομία (ירש in Heb.) appears in 1 Macc. 2.56b.[44] Most commentators note these verses in conjunction with Num. 13.30 and 14.6-9 for 1 Macc. 2.56a. Note, however, that a majority of commentators further refer to Josh. 14.15-16 where Hebron is specifically stated as Caleb's portion of the promised land.[45]

---

44. Num. 14.24, 'But my servant Caleb, because he has a different spirit and has followed me fully, I will bring into the land into which he went, and his descendants shall *possess/inherit* it'.

45. Grimm, 48; Keil, 67; Fairweather and Black, 85; Oesterley, 1:74; Goldstein, 240; Doran, 4:51; Tilly, 107.

Biblical Sources	1 Maccabees	Grimm	Keil	F. & B.	Oesterley	Abel	Zeitlin	Dancy	Bartlett	Goldstein	Collins	Doran	Rappaport	Tilly
2 Sam. 7.1-17	2.57	+	+	+	+	+	+	+	+	+		+		+

1 Maccabees 2.57, like other verses in Mattathias' deathbed blessing, has two parts, the deed and the reward of David, but Lange and Weigold only deal with the latter by referring to 2 Sam. 7.17. The second clause, '[David] inherited the throne of a kingdom forever', is undoubtedly an allusion to 2 Sam. 7.1-17, the cardinal passage regarding the divine legitimation of the Davidic dynasty, containing all the key words in parallel. The commentators are also in agreement.[46] The first clause, 'David, in his mercy', however, has no identified cross-reference in the list of Lange and Weigold, but requires attention. The association between the Greek word ἔλεος ('mercy') and David is uncommon in the Hebrew Bible, and commentators have noted this peculiarity.[47] Most commentators associate this Greek word with the Hebrew חסד, a word frequently described in the Hebrew Bible as a characteristic of God. The word is occasionally attributed to humans,[48] and the same usage is taken in 1 Maccabees to describe either David's goodness, piety or faithfulness, just as the author evidentially translated חסד (God's 'faithfulness') with ἔλεος in 3.44. Some commentators emphatically take the meaning of David's piety toward God, though without any reference (see my comment under the verse), as opposed to his general loyalty, such as that toward Saul in 1 Sam. 24.4-8, 26.5-12,[49] whilst others do not make such separation.[50] Abel, on the other hand, emphatically takes the more general meaning as opposed to piety toward God.[51] He suggests מרפא, which usually means 'calmness',

---

46. Regarding the interpretation of 1 Macc. 2.57 and the scholarly dispute about the validity of the Davidic covenant from the perspective of 1 Maccabees, see 'Literature Review' in Chapter 1, and Chapter 5.

47. Collins, 170, says that the association is made 'oddly enough', and Dancy, 51, regards the Greek word as 'out of place'.

48. Jer. 2.2; Hos. 6.4, 6.

49. Grimm, 48; Keil, 67.

50. Fairweather and Black, 85; Zeitlin, 86; Dancy, 87; Bartlett[2], 1563; Goldstein, 240; Doran, 4:51, calling it 'covenant faithfulness'; Tilly, 104.

51. Abel, 49.

or 'gentleness',[52] and which especially appears paired with חסד in Sir. 36.28,[53] indicating their synonymous relation. Abel further observes the Septuagint version of Psalm 131's insertion of πραΰτης in the description of David.[54] There is, however, lack of a clause to determine the meaning of David's ἔλεος.

Biblical Sources	1 Maccabees	Grimm	Keil	F. & B.	Oesterley	Abel	Zeitlin	Dancy	Bartlett	Goldstein	Collins	Doran	Rappaport	Tilly
1 Kgs 19.10, 14	2.58				+	+				+		+		+

1 Maccabees 2.58a, 'Elijah, by becoming greatly zealous for the law' (Ηλιας ἐν τῷ ζηλῶσαι ζῆλον νόμου): Lange and Weigold identify the phrase with 1 Kgs 19.10 and 19.14, where Elijah, in the dialogue with God on Mount Horeb, repeatedly utters a similar phrase, קנא קנאתי ליהוה. Provided 1 Macc. 2.58a is another example of the author's characteristic replacement of the Tetragrammaton, replaced with νόμος in this case, Elijah's repeated expression in 1 Kings may well be alluded to in 1 Macc. 2.58a. Several commentators point out these verses,[55] although others only pick up various passages which may exemplify Elijah's zeal.[56]

Biblical Sources	1 Maccabees	Grimm	Keil	F. & B.	Oesterley	Abel	Zeitlin	Dancy	Bartlett	Goldstein	Collins	Doran	Rappaport	Tilly
2 Kgs 2.1, 11	2.58	+	+		+	+			+	+		+		+

1 Maccabees 2.58b, '[Elijah] was taken up into heaven' (ἀνελήμφθη εἰς τὸν οὐρνόν): Lange and Weigold point out 2 Kgs 2.1 and 2.11, where similar phrases appear. Although our list above will note all the commentators

---

52. E.g. Prov. 15.4; Eccl. 10.4.
53. In Greek, ἔλεος καὶ πραΰτης.
54. Ps.^GK 131.1, 'O Lord, remember David and all his *meekness* (πραΰτης)'.
55. Oesterley, 1:74; Abel, 49, even calling the expression in 1 Kgs 19.10 and 19.14 'Elijah's motto' ('la devise d'Élie'); Goldstein, 241; Doran, 4:51; Tilly, 107.
56. E.g. 1 Kgs 18.10-40; 21.17-29; 2 Kgs 1.10-12.

who mention either of the two verses, some commentators note 2 Kgs 2.1 only,[57] and some both verses,[58] whilst others note only 2 Kgs 2.11.[59] On morphological grounds, however, 2 Kgs 2.1 should be discarded from our consideration. Both 2.1 and 2.11 in the Septuagint contain εἰς τὸν οὐρανόν, but v. 1 renders the active form of ἀνάγω compared to v. 11 which contains the same verb ἀναλαμβάνω in the same passive form, just as in 1 Maccabees. Both verbs are rendered in the Masoretic text with עלה, which creates the possibility that the original author of 1 Maccabees alluded to both verses and the Greek translator was not influenced by the Greek form of 2 Kings. None of the two verses contain *niphal* form of עלה (*hiphil* infinitive in v. 1 and *qal waw*-consecutive in v. 11). It seems, therefore, most plausible to choose 2 Kgs 2.11 as the scriptural source for 2.58b, and to infer that the Greek translator of 1 Maccabees is here consulting the Greek text of 2 Kings.

Biblical Sources	1 Maccabees	Grimm	Keil	F. & B.	Oesterley	Abel	Zeitlin	Dancy	Bartlett	Goldstein	Collins	Doran	Rappaport	Tilly
Dan. 3.1-30	2.59	+	+	+	+		+		+	+		+		+

1 Maccabees 2.59, 'Hananias, Azarias and Misael, because of their faith, were saved from fire': this verse is undoubtedly an allusion to the story of the trial Daniel and his three friends received from Nebuchadnezzar in Dan. 3.1-30, although the three names are found on multiple occasions.[60] Note, however, that Lange and Weigold fail to clarify the fact that the mention of their Hebrew names within Dan. 3.1-30 is only found in the Old Greek version of Dan. 3.24. Thus, if one takes the view that this passage is another example of the Greek version of Scripture's influence on the Greek translation of 1 Maccabees, the Old Greek version of Daniel 3 (particularly with Dan.[GK (OG)] 3.24) can be seen as the scriptural material. If, however, such an influence does not seem necessary, one must add, just as most commentators do, other verses which mention the

57. Grimm, 49; Keil, 68.
58. Abel, 49; Goldstein, 241; Doran, 4:51.
59. Oesterley, 1:74; Bartlett[2], 1563; Tilly, 107.
60. E.g. for later Jewish and Christian traditions referring to the story, see 3 Macc. 6.6; 16.21; 18.12; Heb. 11.33-34; cf. for the reference to the three friends in their Hebrew name, Dan. 1.6-7, 11, 19; 2.17; Dan.[GK] 3.24; Dan.[GK] 3.88; their Greek names, Sedrach, Misach and Abdenago, e.g. Dan. 1.7; 2.49; 3.12-30.

3. Philological Parallels

Hebrew names of Daniel's friends, such as Dan. 1.6-7. As regards Dan. 3.1-30, most commentators note the passage being alluded to in 1 Macc. 2.59, except for Abel,[61] who pays attention to the Theodotion's Greek version of Daniel which reads at 3.95, 'And Nabouchodonosor answered and said, "Blessed be the God of Sedrach, Misach, Abdenago, who has sent his angel and delivered his servants, *because they trusted in him*"' (ὅτι ἐπεποίθεισαν ἐπ'αὐτῷ).[62] The different verbs, however, make the suggestion unconvincing.

Biblical Sources	1 Maccabees	Grimm	Keil	F. & B.	Oesterley	Abel	Zeitlin	Dancy	Bartlett	Goldstein	Collins	Doran	Rappaport	Tilly
Dan. 6.17-24	2.60	+	+	+	+	+			+	+		+		+

1 Maccabees 2.60, 'Daniel, by his simplicity, was rescued from the mouth of lions': Daniel's rescue from lions is narrated in Dan. 6.17-24. Clarification about the use of ἁπλότης ('simplicity' or 'sincerity')[63] can determine its scriptural source between different versions of Daniel. Some commentators suggest Dan. 6.22 as a key verse suggesting ἁπλότης of Daniel, but none of them discusses it further.[64] In Dan. 6.22, Daniel explains to the Persian king, Darius, the reason he was rescued from lions. The Old Greek version says that it was because of Daniel's δικαιοσύνη ('righteousness'), whilst the Theodotion's version renders εὐθύτης ('uprightness'). The Masoretic version has זכו ('innocence'). The immediate observation of the Greek words is that the translator of 1 Maccabees did not seem to be influenced by the Greek version of Daniel, but translated the verse independently. Regarding the original Hebrew word for ἁπλότης in 1 Macc. 2.60, the word is not so popular in the Septuagint,[65] and it is translated from תמם in 2 Sam. 15.11 ('innocence') or from ישׁר in 1 Chron. 29.17 ('uprightness'), either of which may have been the original Hebrew word used in 1 Macc. 2.60.

---

61. Abel, 49.
62. Cf. the Old Greek version which reads τοὺς ἐλπίσαντας ἐπ'αὐτόν.
63. Also in the description of the Jewish martyrs on the Sabbath day in 1 Macc. 2.37.
64. Fairweather and Black, 85; Abel, 49.
65. 2 Sam[GK] 15.11; 1 Chron.[GK] 29.17; 1 Macc. 2.37, 60; 3 Macc. 3.21; Wis. 1.1; Sus.[OG] 63.

Biblical Sources	1 Maccabees	Grimm	Keil	F. & B.	Oesterley	Abel	Zeitlin	Dancy	Bartlett	Goldstein	Collins	Doran	Rappaport	Tilly
Ps. 146.4	2.63	+	+	+	+	+				+		+		+

1 Maccabees 2.63, 'Today they will be elevated, but tomorrow they will not be found, because *they will have returned to their dust and their counsels will be lost*' (ἐπέστρεψεν εἰς τὸν χοῦν αὐτοῦ, καὶ ὁ διαλογισμὸς αὐτοῦ ἀπολεῖται): commentators unanimously identify Ps. 146.4 (Ps.^{GK} 145.4) as the scriptural material clearly alluded to in this verse.[66] The Greek form of the psalm is taken as the source by Lange and Weigold, as well as by many other commentators: '…he will return to his earth; in that very day, all their designs will perish' (ἐπιστρέψει εἰς τὴν γῆν αὐτοῦ· ἐν ἐκείνῃ τῇ ἡμέρᾳ ἀπολοῦνται πάντες οἱ διαλογισμοὶ αὐτῶν). The implication of this identification is that the Greek translator of 1 Maccabees consulted the Greek version of the psalm and followed its rendering. However, the matter is not simple. The Hebrew word for 'counsel/design', עשתנו, is a *hapax legomenon*,[67] and is rendered in plural form with the third person masculine singular pronominal suffix, עשתנתיו, and the Greek translator of the psalm seems to confuse the correct rendering and suddenly changes the number of the pronominal suffix of this noun from singular to plural by supplying the third person plural possessive pronoun in Greek (i.e. 'he will return to his earth… their [αὐτῶν] designs will perish'). This absurd, inconsistent change indicates that the translator confused ו with the final form of נ, and read the suffix as the plural feminine possessive pronoun. The translator of 1 Maccabees, on the other hand, does not repeat the same error. Or, put differently, the second clause, ὁ διαλογισμὸς αὐτοῦ ἀπολεῖται, is consistently using the third person singular pronoun throughout, rather than following the inconsistent pattern of the Greek psalm. I suggest that this verse is another example where the Greek translator is independent from the influence of the Greek version of Scripture, and the scriptural source is specifically the Hebrew version of Ps. 146.4.

---

66. Cf. Bartlett[1], 44, who adds Ps. 37.35-36 which provides the answer to the question of 'why the wicked seem to prosper'; Goldstein, 241, adds Isa. 14.4-22; 51.12-13; Dan. 11.9; these cross-references are less decisive due to their lack of morphological association.

67. Only Abel, 50, notes this, but without taking it further.

3. Philological Parallels

Biblical Sources	1 Maccabees	Grimm	Keil	F. & B.	Oesterley	Abel	Zeitlin	Dancy	Bartlett	Goldstein	Collins	Doran	Rappaport	Tilly
1 Sam. 7.5-6	3.46	+	+	+	+	+	+	+	+	+	+	+	+	+

1 Maccabees 3.46 states that Judas gathered the Judeans at Mizpah to offer a prayer before the battle. Lange and Weigold identify 1 Sam. 7.5-6 in which a few words draw a linguistic connection between the two texts, such as gather (συνάγω) in 1 Maccabees / gather (קבץ; συνάγω) in 1 Samuel and its Greek rendering; 'Massepha' (Μασσηφα) / 'Mizpah' (מצפה; Μασσηφαθ); 'prayer' (προσευχή) / 'pray' (פלל; προσεύχομαι); 'for Israel' (τῷ Ισραηλ) / 'for you [Israel]' (בעדכם [ישראל]; περὶ ὑμῶν [Ισραηλ]). This connection is also unanimous amongst commentators. Some add 1 Sam. 10.17 which also shows Samuel going to Mizpah, gathering Israel to choose their king by lot, but this passage lacks the same imagery of offering prayer in an urgent occasion.[68] Some also suggested Judg. 20.1 and 2 Kgs 25.23, in which Israel is gathered at Mizpah for a meeting or discussion.[69] These references are different from offering urgent prayer.

Biblical Sources	1 Maccabees	Grimm	Keil	F. & B.	Oesterley	Abel	Zeitlin	Dancy	Bartlett	Goldstein	Collins	Doran	Rappaport	Tilly
Num. 6.13	3.49	+	+	+		+		+	+		+			+

1 Maccabees 3.49 states that Nazirites who fulfilled their vows were raised and called to join the Hasmoneans' battle against Gorgias and the Seleucid army. The law regarding the Nazirites' vow and its fulfilment is found in Num. 6.1-21, including v. 13, where the fulfilment is described, which is taken as a cross-reference by Lange and Weigold.[70] A majority of commentators also make note of the reference.[71]

---

68. Abel, 68; Dancy, 94; Tilly, 125.
69. Zeitlin, 97; Doran, 4:63.
70. The Nazirites' vow can also be found in Acts 21.23, 26; *m. Meg.* 1.10-11.
71. Cf. Bartlett[1], 55, who further suggests the fulfilment of the Nazirites' vow in 1 Macc. 3.49 as an allusion to Samson, 'a champion of Israel against the Philistines'.

Biblical Sources	1 Maccabees	Grimm	Keil	F. & B.	Oesterley	Abel	Zeitlin	Dancy	Bartlett	Goldstein	Collins	Doran	Rappaport	Tilly
Num. 10.8-9	3.54	+	+	+	+	+		+	+		+	+	+	

1 Maccabees 3.54 narrates the act of trumpet-blowing before the battle, which is set out as a commandment in Num. 10.8-9. The act in fact appears numerously in 1 Maccabees.[72] Commentators almost unanimously accept the view that the Hasmoneans' blowing of the trumpet follows the manner of Jewish traditions, noting Num. 10.8-9 as a cross-reference. Grimm makes an ambiguous comment that the trumpet-blowing indicates an impending departure for battle.[73] The sense of impending departure may be found in 1 Macc. 9.12, where the Seleucid general Bacchides blew the trumpet first to engage in battle, and Judas blew it in response, but the Hasmoneans' consistent act of trumpet-blowing in a war context makes it more plausible to assume their motif to be in accordance with Jewish traditions. As for Num. 10.8-9, however, it should be noted that the act of trumpet-blowing is also found frequently in historical books of the Hebrew Bible,[74] and there is a possibility that Judas' act imitates biblical figures and events found in historical books.

Biblical Sources	1 Maccabees	Grimm	Keil	F. & B.	Oesterley	Abel	Zeitlin	Dancy	Bartlett	Goldstein	Collins	Doran	Rappaport	Tilly
Exod. 18.21, 25	3.55	+	+	+		+		+		+		+	+	+

1 Maccabees 3.55 describes Judas' military formation in which he appoints leaders of thousands, hundreds, fifties and tens.[75] This picture is

---

72. 1 Macc. 3.54; 4.40; 5.33; 6.34-35; 9.12; 16.8; the latter three are omitted in Lange and Weigold's list, but these verses still consistently show that the trumpet-blowing is one of the characteristics of the Hasmonean wars with a demonstration of observing Jewish traditions and following divine order.

73. Grimm, 64; see Keil's critique of Grimm (Keil, 82).

74. Judg. 3.27; 6.34-35; 7.18-22; 1 Sam. 13.3; cf. 1QM 2.15–3.11; 10.7-8.

75. Cf. 2 Macc. 8.21-22 states that Judas rather divided his army into four parts.

reminiscent of Moses' administration of Israel in the wilderness, as advised by his father-in-law, Jethro (Exod. 18.21, 25), as identified by Lange and Weigold. It should first be noted that Moses' case was not precisely of military occasion, but caused by the inefficiency of Moses' administration of Israel in juridical matters (Exod. 18.13-15). The hierarchical structure, mostly in military terms, is found throughout the history of Israel,[76] and in the Second Temple period.[77] However, it is only in Exod. 18.21, 25 and Deut. 1.15 that the division of 1000, 100, 50, 10 is referenced, which Judas identically imitated.[78] Moreover, it is only in Exod. 18.25 that the actual appointment of hierarchical structure is found, and the imitative act of appointment under Judas' order bears a strong echo of Moses' act. Most commentators make note of the Exodus references amongst biblical and other cross-references, but only a few emphasize the singularity of Exod. 18.25 as an allusion.[79] Regarding Deut. 1.15, where Moses commands Israel to form their structure in accord with the same hierarchical system as in Exod. 18.21, 25, this reference may still be considered as a scriptural source of 1 Macc. 3.55 on the grounds that Deuteronomic legacies evidentially play an important role in Judas' administration in general (see our discussion on 1 Macc. 3.56, below), hence Collins puts it, 'Judas behaves like Moses in Deuteronomy, appointing his officers (compare Deut. 1.15) and in accordance with the prescriptions of the law of Moses in sending home those who were betrothed, engaged in building or planting, or fainthearted (compare Deut. 20.5-8)'.[80] There is, however, a subtle difference between the two figures: Moses only commanded to Israel before his departure, and it was Joshua who in fact led Israel into the promised land, whereas Judas' act shows his fulfilment of the command. In other words, rather than portraying Judas as Moses, the author seems to portray the former as faithfully carrying out the legacy of Moses, or Deuteronomy. In this way, Judas behaves more like Joshua.

---

76. Num. 31.14; Deut. 1.15; Judg. 20.10; 1 Sam. 8.12; 2 Sam. 18.2-3; 2 Kgs 1.9-16; 11.4; 2 Chron. 25.5.
77. 1QM 2.15-17; 1QS 2.19-22; Josephus, *War* 2.577-78; cf. similar division systems which were found in Ptolemaic as well as Roman armies (Abel, 71); see also, Bar-Kochva, *Judas Maccabaeus*, 256–7.
78. Cf. the Qumran community shares this system (1QS 2.21-22).
79. Grimm, 64; Fairweather and Black, 102.
80. Collins, 179.

Biblical Sources	1 Maccabees	Grimm	Keil	F. & B.	Oesterley	Abel	Zeitlin	Dancy	Bartlett	Goldstein	Collins	Doran	Rappaport	Tilly
Deut. 1.13, 15	3.55	+	+			+				+	+	+	+	

See the footnote under Exod. 18.21, 25.

Biblical Sources	1 Maccabees	Grimm	Keil	F. & B.	Oesterley	Abel	Zeitlin	Dancy	Bartlett	Goldstein	Collins	Doran	Rappaport	Tilly
Deut. 20.5-8	3.56	+	+	+		+	+		+	+	+	+	+	+

1 Maccabees 3.56 continues describing Judas' administration in war time by having him return all those men who were building new houses, engaged to be married, cowards or planting a vineyard. These four types of soldiers, called to return home, is a clear allusion to Deut. 20.5-8, where Moses commands Israel in the same way (only the order is slightly changed: building new houses, planting a vineyard, engaged or cowards). Note the phrase κατὰ τὸν νόμον, which similarly functions as a quotation formula, and indicates Judas' fulfilment of the law. Some scholars also make note of Gideon's similar act, sending home all who are 'fearful and trembling' (Judg. 7.3), and Rappaport makes the claim that Judas is imitating Gideon in this passage.[81] The similarities between Judas and Gideon are considerable.[82] However, the inclusion of all four types of soldiers being instructed to return home in 1 Macc. 3.55 and Deut. 20.5-8 makes their connection stronger.

81. Rappaport, 717.
82. E.g. Judas' battle with Nicanor in ch. 7 which has multiple points in parallel with the battle of Gideon in Judg. 5 which will be discussed in detail in the next chapter.

3. Philological Parallels

Biblical Sources	1 Maccabees	Grimm	Keil	F. & B.	Oesterley	Abel	Zeitlin	Dancy	Bartlett	Goldstein	Collins	Doran	Rappaport	Tilly
2 Sam. 2.7	3.58	+	+	+	+	+					+			

1 Maccabees 3.58, 'Gird yourselves, and become strong sons' (Περιζώσασθε καὶ γίνεσθε εἰς υἱοὺς δυνατούς): Lange and Weigold identify this with David's speech after Saul's death in 2 Sam. 2.7 ('let your hands be strong, and be valiant' [תחזקנה ידיכם והיו לבני־חיל; κραταιούσθωσαν αἱ χεῖρες ὑμῶν καὶ γίνεσθε εἰς υἱοὺς δυνατούς]). However, only the phrase γίνεσθε εἰς υἱοὺς δυνατούς appears identically in the two texts, and this phrase is also used by Absalom in 2 Sam. 13.28 ('Be courageous and be valiant'; חזקו והיו לבני־חיל; ἀνδρίζεσθε καὶ γίνεσθε εἰς υἱοὺς δυνάμεως), and several commentators who note 2 Sam. 2.7 also add 13.28. The encouragement given by Absalom to his servants, however, relates to his plot to kill his brother Amnon, and it is highly unlikely for such an allusion to family treachery to be made by Judas to his soldiers before the battle. Nor is it likely that Absalom's use of the phrase is meant to echo David's encouragement of Saul's servants. The phrase simply seems to be an idiomatic Hebrew expression for 2 Sam. 13.28, and 1 Maccabees' use of 2 Sam. 2.7 remains less decisive because the expression may only indicate a use of Hebrew idiom.[83] Besides, Doran suggests Deut. 20.2-4 as an allusion in which Moses encourages Israel to be strong.[84] Despite the lack of any morphological similarity, this is a valid suggestion because the whole context of Deut. 20.1-9 is relevant and echoing in the portrayal of Judas' acts in 1 Macc. 3.55-60.[85] Some commentators heed the verb περιζωννύω ('to gird') and suggest Isa. 8.9 and Lk. 12.35,[86] and Exod. 12.11,[87] as cross-references.

---

83. Cf. 1QM 15.7 has the same expression; חזקו והיו לבני חיל.
84. Doran, 4:99.
85. Also, Goldstein, 262.
86. Fairweather and Black, 103; Zeitlin, 99.
87. Abel, 72.

Biblical Sources	1 Maccabees	Grimm	Keil	F. & B.	Oesterley	Abel	Zeitlin	Dancy	Bartlett	Goldstein	Collins	Doran	Rappaport	Tilly
Exod. 34.2	3.58	+	+	+	+	+								

1 Maccabees 3.58, 'Be ready in the morning' (γίνεσθε ἕτοιμοι εἰς πρωὶ): Lange and Weigold find the same expression in Exod. 34.2, where God commands Moses to come up to Mount Sinai. The expressions are identical between the two texts, but there is little clue as to the need of any allusion to Exod. 34.2. It is possible that the act of getting ready early in the morning may bear some significance, but commentators do not suggest any contextual connection either. What is interesting from our list of commentators is the fact that whilst old commentaries point out Exod. 34.2 (as well as Exod. 19.5, where a similar expression appears, 'Be ready for the third day'), the commentaries from the mid-1900s ignore it. Whether this change amongst commentaries indicates a growing awareness of unnecessary connection between the Exodus reference and 1 Macc. 3.58 or not, I cannot infer any reason behind using the Exodus material, if it was used. Instead, it may well be that this expression indicates nothing more than being idiomatic.

Biblical Sources	1 Maccabees	Grimm	Keil	F. & B.	Oesterley	Abel	Zeitlin	Dancy	Bartlett	Goldstein	Collins	Doran	Rappaport	Tilly
Deut. 7.18-19	4.8-9													

1 Maccabees 4.8-9 contains Judas' battle speech given before the overwhelming expanse of the Seleucid general Gorgias' army, in which he encourages the Judeans not to fear but to remember the miraculous story of their ancestors' deliverance from Pharaoh at the Red Sea.[88] No commentators from our list, however, refer to Deut. 7.18-19, which Lange and Weigold identify as an allusion. Instead, a majority of commentators

---

88. Cf. the parallel passage in 2 Macc. 8.16-20 which has Judas instead refer to Jerusalem's deliverance from Sennacherib.

identify Exodus 14 in which the miraculous story is narrated.[89] These commentators are certainly correct in placing 1 Macc. 4.8-9 within the traditions in which Israel/Jews' remembrance of the miraculous story at the Red Sea,[90] or the divine deliverance of Israel from the oppression of Pharaoh as a whole can be found.[91] However, Lange and Weigold's reference to Deut. 7.18-19 requires attention. Between this passage and 1 Macc. 4.8-9, the combination of particular elements – public speech + audience fearful of great enemies (gentile nations) + urge to remember + the divine deliverance of Israel from Pharaoh at the Red Sea – is paralleled. The use of Scripture can thus be seen in double layers: first, the famous story of Israel's miraculous deliverance from Pharaoh at the Red Sea in Exodus 14 is explicitly referred to; second, more implicitly, Judas imitates the imagery in Deut. 7.18-19 in which Moses encourages Israel before the multitude of enemy and urges them to remember the divine deliverance at the Red Sea.

Biblical Sources	1 Maccabees	Grimm	Keil	F. & B.	Oesterley	Abel	Zeitlin	Dancy	Bartlett	Goldstein	Collins	Doran	Rappaport	Tilly
Ps. 118.1, 29	4.24	+	+	+	+	+		+	+				+	+

1 Maccabees 4.24, '…they sang hymns and blessed heaven, "for he is good, for his mercy is forever"' (ἐπιστραφέντες ὕμνουν καὶ εὐλόγουν εἰς οὐρανὸν ὅτι καλόν, ὅτι εἰς τὸν αἰῶνα τὸ ἔλεος αὐτοῦ): returning in victory, Judas and the Judeans sang ὕμνουν ('hymns'), which Lange and Weigold identify as the famous phrase repeated at the beginning and the end of Psalm 118 (vv. 1, 29): 'Give thanks to the Lord, for his is good; for his steadfast love endures forever' (הודו ליהוה כי־טוב כי לעולם חסדו). Its Septuagint rendering is almost identical to the phrase sung in 1 Macc. 4.24: …ὅτι ἀγαθός, ὅτι εἰς τὸν αἰῶνα τὸ ἔλεος αὐτοῦ ('for he is good, and his mercy endures forever'). The function of ὕμνουν can be seen as something

---

89. Grimm, 66; Keil, 84; Fairweather and Black, 105; Abel, 75; Bartlett[1], 57; Goldstein, 264; Doran, 4:66.
90. E.g. Josh. 4.23; 24.6; Neh. 9.9-10; Pss. 106.9; 136.15; Jdt 5.13; Wis. 10.18; 19.7; 1QM 11.9-10; also Heb. 11.29.
91. E.g. Deut. 6.21-22; 7.8; 11.3-4; Ps. 135.9.

similar to κατὰ τὸν νομόν (1 Macc. 3.56; 4.47) or κατὰ τὸ κρίμα (1 Macc. 2.24), as an explicit allusion to the psalm. As for the cited version of the psalm, the fact that 1 Maccabees has καλός rather than ἀγαθός in the Greek version suggests that the translator is here independently translating the original Hebrew wording without consulting the Greek text of the psalm. The phrase, however, appears several times in Psalms (106.1; 107.1; 136.1), as well as in 1 Chronicles (16.41), Jeremiah (33.11), and Ezra (3.11), but only Fairweather and Black and Tilly suggest these latter three references.[92] Goldstein heeds the phrase 'give thanks' and unconvincingly connects 1 Macc. 4.24 to Isa. 12.1, ignoring the aforementioned references which bear morphological association.[93] If ὕμνουν functions as a quotation formula, the three other references in Psalms should equally be considered. Moreover, the imagery of the restoration of the Temple foundation in Ezra may have echoed in the early stage of the Hasmonean triumph, and in this way the hymnic phrase in Ezra 3.11 may be alluded to. Furthermore, Jeremiah's prophecy of Israel's restoration in which singing of the hymnic phrase is specifically prophesied may be seen as fulfilled in the Jews' singing of the hymn in 1 Maccabees. These options should all be considered plausible due to the popularity of the hymnic phrase in Jewish traditions, and because there is no further clue to narrow down scriptural sources.

Biblical Sources	1 Maccabees	Grimm	Keil	F. & B.	Oesterley	Abel	Zeitlin	Dancy	Bartlett	Goldstein	Collins	Doran	Rappaport	Tilly
1 Sam. 14.23, 45	4.25				+		+	+		+				+

1 Maccabees 4.25, 'And a great salvation came about in Israel on that day' (καὶ ἐγενήθη σωτηρία μεγάλη τῷ Ισραηλ ἐν τῇ ἡμέρᾳ ἐκείνῃ): after his victory from the battle with Gorgias and the Seleucid army, Judas and his soldiers return to Judea and the passage ends with this phrase. Lange and Weigold identify it with 1 Sam. 14.23, an ending statement of the battle scene of Saul and Jonathan with the Philistines (v. 23) and reiterated in v. 45. The Hebrew wording in v. 23 has ויושע יהוה היום ההוא, and its Greek

---

92. Fairweather and Black, 108; Tilly, 131.
93. Goldstein, 265–6.

rendering, ἔσωσεν κύριος ἐν τῇ ἡμέρᾳ ἐκείνῃ τὸν Ισραηλ, has some morphological affinity with 1 Macc. 4.25, although it is not identical. The change of ἔσωσεν κύριος into ἐγενήθη σωτηρία, hence omitting the direct reference to God, is presumably considered by Lange and Weigold as a typical linguistic pattern of 1 Maccabees. The adjective μεγάλη is absent in v. 23 but instead appears in v. 45 which in turn omits other words that appear in v. 23: '…Shall Jonathan die, who has worked this *great salvation* (הישועה הגדולה; ἡ σωτηρία ἡ μεγάλη) in Israel?' (v. 45). Moreover, the structures of the sentences in 1 Sam. 14.23 and 1 Macc. 4.25 are different from each other. It should also be noted that several commentators suggest the popularity of the phrase in the historical books in the Hebrew Bible[94] which suggests that the phrase in 1 Macc. 4.25 can be seen as modelled by the scriptural tradition, emphasizing theological understanding of the course of history rather than alluding to a single biblical reference.

Biblical Sources	1 Maccabees	Grimm	Keil	F. & B.	Oesterley	Abel	Zeitlin	Dancy	Bartlett	Goldstein	Collins	Doran	Rappaport	Tilly
1 Sam. 17.1-58	4.30	+	+	+	+	+	+		+	+	+	+	+	+

1 Maccabees 4.30 contains Judas' prayer in his battle with Lysias in which he mentions God's deliverance of Israel from 'the attack of the powerful one' (τὸ ὅρμημα τοῦ δυνατοῦ) by David, and 'the camps of the Philistines' by Jonathan, son of Saul and his armour-bearer. The original Hebrew word for ὁ δυνατός was probably גבור, referring to Goliath in 1 Samuel 17.[95] Likewise, the battle of Jonathan and his armour-bearer with the Philistines is found in 1 Sam. 14.1-23. Commentators unanimously make the same observation on 1 Macc. 4.30 and the two references from 1 Samuel.

---

94. E.g. Exod. 14.13, 30; Judg. 15.18; 1 Sam. 11.13; 19.5; 2 Sam. 23.10; 2 Kgs 13.5; 1 Chron. 11.14.
95. E.g. 1 Sam.[GK] 17.4, '…a mighty man (ανὴρ δυνατός) came out from the ranks of the Philistines…'; 1 Sam. 17.51, '…their mighty one (גבורם; ὁ δυνατὸς αὐτῶν) was dead…'; the story of David's defeat of Goliath is widely remembered in Jewish traditions; 1QM 11.1-3; *m. Soṭah* 8.1.

Biblical Sources	1 Maccabees	Grimm	Keil	F. & B.	Oesterley	Abel	Zeitlin	Dancy	Bartlett	Goldstein	Collins	Doran	Rappaport	Tilly
1 Sam. 14.1-23	4.30	+	+	+	+	+	+		+	+	+	+	+	+

See the footnote under 1 Macc. 4.30 (1 Sam. 17.1-58).

Biblical Sources	1 Maccabees	Grimm	Keil	F. & B.	Oesterley	Abel	Zeitlin	Dancy	Bartlett	Goldstein	Collins	Doran	Rappaport	Tilly
Num. 10.8-9	4.40		+	+	+	+	+		+	+		+		

See the footnote under 1 Macc. 3.54 (Num. 10.8-9).

Biblical Sources	1 Maccabees	Grimm	Keil	F. & B.	Oesterley	Abel	Zeitlin	Dancy	Bartlett	Goldstein	Collins	Doran	Rappaport	Tilly
Lev. 14.40, 45	4.43											+		

1 Maccabees 4.43 has Judas purify the temple and move the defiled stones to an unclean place.[96] Lange and Weigold identify this action with Lev. 14.40, 45, in which the law of Moses instructs that any house deemed by a priest as unclean has to be treated as such. Thus, Judas' purification of the Temple in this way shows another example of his keen observance of the law. However, the references to Lev. 14.40, 45 are almost completely unnoticed by most commentators (with Doran as the only exception).[97] Part of the reason may be that the law regarding purifying one's unclean house in Leviticus is not exactly an instruction for cleansing the Temple,

---

96. The often-suggested places are the Hinnom valley (Jer. 19.13-14; specifically a place called תפת in the valley) and the Kidron valley (2 Kgs 23.4, 6, 12).

97. Doran, 4:71.

although the principle may well have been extended to matters relating to the Temple. A similar instruction can be found in the laws regarding keeping military camps clean.[98] Instead, there are other similar cases in the reforming acts of Davidic kings in the Hebrew Bible, and these reforming imageries are generally quite similar to Judas' cleansing and purification of the Temple.[99] During his first year of reign in Judah, Hezekiah, along with priests and Levites, carried out a reforming project for the Jerusalem Temple (2 Chron. 29.3-19) which included the Levites' disposal of 'all the uncleanness' from the Temple into the Kidron valley (2 Chron. 29.16). Likewise, Josiah, upon reading the book of the law found by high priest Hilkiah, repented of the nation's sins (2 Kgs 22.11–23.3), and carried out a similar reforming project with Hilkiah and a group of priests (2 Kgs 23.4-7), which included taking out the Asherah and throwing it into the Kidron valley (2 Kgs 23.6). These reforming acts were clearly the expression of the national leaders' devotion to the law of Moses, by which they repented to God of the sins the nation committed and expressed their entreaties for the renewal of the covenant with God which had previously been defiled. As we have seen and will continue to see in the next chapter, Judas' acts and those of other Hasmoneans are portrayed as following Deuteronomic legacies in which they show zeal for observing the law of Moses and renewing the covenant of YHWH previously defiled by the pro-Seleucid Judeans and Antiochus IV Epiphanes' imposition of gentile cults. Thus, these Judaic kings' cleansing acts may well be seen as allusions in 1 Macc. 4.43.

Biblical Sources	1 Maccabees	Grimm	Keil	F. & B.	Oesterley	Abel	Zeitlin	Dancy	Bartlett	Goldstein	Collins	Doran	Rappaport	Tilly
Exod. 20.25	4.47	+	+	+	+	+	+	+	+	+	+	+		+

1 Maccabees 4.47 states that a new altar was made by using whole stones rather than hewn ones, adding a formulaic phrase, κατὰ τὸν νόμον ('according to the law'). Lange and Weigold rightly identify Exod. 20.25 and Deut. 27.5-6 here. Commentators almost unanimously make note of these two references, and the formulaic phrase clearly confirms the references to the law of Moses. There is, however, another reference suggested

---

98. Deut. 23.12-14; noted by Osterley, 81; Tilly, 136.
99. Noted by Abel, 83; Dancy, 100; Tilly, 136.

by a few commentators.[100] In Josh. 8.31, Joshua builds an altar at Mount Ebal to offer a peace offering after his conquest of Ai, and the verse says, 'just as Moses the servant of the Lord had commanded the people of Israel, as it is written in the Book of the Law of Moses, "an altar of uncut stones, upon which no man has wielded an iron tool"'. The imageries of Joshua and Judas overlap with each other by the act of building an altar with uncut stones. Here, then, is another case where scriptural allusion has a dual-aspect (see also 1 Macc. 4.43).

Biblical Sources	1 Maccabees	Grimm	Keil	F. & B.	Oesterley	Abel	Zeitlin	Dancy	Bartlett	Goldstein	Collins	Doran	Rappaport	Tilly
Deut. 27.5-6	4.47	+	+	+	+	+	+		+	+		+		+

See the footnote under 1 Macc. 4.47 (Exod. 20.25).

Biblical Sources	1 Maccabees	Grimm	Keil	F. & B.	Oesterley	Abel	Zeitlin	Dancy	Bartlett	Goldstein	Collins	Doran	Rappaport	Tilly
Exod. 40.4-5	4.49													

1 Maccabees 4.49 gives details of furnishing the Temple in which new vessels, the lamp stand, the altar of incense, and the table were brought into the shrine. Lange and Weigold identify Exod. 40.4-5 as a cross-reference in which the instruction for furnishing the Temple is almost identical to the details carried out by Judas and priests. Whilst commentators generally discern that the process of restoring the Temple and its furniture shows that Judas fulfilled the requirement of the law, no commentator gives a specific reference.[101] The fact that the process taken by Judas and the priests closely parallels God's command to Moses in

---

100. Grimm, 74; Abel, 84; Collins, 183.

101. Cf. Bartlett[1], 65, and Doran, 4:72, mentions Exod. 25–27 in which God instructs Moses how to produce those Temple objects, but not the process of furnishing.

Exod. 40.4-5, however, should suggest that the Judeans are observing this specific law.

Biblical Sources	1 Maccabees	Grimm	Keil	F. & B.	Oesterley	Abel	Zeitlin	Dancy	Bartlett	Goldstein	Collins	Doran	Rappaport	Tilly
Exod. 30.8	4.50													

1 Maccabees 4.50 states that Judas and the priests burned incense on the altar and 'gave light in the shrine'. Whilst no commentator suggests any biblical reference related to it, Lange and Weigold suggest Exod. 30.8 in which God commands Moses that Aaron has to light incense on the altar twice daily, every morning and at twilight (30.7-8). Considering that there are several deliberate echoes to the law of Moses relating to Temple matters made in Judas' reforming project of the Temple,[102] the imagery of burning incense on the altar and lighting the shrine may well be seen as fulfilment of the commandment in Exod. 30.8, even though there is a lack of morphological association.

Biblical Sources	1 Maccabees	Grimm	Keil	F. & B.	Oesterley	Abel	Zeitlin	Dancy	Bartlett	Goldstein	Collins	Doran	Rappaport	Tilly
Exod. 25.30	4.51													

1 Maccabees 4.51 states that the procedure of setting up Temple furniture ends with placing the bread on the table and spreading out the curtains. These are instructed in Exod. 25.30 (setting up the bread) and 26.33 (setting up the curtains), as rightly identified by Lange and Weigold. Commentators do not provide any cross-references here, but are all aware of the Judeans' conspicuous display of observing the law in setting up furniture in the Temple.[103] Bartlett[2] suggests that the completion of the

---

102. E.g. 1 Macc. 3.43, 47, 49.
103. Cf. Fairweather and Black, 113, suggest Lev. 24.5-9 and Exod. 26.36, and Bartlett[2], 1568, Exod. 26.1–10, 31–35; these can all be considered as the commands regarding setting up the bread and the curtains which are fulfilled by Judas and the priests.

project, expressed as '*finished* all the works which they made', echoes the completion of Moses' work in Exod. 40.33.[104]

Biblical Sources	1 Maccabees	Grimm	Keil	F. & B.	Oesterley	Abel	Zeitlin	Dancy	Bartlett	Goldstein	Collins	Doran	Rappaport	Tilly
Exod. 26.33	4.51						+							

See the footnote under 1 Maccabees 4.51 (Exod 25.30).

Biblical Sources	1 Maccabees	Grimm	Keil	F. & B.	Oesterley	Abel	Zeitlin	Dancy	Bartlett	Goldstein	Collins	Doran	Rappaport	Tilly
Exod. 29.38-42	4.53		+	+						+		+		+

1 Maccabees 4.53 has the Judeans make a whole burnt offering on the new altar the morning after the completion of the reforming project of the Jerusalem Temple (hence, the beginning of the festival of Hanukkah) which they did 'according to the law' (κατὰ τὸν νόμον). Lange and Weigold identify Exod. 29.38-42 as the command of daily burnt offering which is fulfilled in this occasion, although a few commentators rightly point out Num. 28.3-7, where the same command is given.[105]

Biblical Sources	1 Maccabees	Grimm	Keil	F. & B.	Oesterley	Abel	Zeitlin	Dancy	Bartlett	Goldstein	Collins	Doran	Rappaport	Tilly
2 Chron. 7.9	4.56				+		+						+	

1 Maccabees 4.56 states the Judeans' rededication of the new altar in eight days, performed with burnt offering and gladness, the sacrifice an offering of salvation and praise. Lange and Weigold find in this verse an allusion to Solomon's dedication of the Temple in 2 Chronicles 7, especially v. 9

104. Bartlett², 1568.
105. Keil, 93; Tilly, 137.

3. *Philological Parallels* 129

containing words such as 'the eighth day' and 'the dedication of the altar' ('gladness' in v. 10). However, the dedication, and re-dedication, of the altar in eight days with gladness can also be found in the time of Hezekiah (2 Chron. 29.17-18) and Ezra (Ezra 6.16-17), and similarly in the Mosaic era (Num. 7.10, 84). The reference to Solomon's case in 2 Chron. 7.9 is noted by a few scholars.[106] A few scholars rightly point out these multiple scriptural precedents of the re-dedication of the altar.[107]

Biblical Sources	1 Maccabees	Grimm	Keil	F. & B.	Oesterley	Abel	Zeitlin	Dancy	Bartlett	Goldstein	Collins	Doran	Rappaport	Tilly
Joel 4.4	5.15													

1 Maccabees 5.15, 'there was gathered against them, from *Ptolemais and Tyre and Sidon and even all the Galilee of the allophyles*, to annihilate us': as I have already explained in detail previously (see §2.1), the phrase 'Tyre and Sidon and even all the Galilee of the allophyles' (Τύρου καὶ Σιδῶνος καὶ πᾶσαν Γαλιλαίαν ἀλλοφύλων) clearly shows the Greek translator's use of Joel 4.4 (3.4 in English translations), on the grounds that the translator not only repeats the same phrase in the Greek version (Τύρου καὶ Σιδὼν καὶ πᾶσα Γαλιλαία ἀλλοφύλων, translated from צר וצידון וכל גלילות פלשת), but also repeats the same error of reading גלילות, which stems from גלל ('region'), as גליל(ה) ('Galilee'). As some forms of the word גלל can be very confusing with the proper noun for 'Galilee', and the translators of Greek biblical texts evidentially struggled with them,[108] one can infer that the Greek translator of 1 Maccabees felt the need for consulting the Greek rendering of the word. As for the original Hebrew author, his mention of Tyre and Sidon, and the inclusion of those regions probably between and around the two regions, follow the pattern of regional reference also found in Joel 4.4. Starting with Grimm, a majority of commentators identify Isa. 8.23 which has a similar term,

---

106. Abel, 87; Dancy, 100; Rappaport, 718; cf. on referring to the same account in 1 Kgs 8.65-66 only, Fairweather and Black, 114; Bartlett², 1568; Doran, 4:72; Tilly, 138.

107. Abel, 87; Dancy, 100; Bartlett², 1568; Rappaport, 718; Tilly, 138; cf. Zeitlin, 52, also notes the dedication of the altar in the times of Moses, Solomon and Ezra, but claims that these precedents were kept for seven days whereas Judas' re-dedication took eight days, hence, only identifying Hezekiah's dedication of the altar, which explicitly says 'eight days' in 2 Chron. 29.17.

108. See §2.1.4 for more examples in this regard.

'Galilee of the nations' (גליל הגוים; Γαλιλαία τῶν ἐθνῶν).[109] However, in my judgement, they fail to recognize the following observation. As well as my argument above, 1 Maccabees typically favours the term ἀλλόφυλοι ('foreigners') to refer to the gentile nations around them, and 5.15 uses this term. Isaiah 8.23, in contrast, has ἔθνη, and the structure of the phrase is also different from 1 Macc. 5.15. In comparison, the phrase in Joel[GK] 4.4 is strikingly the same as 1 Macc. 5.15. In sum, Lange and Weigold rightly makes the connection between 1 Macc. 5.15 and Joel 4.4. The context of Joel 4.4, however, seems less relevant in 1 Macc. 5.15. The repayment these gentile regions owe to YHWH and the tone of divine judgement do not help us understand the imagery of these regions' anti-Semitic attitude in 1 Macc. 5.15, other than the fact that they are classified as enemies of Israel/Jews. It is possible that the author's use of Joel 4.4 is an imitation of style.

Biblical Sources	1 Maccabees	Grimm	Keil	F. & B.	Oesterley	Abel	Zeitlin	Dancy	Bartlett	Goldstein	Collins	Doran	Rappaport	Tilly
1 Sam. 5.12	5.31					+				+		+		+

1 Maccabees 5.31, 'And Judas saw that the battle had begun, and *the screaming of the city went up as far as heaven* (ἡ κραυγὴ τῆς πόλεως ἀνέβη ἕως οὐρανοῦ) with trumpeting and great screaming': Lange and Weigold, amongst other commentators, identify the italicized phrase with 1 Sam. 5.12 (ותעל שועת העיר השמים; ἀνέβη ἡ κραυγὴ τῆς πόλεως εἰς τὸν οὐρανόν). The problem with the connection, however, is that the context of 1 Macc. 5.31 makes ἡ κραυγή ('the cry') somewhat different from the phrase used in 1 Sam. 5.12. In 1 Macc. 5.15, ἡ κραυγή is associated with the trumpeting and great screaming. Given that Judas and his army woke up in the morning discovering the massive army of the Seleucid general, Timothy, carrying ladders and engines of war to attack them, the cry may have referred to the fear felt by the Judeans. The cry in 1 Sam. 5.12, on the other hand, is heard from the people of gentile regions, Ashdod and Ekron, where the Ark of God was detained. This latter passage rather generates the theme of God's punishment upon gentile nations. Alternatively, some important Latin texts (X, G, V) change the wording of 1 Macc. 5.31 by

---

109. Grimm, 81; Keil, 99; Fairweather and Black, 120; Oesterley, 1.84; Zeitlin, 113; Bartlett[1], 70; Goldstein, 299; Rappaport, 718; Doran, 4:77; Tilly, 145; these commentators suggest the term 'Galilee of allophyles' or 'Upper Galilee' as a region inhabited by a mixture of ethnic groups.

moving 'the city' to the end of the verse and altering 'with trumpeting' to 'like trumpeting', hence, *sicut tuba et clamor magnus de civitate*.[110] If this reading is preferred, the phrase in 1 Macc. 5.31 lacks any considerable association with 1 Sam. 5.12. Goldstein, for instance, opens these two possibilities of reading, and suggests Isa. 66.6 as a scriptural association with *magnus de civitate* ('cry of the city'), in the case of the alternative reading.[111] However, I suggest, as another option, that just like the agony felt by the Philistines in 1 Sam. 5.12, the author of 1 Maccabees describes the extreme situation faced by Judas and his soldiers which is then immediately overcome by Judas' encouragement in the following verse, 'Fight today for our kindred' (1 Macc. 5.32), finally leading to victory (5.34). In this way, the phrase borrowed from 1 Sam. 5.12 functions as an expression of overwhelming distress, showing the fear and cowardice of Jewish soldiers in contrast to Judas' heroic bravery.

Biblical Sources	1 Maccabees	Grimm	Keil	F. & B.	Oesterley	Abel	Zeitlin	Dancy	Bartlett	Goldstein	Collins	Doran	Rappaport	Tilly
Num. 10.8-9	5.33									+				

See the footnote under 1 Macc. 3.54 (Num. 10.8-9). This verse, in particular, resembles the image of Gideon in Judg. 7.16, the reference noted by most commentators.[112] See also our discussion on the multiple similarities between 1 Maccabees and Judges in the next chapter.

Biblical Sources	1 Maccabees	Grimm	Keil	F. & B.	Oesterley	Abel	Zeitlin	Dancy	Bartlett	Goldstein	Collins	Doran	Rappaport	Tilly
Num. 20.14-20	5.48	+	+		+	+				+		+	+	+

1 Maccabees 5.48 has Judas and all his companies attempt to pass by Ephron peacefully for which Judas asks the people at Ephron to allow them to pass the city. The city remains blocked and Judas makes war with

110. See de Bruyne, *Machabées*, 31.
111. Goldstein, 302.
112. Hence, most commentators' lack of reference to Num. 10.8-9; cf. Goldstein, 302, who suggests 1 Sam. 11.11 as the most probable candidate for scriptural allusion.

the city and passes by force. Lange and Weigold suggest similar incidents with Moses, one with the Edomites (Num. 20.14-20), and another with Amorites (Num. 21.21-23), as well as his recalling of the second incident in Deut. 2.26-30 (with Sihon, the king of Heshbon). Several commentators identify those passages from Numbers as echoing in 1 Macc. 5.48.[113] However, we will only count the actual incidents, Num. 20.14-20 and 21.21-23, rather than later generations' remembrance of them, such as in Deut. 2.26-30 and Judg. 11.12-27, since the allusion in 1 Macc. 5.48 is made to the act of passing through the city.

Biblical Sources	1 Maccabees	Grimm	Keil	F. & B.	Oesterley	Abel	Zeitlin	Dancy	Bartlett	Goldstein	Collins	Doran	Rappaport	Tilly
Num. 21.23	5.48	+	+	+	+	+		+	+		+	+		+

See the footnote under 1 Macc. 5.48 (Num. 20.14-20).

Biblical Sources	1 Maccabees	Grimm	Keil	F. & B.	Oesterley	Abel	Zeitlin	Dancy	Bartlett	Goldstein	Collins	Doran	Rappaport	Tilly
Deut. 2.26-30	5.48													

See the footnote under 1 Macc. 5.48 (Num. 20.14-20).

Biblical Sources	1 Maccabees	Grimm	Keil	F. & B.	Oesterley	Abel	Zeitlin	Dancy	Bartlett	Goldstein	Collins	Doran	Rappaport	Tilly
1 Kgs 22.27	5.54			+										

113. Cf. Goldstein, 303, who rightly adds Jephthah's message to the king of the Ammonites (Judg. 11.12-27) in which those two incidents are recalled (vv. 17, 19); cf. Dancy, 107, and Doran, 4:80, who suggest Deut. 20.10-18, a command of Moses regarding attacking a city, but strictly speaking, this passage is an instruction concerning intended war rather than on peaceful movement through a city.

1 Maccabees 5.54 has the Judeans celebrate upon the safe return of Judas' army, stating that they rejoiced because no-one fell 'until they returned in peace' (ἕως τοῦ ἐπιστρέψαι ἐν εἰρήνῃ). Lange and Weigold point out the command given by King Ahab in which, after his conversation with Micaiah, he orders Micaiah to be imprisoned until he returns in peace. It is at the end of his order where an almost identical clause is used, 'until I return in peace' (ἕως τοῦ ἐπιστρέψαι με ἐν εἰρήνῃ, 1 Kgs 22.27; 2 Chron. 18.26; עד באי בשלום in Heb.). Most commentators do not make note of 1 Kgs 22.27.[114] An immediate observation on the connection between 1 Macc. 5.54 and 1 Kgs 22.27 is that the context of 1 Kings/2 Chronicles has little bearing on the theme of enchanting return from victory, as is the case in the context of 1 Macc. 5.54. Two options are possible: first, 1 Kgs 22.27/2 Chron. 18.26 have no relevance, and the phrase in parallel is nothing more than a Hebrew idiom; second, the author of 1 Maccabees borrowed the phrase from Kings/Chronicles and alluded to its context with an intention of contrast, that is, the contrast between the pious Hasmoneans and the unlawful Ahab. The problem with the latter option, however, is that Ahab does not receive any attention within Judas' campaigns and return episode (1 Macc. 5) or in the rest of 1 Maccabees, and the choice of Ahab's words appears a random one.

Biblical Sources	1 Maccabees	Grimm	Keil	F. & B.	Oesterley	Abel	Zeitlin	Dancy	Bartlett	Goldstein	Collins	Doran	Rappaport	Tilly
2 Chron. 18.26	5.54			+										

See the footnote under 1 Macc. 5.54 (1 Kgs 22.27).

---

114. The only exception being Fairweather and Black (129), but without necessary explanation about the contextual inconsistency between the two texts; cf. Goldstein, 304, who suggests for the image of war victory and joyful return in 1 Macc. 5.54 an echo of multiple passages from Isa. 25; 35.10; 51.11; 52.11-12, none of which are morphologically identifiable, but thematically relevant; on the theme of war victory followed by joyful return to Zion, commentators also offer other biblical references such as Joel 1.16; Prov. 29.26; Est. 9.17-19.

Biblical Sources	1 Maccabees	Grimm	Keil	F. & B.	Oesterley	Abel	Zeitlin	Dancy	Bartlett	Goldstein	Collins	Doran	Rappaport	Tilly
Exod. 34.13	5.68													+

See the footnote under 1 Macc. 2.25-26 (Exod. 34.13-14). Most commentators appear to ignore possible allusions to Exod. 34.13 and Deut. 7.5, but they recognize these biblical references as alluded to in 1 Macc. 2.25-26, where a similar act is delivered by Mattathias. Lange and Weigold's reference to these two biblical materials is convincing, as I have previously shown, and Judas' acts consistently show his devoted observance of the Mosaic law. However, it should be repeated here that this zealous, reforming act of piousness is frequently found in historical books in the Hebrew Bible which may equally be considered as allusions through which the Hasmonean achievements overlap with those of biblical heroes.

Biblical Sources	1 Maccabees	Grimm	Keil	F. & B.	Oesterley	Abel	Zeitlin	Dancy	Bartlett	Goldstein	Collins	Doran	Rappaport	Tilly
Deut. 7.5	5.68									+				+

See the footnotes under 1 Macc. 2.25-26 (Exod. 34.13-14) and 1 Macc. 5.68 (Exod. 34.13-14).

Biblical Sources	1 Maccabees	Grimm	Keil	F. & B.	Oesterley	Abel	Zeitlin	Dancy	Bartlett	Goldstein	Collins	Doran	Rappaport	Tilly
Ps. 79.2-3	7.17	+	+	+	+	+	+	+	+	+	+	+	+	+

1 Maccabees 7.17, 'The flesh of your holy ones and their blood they poured out around Jerusalem, and there was no one to bury them': this verse is unanimously recognized as a direct, slightly abbreviated quotation of Ps. 79.2-3:

They have given the bodies of your servants to the birds of the heavens for food, the flesh of your faithful to the beasts of the earth. They have poured out their blood like water all around Jerusalem, and there was no one to bury them.

The allusion is especially clear because the quotation is preceded by the quotation formula, κατὰ τὸν λόγον, ὃν ἔγραψεν αὐτόν ('according to the word which was written', NETS; literally, 'according to the word which *he* wrote'). Whilst commentators have no problem reading this formulaic term with the assumption of the Psalmist as the implied subject, Goldstein proposes that αὐτόν indicates Alcimus, hence identifying him as the author of the psalm and translating the phrase as 'in accordance with the verse which he himself wrote'.[115] He argues that the phrase ὃν ἔγραψεν αὐτόν cannot but be translated from הוא כתב אשר.[116] If ὃν ἔγραψεν αὐτόν is taken as the original wording, a view which is almost unanimous amongst scholars, the personal pronoun αὐτόν can be, as Goldstein argues, an emphatic reference to Alcimus who appears to be the subject in the preceding verse (otherwise no-one is introduced as the subject in the sentence). However, the following textual consideration does not give such confirmation to Goldstein's conclusion. To start with, other commentators find the phrase typically Hebraic.[117] In my judgement, Goldstein is right in questioning the term. The Septuagint contains the combination of either γράφω + αὐτός (20 times)[118] or ὅς + γραφάω (12 times),[119] but never the combination of all three words ὅς + γράφω + αὐτός.[120] The manuscripts of 1 Maccabees render such a divergent range of readings on this verse, and only Sinaiticus ('S', and some minuscules as per Rahlfs) render τον λογον ον εγραψεν αυτον after κατα. Both Kappler and Rahlfs choose it as the preferred reading. Other textual witnesses include: τους λογους ους εγρ. (A, q, 62, 46, 58, 106, 340); τον λ. ον εγρ. (V, La^L); τον λ. ον εγρ. ο προφητης (S^CA, *L-19-93*, 311, SyI); τους λογους ους εγρ. ο προφητης (542); τους λογους ους εγρ. ασαφ ο προφητης (55); τους λογους ους εγρ. δαδ (56); τον λογον ασαφ ον εγραψεν (Eusebius, *Dem. ev.* 10.1.12); *verbum asaph*

---

115. Goldstein, 332–6, and 327 for the quotation.
116. He refers to 1 Sam. 22.18 as an example here, but the verse has no relevance.
117. Fairweather and Black, 150; Abel, 134; Dancy, 122.
118. E.g. Josh. 18.9; 1 Chron. 24.6.
119. Notably Josh. 8.32 mentioning Moses as the subject earlier in the same verse; 2 Kgs 17.37, mentioning God as the subject in v. 34.
120. Cf. some cases contain ὅς + γράφω + the subject: e.g. Jer. 36.27 (ברוך אשר כתב, 'which Baruch wrote').

profetae (La^G); *verbum quod scriptum est* (La$^{X\ V}$, SyII); *quod scriptum est* (La^B). Whilst most readings may well be seen as copyist editions, the reading, τον λογον ον εγραψεν, which omits the enigmatic αυτον, is worth consideration. It is only de Bruyne who prefers this reading,[121] and I suggest this reading is preferable to the reading of S (and in which case, the original Hebrew would be כדבר אשר כתב). It can be argued that the copyists of various manuscripts supplied the subject in various terms, including αυτον, corresponding with the rule that if a reading is more explanatory than others, it may be a sign of the copyist's improvement of the text. The variant, τους λογους ους εγραψεν, as attested by several important manuscripts (A, *q*, 62, 46, 58, 106, 340), may show the modification of the singular τον λογον into the plural, without needing to supply the subject of γράφω. As for the original Hebrew rendering, there is not enough evidence to identify the subject. Goldstein's proposition is not convincing because his proposition creates another issue, namely that the author of 1 Maccabees in this case makes Alcimus like a true prophet, predicting the future. This idea, of course, is hardly acceptable since Alcimus is clearly an antagonist to the Hasmoneans, and his high priesthood is proven to be illegitimate by his deceit of pious Jews. Worth mentioning is that it is not impossible for the author to have meant the *qal* passive voice of כתב, but rather than the usual rendering כתוב (e.g. Deut. 28.61, אשר לא כתוב ['which was not written']; Josh. 8.31, ככתוב בספר תורת ['as it is written in the book of the law']), he may have meant כָּתַב, which the translator could not distinguish from the active voice and rendered as ἔγραψεν. This cannot be proven, since the passive voice of כתב in the Hebrew Bible always inserts ו.

Biblical Sources	1 Maccabees	Grimm	Keil	F. & B.	Oesterley	Abel	Zeitlin	Dancy	Bartlett	Goldstein	Collins	Doran	Rappaport	Tilly
1 Kgs 8.29-30, 43	7.37	+	+	+	+	+		+	+	+		+		+

1 Maccabees 7.37 has Jerusalem priests mourn over the threat and defilement which the Seleucid general, Nicanor, had upon the Temple, and their prayer is clearly reminiscent of Solomon's prayer in 1 Kings 8. Lange and Weigold rightly observe 1 Kgs 8.29-30, 43, where similar

---

121. De Bruyne, *Machabées*, 43.

language concerning the Temple as the dwelling place for God's name appears. However, it is more appropriate to assume that the whole prayer of Solomon is alluded to, which contains the themes of God's name dwelling, prayers of people and the king being offered and heard, and divine supplication and providence. Thus, most commentators pick up various verses within the passage including 1 Kgs 8.29, 30, 38, 59; 9.3, all of which resonate in the Jerusalem priests' mourning in 1 Macc. 7.37.[122] Note that the parallel passage in 2 Chronicles 6 is overlooked by most commentators, but is rightly referenced by Lange and Weigold.

Biblical Sources	1 Maccabees	Grimm	Keil	F. & B.	Oesterley	Abel	Zeitlin	Dancy	Bartlett	Goldstein	Collins	Doran	Rappaport	Tilly
2 Chron. 6.20-21, 33	7.37				+									

See the footnote under 1 Macc. 7.37 (1 Kgs 8.29-30, 43).

Biblical Sources	1 Maccabees	Grimm	Keil	F. & B.	Oesterley	Abel	Zeitlin	Dancy	Bartlett	Goldstein	Collins	Doran	Rappaport	Tilly
2 Kgs 18.17ff. (19.35)	7.41	+	+	+	+	+	+	+	+	+		+		+

1 Maccabees 7.41 has Judas directly referring to the story of divine protection of Jerusalem from Sennacherib's invasion, clearly indicated by the figure of 185,000 casualties from the Assyrian troop (cf. 2 Macc. 8.19; 15.22). Lange and Weigold refer to the incident narrated in 2 Kgs 18.17–19.37 and Isa. 36.2–37.38 with specific verses (2 Kgs 19.35; Isa. 37.36) where the number of Assyrian casualties is mentioned. Note that Lange and Weigold exclude the parallel account in 2 Chron. 32.1-22, presumably due to the Chronicler's omission of the number 185,000. Only

---

122. Cf. Abel, 141, adds that the themes of prayer and demand often go hand in hand in the Hebrew Bible: 1 Kgs 49.54; 2 Chron. 6.29, as well as in the New Testament, Eph. 6.18; Phil. 4.6.

a few commentators add the passage in Isaiah, but the passage should be included in the list in order that the specific reference to the number in those two passages, and not in 2 Chron. 32.1-22, can be highlighted.

Biblical Sources	1 Maccabees	Grimm	Keil	F. & B.	Oesterley	Abel	Zeitlin	Dancy	Bartlett	Goldstein	Collins	Doran	Rappaport	Tilly
Isa. 36.2ff. (37.36)	7.41									+				+

See the footnote under 1 Macc. 7.41 (2 Kgs 18.17–19.37 [19.35]).

Biblical Sources	1 Maccabees	Grimm	Keil	F. & B.	Oesterley	Abel	Zeitlin	Dancy	Bartlett	Goldstein	Collins	Doran	Rappaport	Tilly
Num. 22.3	9.6													

1 Maccabees 9.6 describes Judas' army fearing a great size of Bacchides' army. Lange and Weigold connect this verse with the Moabites' fear of the size of the Israelite army in Num. 22.3. This connection, however, identifies the Hasmonean army with Israel's frightened enemy which, at a glance, seems inconceivable for the pro-Hasmonean writer. Alternatively, however, the author might have meant to exaggerate the fear of Judas' army. Noting that it is the last battle of Judas which he goes on to lose and in which he is weakened[123] and is killed, the biblical imagery of the Moabites' fear might have been used to anticipate the fall of Judas and his army. Commentators are ignorant of any morphological association between 1 Macc. 9.6 and Num. 22.3. Goldstein makes a contrast between 1 Macc. 9.6 and 2 Chron. 20.15 (the battle speech of Jahaziel) and 2 Chron. 32.7 (the battle speech of Hezekiah).[124] Doran and Tilly suggest that the Judeans' fear of the enemy and their reluctance to leave their

---

123. 1 Macc. 9.8 reads 'he became faint', ἐξελύθη contrasting Moses' command in Deut. 20.3, 'do not faint' (Gk. Μὴ ἐκλυέσθω].

124. Goldstein, 374.

camp for battle contrasts the image of Moses' commandment in Deut. 20.1-9.[125] This passage, which concerns instructions for war, may indeed be relevant, but there is no further, decisive clue that the passage was alluded to in Judas' battle in 1 Maccabees 9.

Biblical Sources	1 Maccabees	Grimm	Keil	F. & B.	Oesterley	Abel	Zeitlin	Dancy	Bartlett	Goldstein	Collins	Doran	Rappaport	Tilly
Amos 8.10	9.41				+		+	+						+

1 Maccabees 9.41, 'And the wedding changed to mourning, and the sound of their musicians to lamentation' (καὶ μετεστράφη ὁ γάμος εἰς πένθος καὶ φωνὴ μουσικῶν αὐτῶν θρῆνον): this is a lamentation of the sons of Iambri caused by the Hasmoneans' revenge for their brother, John, who was killed by them (1 Macc. 9.36). Lange and Weigold connect this verse with Amos 8.10 which similarly renders, 'I will turn your feasts into mourning and all your songs into lamentation'. Their morphologies are remarkably similar, although not identical: καὶ μεταστρέψω τὰς ἑορτὰς ὑμῶν εἰς πένθος καὶ πάσας τὰς ᾠδὰς ὑμῶν εἰς θρῆνον.[126] Given that 'the sound of the musicians' in 1 Maccabees is more or less equivalent to 'the songs' in Amos, the only difference is between 'the wedding' in 1 Maccabees and 'the feast' in Amos, which again shares the connotation of a merry time preceding catastrophe. The problem of this connection, however, is the contextual contrast between the two passages; the recipients of misfortune are opposite to each other – Israel's enemy (1 Maccabees) and Israel herself (Amos). An inference can be made that the author of 1 Maccabees is consciously borrowing the Amos prophecy against Israel to describe instead the misfortune falling upon the enemy of the Hasmoneans and the Judeans, as if a reverse fulfilment of the prophecy. This inference may be supported by the fact that 1 Macc. 1.39 also potentially alludes to Amos 8.10, this time describing the misfortune upon the Judeans as a result of their defilement of the covenant (see my comment under the verse). The Hasmoneans' revenge upon their gentile enemies, the sons of Iambri in this case, may highlight the reverse of misfortune: the misfortune

---

125. Doran, 4:110, and Tilly, 194.
126. The Greek rendering is cited for the convenience of comparison, and is correspondent to the Hebrew rendering without change.

of the Judeans is turned into triumph, the triumph of their enemy into misfortune. Quite a few commentators regard 1 Macc. 9.41 as an allusion to Amos 8.10.

Biblical Sources	1 Maccabees	Grimm	Keil	F. & B.	Oesterley	Abel	Zeitlin	Dancy	Bartlett	Goldstein	Collins	Doran	Rappaport	Tilly
Deut. 3.5	9.50													

1 Maccabees 9.50 describes Jonathan's fortification of Judean cities after his victory over Bacchides' army. The expression that he fortified Judean cities 'with high walls, gates and bolts' (ἐν τείχεσιν ὑψηλοῖς καὶ πύλαις καὶ μοχλοῖς) led Lange and Weigold to suggest Deut. 3.5 as the allusion, 'All these were cities fortified with high walls, gates, and bars...' (חומה גבהה דלתים ובריח; τείχη ὑψηλά, πύλαι καὶ μοχλοί), which in fact describes Israel's defeated enemy with the same phrase. It is difficult to see any connection between the two verses other than that the expression is a Hebrew idiom, and commentators likewise make no scriptural connection with 1 Macc. 9.50.[127]

Biblical Sources	1 Maccabees	Grimm	Keil	F. & B.	Oesterley	Abel	Zeitlin	Dancy	Bartlett	Goldstein	Collins	Doran	Rappaport	Tilly
Joel 4.17	10.31													

As part of the letter sent to the Judeans from Demetrius I, 1 Macc. 10.31 states that Jerusalem is to be holy (Ιερουσαλημ ἔστω ἅγια) and exempt from taxes and tithes. Lange and Weigold suggest an allusion to Joel 4.17, where a similar expression, 'Jerusalem city shall be holy' (ἔσται Ιερουσαλημ πόλις ἁγία) can be found. However, there are some complexities in this verse. The verse is part of Demetrius I' letter sent to the Judeans in which he addresses himself with the first person pronoun throughout (10.25-45), and two explanations for the expression arise. First, if the expression was originally from Demetrius, it cannot be an allusion to

---

127. See also the footnote to my comment on 1 Macc. 13.33 (2 Chron. 14.6).

Joel 4.17 (3.17 in English translations), although he could possibly have been aware of Jewish traditions regarding the holiness of the Jerusalem Temple and expressed his respect for it. Second, if the expression was interpolated by the author, we should still distinguish whether it is an allusion to the Joel prophecy or an attestation to the Mosaic law concerning the holiness of God's dwelling place (e.g. Exod. 29–30). Commentators are divided on the originality of the details of the letter, although the existence of the letter has generally been accepted.[128] Grimm notes that the phrase resembles those inscriptions on the coins found in Seleucid cities from the time of Antiochus III, indicating that the cities' sanctuaries received some grants of independence from the Empire.[129] Regardless of Josephus' addition of 'inviolable' to 1 Maccabees' version of the letter, this observation allows the possibility of the authenticity of the phrase. On the other hand, the whole letter is rather freely paraphrased by Josephus,[130] in accordance with his intention of describing Demetrius' grant upon the Judeans on Jewish terms.[131] In all cases, however, 1 Macc. 10.31 lacks any substantial morphological association with Joel 4.17 because the expression 'Jerusalem is to be holy' can be a generic expression, without necessarily referring to the Joel prophecy, and the second clauses are somewhat different from each other.[132] It is not surprising that no commentators suggest an allusion to the Joel prophecy.

---

128. Oesterley, 1:63, questions the originality of some details, including v. 31, saying 'a thing which would have been impossible for the Seleucid king to grant if he was to have any real hold upon this part of his kingdom, a Seleucid garrison in Jerusalem being essential to his overlordship'; also Zeitlin, 47; in contrast, Dancy, 6–7, quoted from 144, claims that Demetrius' grant of the title 'holy' was 'an event of political, not religious, significance…[and] marked one of the stages along the road to the independence of the city'; Goldstein, 408, denotes the title 'holy' as protection of the city from attack in time of peace and some exemption from taxation). Josephus cites the letter as well in his paraphrase of 1 Maccabees, and renders the phrase as Ἱεροσολυμιτῶν πόλιν ἱερὰν καὶ ἄσυλον εἶναι βούλομαι ('the city of Jerusalem shall be sacred and inviolable').

129. Grimm, 155.

130. E.g. Marcus, *Josephus*, 253.

131. E.g. Josephus' paraphrase of 1 Macc. 10.38 adds '…and that it shall be the concern of the high priest that not a single Jew shall have any temple for worship other than that at Jerusalem'.

132. Prohibition of foreigners' access (Joel) compared to exemption of taxes and tithes (1 Maccabees).

Biblical Sources	1 Maccabees	Grimm	Keil	F. & B.	Oesterley	Abel	Zeitlin	Dancy	Bartlett	Goldstein	Collins	Doran	Rappaport	Tilly
Deut. 32.26	12.53	+	+	+										

1 Maccabees 12.53, 'And all the nations around them [the Judeans] sought to annihilate them, for they said, "They have no ruler or helper. Now then, let us do battle with them and *wipe out the memory of them from people* (ἐξάρωμεν ἐξ ἀνθρώπων τὸ μνημόσυνον αὐτῶν)"': Lange and Weigold find a similar idiomatic expression in the final song of Moses in Deuteronomy (Deut. 32.26), 'I will wipe them from human memory' (אשביתה מאנוש זכרם) which almost resembles the wording of the Septuagint, παύσω δὴ ἐξ ἀνθρώπων τὸ μνημόσυνον αὐτῶν. Some commentators point out Deut. 32.26 as a cross-reference,[133] but they also rightly note other references where a similar expression appears, such as Ps. 34.17, 109.15 and Sir. 10.17, although these references have 'from the earth' (מארץ; ἀπὸ γῆς) instead of 'from people'. Concerning the immediate context to which the expression belongs, the object of such extirpation in Deut. 32.26 is Israel, given as a warning against their sin, and any ungodly person in the Psalms and Ben Sira, whereas 1 Maccabees only says that Judea is now left without a leader. However, it is attractive to infer that the use of the Deuteronomic material in this verse might indicate a similar pattern found in Judges, namely that every time a judge fell and Israel had no leader, people did what was evil and provoked God's anger, and the anger was expressed by means of gentile threats upon Israel (Judg. 2.11-23). As we will see in the next chapter, this pattern recurs in the narrative of 1 Maccabees, and is based on, what I will call, the Deuteronomic covenantal framework. Worth noting is 1 Macc. 3.35, where a similar expression is used: ἆραι τὸ μνημόσυνον αὐτῶν ἀπὸ τοῦ τόπου ('to remove the memory of them from the place'). The fact that Jonathan is described explicitly as a judge in 1 Macc. 9.73 may further support such a connection. Therefore, Deut. 32.26, which evokes the imagery of national calamity as a result of Israel's sin, is likely to be alluded to in 1 Macc. 12.53.

---

133. Grimm, 195; Keil, 210; Fairweather and Black, 225; cf. Oesterley, 1:113, only points out Sir. 10.17.

Biblical Sources	1 Maccabees	Grimm	Keil	F. & B.	Oesterley	Abel	Zeitlin	Dancy	Bartlett	Goldstein	Collins	Doran	Rappaport	Tilly
2 Chron. 14.6	13.33													

1 Maccabees 13.33 has Simon fortify Judean cities with high towers, walls, gates and bolts, as well as supplying them with food. Lange and Weigold's reference to 2 Chron. 14.6 shows no morphological connection other than it describes a similar act of fortification of Judah under King Asa. No commentator refers to 2 Chron. 14.6,[134] but a few of them rightly comment on the repeated pattern of fortification under the Hasmoneans in 1 Macc. 9.50, 52; 11.66; 12.35, 38; 14.33-34.[135]

Biblical Sources	1 Maccabees	Grimm	Keil	F. & B.	Oesterley	Abel	Zeitlin	Dancy	Bartlett	Goldstein	Collins	Doran	Rappaport	Tilly
Exod. 34.24	14.6				+				+		+		+	

1 Maccabees 14.6, 8, 9, 12 are all part of Simon's eulogy, discussion of which is reserved for the second part of this chapter. Here, it is sufficient to say that Lange and Weigold's identification of biblical references in these verses is plausible, and they are all noted by most commentators. The issue, however, is whether they are the only candidates for scriptural allusion. Many commentators rightly note multiple biblical references in each of these verses, and I will contend that there are several cases in this regard in 1 Maccabees, and that they suggest thematic association.

---

134. Cf. Abel, 241–2, points out Deut. 3.5 for the fortification and 2 Chron. 11.11 for the food supply; see my footnote under 1 Macc. 9.50 (Deut. 3.5).

135. Dancy, 175; Bartlett[2], 1591; Rappaport, 730; Tilly, 268.

Biblical Sources	1 Maccabees	Grimm	Keil	F. & B.	Oesterley	Abel	Zeitlin	Dancy	Bartlett	Goldstein	Collins	Doran	Rappaport	Tilly
Zech. 8.12	14.8				+	+				+	+	+		+

See my comment under 1 Macc. 14.6 (Exod. 34.24).

Biblical Sources	1 Maccabees	Grimm	Keil	F. & B.	Oesterley	Abel	Zeitlin	Dancy	Bartlett	Goldstein	Collins	Doran	Rappaport	Tilly
Zech. 8.4-5	14.9	+	+	+	+	+		+	+	+	+	+		+

See my comment under 1 Macc. 14.6 (Exod. 34.24).

Biblical Sources	1 Maccabees	Grimm	Keil	F. & B.	Oesterley	Abel	Zeitlin	Dancy	Bartlett	Goldstein	Collins	Doran	Rappaport	Tilly
Mic. 4.4	14.12	+	+	+	+	+	+		+	+	+	+		+

See the footnote under 1 Macc. 14.6.

Biblical Sources	1 Maccabees	Grimm	Keil	F. & B.	Oesterley	Abel	Zeitlin	Dancy	Bartlett	Goldstein	Collins	Doran	Rappaport	Tilly
Zech. 1.7	16.14	+	+	+	+	+								

1 Maccabees 16.14 begins the incident of Simon's murder, in which it says 'the 177th year in *the eleventh month; this is the month Sabat*'. Lange and Weigold refer to Zech. 1.7, '24th day of *the eleventh month, which is the month of the Sabat*', referring to the time Zechariah received words from God. There is little possibility that the author of 1 Maccabees had any intention of referring to Zech. 1.7 since their contexts are markedly irrelevant to each other, and their morphological similarity seems to be

almost purely coincidental. On the other hand, it is only in Zech. 1.7 that the eleventh month is explained as the month of the Sabat, and this singularity of Zech. 1.7 is noted by most commentators (although none of them suggests any sense of allusion intended by the author). It may be possible that the author, who is evidentially well versed in Scripture, knew this phrase from Zechariah by heart, and used it without consciousness, or that he inserted the phrase in order that the general literary style of his work resembled Scripture. These inferences lack supporting evidence, and we should conclude that the use of Zech. 1.7 is generally for stylistic reasons.

3.3. Results

3.3.1. Features of philological parallels

The analysis of the philological parallels between 1 Maccabees and biblical literature generates the following results for discussion. First, the relationship between 1 Maccabees – the posterior text – and those identified scriptural sources – the anterior texts – can be categorized in three ways: (1) a majority of cases show that use of Scripture is intended to import certain aspects of the anterior text into the posterior text so that, for example, expressions, themes, characters, or events of the anterior text either become analogous with those of the posterior text, or are seen as being fulfilled in the development of the narrative plot in the posterior text. Examples include the Antiochan regime in Judea, the Judean domestic political affairs, and the background and process of the establishment of the Hasmonean institution. Utilization of Scripture helps the author not only to venerate national heroes, but also to support his pro-Hasmonean rhetoric. (2) There are occasionally cases where the philological parallel can only be suggested as a Hebrew idiom. 1 Maccabees 3.58, 'Gird yourselves, and become strong sons', for example, can be found in multiple texts such as 2 Sam. 2.7, 13.28 and 1QM 15.7, to name three. However, the contexts in which the expression appears vary and are unrelated to each other. One can only conclude that the expression is idiomatic without any intention of importing the meaning within the context(s) of the anterior text(s). These idiomatic cases are in fact many,[136] and show evidence of 1 Maccabees' Hebraism. (3) Some cases lack necessary clues to determine whether the author is using any particular scriptural materials. Where a specific anterior text can be identified, the intention still seems unclear. For instance, 1 Macc. 14.6 explains 'the eleventh month' as 'the month of the Sabat'. The same phrase is found only in Zech. 1.7,

---

136. See §2.1.

and yet, 'the month of the Sabat' in this case refers to the time when the prophet received words from God. On the contrary, 1 Maccabees has it as the time when Simon was murdered. One can only infer that the biblical phrase is here not more than being stylistic.

Second, the first five chapters of 1 Maccabees contain more scriptural references and allusions than later chapters of the text, as per Lange and Weigold. In the meantime, this corresponds to the events of calamities in Judea, the outbreak of the Hasmonean revolt, and to the early- and middle-stages of Judas' leadership career, marked by battle preparations, speeches, victories and Temple rededication. A recurrent pattern of using Scripture in these chapters is both direct and indirect allusion to Mosaic materials, creating a strong imagery of Torah-abiding Hasmoneans with the implication that one's success depends on their faithfulness to the covenant with God.

The list of biblical references produced by Lange and Weigold, however, requires revision in light to the analysis above. Several of the references included in their list are not eligible as scriptural allusions. Moreover, we will continue to see in the next chapter that several important cases are omitted from their list. Integrated into our list, these cases help understand the functionality of Scripture in 1 Maccabees.

3.3.2. *Classification of the parallels*

There are several studies available concerning classification of the types of scriptural references and allusions appearing in 1 Maccabees,[137] but two studies in particular – Lange and Weigold's, and Devorah Dimant's[138] –

---

137. Studying the use of Scripture has become an area of prominence in biblical studies in recent decades, and has enabled multiple propositions on classification, some of which are either schematic and facile or more sophisticated and various than the one adopted in the present study. Examples include: Michael A. Fishbane's seminal study, *Biblical Interpretation in Ancient Israel* (Oxford: Clarendon, 1985), a summary of which can be found, among multiple essays, in Fishbane, 'Types of Biblical Intertextuality', in *Congress Volume: Oslo 1998*, ed. A. Lemaire and M. Sæbø, VTSup 80 (Leiden: Brill, 2000), 39–44. Here, Fishbane defines four categories of exegesis: scribal, legal, haggadic and mantological. Alternatively, see Sommer, *Isaiah 40–66*, in which Sommer comes up with various categories of the ways Isaiah uses different biblical texts such as the Pentateuch, prophetic writings, and so forth. Both of these studies offer useful tools, but their tools are less suitable for studying 1 Maccabees. For critique of Fishbane's categorization, see James L. Kugel, review of *Biblical Interpretation*, by Michael Fishbane, *Prooftexts* 7 (1987): 269–305.

138. Lange and Weigold, *Quotations and Allusions*, 23–9; Dimant, 'Mikra', 379–419.

are especially relevant to the present discussion. The following is a critical adaptation of these two studies.

To start with, our analysis of the philological parallels, based on Lange and Weigold's study, can be summarized into seven types of appearance of scriptural pretexts:

1. An expression from Scripture is clearly quoted with a formulaic term (and it appears only once, in 7.16-17, quoting an abbreviated version of Ps. 79.2-3, and is explicitly marked by a quotation formula, κατὰ τὸν λόγον ὃν ἔγραψεν αὐτόν).
2. With a formulaic term such as κατὰ τὸν νόμον, Mosaic materials are clearly alluded to in the actions of the Hasmoneans on legal, ritual and military issues, thus implying fulfilment of the law. However, despite the referential nature of the term which makes the reference to specific Mosaic materials explicit, this type is to be differentiated from an actual explicit quotation.
3. Characters and events from Scripture are explicitly mentioned, to the extent that the whole story about the character or a particular story is referred to.
4. An extensive phrase from biblical prophetic material is quoted, but there is no quotation formula nor any other indication that the expression is actually borrowed from Scripture.
5. A linguistic parallel between the posterior and anterior texts can be made, but without any explicit indication or quotation formula.
6. A linguistic parallel between one posterior text and several anterior texts can be made.
7. Despite a morphological parallel with some biblical materials, the phrase is nothing more than an idiomatic Hebrew expression.

Both Lange/Weigold and Dimant generally agree on what they call 'explicit quotation' (EQ) and 'implicit quotation' (IQ). They agree that 'explicit quotation' is marked primarily by a quotation formula followed by an actual quotation of at least two or three words.[139] 1 Maccabees contains a single case of explicit quotation in this regard, that is, the first of the seven types above. For 'implicit quotation', these scholars more or less agree that a parallel of three (Dimant) or four (Lange/Weigold) words is present between the posterior and anterior texts, but that there is a lack of any quotation formula. The fourth of the seven types can be regarded as implicit quotation.

---

139. Lange and Weigold, *Quotations and Allusions*, 27; Dimant, 'Mikra', 385.

On the third and fifth types of using Scripture in 1 Maccabees, Dimant's classification is more relevant than that of Lange and Weigold. As well as EQ, Dimant includes in 'explicit use of Mikra' what she calls 'explicit mention of persons and circumstances' (EMPC).[140] These are different from what Lange and Weigold call 'explicit allusion' (EA), which generally contain a linguistic parallel of two to three words without any clear morphological identification, but which contain a quotation formula or a special term.[141] The EA is more suitable for the second of the seven types above, in which κατὰ τὸν νόμον functions as a special term to identify a specific scriptural source, and the posterior text contains an action carried out in acknowledgement of that material. The EMPCs are, on the one hand, as explicit as an 'explicit allusion' in that a biblical character and their deed, or a related event, is clearly referenced and thus isolates a specific biblical passage (e.g. David and Jonathan, son of Saul, in 1 Macc. 4.30 unmistakably referring to 1 Sam. 17.1-58 and 1 Sam. 14.1-23). On the other hand, EMPCs do not require a quotation formula or a special term, and are not allusions. The third of seven types above will be labelled as EMPC.

'Allusion' is a difficult term, and our analysis further requires a fairly precise definition. Lange and Weigold define 'implicit allusion' (IM) as a linguistic parallel just like EA, but which lacks any quotation formula.[142] Dimant, in addition to this, observes that some allusions appear in inversion of the motifs in the anterior text, or in small terms and phrases borrowed from a running text.[143] In light of the analysis above, we should add cases in which one posterior text contains a phrase or term in parallel with multiple anterior texts. These cases, represented in the fifth and sixth of the seven types, will be called 'implicit allusion', but with a slightly different definition to that of Lange and Weigold.

Idiomatic expressions, as in the seventh type in our list, can be considered as part of IQ or IA due to their morphologically identifiable character. However, our list will distinguish them from the rest and is labelled as 'Idiom', mainly because in this type, use of Scripture is not intended to point to a specific text but only the expression.

---

140. Dimant, 'Mikra', 391–9.
141. Lange and Weigold, *Quotations and Allusions*, 26.
142. Lange and Weigold, *Quotations and Allusions*, 26. On the other hand, they define 'explicit allusion' as a linguistic parallel with an inclusion of a quotation formula or a special term. However, such a type cannot be an allusion.
143. For examples, see Dimant, 'Mikra', 409–17.

3.3.3. Result: a revised list of philological parallels

Below is a revised list of Lange and Weigold's philological parallels between 1 Maccabees and biblical literature. References in bold are additions to their list, and references deemed to be irrelevant are excluded.[144] The mark '+++' indicates multiple references of three and more.

3.3.3.1. Order of 1 Maccabees

Biblical Sources	1 Maccabees	Type	Grimm	Keil	F. & B.	Oesterley	Abel	Zeitlin	Dancy	Bartlett	Goldstein	Collins	Doran	Rappaport	Tilly
2 Kgs 17.17	1.15	IA									+				
Amos 8.10	1.39	IQ	+	+	+	+	+			+	+		+		+
Lam. 5.15-18	1.39	IA									+	+			
Lev. 11.43	1.48	IA		+	+		+	+			+		+		+
Lev. 20.25	1.48	IA		+	+		+				+		+		+
Dan. 9.27	1.54	IA	+	+	+		+	+	+		+	+	+		+
Dan. 11.31	1.54	IA	+	+	+	+	+	+	+	+	+	+	+	+	+
Dan. 12.11	1.54	IA	+	+	+	+	+		+	+	+				+
Lam. 2.11, 21	2.9	IA				+			+	+					+
Num. 25.6-15	2.24, 26	EA	+	+	+	+	+	+	+	+	+	+	+	+	+
Exod. 34.13-14 +++	2.25-26	EA		+				+							+
Gen. 22.1-19	2.52a	EMPC	+	+	+	+	+	+	+	+	+	+	+	+	+
Gen. 15.6	2.52b	EMPC	+	+	+	+	+			+	+		+		+
Gen. 39.7-12	2.53a	EMPC	+		+	+		+			+		+		+
Gen. 41.39-45	2.53b	EMPC											+		+
Num. 25.11-13	2.54	EMPC	+	+	+	+	+	+	+	+	+		+		
Num. 27.16-23	2.55a	EMPC	+	+	+		+		+				+		+
Josh. 1.2-10	2.55a	EMPC	+		+								+		+
Josh. 24.25	2.55b	EMPC											+		

---

144. The excluded references are Jer. 49.26 and 50.30 (1 Macc. 2.9); Num. 32.12 (1 Macc. 2.55); Lev. 14.40, 45 (1 Macc. 4.43); Deut. 2.26-30 (1 Macc. 5.48); Joel 4.17 (1 Macc. 10.31); 2 Chron. 14.6 (1 Macc. 13.33); cf. 1 Kgs 8.29-30 and 2 Chron. 6.20-21, 33 (1 Macc. 7.37) are replaced with the entire chapters to which they belong.

Biblical Sources	1 Maccabees	Type	Grimm	Keil	F. & B.	Oesterley	Abel	Zeitlin	Dancy	Bartlett	Goldstein	Collins	Doran	Rappaport	Tilly
Num. 13.30; 14.6-9	2.56a	EMPC	+	+	+	+	+		+	+	+		+		+
Num. 14.24, 30	2.56b	EMPC	+	+	+	+	+		+	+	+		+		+
Josh. 14.15-16	2.56b	EMPC	+	+	+	+					+		+		+
2 Sam. 7.1-17	2.57b	EMPC	+	+	+	+	+	+	+	+	+		+		+
1 Kgs 19.10, 14	2.58a	EMPC				+	+				+		+		+
2 Kgs 2.1, 11	2.58b	EMPC	+	+		+	+			+	+		+		+
Dan. 3.1-30	2.59	EMPC	+	+	+	+		+		+	+		+		+
Dan. 1.6-7	2.59	EMPC	+	+	+	+		+					+		+
Dan. 6.17-24	2.60	EMPC	+	+	+	+	+			+	+		+		+
Ps. 146.4	2.63	IQ	+	+	+	+	+				+		+		+
1 Sam. 7.5-6	3.46	IA	+	+	+	+	+	+	+	+	+	+	+	+	+
Num. 6.13	3.49	IA	+	+	+		+		+	+	+		+		+
Num. 10.8-9 +++	3.54	IA	+	+	+	+	+			+	+		+	+	+
Exod. 18.21, 25	3.55	IA	+	+	+		+		+		+		+	+	+
Deut. 1.13, 15	3.55	IA	+	+			+			+		+	+	+	+
Deut. 20.5-8	3.56	EA	+	+	+		+	+		+	+	+	+	+	+
2 Sam. 2.7	3.58	Idiom	+	+	+	+	+						+		
Exod. 34.2	3.58	Idiom	+	+	+	+	+								
Deut. 20.2-4	3.58	Idiom									+		+		
Deut. 7.18–19	4.8-9	IA													
Exod. 14.5-31	4.8-9	EMPC	+	+	+		+			+	+				+
Ps. 118.1, 29 +++	4.24	IQ	+	+	+	+	+		+	+				+	+
1 Sam. 14.23, 45 +++	4.25	IA					+			+	+		+		+
1 Sam. 17.1-58	4.30	EMPC	+	+	+	+	+	+		+	+	+	+	+	+
1 Sam. 14.1-23	4.30	EMPC	+	+	+	+	+			+	+	+	+	+	+

3. *Philological Parallels*

Biblical Sources	1 Maccabees	Type	Grimm	Keil	F. & B.	Oesterley	Abel	Zeitlin	Dancy	Bartlett	Goldstein	Collins	Doran	Rappaport	Tilly
Num. 10.8-9 +++	4.40	IA		+	+	+	+	+		+	+		+		
2 Kgs 23.6	4.43	IA				+		+							+
2 Chron. 29.16	4.43	IA				+		+							+
Exod. 20.25	4.47	EA	+	+	+	+	+	+	+	+	+	+	+		+
Deut. 27.5-6	4.47	EA	+	+	+	+	+	+		+	+		+		+
Josh. 8.31	4.47	IA	+			+						+			
Exod. 40.4-5	4.49	IA													
Exod. 30.8	4.50	IA													
Exod. 25.30	4.51	IA													
Exod. 26.33	4.51	IA									+				
Exod. 29.38-42	4.53	IA		+	+						+		+		+
Num. 28.3-7	4.53	IA		+											+
2 Chron. 7.9 +++	4.56	IA				+		+					+		
Joel 4.4	5.15	IA													
1 Sam. 5.12	5.31	IA				+				+		+			+
Num. 10.8-9 +++	5.33	IA									+				
Num. 20.14-20	5.48	IA	+	+		+	+			+		+	+	+	
Num. 21.21-23	5.48	IA	+	+	+	+	+		+	+		+	+		+
1 Kgs 22.27	5.54	Idiom		+											
2 Chron. 18.26	5.54	Idiom		+											
Exod. 34.13 +++	5.68	IA													+
Deut. 7.5 +++	5.68	IA											+		+
Ps. 79.2-3	7.17	EQ	+	+	+	+	+	+	+	+	+	+	+	+
1 Kgs 8.1-66	7.37	IA	+	+	+	+	+		+	+	+		+		+
2 Chron. 6.1-42	7.37	IA					+								

Biblical Sources	1 Maccabees	Type	Grimm	Keil	F. & B.	Oesterley	Abel	Zeitlin	Dancy	Bartlett	Goldstein	Collins	Doran	Rappaport	Tilly
2 Kgs 18.17ff. (19.35)	7.41	EMPC	+	+	+	+	+	+	+	+	+		+		+
Isa. 36.2ff. (37.36)	7.41	EMPC									+				+
Num. 22.3	9.6	IA													
Amos 8.10	9.41	IQ				+			+	+					+
Deut. 3.5	9.50	Idiom													
Deut. 32.26	12.53	IA	+	+	+										
Deut. 3.5	13.33	Idiom					+								
Exod. 34.24	14.6	IQ					+				+		+		+
Zech. 8.12	14.8	IQ			+	+					+	+	+		+
Zech. 8.4-5	14.9	IQ	+	+	+	+	+		+	+	+	+	+		+
Mic. 4.4	14.12	IQ	+	+	+	+	+	+		+	+	+	+		+
Zech. 1.7	16.14	IA	+	+	+	+	+								

3.3.3.2. Order of the Hebrew Bible

Biblical Sources	1 Maccabees	Type	Grimm	Keil	F. & B.	Oesterley	Abel	Zeitlin	Dancy	Bartlett	Goldstein	Collins	Doran	Rappaport	Tilly
Gen. 15.6	2.52b	EMPC	+	+	+	+	+			+	+		+		+
Gen. 22.1-19	2.52a	EMPC	+	+	+	+	+	+	+	+	+	+	+	+	+
Gen. 39.7-12	2.53a	EMPC	+		+	+		+			+		+		+
Gen. 41.39-45	2.53b	EMPC											+		+
Exod. 14.5-31	4.8-9	EMPC	+	+	+		+			+	+				+
Exod. 18.21, 25	3.55	IA	+	+	+		+		+		+		+	+	+
Exod. 20.25	4.47	EA	+	+	+	+	+	+	+	+	+	+			+
Exod. 25.30	4.51	IA													
Exod. 26.33	4.51	IA							+						

3. *Philological Parallels* 153

Biblical Sources	1 Maccabees	Type	Grimm	Keil	F. & B.	Oesterley	Abel	Zeitlin	Dancy	Bartlett	Goldstein	Collins	Doran	Rappaport	Tilly
Exod. 29.38-42	4.53	IA		+	+						+		+		+
Exod. 30.8	4.50	IA													
Exod. 34.2	3.58	Idiom	+	+	+	+	+								
Exod. 34.13-14 +++	2.25-26	EA			+				+						+
Exod. 34.13 +++	5.68	IA													+
Exod. 34.24	14.6	IQ					+				+		+		+
Exod. 40.4-5	4.49	IA													
Lev. 11.43	1.48	IA		+	+		+	+			+		+		+
Lev. 20.25	1.48	IA		+	+		+				+		+		+
Num. 6.13	3.49	IA	+	+	+		+		+	+	+		+		+
Num. 10.8-9 +++	3.54	IA	+	+	+	+	+			+	+		+	+	+
Num. 10.8-9 +++	4.40	IA		+	+	+	+	+		+	+		+		
Num. 10.8-9 +++	5.33	IA									+				
Num. 13.30; 14.6-9	2.56a	EMPC	+	+	+	+	+		+	+	+		+		+
Num. 14.24, 30	2.56b	EMPC	+	+	+	+	+		+	+	+		+		+
Num. 20.14-20	5.48	IA	+	+		+	+				+		+	+	+
Num. 21.21-23	5.48	IA	+	+	+	+	+		+	+		+	+		+
Num. 22.3	9.6	IA													
Num. 25.6-15	2.24, 26	EA	+	+	+	+	+	+	+	+	+	+	+	+	+
Num. 25.11-13	2.54	EMPC	+	+	+	+	+	+	+	+	+		+		
Num. 27.16-23	2.55a	EMPC	+	+	+		+		+				+		+
Num. 28.3-7	4.53	IA		+											+
Deut. 1.13, 15	3.55	IA	+	+			+			+		+	+	+	+
Deut. 3.5	9.50	Idiom													
Deut. 3.5	13.33	Idiom					+								

Biblical Sources	1 Maccabees	Type	Grimm	Keil	F. & B.	Oesterley	Abel	Zeitlin	Dancy	Bartlett	Goldstein	Collins	Doran	Rappaport	Tilly
Deut. 7.5 +++	5.68	IA											+		+
Deut. 7.18-19	4.8-9	IA													
Deut. 20.2-4	3.58	Idiom								+			+		
Deut. 20.5-8	3.56	EA	+	+	+		+	+		+	+	+	+	+	+
Deut. 27.5-6	4.47	EA	+	+	+	+	+	+		+	+		+		+
Deut. 32.26	12.53	IA	+	+	+										
Josh. 1.2-10	2.55a	EMPC	+		+								+		+
Josh. 8.31	4.47	IA	+				+					+			
Josh. 14.15-16	2.56b	EMPC	+	+	+	+					+		+		+
Josh. 24.25	2.55b	EMPC											+		
1 Sam. 5.12	5.31	IA					+				+		+		+
1 Sam. 7.5-6	3.46	IA	+	+	+	+	+	+	+	+	+	+	+	+	+
1 Sam. 14.1-23	4.30	EMPC	+	+	+	+	+	+		+	+	+	+	+	+
1 Sam. 14.23, 45 +++	4.25	IA					+			+	+		+		+
1 Sam. 17.1-58	4.30	EMPC	+	+	+	+	+	+		+	+	+	+	+	+
2 Sam. 2.7	3.58	Idiom	+	+	+	+	+				+				
2 Sam. 7.1-17	2.57b	EMPC	+	+	+	+	+	+	+	+	+		+		+
1 Kgs 8.1-66	7.37	IA	+	+	+	+	+		+	+	+		+		+
1 Kgs 19.10, 14	2.58a	EMPC				+	+				+		+		+
1 Kgs 22.27	5.54	Idiom		+											
2 Kgs 2.1, 11	2.58b	EMPC	+	+		+	+			+	+		+		+
2 Kgs 17.17	1.15	IA									+				
2 Kgs 18.17ff. (19.35)	7.41	EMPC	+	+	+	+	+	+	+	+	+		+		+
2 Kgs 23.6	4.43	IA					+		+						+
Isa 36.2ff. (37.36)	7.41	EMPC									+				+
Joel 4.4	5.15	IA													
Amos 8.10	1.39	IQ	+	+	+	+	+			+	+		+		+

3. Philological Parallels

Biblical Sources	1 Maccabees	Type	Grimm	Keil	F. & B.	Oesterley	Abel	Zeitlin	Dancy	Bartlett	Goldstein	Collins	Doran	Rappaport	Tilly
Amos 8.10	9.41	IQ					+		+	+					+
Mic. 4.4	14.12	IQ	+	+	+	+	+	+		+	+	+	+		+
Zech. 1.7	16.14	IA	+	+	+	+	+								
Zech. 8.4-5	14.9	IQ	+	+	+	+	+		+	+	+	+	+		+
Zech. 8.12	14.8	IQ				+	+				+	+	+		+
Ps. 79.2-3	7.17	EQ	+	+	+	+	+	+	+	+	+	+	+	+	+
Ps. 118.1, 29 +++	4.24	IQ	+	+	+	+	+		+	+				+	+
Ps. 146.4	2.63	IQ	+	+	+	+	+				+		+		+
Lam. 2.11, 21	2.9	IA					+			+	+				+
Lam. 5.15-18	1.39	IA									+		+		
Dan. 1.6-7	2.59	EMPC	+	+	+	+		+					+		+
Dan. 3.1-30	2.59	EMPC	+	+	+	+		+		+	+		+		+
Dan. 6.17-24	2.60	EMPC	+	+	+	+	+			+	+		+		+
Dan. 9.27	1.54	IA	+	+	+		+	+	+		+	+	+		+
Dan. 11.31	1.54	IA	+	+	+	+	+	+	+	+	+	+	+	+	+
Dan. 12.11	1.54	IA	+	+	+	+	+		+	+	+	+			+
2 Chron. 6.1-42	7.37	IA					+								
2 Chron. 7.9 +++	4.56	IA					+		+					+	
2 Chron. 18.26	5.54	Idiom		+											
2 Chron. 29.16	4.43	IA					+		+						+

Chapter 4

THE USE OF SCRIPTURE IN 1 MACCABEES: CONCEPTUAL PARALLELS

The previous chapter discussed the use of Scripture in 1 Maccabees on a morphological ground, i.e. the appearance of at least a couple of words constructed in the same way as they appear in biblical texts. However, I have also emphasized, in the form of critical comment on Lange and Weigold's methodology, that thematic resemblance between the anterior and posterior texts should also be appreciated in order to grasp a fuller understanding about the use of Scripture in 1 Maccabees. In this chapter, therefore, I will explore scriptural themes, particularly with regards to Deuteronomy and Judges. These themes have been chosen for the following reason. Scholars have already paid attention to resonance of the ideologies of the two books (see below for details). However, in Deuteronomy's case, the focus was heavily on the Mosaic law and how this theme shaped 1 Maccabees' ideology. I, on the other hand, will propose the paramount importance of the Deuteronomic theme of the covenant between Israel and God for understanding 1 Maccabees' thematic use of Scripture. As for the use of Judges, scholars who recognize a special role of Judges in 1 Maccabees make surprisingly brief notes without in-depth discussion. By discussing these two themes, I will further elaborate the ways in which use of Scripture contributes to the shaping of the role of the Hasmoneans in 1 Maccabees.

4.1. *The Deuteronomic covenantal framework*

The book of Deuteronomy lays a legacy that perpetuates not only throughout biblical literature, most notably the Former and the Latter Prophets,[1] but also Jewish literature contemporary to the Hasmonean

---

1. The scope of scholarly discussion on the topic of 'covenant' in the field of the Hebrew Bible (or the Old Testament) has been immense in the past two centuries,

era, such as Jubilees, the Testament of Moses, and 2 Maccabees.[2] To this list one can add 1 Maccabees by showing that the text has multiple points in contact with the Deuteronomic legacy, namely that in view of the causality of Israel's history, Israel's fortune and misfortune are seen as a covenantal blessing and curse, consequences of either the Jews' defilement of the covenant or their faithfulness to it. This theme of Israel's covenant with YHWH in this way functions as a framework to reflect, interpret and predict the course of history. In this section, we will show this by discussing Deuteronomy 28–30, where Israel's fortune and misfortune is most delineated. We will observe how 1 Maccabees imitates the same pattern found there for the course of history.

4.1.1. *Deuteronomy*

As a point of departure, Deuteronomy sets out teachings on Israel's covenant with YHWH, emphasizing the centrality of the covenantal fidelity and the fatal consequences of infidelity. The author identifies

---

and will not be repeated in the present study. See a survey of OT scholarship on the topic, as well as a renewal of the emphasis on the importance of the topic in biblical studies, in Ernest W. Nicholson, *God and His People: Covenant and Theology in the Old Testament*, repr. (Oxford: Clarendon, 2002). Nicholson's thesis is that 'covenant' was not functioning to unite diverse tribes in the land, but to provide an ideal model for the people of God with a presupposition of 'Israel' as a unity of the tribes. The interest in the topic is strangely marginal within the field of Second Temple Jewish studies, although there is an important exception: Stanley E. Porter and Jacqueline C. R. de Roo, eds., *The Concept of the Covenant in the Second Temple Period*, JSJSup 71 (Leiden: Brill, 2003). This edited volume discusses the development of the concept of 'covenant' in Second Temple Judaism.

2. Nickelsburg, *Jewish Literature*, 77–83. On Jub. 1, Nickelsburg notes 'unmistakable echoes' of Deut. 28 (78). Concerning the passage on the eschatological addition in 23.16-32, he rightly notes the Deuteronomic covenantal framework as an interpreting tool for the past, present and future of Israel: Defilement (vv. 16-21; 'Sin' in Nickelsburg's term); Curse (vv. 22-25; 'Punishment'); Repentance (v. 26; 'Turning Point'); Blessing (vv. 27-31; 'Salvation'). Verse 32, the closing verse, is reminiscent of Deut. 31.19 as well as the whole of chs. 28–32. Likewise, the Testament of Moses contains a narrative pattern that resembles this Deuteronomic covenantal cycle: D (ch. 2); C (3.1-4); R (3.5–4.4); B (4.5-9); D (5.1-6); C (ch. 8); R (ch. 9); B (ch. 10). On 2 Maccabees, see also Nickelsburg Jr., '1 & 2 Maccabees – Same Story, Different Meaning', *CTM* 42 (1971): 515–26 (521–2). For a similar emphasis on the covenantal relationship between God and Israel as the dominant theme, see Susan Docherty, *The Jewish Pseudepigrapha: An Introduction to the Literature of the Second Temple Period* (London: SPCK, 2014), 19–23 (on Jubilees); 111–14 (on the Testament of Moses).

apostasy as Israel's primary sin in retrospect of the Babylonian exile,[3] and throughout the book he reminds the reader of the legacy of Israel's covenantal relationship with YHWH, namely the covenant between God and the Patriarchs, the Sinai covenant between Israel and God which was a continuation of the same covenant (4.10-14; 5.2-4), and their renewed covenant in Moab (29.1, 9-15).[4]

The teaching on the covenant is climaxed in chs. 28–30, where Israel's requirement of upholding the covenant with her God is reinforced by the exposition of two polarized outcomes: blessing and curse.[5] The section comprises the following units: a description of blessing (28.1-14); a description of curse (28.15-68); the covenant previously made at Horeb now renewed in Moab (hence, the Moabite covenant, 29.2-15); the return of blessing (30.1-10); and a conclusive remark (30.11-20). What is notable in this whole section is a tendency to systematize the course of Israel's history as corresponding to the relationship between the covenant-bound

---

3. Anthony Philips, *Deuteronomy*, CBC (Cambridge: Cambridge University Press, 1973), 8–9.

4. Edward J. Woods, *Deuteronomy*, TOTC 5 (Downers Grove, IL: Inter Varsity Press, 2011), 59, 60.

5. Timothy H. Lim, 'Deuteronomy in the Judaism of the Second Temple Period', in *Deuteronomy in the New Testament: The New Testament and the Scriptures of Israel*, ed. Maarten J. J. Menken and Steve Moyise, LNTS 358 (London: T&T Clark, 2007), 6–26. Lim stresses that most Hebrew manuscripts found at Qumran are fragmentary (with an exception of the so-called proto-MT text in 4QDeut^c [4Q30] which contains over 120 verses encompassing 19 chapters of Deuteronomy). Also, the Masoretic Text exists in multiple versions, which complicates the Judeo-Christian reception history of Deuteronomy. These textual concerns, however, should not deter our approach to the passage, namely that the detailed blessing and curse are part of one package associated with covenantal obligation. Ever since the pioneering work of George E. Mendenhall ('Covenant Forms in Israelite Tradition', *BA* 17 [1954]: 50–76), it has long been recognized that Deuteronomy resembles the so-called treaty language that was already prevalent in the ancient Near East. The pattern in chs. 28–30, where blessing and curse are juxtaposed, is typical of the treaty documents of the ancient Near East (e.g. the Law Code of Hammurabi, Hittite treaties). On the similarities between Deuteronomy and the ancient Near East, see, for instance, S. J. McCarthy, *Treaty and Covenant*, 2nd edn, AB 21b (Rome: Pontifical Biblical Institute, 1981); Gordon J. Wenham, 'The Structure and Date of Deuteronomy' (PhD diss., University of London, 1969). Nevertheless, following G. von Rad's *Deuteronomy* (OTL [London: SCM, 1966]), these writers affirm that the overall linguistic style of Deuteronomy is generally seen as a typical farewell speech. A helpful overview of scholarship on this topic is offered by Woods, *Deuteronomy*, 41–7.

people and her covenantal God. Israel's faithfulness to the covenant will bring about safety and security in the community, as well as prosperity of its population, agricultural production and abundance of the livestock. The scope of blessing will also be extended to Israel's gain of international renown and defeat of enemies. Their defilement of the covenant, however, will precipitate contrasting effects: devastation of the society and deprivation of the population, its agricultural production and its livestock through natural disasters and foreign attacks. The passage also gives a lengthy description of the process of exile and dispersion of the people from their land, bringing international shame (28.45-68). The promise of blessing is then reiterated in ch. 30, after a renewal of the covenant between every member of Israel's community under Moses' lead. The opening verses read:

> ¹ And when all these things come upon you, the blessing and the curse, which I have set before you, and you call them to mind among all the nations where the Lord your God has driven you, ² and return to the Lord your God, you and your children, and obey his voice in all that command you today, with all your heart and with all your soul... (Deut. 30.1-2)

The blessing in this case is restoration of the cursed state of Israel, the society, its production and the livestock, reverting to the previous blessed condition. Highlighted in this restoration is Israel's repentance which precedes the restoration process, with expressions such as 'you call them to mind' and 'return to the Lord your God'. It is through repentance that the former blessing will return.[6] In this way, Israel's blessed state journeys through a cycle of four events: defilement, curse, repentance, and returning to blessing. I will call this cycle 'the covenantal DCRB'. In the following we will see that this Deuteronomic covenantal framework, in which curse is precipitated by defilement, or blessing brought by repentance, runs throughout the following history of Israel and continues to shape the history of the Hasmonean revolt.

---

6. Woods, *Deuteronomy*, 190–1, helpfully summarizes three different approach to the interpretation of Deut. 30: (1) the promise of covenantal blessing in reversal of curse is based on YHWH's circumcision, i.e. 30.6; (2) the promise is based on Israel's repentance; (3) both YHWH's grace and Israel's repentance should be balanced as a pre-condition for the blessing. Thus, P. C. Craigie, *The Book of Deuteronomy*, NICOT (Grand Rapids: Eerdmans, 1976), 361, in advocating the first approach, translates 30.2 as 'then you shall return to your senses among all the nations to which the Lord your God banished you'.

4.1.2. *1 Maccabees*

In view of the Deuteronomic covenantal legacy in Jewish literature, Nickelsburg rightly points out that such a connection is also found in 2 Maccabees.[7] However, he does not observe the same Deuteronomic connection in 1 Maccabees (as alluded to in his title, '1 & 2 Maccabees: Same Story, Different Meaning'). To a certain extent, this difference may be legitimate since in 2 Maccabees Nickelsburg rightly points out a clear narrative division: 'Two prefixed letters – the epitomizer's prologue – *Blessing – Sin – Punishment – Turning Point – Judgment and Salvation –* the epitomizer's epilogue'.[8] 1 Maccabees, on the other hand, has its narrative more explicitly divided by the story of each Hasmonean leader: 'The calamities in Judea – *Rise of Mattathias – Judas – Jonathan – Simon – the succession of John Hyrcanus as an epilogue*'. However, I will propose in this section that 1 Maccabees also carefully follows the Deuteronomic covenantal legacy in its depiction of second-century Jewish history[9] by examining how the Deuteronomic concept of 'covenant', 'making a covenant', or 'breaching it' is imbedded in 1 Maccabees through its particular use of the word διαθήκη. The narrative development of the book, in which the Deuteronomic covenantal framework plays a central role, will also be examined.

4.1.2.1. Διαθήκη *as a connotation of Israel's covenant with YHWH*

The term διαθήκη goes back to the original author's use of ברית, and the Greek translator places eight out of ten references to διαθήκη[10] within chs. 1–2 which set the scene of the narrative, namely the pro-Seleucid Jerusalem authorities' implementation of Hellenistic customs in Judea,

---

7. Nickelsburg, 'Same Story', 521.
8. Nickelsburg, 'Same Story', 522.
9. Francis Borchardt has rightly offered a helpful observation on 1 Maccabees' citation of Deuteronomy and the occurrences of the Deuteronomic phraseology in 'Deuteronomic Legacy in 1 Maccabees', 297–320. For citation of Deuteronomy, Borchardt includes: Deut. 20.5-8 in 1 Macc. 3.56; Deut. 27.5-6 in 1 Macc. 4.47; and Deut. 13.7-12 in 1 Macc. 2.24. For the Deuteronomic phraseology, he includes (1) idolatry (e.g. 1 Macc. 1.43, 47, 54; 6.7); (2) covenant and election of Israel (e.g. 1 Macc. 2.22, 53; 7.37); and (3) observance of the law (e.g. 1 Macc 1.56; 3.48). Likewise, Brent Nongbri argues that 'the covenant of the fathers' was the Hasmoneans' justifying motive, placing them in competition with other Jewish groups like the Qumran sect, who made the same claim. See Nongbri, 'The Motivations of the Maccabees and the Judean Rhetoric of Ancestral Tradition', in Bakhos, ed., *Ancient Judaism*, 85–111 (especially, 87, 105, 109–11, 110 n. 84).
10. None of the ten references to διαθήκη has any textual variance for the word.

the Antiochan persecution, and the beginning of the Hasmonean revolt. I have discussed earlier the careful rendering of a Hebraic form of Greek vocabulary in 1 Maccabees, evident from the transliteration and the preservations of Hebrew idioms and word order.[11] Here, again, the translator carefully selects the term διαθήκη to resonate with the Deuteronomic concept of covenant, namely the centrality of its role in determining Israel's destiny.[12] Consider the first set of references:

1.11 In those days out of Israel came sons, transgressors of the law, and persuaded many, saying, 'Let us go and make a *covenant* (διαθήκη) with the nations around us, because from the time we separated ourselves from them many evils have found us'.

1.15 and they fashioned foreskins for themselves and apostatized from the holy *covenant* (διαθήκη) and joined themselves to the nations and sold themselves to do evil…

1.57 and wherever there was found in someone's possession a book of *the covenant* (διαθήκη), or if someone was conforming to the law, the judgement of the king put them to death…

1.63 and they preferred to die so as not to be contaminated by food and not to defile the holy *covenant* (διαθήκη), and they died.

11. See §2.1.
12. Surprisingly, most commentators and scholars of 1 Maccabees do not discuss the significantly consistent use of the word διαθήκη and the role it takes in the narrative. I have only come across two scholars: Lester L. Grabbe, 'Did All Jews Think Alike? "Covenant" in Philo and Josephus in the Context of Second Temple Judaic Religion', in Porter and de Roo, eds., *Concept of the Covenant*, 251–66, and Dongshin Don Chang, *Phinehas, The Sons of Zadok, and Melchizedek: Priestly Covenant in Late Second Temple Texts*, LSTS 90 (London: T&T Clark, 2016), 24–44. Grabbe rightly observes, though briefly, the particular way in which διαθήκη is used in 1 Maccabees, that is, 'almost always used of the covenant with God' (206). He also offers a brief survey on the use of the word 'covenant' in a wide range of Second Temple Jewish literature. Recently, Chang offered a structural analysis on the term διαθήκη in 1 Maccabees, rightly arguing, in my judgement, the author's deliberate employment of the covenant concept for his pro-Hasmonean agendas. In particular, he proposes a close relation between the covenantal terminology and the legitimation of the Hasmonean high priesthood. One may pose the questions of whether the use of διαθήκη in 1 Maccabees is restricted to the concept of priestly covenant, or whether it should more broadly be regarded as a symbol of the divine covenant within the Jewish tradition. I am inclined to choose the latter option, and consider the legitimation of high priesthood as a part.

The pro-Seleucid Judeans' exhortation in the first reference is itself an ironic echo of the emphatic phrase in Deuteronomy 13 (repeated three times in vv. 2, 6 and 13); what was solemnly prohibited and illegal, as far as the covenantal relationship between Israel and God is concerned, is in fact being committed publicly by Jerusalem authorities.[13] With the erection of a Greek gymnasium in Jerusalem and the spread of Greek practices, Judeans hid the mark of circumcision, thereby deserting the covenant (note the adjective ἅγιος, 'holy', to describe the covenant with God). Antiochan persecution was then initiated in Jerusalem and extended to other Judean regions, suppressing anything that/anyone who sustained the Jewish covenantal tradition by extinguishing 'the book of covenant' and massacring anyone upholding διαθήκη. Thus, the Judeans' covenant with God was abandoned by the Judeans themselves, the result of which was national catastrophe. This series of scenes holds deep theological implication, and the Deuteronomic idea of Israel's covenant with God in particular.

The second set of references occurs in ch. 2:

2.20   ...both I and my sons and my brothers will walk in *the covenant* (διαθήκη) of our fathers...

2.27   And Mattathias cried out in the city with a loud voice, saying, 'Let everyone who is zealous in the law and is upholding *the covenant* (διαθήκη) follow me'.

2.50   Now, children, be zealous in the law, and give your lives for *the covenant* (διαθήκη) of our fathers...

2.54   Phinehas our father, by becoming zealous with zeal, received *a covenant* (διαθήκη) of everlasting priesthood.

Shifting the scene, ch. 2 introduces the birth of the Maccabean revolt in which Mattathias, a leading priest in a Judean village called Modein, stands up against the Seleucid king's command to paganize the Jewish cult in his village by exclaiming words as cited in 2.20 (above). The emphasis on 'the covenant of our fathers' suggests that the motivation for the revolt is essentially associated with the tradition of Israel's covenant with YHWH. Note that Mattathias' speech ends with the following words: 'we will not obey the words of the king nor deviate from our religion to the right or to

---

13. Abel (*Maccabées*, 6) suggests Deut. 7.2 as an allusion. Doran ('Maccabees', 4:32) also acknowledges the resonance of Deut. 13 in the term διαθήκη in 1 Macc. 1.11 and 1.15. Cf. Fairweather and Black, *Maccabees*, 58–9, who view the act of the renegades in v. 11 as a defilement of the commandment in Exod. 23.32.

the left' (2.22). Doran rightly identifies the words as Deuteronomic (Deut. 5.32-33).[14] Likewise, Mattathias' hortatory speech to Jewish fellows in 2.27 (above) again reiterates διαθήκη as the reason for fight. Furthermore, on his deathbed, Mattathias gives a blessing to his sons in which he sets out his legacy (2.50, above). The main point of the legacy is again preservation of the covenant with God, emphatically restating the term διαθήκη.[15] In Mattathias' list of biblical heroes, Phinehas is said to receive a covenant (διαθήκη) of everlasting priesthood. This case, although exceptionally addressing an individual's covenant with God, nevertheless broadly falls under the same category since Phinehas' zeal and action should be seen as motivated by Israel's covenantal requirements.

There are two more occurrences. In the early stage of Judas' career as leader, he prepares for a battle against Gorgias, who came with a large army, by delivering a speech to his men by saying:

> And now let us cry out to heaven, if he will desire us and will remember *the covenant* (διαθήκη) of our fathers and will smash this company in front of us today. And all the nations will know that there is one who redeems and saves Israel. (4.10-11)

14. Doran, 'Maccabees', 4:44; also, Tilly (*Makkabäer*, 96), who adds Deut. 17.10-11 and Jub. 23.16. See Moshe Weinfeld, *Deuteronomy and the Deuteronomic School*, repr. (Oxford: Clarendon, 1983). Weinfeld provides an important reference tool in an appendix (320–65), in which the term 'to turn right or left', along with other similar terms (e.g. 'to turn aside from the way', 'to turn away from Yahweh'), is a typical Deuteronomic phrase (339–40). In fact, several phrases I discuss in relation to the Deuteronomic covenantal framework in the present chapter are found in Weinfeld's list of Deuteronomic phraseology. See also Borchardt ('Deuteronomic Legacy', 297–320) who has already provided a handful of Deuteronomic phrases in 1 Maccabees.

15. Compare Bartlett (*Books of the Maccabees*, 42), who places emphasis on 'the law' rather than 'the covenant'; '*the law* in particular is constantly referred to throughout the speech' (his italic). This statement seems difficult to appreciate. The opening statement of Mattathias addresses 'the law and the covenant' (using νόμος and διαθήκη) in v. 50, and the mention of νόμος within the ancestral list occurs only once in the description of Elijah in v. 58 ('in his zeal for the law', ἐν τῷ ζηλῶσαι ζῆλον νόμου). Joseph's case, where it reads, 'Joseph...observed commandments' (ἐφύλαξεν ἐντολήν), is ambiguous due to the use of ἐντόλη. Νόμος may have been translated from תורה, and ἐντόλη from מצוה. The original Hebrew author's consistent use of תורה in both occasions (vv. 53, 58), as well as v. 50, is possible, but the chances are small because the Greek translator generally shows consistency in his translation of important terms. That is not to overlook the prominence of 'the law' in 1 Maccabees in general, but to emphasize the importance of the covenantal relationship between Israel and their God in the legacy of Mattathias to his children.

Despite being replaced with a personal pronoun, Judas makes it clear that it is the covenantal God who would fight for them, and it is their covenantal commitment by which the Jewish soldiers are bound to offer their lives willingly. Διαθήκη is again combined with 'fathers', just as in 2.20 and 2.50, and consistently resonates with the covenant ideology as the motivation for fight. The last occurrence, which is remotely located from the others, appears in 11.9, and is perhaps considered as exceptional due to its context of international treaty:

> And he sent ambassadors to Demetrius the king, saying, 'Come, let us conclude *a covenant* (διαθήκη) between ourselves, and I will give you my daughter, whom Alexander has, and you will rule over the kingdom of your father...'

Here, the term refers to a political treaty that Ptolemy made with Demetrius II in his scheme to hold Alexander in check. The rationale behind this irregular choice is unclear. Nevertheless, the other nine occurrences of διαθήκη still cumulatively and uniformly resonate with the context of Israel's covenantal relationship with God. This is especially outstanding since on multiple other occasions, where treaties and friendships are made between nations, it is never διαθήκη but always another term that is used: συμμαχία, συνθήκη, φίλια, ἵστημι, συντρίθημι.[16] Notably, there are several occasions relating to the Judeans' treaties with nearby nations,[17] but they are considered as a part of military strategy, crucially without affecting the Jewish ways of life, such as covenantal obligation or observance of the law, and no single occurrence of διαθήκη is found.[18]

In short, the author cumulatively employs the term διαθήκη as a specific reference to the Jewish ancestral covenant (or, in the case of 1.11, an antithetical, defiling act of Israel). The term is purposely used consistently in the depiction of the course of events relating to the pro-Seleucid Judeans' political acts, their implementation of Greek customs and the catastrophic repercussions in Judea, as well as the rise of the Hasmonean family and their motives. In the next section, we shall see that the narrative as a whole is shaped by the Deuteronomic covenantal framework, thus imitating historical books in the Bible.

---

16. 1 Macc. 8.1, 7, 17, 20, 29; 9.70; 10.54; 12.1; 14.18, 24.
17. 1 Macc. 8.26, 28; 10.26; 11.33; 13.38; 15.27.
18. Instead, terms such as ἵστημι and συνθήκη are used on these occasions.

4.1.2.2. *Covenantal framework as a narrative pattern*

We have seen that Deuteronomy 28–30 frames the course of Israel's history in accordance with the covenantal DCRB pattern which subsequently recurs in historical and prophetic writings of biblical literature, as well as Jewish literature around the Hasmonean era. In 1 Maccabees, basically the same pattern governs the narrative development even though the arrangement of the covenantal DCRB does not seem obvious. I will present some observations on the cycle of the covenantal DCRB in the text.

1. Defilement: in the beginning of the narrative, after a brief history of the Greek Empire, the author has those pro-Seleucid Judeans directly imitate the claim, 'let us make a covenant with gentiles around us…' (1.11), which appears identically in Deuteronomy 13, and which is solemnly prohibited in the context, by repeating the prohibition three times (vv. 2, 6, 13).[19] The agreement between the pro-Seleucid Judeans and Antiochus IV Epiphanes leads to the building of a gymnasium and engaging in associated activities, and in consequence, denouncing the Jewish tradition of circumcision (1.12-15). The passage ends with the author's comment that such an incident was an act of apostasy of the holy covenant: '[the pro-Seleucid Judeans] removed the marks of circumcision, and *apostatized from the holy covenant* and joined themselves to the nations and *sold themselves to do evil*' (1.15), using the Deuteronomic phraseology discussed above.[20]

---

19. According to Weinfeld (*Deuteronomic School*, 320), this phrase is a typical Deuteronomy phrase. For the full list of Deuteronomic phraseology in Deuteronomy and the rest of the Hebrew Bible, see his appendix (320–65). Surprisingly, not many commentators heed scriptural allusion in this verse. Only Doran makes this connection; see 'Maccabees', 4:32. Cf. Abel (*Maccabées*, 6) connects 1 Macc. 1.11 with Deut. 7.2. The commandment of 'not making a covenant with the inhabitants of the land' in Deut. 7.2 is, on the whole, the same as Deut. 13, but the use of the actual phrase of Deut. 13 makes the latter a stronger candidate for a scriptural source. See also Rappaport, who suggests the phrase 'let us go…found us' as a 'manifesto' of the pro-Seleucid party in Jerusalem; see 'Maccabees', 713.

20. According to Weinfeld's survey of Deuteronomic phraseology: התמכר לעשות הרע, 'to sell oneself to do evil' (1 Kgs 21.20, 25; 2 Kgs 17.17; cf. Deut. 28.68). 'Apostatizing from the holy covenant', literally, 'withdrawing from the holy covenant' (ἀπέστησαν ἀπὸ διαθήκης ἁγίας) is not immediately found in the Hebrew Bible. Ἀφίστημι is usually rendered as סור, and is often associated with apostasy: 'to turn away' (e.g. Deut. 11.16; 1 Sam. 12.21); 'to turn aside from the way' (e.g. Deut.

2. Curse: the rest of ch. 1 painstakingly details the catastrophes that fell upon Jerusalem and the entire Judean regions.[21]
3. Repentance: the rise of the Hasmonean family changes the direction of the narrative development. Mattathias appears in the scene and delivers a lengthy lamentation over the devastation of the land, captivity of the people and defilement of the sacred places (2.7-13). Especially emphasized in his lament is the removal of the glory of the Jerusalem Temple, the sacred centre of the Jewish cults and the symbol of the dwelling of their covenantal God. His family then gather together, tear their clothes, put on sackcloth, and intensely mourn (2.14).[22] Upon the visit of the Seleucid king's agent to his village to command paganization of their local Jewish altar and the local Judeans' compromise, Mattathias rises in fury, kills the Jewish renegade and the Seleucid agent, and organizes a rebel group; the revolt begins. As mentioned previously, Mattathias' slogan is notable, repetitively using the term διαθήκη which deliberately anchors the rebel movement in the context of preserving the ancient covenant (2.20, 27, 50). In other words, Mattathias' reaction to the threat of covenantal defilement, such as his lamentation, killing of the two individuals (which is fulfilment of Deuteronomic obligation), and organizing a group to uphold the covenantal values, is a form of repentance and return to the covenant, perhaps in fulfilment of Deuteronomy 13.

9.12, 16; 11.28; 31.29; Judg. 2.17; 1 Kgs 22.43); 'to turn away from YHWH' (e.g. 1 Sam. 12.20; 2 Kgs 18.6). Apostatizing from Διαθήκη (ἁγίας) may be found in the form of לעבור ברית (e.g. Deut. 17.2; Josh. 23.16; Judg. 2.20; 2 Kgs 18.12; 'transgressing the covenant', and usually rendered in Greek using παραβαίνω for עבר). It might be that the original author of 1 Maccabees rendered either 'turned away from the holy covenant' (replacing YHWH with 'the holy covenant' as replacing/silencing terms for 'God' is customary in 1 Maccabees), or 'transgressed the holy covenant', which is a typical Deuteronomic phrase and which the Greek translator may have rendered with ἀφίστημι supplied by ἀπὸ rather than rendering παραβαίνω.

21. The catastrophes in Judea are described particularly using Deuteronomic phraseology as Borchardt already observed through Weinfeld's list of Deuteronomic phraseology, see Borchardt, 'Deuteronomic Legacy', 297–320.

22. This act may be seen as a non-specific term, rather generally describing an act of mourning (e.g. Jacob's act as a response to the report of Joseph's death in Gen. 37.34; David's act in response to Abner's death in 2 Sam. 3.31). Within the Deuteronomic covenantal framework, DCRB, Mattathias' act has a strong echo of Deut. 30.1, i.e. 'returning to God'.

4. Blessing: the Hasmoneans' zeal for the covenant is then rewarded through the initial victories of the Hasmoneans and their early-stage supporters, such as the Hasidim. This Hasmonean triumph is then amplified throughout the rest of the narrative by recovery of their traditional ritual system, victory of wars, and fortification of Judean territories. The outcomes of the revolt mark the culmination of the Deuteronomic promise of covenantal blessing.

4.1.3. *Summary*

The author of 1 Maccabees ingrains the Deuteronomic covenantal motif in his account of the Hasmonean revolt. The pro-Seleucid Judeans' treaty with Antiochus IV Epiphanes and their implementation of Hellenistic customs at the cost of their ancestral covenant with God, along with the Antiochan persecution and the aftermaths in Judea, the rise of Mattathias' family, and their triumphs over the gentile overload, are all shaped and inter-connected by the Deuteronomic theme most clearly found in Deuteronomy 28–30. These historical events in Judea are thus comprehended in theological terms. The mis/fortune of the Judeans is depicted as solely dependent upon their attitude to the ancestral covenant. The pro-Hasmonean perspective is thus part and parcel of the Deuteronomic tradition, particularly emphasizing the covenantal fidelity of the Hasmonean party.

4.2. *Biblical judges*

Similarities between the Hasmoneans in 1 Maccabees and the biblical judges have already been suggested by several scholars.[23] This suggestion, just like the view of kingship, provides an important clue to the intended role of the Hasmoneans in the book. In this section, I will propose that unlike the theme of Hasmonean kingship in replacement of Davidic kingship, the connection between the biblical judges of Judges and the Hasmoneans in 1 Maccabees can be demonstrated. This conceptual parallel is found in three ways: morphological parallels, a parallel of the narrative pattern, and a parallel of leadership models.[24]

---

23. See §1.2 for more details.

24. Concerning the text of Judges, I will consider the last form of Judges as the same one available by the time of 1 Maccabees' composition. Scholars often claim that the Masoretic Text of Judges is 'generally pure' in that it is best among other books within the Former Prophets. See J. Alberto Soggin, *Judges*, trans. John Bowden, 2nd edn, OTL (London: SCM, 1981), 12–13; E. J. Revell, 'Masoretic Text', *ABD* 4:597–9 (598). On its Greek text, there are some complexities arising from the

4.2.1. *Morphological association*

The first kind of association between 1 Maccabees and Judges can be made on morphological grounds. We will consider three cases. First, 1 Maccabees describes the land of Judea as 'being quiet' or 'resting', the expression uniquely echoing the same imagery in Judges. The phrase occurs as many as three times in 1 Maccabees:

7.50   And *the land of Judah became quiet for a few days* (ἡσύχασεν ἡ γῆ Ιουδα ἡμέρας ὀλίγας).

9.57   And Bacchides saw that Alcimus had died, and he returned to the king, and *the land of Judah was quiet for two years* (ἡσύχασεν ἡ γῆ Ιουδα ἔτη δύο).

14.4   And *the land became quiet all the days of Simon...* (ἡσύχασεν ἡ γῆ πάσας τὰς ἡμέρας Σίμωνος...).[25]

---

marked differences among textual variant groups. As a result, Rahlfs' edition of the Septuagint contains two versions of Judges[Gk], named Text A and B. Text A follows Codex Alexandrinus and represents the recension of Origen (O) and Lucian (L), and Text B follows Codex Vaticanus. I follow an increasing majority of scholars discarding the idea that these two markedly different textual traditions represent two independent translations. I will regard these textual traditions as the evidence of, using Soggin's term, 'successive revisions of the same text' (Soggin, *Judges*, 13). This view is notably proposed by J. Soisalon-Soininen, *Die Textformen der Septuaginta-Übersetzungen* (Helsinki: Suomalainen Tiedeakatemia, 1951), 31–3, 102–5; see also Jellicoe, *Septuagint*, 280–3; B. Lindars, 'Some Septuagint Readings in Judges', *JTS* 22 (1971): 1–14; cf. M. K. H. Peters suggests multiple translations, see Peters, 'Septuagint', *ABD* 5:1093–1104 (1100). A few Hebrew fragments of Judges survived and were found at Qumran, and F. M. Cross suggested that they might provide 'the better Septuagint tradition', a claim critiqued by R. G. Boling, *Judges: Introduction, Translation and Commentary*, AB (New York: Doubleday, 1975), 40–1.

25. Abel (*Maccabées*, 144) rightly identifies these three references in 1 Maccabees and associates them with Judges. Also, see Fairweather and Black, *Maccabees*, 156. Doran ('Maccabees', 4:101) rightly notes 'a formula known well from Judges', but ignorantly, in my opinion, adds 11.38, 52, in which a similar phrase is used, but is describing gentile kings' reigns which leads to their coveting of self-reputation. See below in the present section. Note Goldstein (*1 Maccabees*, 393–4), who surprisingly identifies 9.57 only (in which the phrase in question is attributed to Jonathan) as bearing resemblance to Judges and completely ignores the other two references, 7.50 and 14.4, which are conspicuously identical to 9.57. One may infer that this inconsistency reflects Goldstein's overall thesis that the pro-Hasmonean author, or 'the Hasmonean propagandist' in his term, depicts the Hasmonean institution as

Recurrent in these three verses is the formulaic term 'ἡσυχάζω + ἡ γῆ + (Ιουδα)[26] + duration', whose Hebrew form was probably 'duration + ארץ + שקט'. The peaceful states of the Judean land under the Hasmoneans are the result of notable victories of the family over the Seleucids in the first two references: Judas' defeat of Nicanor and Jonathan's first victory in his leadership career. The third reference is even more notable in that the duration of the peace in the land is extended to 'all the days' of Simon's rule. All three major Hasmonean leaders in the narrative are attributed with this particular term. Interesting is a similar phrase, ἡσύχασεν ἡ γῆ ἐνώπιον αὐτοῦ, 'the land was quiet before him', attributed to antagonistic Hellenistic kings: Alexander the Great in 1.3, and Demetrius I in 11.38 and 11.52. The peaceful states of their lands inspire them to covet self-aggrandization, providing a vividly contrasting function of the temporal phrase.[27] In sum, the phrase in question is deliberately designed to characterize the Hasmoneans in 1 Maccabees.

In biblical literature, it is singularly in Judges that the same phrase functions to describe the achievements of the judges. The phrase 'duration + ותשקט + הארץ' notably occurs after the acts of Othniel (Judg. 3.11), Ehud (3.30), Deborah (5.31b), and Gideon (8.28). The basic term שקט + ארץ is not so unique,[28] and the thematically relevant passages are numerous in biblical literature.[29] There is even a similar phrase, 'duration + שקטה הארץ', in 2 Chron. 14.1 (Heb. 13.23). However, the frequency of the phrase's occurrence in Judges cannot be overlooked. The combination of the feminine singular, *waw*-consecutive, *qal* verb with 'the land' and

---

a legitimate replacement of Davidic dynasty rather than biblical judges. It is only concerning Jonathan, who is explicitly identified as a judge (9.73; see below for details), that Goldstein admits an association with Judges. This may explain his identification of 9.57 with Judges.

26. Ιουδα in 14.4 is omitted by Kappler, contrary to Rahlfs. Many significant manuscripts –Sinaiticus and Venetus, the minuscule 55, as well as La^L, La^x and the Vulgate – include it, and Kappler is probably following Codex Alexandrinus on this occasion. Kappler's decision is probably based on the inference that because 7.50 and 9.57b both include the word without textual variants, those key manuscripts' inclusion of the word in 14.4 should be seen as a later attempt to smooth out inconsistency.

27. 1 Macc. 1.3, '...and he [Alexander the Great] was exalted and his heart was uplifted'; 11.38, '...and no one opposed him [Demetrius I] and he dismissed all his forces...'; 11.52, 'but he [Demetrius I] falsified everything he had said and became alienated from Jonathan...'

28. Josh. 11.23, ארץ שקטה; Josh. 14.15, והארץ שקטה.

29. E.g. Judg. 18.7; 2 Kgs 11.20; Isa. 14.7; Jer. 30.10; 46.27; Ezek. 38.11; Zech. 1.11; 1 Chron. 4.40; 2 Chron. 14.6 (Heb. 14.5); Ps. 76.9.

with duration occurs four times. Similarly, the same combination recurs three times in 1 Maccabees. In both books, the phrase is attributed to the main narrative characters.[30]

Second, in 1 Macc. 5.62, one finds a famous sentence that is often considered as chief evidence of the author's pro-Hasmonean attitude.[31] The Jerusalem priests Joseph and Azariah, jealous of the Hasmoneans' fame, attempted to lead the battle which Judas prohibited, but failed, resulting in a great loss of Judean soldiers, followed by the author's comment:

> 'But they [Joseph and Azariah] were not from the seed of those men [the Hasmonean family] to whom salvation of Israel is given by their hand' (1 Macc. 5.62; αυτοὶ δὲ οὐκ ἦσαν ἐκ τοῦ σπέρματος τῶν ἀνδρῶν ἐκείνων, οἷς ἐδόθη σωτηρία Ισραηλ διὰ χειρὸς αὐτῶν).

The combination 'δίδωμι + σωτηρία + Ισραηλ + διὰ χειρὸς + of a person' was often associated, especially by the proponents of the Hasmonean kingship propaganda,[32] with 2 Sam. 3.18 in which Abner claims:

> ...the Lord has promised David, saying, 'By the hand of my servant David I will save my people Israel (ביד דוד עבדי הושיע את־עמי ישראל; in the Septuagint, ἐν χειρὶ τοῦ δούλου μου Δαυιδ σώσω τὸν Ισραηλ) from the hand of the Philistines, and from the hand of all their enemies'.

There is a difference between the verb σῴζω in 2 Samuel and the noun σωτηρία in 1 Maccabees, of which Goldstein argues that the noun form is 'an instance of the Hasmonean propagandist's habitual avoidance of speaking directly of God', and that the writer deliberately echoed the verse in 2 Samuel.[33] In this way, Goldstein believes 5.62 is supporting evidence that the author of 1 Maccabees is legitimizing the replaced kingship of Judea under the Hasmoneans.

However, the association with 2 Samuel seems less strong than with that of Judges where the phrase appears in two passages:

---

30. Himmelfarb ('He Was Renowned', 81), noting 1 Macc. 14.4 with Judg. 3.30 and 5.31.

31. Surprisingly, many major commentators of 1 Maccabees ignore any scriptural connection with 1 Macc. 5.62 (Abel, Bartlett, Fairweather and Black, who otherwise provide biblical materials as potential sources on several occasions). Alternatively, Doran ('Maccabees', 4.81) mentions that the phrase 'not of the seed of...' is found in Num. 16.40.

32. E.g. Goldstein, 'Messianic Promises', 80, 93–4 nn. 61–2; *1 Maccabees*, 305.

33. Goldstein, 'Messianic Promises', 80.

³⁶ Then Gideon said to God, '*If you will save Israel by my hand*, as you have said, ³⁷ behold, I am laying a fleece of wool on the threshing floor. If there is dew on the fleece alone, and it is dry on all the ground, then I shall know that *you will save Israel by my hand*, as you have said.' (Judg. 6.36-37)

And he [Samson] was very thirsty, and he called upon the Lord and said, '*You have granted this great salvation by the hand of your servant*, and shall I now die of thirst and fall into the hands of the uncircumcised?' (Judg. 15.18)

Here, the phrase which contains essentially the same components, 'save + Israel + by hand of someone', is twice attributed to the judges. In fact, the phrase, with some variations, occurs in multiple passages within Judges.³⁴

Third, in 1 Macc. 9.73 the author describes Jonathan as a judge:

Thus the sword ceased from Israel. Jonathan settled in Michmash and *began to judge the people* (ἤρξατο Ιωναθαν κρίνειν τὸν λαὸν); and he destroyed the godless out of Israel.

The explicit mention of 'judging the people' and its echo of biblical judges is already noted by many scholars.³⁵ The word κρίνω occurs in two other occasions, but is irrelevant to this context.³⁶ The phrases 'to judge the people' or 'to judge Israel' occur numerously in the Hebrew Bible by using either שפט or דין as the verb. Their subjects can be as diverse as kings, priests, God, or other figures.³⁷ However, the prevailing occurrences of a phrase which contains 'a person + to judge + a mass of people' are notably found, occurring eleven times, in Judges.³⁸

The underlining feature in the three presented cases is that the correspondent anterior texts in Judges are significantly recurrent within the

---

34. Judg. 2.16, 18; 3.9-10; 6.14; 13.5; see also 3.15; 10.1 for a shorter version, 'a person + save + people (of Israel)'.

35. Pfeiffer, *History*, 493; Bartlett, *Books of the Maccabees*, 127; Klaus-Dietrich Schunck, *I. Makkabäerbuch*, JSHRZ (Gütersloh: Gerd Mohn, 1980), 338; Rappaport, 'The Use of the Bible', 176; van Henten, 'The Hasmonean Period', 21. In contrast, see Goldstein, 'Messianic Promises', 78. Goldstein backs up his view (i.e. Hasmonean kingship propaganda) by commenting that the author nevertheless does not echo similar expressions in Isaiah concerning the coming of Judges, '…I will set up your Judges as at the former time…' (Isa. 1.26). This could be the case on thematic grounds but is difficult to prove.

36. In 1 Macc. 7.42 Judas prayed that God judge Nicanor according to his wickedness; in 11.33 the Romans write to the Judeans saying that they judged (or decided) to make friendship with the latter and support them.

37. E.g. Gen. 49.16; Exod. 18.13; 1 Sam. 4.18; 1 Kgs 3.28; 2 Chron. 19.8.

38. Judg. 3.10, 30; 4.4; 10.2, 3; 12.7, 8, 11, 13; 15.20; 16.31.

book with the expressions 'the land became quiet...', 'to save Israel by the hand of someone...', and 'to judge the people/Israel', appearing there several times, unlike other biblical books where they are found infrequently. Crucially, the fact that these expressions are predominantly attributed to judges, rather than David or Davidic dynasty, has implications for the dispute about the Hasmoneans' role in 1 Maccabees. Our argument against the Hasmonean kingship propaganda has been cumulative in that there is no explicit evidence for a monarchical role of the family in the book, that those references suggested by the proponents of the view are unconvincing, and that the family's role seems to be primarily associated with biblical judges, the point which we will continue to see in this section.

4.2.2. *Narrative development*

We have already suggested that 1 Maccabees' narrative plot is developed through the covenantal DCRB: the defilement of the covenant committed by pro-Seleucid Jerusalem authorities and their implementation of Greek customs (1.11-15), the ensuing national catastrophes upon the Judeans (1.16-64), the lament and rise of Mattathias and his five sons (ch. 2), and their gradual triumphs over the Seleucids (chs. 3–16). What recurs within these last fourteen chapters is the return of gentile threat and national crisis upon the Judeans. I have remarked in the previous section that this pattern essentially fits the promise of covenantal blessing in Deuteronomy, and will add here that there are sub-cycles of crisis-resolution within the progressive Hasmonean triumphs. Thus, when Judas faced death in battle, the previous horror flared up again in Judea, of which the author comments: 'And it happened after the death of Judas, the lawless came forth in all the regions of Israel, and all those who worked injustice arose... And Bacchides selected the impious men and established them as masters of the country... And there was a great affliction in Israel such as had not been since the day that a prophet was not seen among them' (1 Macc. 9.23-27). In this passage, defilement of the covenant of God is reintroduced through the rise of 'the lawless...who worked injustice' (v. 23). There was famine (v. 24) and gentile oppression (v. 25). This passage is followed by the succession of Jonathan. Jonathan's death, too, is followed by the rise of lawless men in Judea, and neighbouring gentile nations who threaten the Judean nation: 'And all the nations around them sought to annihilate them, for they said, "They have no ruler or helper. Now then, let us do battle with them and wipe out the memory of them from people"' (12.53). Simon's death, likewise, was followed by Ptolemy, his son-in-law reigning in Jerusalem, and his pro-Seleucid attitude and coveting of leadership in Judea suggest a looming national crisis. Thus, the sub-cycles of crisis-resolution in 1 Maccabees essentially share the rise of a heroic leader and resolution to the national vulnerability to gentile invasion and violation of the covenant and the law.[39]

Judges plainly sets out the narrative pattern in ch. 2. It reads:

> [11] And the people of Israel did what was evil in the sight of the Lord and served the Baals. [12] And they abandoned the Lord, the God of their fathers, who had brought them out of the land of Egypt... [14] So the anger of the Lord was kindled against Israel, and he gave them over to plunderers, who plundered them... [15] ...And they were in terrible distress... Then the Lord raised up judges, who saved them out of the hand of those who plundered them... [18] *Whenever the Lord raised up judges for them, the Lord was with the judge, and he saved them from the hand of their enemies all the days of the judge...* [19] *But whenever the judge died, they turned back and were more corrupt than their fathers, going after other gods, serving them and bowing down to them...* (Judg. 2.11-20)

On the grounds of the conspicuously Deuteronomic covenantal framework,[40] the passage summarizes the motif of the narrative of Judges. Israel defiled their covenant with YHWH by following gentile customs in the land,[41] and a curse fell upon them.[42] Heroic judges arose among the people and delivered the people from crisis.[43] Whenever judges died, the people returned to apostasy and calamities were repeated. In other

---

39. Collins (*Maccabees*, 233) rightly makes a connection between the narrative of 1 Maccabees and that of Judges by saying, '1 Maccabees wishes to evoke the recurring crises of the book of Judges'. Likewise, Doran ('Maccabees', 4:16–17) draws a connection between the two books under the concept of destroying the entire city in war.

40. Soggin (*Judges*, 40) refers to 2.6–3.6 as 'abundant [with] terms and expressions typical of the Dtr history'. For instance, the phrase 'serving other Baal/other gods' in vv. 11, 13, 19 is a formula characteristic of the Deuteronomist and the Deuteronomist History (39). Similarly, see Barnabas Lindars, *Judges 1–5: A New Translation and Commentary* (Edinburgh: T. & T. Clark, 1995), 102. See more on the formula in Weinfeld, *Deuteronomic School*, 320–65.

41. E.g. Judg. 2.3, 11-15; 3.7-8, 12.

42. E.g. Judg. 2.3, 14-15; 3.8, 12; 4.2; 6.2-6; 10.7-9; 13.1.

43. E.g. Judg. 2.16, 18; 3.9-11, 15-30; 6.14; 10.1; 13.5. Soggin (*Judges*, 43–4) rightly observes in the whole section, 2.6–3.6, that the pattern, Israel's sin–divine judgement–Israel's penitence–calling of the judge-saviour, appears 'throughout the book and already seems to be clearly outlined here'. Also, Boling (*Judges*, 74) comments on 2.11-23 that '[t]his segment of the introduction describes a pattern of apostasy, hardship, moaning, and rescue, a pattern to be illustrated for various segments of Israel in the stories which follow...'

words, the Israelite community's fortune depended upon the rise of a judge. Note the pattern: doing what is evil (following gentile customs), terrible distress in Israel (gentile invasion and oppression), rise of judges and deliverance of Israel, judges' death/absence and the previous distress rekindled. This narrative pattern is precisely one that governs 1 Maccabees, as observed above, and the structure of Judges is composed in the same manner.

Special attention is to be paid on the roles of the Hasmoneans and judges. In the honorary decree which Simon received from the Romans, the motive of the Hasmoneans heroic deeds is described as follows:

> ...when many times wars came about in the country...Simon...and his brothers put themselves in danger and stood up against the opponents of their nation so that their holy places and the law could endure, and they glorified their nation with great glory. (1 Macc. 14.29)

The public recognition of the Hasmonean family was based on their willingness to volunteer to fight for the nation and preserve the Jewish tradition. This attribute of the Hasmoneans is readily found throughout the narrative. For instance, in his aspiring speech to the people who have just lost Jonathan, Simon reminds them of how he and his family have stood up for the nation, willing to sacrifice their own lives for its sake (13.2-6). In the same way, Simon passes on to his children the legacy of him and his predecessors by saying: '...I and my brothers and the house of my father have fought the enemies of Israel from our youth until this very day... Become my replacement and my brother's; then go out, and fight for our nation, and may the help from heaven be with you' (16.2-3). Likewise, Mattathias' initiation of revolting against Antiochus IV Epiphanes, who threatened their covenant and the law, can be seen as another example of one's willingness to offer oneself for the nation: 'Now, children, be zealous in the law, and give your lives for the covenant of our fathers' (2.50).

In Judges the main attribute of most judges is also voluntary self-sacrifice to fight for Israel. In particular, in the so-called Deborah's Song of ch. 5, one finds two expressions, almost identical to each other, which describe judges in this way:

5.2 That the leaders took the lead in Israel, that the people *offered themselves willingly* (בהתנדב), bless the Lord!

5.9 My heart goes out to the commanders of Israel *who offered themselves willingly* (המתנדבים) among the people. Bless the Lord.

The verb נדב is used elsewhere in the Hebrew Bible to refer to a voluntary act of offering goods to God,[44] but in these two references the word describes a voluntary self-sacrificial act of national heroes.[45] Note in 5.2 that the subject of the second clause is ambiguous. Unlike the ESV's identification of it as עם ('people'), it is possible that the subject is still פרעות, the subject of the first clause. Thus, the judges who took the lead in Israel are also the ones who offered themselves willingly. This interpretation can be supported by the fact that vv. 2 and 9 are essentially identical and possibly designed to repeat.[46] The repetition of the imperative 'bless the Lord' likewise adds a sense of repetition. This voluntary act of heroic leaders of ancient Israel resonates through the stories of the Hasmonean leaders in 1 Maccabees.

In summary, the voluntary self-sacrificial leadership can be found in both 1 Maccabees and Judges, and their narrative developments are formed accordingly. From the pro-Hasmonean perspective, just like the judges, the role of the Hasmoneans is seen as determining the narrative development to resemble the Deuteronomic covenantal DCRB. Regarding 1 Maccabees' use of Scripture, it follows that our proposed themes – Deuteronomic covenantal framework and biblical judge-like heroism – are complimentary to each other, but are distinctively distant from the monarchical theme.

---

44. Exodus' account is probably the precedent of this voluntary offering (e.g. Exod. 25.2; 35.21) which is then extended to Ezra 3.5; 7.13, 15, 16 and 1 Chron. 29.5, 6, 9, 14, 17. The motive of such an act is also explained in David's prayer; '…who am I, and what is my people, that we should be able thus to offer willingly? For all things come from you, and of your own have we given you' (1 Chron. 29.14). The verb is also used in Neh. 11.2 to refer to a voluntary act to come back from the foreign land and live in Jerusalem.

45. There is one exception. In the Chronicler's description of the peaceful Judah under the reign of Jehoshaphat, he says Amasiah, the son of Zichri, was 'one who offers voluntarily to the Lord' (המתנדב ליהוה). Such an attitude is probably associated with a military context because his description is coupled with his '200,000 mighty men of valour' (2 Chron. 17.16).

46. The editor of *BHS* (5th edn) footnotes that 5.9 is *probabiliter additum* and potentially *dupliciter ad* v. 2 (814). There are no textual variants noted for the two verses. Among the commentators, only Susan Niditch and Barnabas Lindars recognize the parallel between the two verses; see Niditch, *Judges* (Louisville: Westminster John Knox, 2008), 71; Lindars, *Judges*, 223–7. Lindars, in particular, helpfully offers a detailed literary analysis on these paralleled verses, thereby arguing their identification despite some minor differences.

4.2.3. *The leadership of judges and the legitimacy of the Hasmonean leadership*

We have observed that a significant similarity between the roles of the Hasmoneans and the judges was that they were both generally highlighted as voluntary self-sacrificial leaders. A more specific connection between the two can be suggested, potentially shedding light on the purpose of 1 Maccabees.

Scholars have already found allusions to Gideon in references to Judas.[47] These two characters restored sacrifice in Israel/Judea by crushing Baal's altar/defiled altars erected by Antiochus Epiphanes, and rebuilding a new one (Judg. 6.25-27; 1 Macc. 4.36-58). Second, the acts of trumpet-blowing in the battle scenes of both characters create visual imageries of gathering and harnessing their respective troops with a rallying cry, fervently pursuing and crushing their enemies (Judg. 6.34-35; 7.19-24; 1 Macc. 3.54; 4.14, 40; 5.31, 33; 7.45).[48] Third, Gideon was guided by God to select his small troop of 300 out of a large number of soldiers so that Israel may know that strength comes from God, not by their own ability; his small troop defeated a large number of the Midianites, the Amalekites, and the people from the east (Judg. 7.2; 7.9–8.28). Likewise, Judas led a small troop to successfully defeat a huge Seleucid army during which he exclaimed, 'it is easy for many to be hemmed in by few, for in the sight of heaven there is no difference between saving by many or by few. It is not on the size of the army that victory in battle depends, but strength comes from heaven... He himself will crush them before us...' (1 Macc. 3.18-22).[49] Fourth, in the story of his pursual and defeat of the Midian 'princes' (Judg. 7.19-25), a combination of sequences is notably similar to that of Judas' defeat of Nicanor (1 Macc. 7.45-50): the trumpet-blowing (Judg. 7.19, 20, 22; 1 Macc. 7.45); pursuing the troop (Judg. 7.23; 1 Macc. 7.46); fellow Israelites coming out from surrounding places to help pursue the enemies (Judg. 7.23-24; 1 Macc. 7.46); and capturing and beheading the main enemy (Judg. 7.25; 1 Macc. 7.47). Finally, Gideon's story ends with his burial in his family tombs, and so does that of Judas (Judg. 8.32; 1 Macc. 9.19).

---

47. Bartlett, *Books of the Maccabees*, 77; Deines, 'Matthew', 6.

48. On the imagery of trumpet-blowing as fulfilment of the Mosaic law, as well as discussions on these passages in 1 Maccabees, see Chapter 3.

49. The size of army is considerably smaller in Judas' case, compared to that of Gideon, but the rationale of relying one's victory on divine help is essentially identical in both narratives.

In addition to Gideon, however, the imagery of Jephthah provides another connection, and this is particularly significant in understanding the use of Judges within the pro-Hasmonean agenda of 1 Maccabees. To begin with, is Jephthah portrayed as a positive or negative character in Judges? Elie Assis proposed an argument that Jephthah's portrayal within the narrative of Judges has to be taken negatively. He is 'egocentric' and his negotiations with the Ammonites are rushed, which turns out to be tragic.[50] Contrasted with Gideon's narrative, as per Assis, Jephthah is intentionally seen as a negative figure and is, rather, paralleled with Abimelech who is explicitly portrayed with evil conduct. They share other similarities; for example, they are both born illegitimately of a prostitute (see below). However, this negative reading of Jephthah's story is difficult to accept. First, the passage on his vow (Judg. 11.29-40), which is the main supporting evidence for the negative reading, is far more sophisticated than a mere tale of tragedy, and most commentators interpret the passage to be integral to the overall positive portrayal of Jephthah in Judges.[51] Second, setting a contrast between different judges seems more nuanced than Assis' judgement. If Jephthah was an egocentric man, one could see Gideon as a man full of doubt and lacking of trust in God. He even returned to idolatry later in his life, which 'became a snare to him and his family [i.e. Abimelech]' (Judg. 8.27). This argument cannot be tenable. The judges' individual, personal characters should rather reflect

---

50. Elie Assis, *Self-Interest or Communal Interest: An Ideology of Leadership in the Gideon, Abimelech, and Jephthah Narratives (Judg. 6–12)*, VTSup 106 (Leiden: Brill, 2005), see especially 175–237 for his conclusions.

51. Soggin carefully observes the sophistication of the vow and its fulfilment made by 'a responsible man calculating and particularly skilled at negotiations [with the Ammonites]', thus reading Jephthah's story in a positive light (Soggin, *Judges*, 215–19, the quotation from 216). Soggin also rightly observes that 'the spirit of the Lord' (v. 29) that was bestowed on Jephthah played a major role in his vow (219). Niditch (*Judges*, 130–5) also offers a similar positive portrayal of Jephthah's vow, as well as the overall narrative about him. Boling likewise suggests that Jephthah's fulfilment of the vow is 'psychologically consistent' with the story of his negotiations with the Ammonites, revealing his persisting character (Boling, *Judges*, 210). Barry G. Webb further offers an insightful literary structure of the vow passage in which the spirit of the Lord initiates a sequence of Jephthah's vow, victory and fulfilment of the vow; see Webb, *The Book of the Judges: An Integrated Reading*, JSOTSup 46 (Sheffield: Sheffield Academic, 1987), 60–5. Also notable is the parallel of the work of the spirit of the Lord in a similar sequence of events in Othniel's narrative (Webb, *Judges*, 61). Thus, on the whole, the array of commentators on the passage goes against the negative reading of the passage and Jephthah's story.

the idea that despite their differences and imperfections, they were still adequate to be servants of God by whose hands Israel was delivered from gentile threat. Furthermore, Assis' point concerning similarities between Jephthah and Abimelech seems simplistic. One has to observe some of the stark differences between them wherein the former, full of heroic acts, judged Israel for six years and received the burial, while the latter is depicted with nothing but evil conduct and being crushed by God. In other words, the two have the same dishonourable births but with starkly contrasting life stories and endings. Thus, one must conclude that Assis' negative reading of Jephthah is untenable, and more sophisticated discernments are required for the portrayal of Jephthah in Judges.

This Jephthah has multiple points of connection with the Hasmoneans in 1 Maccabees. To begin with, Jephthah's story begins with an introductory remark that reads:

> Now Jephthah the Gileadite was a mighty warrior, but he was the son of a prostitute. (Judg. 11.1)[52]

There are two things addressed about Jephthah: (1) Jephthah was a mighty warrior, but (2) he was of dishonourable birth. The label, 'a mighty warrior' (גבור חיל; δυνατὸς ἐν ἰσχύι in the Septuagint), is one that also describes Judas in 1 Maccabees (ἰσχυρὸς δυνάμει in 2.66). The Hasmoneans are acclaimed as mighty warriors (Judas as ἰσχυρὸς δυνάμει in 2.66 and Jonathan as δυνατὸς ἰσχύι in 10.19).[53]

It is, however, the second and rather negative image of Jephthah that is more noteworthy. His dishonourable birth caused him to be driven out of the land and rejected by his brothers (11.2), and his eligibility as a leader was disapproved of by Gilead's elders (11.7-8). At the time of the Ammonites' threat, however, these elders came back to Jephthah and requested him to be their leader. It reads,

---

52. I prefer ESV to NRSV because the former discerns the prefixed *waw* in והוא to mean 'but'. Being a mighty warrior and being the son of a prostitute are contradictory statuses, and the story soon unfolds that Jephthah's brothers drive him out of the land due to his dishonourable birth.

53. True, such a term as a 'mighty warrior' is not a very specific term and could generally denote a remarkably strong soldier (elsewhere in the book, mighty warriors refer to the Ασιδαῖοι in 2.42 and even Goliath in 1 Samuel in 4.30). There are also several references to a 'warrior' (without 'mighty'). The point, however, is that for the Hasmoneans, their warrior-like status is interwoven with their negative status as the sons of an 'unclean woman' according to Josephus. Such a combination, when accumulated with other striking similarities, displays a strong case that our author intentionally relates his writing to Judges.

the elders of Gilead said to Jephthah, 'Nevertheless, we have now turned back to you, so that you may go with us and fight with the Ammonites, and become head over us, over all the inhabitants of Gilead… The Lord will be witness between us…' [A]nd Jephthah spoke all his words before the Lord at Mizpah. (Judg. 11.8-11).

Jephthah, once condemned as of dishonourable birth, now becomes the leader of the Gileadites. Of particular note is that his leadership was requested by an assembly of elders gathered at Mizpah during wartime to deal with an urgent matter, and he finally accepted the offer. This model of leadership contrasts to that of other judges who were divinely chosen. He then led battles against the Ammonites successfully, even at the expense of his daughter's life[54] in 11.34-40.

With this image of Jephthah there are some compelling similarities in 1 Maccabees. Jonathan's leadership was requested by an assembly of people called 'all the friends of Judas' (1 Macc. 9.28) who were faced with gentile threat, and he accepted the offer. Simon's appointment of leadership, despite being somewhat different (he willingly offered himself to the people in 13.1-6), is also essentially similar in that it was undertaken after the assembly's approval rather than the result of divine calling, and the decision was made during urgent wartime. Likewise, one also discovers Simon's high priesthood was agreed by a large assembly when the honorary decree was read out (14.27-28). Lastly, and most significantly, the Pharisees' disapproval of the Hasmoneans' high priesthood was based on the latter's birth from a foreign captive woman, a kind of birth which the instruction of Leviticus solemnly prohibits from gaining priestly status. Thus, the Hasmoneans, who were mighty warriors, of illegitimate lineage, and yet appointed as high priests by the assembly in the community, are remarkably similar to Jephthah.

4.2.4. *Summary*

Certain phrases particular to Judges are prominently used in 1 Maccabees, which is hardly a coincidence given that the narratological plot in both books is remarkably similar, complying with the Deuteronomic covenantal cycle of history. Just as the rise of the judges is a driving force of the cycle in Judges, the rise of the Hasmoneans also shapes the narrative of

---

54. It is often said, rather mistakenly, that Jephthah's vow to God is to sacrifice 'whatever first comes out of his house' (11.31). There are no hints within Jephthah's story that display him negatively. His vow should better be understood as led by 'the spirit of the Lord' that came upon him (11.29). Moreover, the passage seems to display Jephthah's faithfulness instead, because in his agony, Jephthah keeps his word to God (11.39).

1 Maccabees in the same way. The leadership of Gideon and (especially) Jephthah in the Israelite community resonates with the role played by the Hasmonean family in Judea. Jephthah's appointment as leader of the nation, despite his dishonourable lineage, resembles the procedure in which the Hasmoneans, despite the dispute about the legitimacy of their title, became high priests in Judea. Even if this suggestion were not convincing, the numerous similarities on morphological and semantic grounds sufficiently suggest that the role of the Hasmonean family is quite similar to that of the biblical judges.

The results in this chapter have an important bearing on the role of the Hasmoneans. The use of the Deuteronomic covenantal concept suggests their role as people who were faithful to their God and to his covenant, fulfilling the promise of God made through Scripture. This salvific role is further shaped by the Hasmoneans' resemblance to the biblical judges. How does this role compare to the Davidic-messianic role of the Hasmoneans claimed by Goldstein and others? The next chapter will deal specifically with this question.

Chapter 5

SCRIPTURE AND THE ROLE OF THE HASMONEANS:
A STUDY ON THE EULOGIES OF JUDAS AND SIMON

In this chapter our discussion will centre on the role of the Hasmoneans in 1 Maccabees with a specific aim to examine the ways in which Scripture is used in the two eulogies attributed to the Hasmoneans – Judas (3.3-8) and Simon (14.4-15) – where poetic language strongly resonates with Scripture.[1] The stories of these two figures receive major attention in the narrative (the story of Judas in 3.1–9.27 and that of Simon in 13.1–16.17),[2] and the eulogies derived from them function as a concise portrayal of the person. In Simon's eulogy particularly, there are multiple expressions present recalling several specific prophecies from Scripture. Furthermore, the seemingly implicit characteristic of using prophetic materials is most vividly found in these eulogies. It is also in these eulogies that the advocates of the so-called Hasmonean-kingship propaganda theory claim to discover important pieces of supporting evidence. Issues affecting the Hasmoneans' legitimate kingship are exclusively dealt with by use of materials related to David and/or the promise of a future

1. On poetic passages in 1 Maccabees, see Neuhaus, *Makkabäerbuch*, 186–226. His list of poetic passages includes: (1) poems of the people (1.25-28, 36-40; 3.45); (2) poems of praise (3.3-9a; 14.4-15); (3) poems of people's prayer (3.50b-53; 4.30b-33); (4) the long poetic pieces in ch. 2 (2.7-13, 49b-68); (5) short poetic pieces (2.44; 4.24a, 38; 7.17; 9.21, 41); and (6) several summative remarks (e.g. 1.26c, 39d; 3.45-46). However, Nils Martola rightly questioned Neuhaus' criteria for poetical passages which are applied to the 'translated text' of 1 Maccabees, referring to the fact that the Greek text of 1 Maccabees is consensually regarded amongst scholars as a translation from an original Hebrew text, the manuscript of which has not survived (see more details in §2.1). See Martola, *Capture and Liberation*, 38.

2. It is surprising that Jonathan's story in 9.28–12.53 generates no eulogy despite his role as the second leader from the Maccabean brothers. The absence may not be significant or it may reflect the author's intention, potentially suggesting his unfavourable view of Jonathan in comparison to Judas and Simon.

king in Scripture, and the analysis here will aim to engage with these issues. Furthermore, some scholars entirely ignore the sense of scriptural or prophetic fulfilment in these eulogies.[3]

5.1. *Judas' eulogy*

Our eulogy is immediately preceded by Mattathias' deathbed blessing (2.49-70), which provides a fitting legacy of Mattathias, or, more precisely, a biblical legacy upon which he himself depended. In his blessing of his sons, Mattathias mentions several biblical figures who wilfully acted for the sake of the law and the covenant. Well informed of the rewards of these individuals, he urges his sons to act in the same way in order to live lives worthy of praise. Indeed, our eulogy projects Judas' image in a way that resonates with biblical heroism.[4] After Judas' eulogy, his fervent heroic career is detailed through a series of wars with gentiles in which he crushes them in several regions in and out of Judea, protecting/ cleansing the Judean cities, as well as the Jerusalem Temple. The careers of Jonathan and Simon also entail essentially the same pattern throughout; all three Hasmoneans take after their father in offering their lives willingly for the law, the covenant, and the people.

Judas' eulogy mainly focuses on his martial bravery, mightiness, and religious zeal. Its clearly poetic form of structure and style of language, as we shall see, is closely related to the similar eulogy attributed to Simon, deliberately employing similar vocabulary, although there is some subtle difference of emphasis between the two. In addition, Bartlett suggests similarities between this eulogy and Ben Sira's description of Joshua in the Praise of the Fathers (Sir. 46.1-6).[5] Their similarities are mainly on the grounds of the emphasis on military achievements of the person.[6]

---

3. Some commentators make their comments on these passages rather too brief (Judas' eulogy in particular). Rappaport ('Maccabees', 716, 731) considers the eulogies to be of 'poetic encomium', each serving as an introduction to the story of the person it is attributed to. Also, Dancy, *Maccabees*, 88, 181. Cf. Bartlett treats Judas' eulogy as an introduction (*Books of the Maccabees*, 45–6), but is more inclined to associate scriptural echoes with Simon's eulogy (190–1). However, his more recent comment on Judas' eulogy emphatically acknowledges scriptural echoes (*Maccabees*, 70).

4. I have contended in the previous chapter that this biblical heroism has a particular focus on biblical judges, rather than kingship.

5. Bartlett, *Books of the Maccabees*, 45.

6. A century ago, there was a creative analysis offered by C. F. Burney in which he proposed an acrostic form of Judas' eulogy. When translated into Hebrew, the beginning letters of each line of the poem forms an acrostic on the name, יהודה המקבה

5. Scripture and the Role of the Hasmoneans 183

5.1.1. Restoration of Israel
A large proportion of the eulogy suggests that use of Scripture functions as a salvific portrayal of Judas' deeds, implying the era of Israel's restoration. However, the passage also suggests that several phrases in the eulogy do not necessarily refer to any specific passage from Scripture. The impression of scriptural fulfilment vis-à-vis Israel's future restoration is ample without pointing to specific and individual biblical materials.

3.3a – 'he magnified glory to his people' (καὶ ἐπλάτυνε δόξαν τῷ λαῷ αὐτοῦ)

This first line of the eulogy opens with the theme of 'glory' (δόξα). The theme is prominent both in Greek and Jewish traditions,[7] and the phrase may be seen as resonating with either Greek or biblical ideas. However, there is a translational issue pertaining to the word δόξα because its attribution is ambiguous, and two possibilities arise: the attribution of glory to people or to Judas. The majority of translators and commentators tend to translate the phrase as 'glory *of* his people', in which case Judas' achievement is such that he not only restored the glory of the nation, but also magnified it.[8] In this regard, Goldstein refers to Isa. 17.4 which reads, 'on that day, the glory of Jacob *will be brought low* (יִדַּל), and the fat of his flesh will grow lean'.[9] Recognizing the unusual combination of πλατύνω and δόξα (literally 'to enlarge glory') in 1 Maccabees, he suggests that the author alluded to this Isaianic reference, implying an overturn of the curse upon Israel through Judas' acts, a reverse application of prophecy. He supports this suggestion by noting that the verb דלל can also mean 'thinning'[10] in that Jacob's glory was increasing rather waning. In this

---

('Yehudah the Maccabee'). See Burney, 'An Acrostic Poem in the Praise of Judas Maccabaeus', *JTS* 21 (1920): 319–25.

7. For 1 Maccabees' concept of 'glory' or 'glorification' in both biblical and Greek cultures, see Himmelfarb, "He Was Renowned', 77–97. Her conclusion, however, is that the concept in 1 Maccabees is characteristically more Greek than Jewish. See also Tomes, 'Heroism', 171–99.

8. E.g. NRSV, NEB (taken by Bartlett, *Books of Maccabees*, 45), and RV (taken by Fairweather and Black, *Maccabees*, 88; Dancy, *Maccabees*, 88) attribute δόξα to the people. See also Oesterley, 'Maccabees', 1:75. Abel (*Maccabées*, 53) translates the phrase as '[i]l dilate le renom de son peuple' ('he dilated the reputation of his people'); Schunck (*Makkabäerbuch*, 309) as '[e]r vergrößerte den Ruhm für sein Volk' ('he magnified the glory of his people').

9. Goldstein, *1 Maccabees*, 244.

10. Goldstein provides no supporting evidence for this meaning דלל. Perhaps he is referring to Isa. 19.6, where the word describes the branches of the Nile diminishing and eventually drying up.

way, δόξα belongs to the people rather than Judas – 'he restored the glory of his people' – and this translation is followed by quite a few scholars.[11] However, the author's reverse use of the Isaianic passage seems rather dubious. From the Greek rendering, ἔκλειψις τῆς δόχης ('a failing of the glory of Jacob'), which keeps the sense of 'leaning' rather than 'thinning', and from the second half of the verse, 'and the fat of his flesh will grow lean', it seems unlikely that the original author of 1 Maccabees or the Greek translator picked up this passage. If the original author had, he would likely have used an antonym of דלל, in the opposite sense of leaning.[12] It is therefore difficult to view this Isaianic prophecy as the scriptural source of 1 Macc. 3.3a.

3.5, 6b – 'as he searched out, he pursued the lawless and burned those who afflicted his people... all who conduct lawlessness were afflicted' (ἐδίωξεν ἀνόμους ἐξερευνῶν καὶ τοὺς ταράσσοντας τὸν λαὸν αὐτοῦ ἐφλόγισε... καὶ πάντες οἱ ἐργάται τῆς ἀνομίας συνεταράχθησαν)

The second case relating to the theme of Israel's restoration shows an act of executing renegades which may well be a part of a reforming scheme recurrent in biblical literature, but here again there is no notable morphological identification. The last phrase, 'those who afflicted his people' (τοὺς ταράσσοντας τὸν λαὸν αὐτοῦ), has been suggested by both Goldstein and Doran to be associated with 1 Kgs 18.18, where Elijah tells Ahab, 'I have not *troubled Israel*, but you have...', and 1 Chron. 2.7, reading 'the son of Carmi, Achan, the *troubler of Israel*...'[13] These verses lack morphological association because the Hebrew word עכר ('to trouble'), in its thirteen occurrences in the Hebrew Bible inclusive of these two, is never rendered as ταράσσω in the Septuagint. However, thematically, Ahab's and Achan's troubles both imply impiety[14] which is also the case for Judas' act of execution. On the other hand, this theme pervades in biblical stories of Israel's religious cleansing and reformation,[15] which makes specific association with Ahab and Achan unwarranted.

11. Goldstein, *1 Maccabees*, 243.
12. Abel (*Maccabées*, 52) suggests רחב as the original Hebrew word.
13. Goldstein, *1 Maccabees*, 245; Doran, 'Maccabees', 4:55.
14. Ahab is condemned of his impiety. He 'abandoned the commandments of the Lord and followed the Baals' (1 Kgs 18.18), and Achan is the trouble-maker of Israel 'who broke faith in the matter of the devoted thing' (1 Chron. 2.7).
15. E.g. Josh. 6.24; Judg. 4.49, 52; Isa. 66.15; Obad. 18. A similar feature may also be found outside of biblical and other Jewish literature. Fairweather and Black (*Maccabees*, 127) suggest Herodotus, *History* 6.80.

Similarly, v. 6b, which reads 'all who conduct lawlessness were afflicted', shares the theme of renegade execution. These two verses seem to be closely related due to a wordplay between the two: Judas burnt those who afflicted (ταράσσω) his people (v. 5), and vengefully afflicted (συνταράσσω) all the renegades in the land (v. 6b). The verb's repetition in its compound form creates a poetic quality within the eulogy itself, without echoing any specific biblical materials. This theme of punishing the ungodliness is also found in Simon's eulogy (14.7, 14b). The author of 1 Maccabees may well be aware of the biblical theme of punishing the ungodliness in the land (e.g. Deut. 13), but does not intend to allude to any specific sources.

3.7a – 'many kings were embittered' (ἐπίκρανε βασιλεῖς πολλούς)

The first part of v. 7, 'many kings were embittered' (ἐπίκρανε βασιλεῖς πολλούς), puts Judas' military achievement in the context of international relation (especially in relation to Antiochus IV Epiphanes, Antiochus V Eupator, and Demetrius I, as well as their officers).[16] Πικραίνω ('embittering') potentially evokes the biblical imagery of Israel's defeat of gentile kings.[17] It should be noted that there is a similar phrase in Simon's eulogy, where a stronger verb, συντρίβω ('crushing'), describes Simon's defeat of gentile kings in the manner found in the Hebrew Bible (see below). The act of 'embittering' may hyperbolically refer to Judas' many victories, but scriptural precedents of this particular act are difficult to identify. Such an inference may explain the fact that none of the major commentators makes any suggestion of associated biblical materials on this. On a morphological level, מרר is possibly the Hebrew original word which is rendered as πικραίνω in a few biblical references in Greek,[18] but these examples are thematically irrelevant to 'embittering gentile kings'.

The word πικραίνω rather directs us to another example of wordplay, just as the wordplay with (συν)ταράσσω does in vv. 5-6. As both Abel and Doran suggest, there are two rhyming verbs in the verse, 'he embittered

---

16. 1 Macc. 3.27; 6.11-13, 28; 7.1.

17. This theme is generally featured in Joshua's campaigns and warfare of judges, as well as David's.

18. Ruth[GK] 1.13, 20; Job[GK] 27.2; Lam.[GK] 1.4. The Septuagint also takes πικραίνω on other Hebrew words such as קצף ('to be angry', e.g. Exod. 16.20; Jer. 37.15), כעס ('to be angry', e.g. Jer. 32.32), רגז ('to be excited', e.g. Isa. 14.9; Jer. 33.9). These words do not quite bear the sense of 'embittering' in the same way as the examples from Ruth, Job and Lamentations referenced above.

(ἐπίκρανε) many kings, and/but gladdened (εὔφρανε) Jacob by his works',[19] and they are antonymous to one another. It should be noted, of course, that the rhyme itself is the translator's literary design, but these two juxtaposed images highlight the effect of Judas' acts on both international and domestic scales (the kind of writing technique which continues in Simon's eulogy as well).

In addition to wordplay, the image of embittered kings may remind the reader of the opening section of 1 Maccabees (1.1-10) which describes the image of those Greek kings who enthroned themselves, multiplied, and prospered in evil. These antagonist kings are consistently caricatured as craving for self-elevation and fame (e.g. Seron in 3.14, Demetrius II in ch. 11). Since 1 Maccabees clearly presents the notion that the arrogant falls while the humble and selfless receive fame, our phrase may underline the same idea.

3.7b – 'he gladdened Jacob by his works' (εὔφρανε τὸν Ιακωβ ἐν τοῖς ἔργοις αὐτοῦ)

The second part of v. 7, 'he gladdened Jacob by his works' (εὔφρανε τὸν Ιακωβ ἐν τοῖς ἔργοις αὐτοῦ), may conveniently be seen as a general term referring to the restoration of Israel. Again, Simon's eulogy contains a similar image with 'gladdening Israel' (1 Macc. 14.11; 'Israel rejoiced with great joy', εὐφράνθη Ισραηλ εὐφροσύνην μεγάλην; see below), and is made more explicit and greater than Judas' image. Whilst the sense of Israel's restoration is clearly communicated, the author consistently fashions Judas' image as relatively moderate compared to Simon's. One could infer that despite Judas' fervent and successful warfare, Judea was still undergoing a turbulent period under his leadership, and a peaceful state was yet to be delivered. The circumstance gradually improves and reaches its climax under the leadership of Simon. In this regard, the subtle difference of language between the two eulogies may be seen to reflect the author's intention of presenting accurate history.[20]

3.7c – 'for ever his memory will be a blessing' (ἕως τοῦ αἰῶνος τὸ μνημόσυνον αὐτοῦ εἰς εὐλογίαν)

In the last part of v. 7, 'forever his memory will be a blessing' (ἕως τοῦ αἰῶνος τὸ μνημόσυνον αὐτοῦ εἰς εὐλογίαν), there is a scriptural expression

---

19. Abel, *Maccabées*, 54; Doran, 'Maccabees', 4:55.
20. None of the major studies on 1 Maccabees seems to heed this subtle difference between the two eulogies, and comparative study on them might be very interesting.

which may be identifiable on morphological grounds. The immortality of the pious' name is a recurrent theme in the Hebrew Bible,[21] and the same theme is underlined in this expression. The biblical references often suggested are as follows: Ps. 112.6 'he [the righteous] will be remembered forever', and Prov. 10.7 'the memory of the righteous is a blessing'. On morphological grounds, Prov. 10.7 is a better candidate for it contains at least two identical words 'memory' and 'blessing'. Both verses, however, underline the same theme. More notably, Ben Sira's description of the biblical judges produces another similar phrase:

> And the judges, each with his own name, whose heart did not commit fornication and who did not turn away from the Lord, may their memorial be for blessings. May their bones sprout anew out of their plot and their name be traded; may it be renowned among the sons of humankind. (Sir. 46.11-12)

Ben Sira's keen interest in the theme of the immortality of the honour of the pious' name is already made clear in the introduction (Sir. 44.1-15) to the Praise of the Fathers (Sir. 44–49/50) and elsewhere in the book.[22] The connection between Ben Sira's description of the judges and Judas' image in 1 Maccabees is especially attractive since Judges has a special place in 1 Maccabees' use of Scripture, as discussed in the previous section.[23] If our author is specifically alluding to Ben Sira's description of judges, this phrase about the immortality of Judas' honour supports the proposition made in the previous section, namely that the role of the Hasmoneans is deliberately overlapped with that of the judges (rather than that of Davidic kingship).[24] Whilst the use of Judges provides a necessary framework through which Sir. 46.11-12 can be identified with 1 Macc. 3.7c, I cannot ascertain this to be the case, especially because all the similar,

---

21. For scholars who highlight this theme and identify the following biblical references, see Abel, *Maccabées*, 54; Fairweather and Black, *Maccabees*, 89; Goldstein, *1 Maccabees*, 245.

22. Ben Sira repeatedly highlights this theme and thus asserts in the introduction of the Praise of the Fathers: 'forever will their [the pious ancestors] seed remain, and their glory will not be blotted out. Their bodies were buried in peace, and their name lives for generations' (Sir. 44.13-14; on the introduction of the Praise of the Fathers, see our previous discussion in §2.5). Elsewhere, Ben Sira also highlights this theme when he delivers an exposition concerning death (Sir. 40–41): 'Have regard for a name, for it will endure for you rather than a thousand great treasures of gold. Of a good life there is a number of days, but a good name will endure forever' (Sir. 41.12-13).

23. See Chapter 4.

24. See Chapter 4.

aforementioned phrases share minor literary affinities (morphologically 'memory' + 'blessing'/'forever') and shared themes on the immortality of the pious' name's honour.

3.8c – 'he turned the wrath away from Israel' (ἀπέστρεψεν ὀργὴν ἀπὸ Ισραηλ)

Lastly, v. 8, 'he turned the wrath away from Israel' (ἀπέστρεψεν ὀργὴν ἀπὸ Ισραηλ), clearly reminds the reader of the last verse of ch. 1, 'there was a very great wrath upon Israel' (ἐγένετο ὀργὴ μεγάλη ἐπὶ Ισραηλ σφόδρα).[25] The phrase ὀργὴ ἐπὶ Ισραηλ is now overturned as ἀπέστρεψεν ὀργὴν ἀπὸ Ισραηλ. 'Wrath' here probably indicates God's wrath, and Israel's act of enduring God's wrath is frequently found in biblical literature.[26] Goldstein specifically points out Phinehas' turning the wrath from Israel by his zealous act, with the implication that our author is describing the Hasmonean family as an heir of the Aaronite priesthood. Thus, Num. 25.11 reads:

> Phinehas the son of Eleazar, son of Aaron the priest, has turned back my wrath from the people of Israel, in that he was jealous with my jealousy among them, so that I did not consume the people of Israel in my jealousy.

The combination of the three words, 'turn', 'wrath' and 'Israel' certainly indicates that the verse is alluded to in the description of Judas, and Goldstein's suggestion that such an allusion fits the pro-Hasmonean agenda, legitimizing the Hasmonean high priesthood, may further strengthen the connection between the two verses. However, there are equally relevant expressions elsewhere.[27] For instance, in his prayer, Jeremiah speaks of his own act of turning the wrath from Israel, 'Remember how I stood before you…*to turn away your wrath from them*' (Jer. 18.20). Ezra and his people apparently deliver the same act to turn the wrath from them, 'Let all in our cities…come at appointed times…until *the fierce wrath of our God* over this matter *is turned away from us*' (Ezra 10.14). Also, in Ps. 106.23 it is Moses to whom such an act is attributed, 'Moses…stood in the breach before him to *turn away his wrath from destroying them*'. Daniel also invokes God for turning his wrath from Jerusalem, 'O Lord… *let your anger and your wrath turn*

---

25. Also, Abel, *Maccabées*, 54; Fairweather and Black, *Maccabees*, 89.

26. Doran ('Maccabees', 4:55) identifies the following list as resembling the expression in the eulogy: Num. 25.4; 2 Chron. 12.12; 29.10; 30.8; Ps. 106.23; Ezek. 10.14; Dan. 9.16; Hos. 14.4; Zech. 1.2.

27. For the same view, see Doran, 'Maccabees', 4:55.

away from your city Jerusalem' (Dan. 9.16). All these biblical references share the three combined words, 'turn', 'wrath/anger', 'Israel/People/ Jerusalem'. Thematically, all these biblical materials uniformly express the theme of Israel's restoration, and it should thus be underlined that the verse might render two layers of meaning: Judas' act brought about Israel's restoration reminiscent of the acts of biblical heroes; simultaneously, the Hasmonean high priestly institution is legitimate.

In summary, Judas' eulogy generally resonates with the biblical theme of Israel's restoration. More precisely, the use of Scripture is neither completely restricted to thematic resonance only nor specifies a single biblical reference that corresponds to every single phrase in the eulogy. The practice of using Scripture seems rather flexible and fluid between the two spectrums. Also characteristic of this practice is its diminished degree and quality of the restoration it describes in comparison to the practice of Simon's eulogy, perhaps reflecting historical accuracy on the achievements of the two Hasmonean leaders. There are yet more verses in the eulogy that fall within the theme of Israel's restoration, but due to their particular associations to other biblical themes, they will be studied separately below.

5.1.2. *Gathering of the dispersed Israel?*

The Hasmoneans' restoration of Judea brought with it the gathering of both Jewish captives, who were deported from their land in the aftermath of the Antiochan persecution, and the diaspora, who were oppressed in their regions. The question asked concerns the implication of this particular act. In this section, I will engage with two views in particular: a view that denies the Jews' physical and symbolic return from foreign captivity and deportation, and a view that not only sees the Jews' return to their promised land as a sign of Israel's restoration but also as messianic and eschatological fulfilment of biblical prophecies.

The first view has been advocated by N. T. Wright in multiple publications, claiming that the Jews across the Second Temple period believed themselves to be living in a *continuing exile* ever since the Babylonian exile in the early sixth century BCE.[28] He sets out this idea in a recent publication:

---

28. Wright, *Faithfulness*, 114–39. See also the previous three volumes, especially the first two, of the same series, in which Wright consistently bases the idea as a hermeneutic tool for the understanding of Second-Temple Jews' worldview: *New Testament and the People of God*, COQG 1 (London: SPCK, 1992); *Jesus and the Victory of God*, COQG 2 (London: SPCK, 1996). The idea of a continuing exile was already expressed by Peter R. Ackroyd, *Exile and Restoration: A Study of Hebrew*

> ...a great many Second-Temple Jews interpreted *that part of the continuing narrative in which they were living* in terms of the so-called Deuteronomic scheme of sin–exile–restoration, with themselves still somewhere in the middle stage, that of 'exile'... The point...is the *theological* awareness of being at a particular stage within the overall continuing narrative, coupled with the *exegetical* awareness of a large-scale Deuteronomic prophecy being worked out.[29]

Whilst I agree that the Second Temple Jews were deeply conscious of their past and regarded the present time and their own story as part of a larger, continuous narrative,[30] Wright's 'exilic' model for the understanding of Jews' perception of their current state of affairs raises objections.[31] On the one hand, the Deuteronomic scheme of sin–exile–restoration ('SER') may well be seen as the backdrop of the Jews' narrative of their history, just as I have shown in the previous chapter (the covenantal DCRB).[32] On the other hand, it is precisely the *paradigm* of that Deuteronomic scheme that recurs in the Jewish history, recalling Ricoeur's 'configured history' or Newsom's 'historical résumés', rather than any single linear process in which the Jews believed they were still in-between '(Babylonian) exile'

Thought of the Sixth Century BC (London: SCM, 1968), 232–47; see also James M. Scott, 'Exile and the Self-Understanding of Diaspora Jews in the Greco-Roman Period', in *Exile: Old Testament, Jewish, and Christian Conceptions*, ed. James M. Scott, JSJSup 56 (Leiden: Brill, 1997), 173–218; Craig A. Evans, 'Jesus and the Continuing Exile', in *Jesus and the Restoration of Israel: A Critical Assessment on N. T. Wright's Jesus and the Victory of God*, ed. Carey C. Newman (Downers Grove, IL: InterVarsity, 1999), 77–100 (especially 78–87); Wright, *Faithfulness*, 139–63. In Wright's case, it can be argued that the concept of the continuing exile is the backbone of his overall thesis on the early Christians' perception of Israel's eschatological hope seen as fulfilled through the Christ event – the birth, death, and resurrection of Jesus of Nazareth.

29. Wright, *Faithfulness*, 140 (his italics).

30. See §2.5.

31. The idea of the continuing exile has received rigorous critical reviews. See Carey C. Newman's edited volume in n. 28 above for more discussions on the topic. See especially the final summary by D. A. Carson, 'Summaries and Conclusions', in *Justification and Variegated Nomism: Vol. 1, the Complexities of Second Temple Judaism*, ed. D. A. Carson, Peter T. O'Brien and Mark A. Seifrid, WUNT 2/140 (Tübingen: Mohr Siebeck; Grand Rapids: Baker Academic, 2001), 505–48; also, Steven M. Bryan, *Jesus and Israel's Traditions of Judgement and Restoration*, SNTSMS 117 (Cambridge: Cambridge University Press, 2002), 12–20 (this is to be read together with Wright's response in Wright, *Faithfulness*, 160–2).

32. See Chapter 4.

and 'restoration'.³³ Moreover, the narrative of 1 Maccabees expresses the Deuteronomic SER pattern, and is in fact expressed in its *full-course*. That is, *both* the exilic language in the description of the calamities in Judea *and* the return language in the subsequent Hasmonean triumphs are juxtaposed, *preceded* by the incidents where the pro-Seleucid Judeans and their actions are seen as 'sin' or 'defilement of the divine covenant'. As I will show below, 1 Maccabees narrates several occasions of the Jews' *actual return from captivity*.³⁴

33. See §2.5. The eschatological depiction of the defeat of Rome in the synagogue paintings in Dura-Europos is often proposed as the evidence for a belief in the continuing exile (Scott, 'Self-Understanding', 193–7; taken up by Wright, *Faithfulness*, 159). Cf. Jonathan A. Goldstein, 'The Judaism of the Synagogues (Focusing on the Synagogue of Dura-Europos)', in *Judaism in Late Antiquity, Part 2: Historical Syntheses*, ed. Jacob Neusner, HO 17 (Leiden: Brill, 1995), 109–57. On the contrary, these synagogue paintings are a prime example of Newsom's 'historical résumé'. The historical experience of the exodus from Egypt synchronized with the later history of the Babylonian exile/return, and was amplified in the narrative of the third-century Jews under Roman oppression, thus rhetorically delivering an *experiential* sense of hope. Just as Ricoeur's 'configured history', God's salvific history configured the narrative of these Jews so that they could envisage the end of their suffering and express their hope in art form. In the wider Second Temple Jewish context, it also seems that the Deuteronomic SER concept becomes a pattern that triggers imagination and provides a hermeneutic for the Jewish writers. The advocates of the 'continuing exile' ignore, or only briefly mention in passing, that multiple applications of the Deuteronomic SER concept can be found. As Martin G. Abegg, Jr. demonstrates, there are imaginative and indeed paradigmatic ways of applying the concept to the historical event of the Babylonian exile, as well as return in the Dead Sea Scrolls, see Abegg Jr., 'Exile and the Dead Sea Scrolls', in Scott, ed., *Exile*, 111–25. Likewise, James C. VanderKam, 'Exile in Jewish Apocalyptic Literature', in Scott, ed., *Exile*, 89–109, whose approach is more sympathetic to seeing the Babylonian exile as a continued condition, nevertheless identifies three types of exile in Jewish apocalyptic literature: (1) a historical event of limited duration, (2) a continuing state, and (3) an object of reflection and meditation. Further, Louis H. Feldman ('The Concept of Exile in Josephus', in Scott, ed., *Exile*, 145–72) demonstrates that Josephus views the concept of exile *positively* and only occasionally associates the term with divine punishment. Feldman seems to assume that Josephus personally believed the Jewish diaspora would eventually return to the land (163), but his intention of mass conversion of the diaspora (who would not view themselves to be under divine punishment) and the presence of the Romans possibly required him to silence his own voice. This assumption is still clearly different from the continuing exile in which 'exile' is profoundly a theological notion rather than a geographic one.

34. The narrative of 1 Maccabees especially contradicts the idea of the continuing exile. Wright asserts, 'the book ends with Simon (and his sons) getting drunk and

The second view I want to highlight is that of the Hasmonean kingship propaganda, which argues in opposition to Wright, namely that the

being murdered, with the remaining son John succeeding him. No sign of the glorious eschaton there' (Wright, *Faithfulness*, 159). But this statement is made without support, and is, in fact, contradictory to a large body, if not a majority, of scholarship on 1 Maccabees which favours the pro-Hasmonean and legitimizing style of the writing. In my judgement, Wright cannot gain support from scholars who suggest that the author's purpose may be less concentrated on legitimizing the Hasmonean dynasty. Schwartz ('Nations Roundabout', 16–38) suggests a composition intended for John Hyrcanus I to gain the domestic, Jewish support before his territorial expansion, but this scheme has little to do with downplaying the Hasmonean position. Pfeiffer (*History*, 493) places an equal emphasis on the role of 'the people' in the drama of restoration, but is nevertheless in support of the majority view of overall pro-Hasmonean rhetoric. Perhaps Doran ('Maccabees', 4:22) comes close when he suggests the composition as generating hostility to the Hasmoneans, composed shortly after Hyrcanus' death (indeed, referring to Simon's death as an element of critiquing the Hasmoneans). This is merely speculative and claimed without evidence or discussion, and is certainly insufficient to support Wright's reading of 1 Maccabees. Does Simon's death leave a negative mark on the triumphant account of the Hasmoneans? In fact, all three Hasmonean brothers faced an unexpected death. Judas lost the battle against Bacchides and was killed, his death followed by great mourning and the discouragement of the people (9.27). Jonathan was deceived and kidnapped by Trypho, and never returned; only his bones were sent to Simon (13.25-26). Likewise, Simon was murdered by Ptolemy, his son-in-law, at a banquet (16.16-17). Consistent in this sequence of deaths, however, is not the misfortune of the Judean nation but precisely the opposite. Their deaths are all followed by triumphant successions leading to rejuvenation of the nation. Judas' death was immediately followed by Jonathan's succession, then Simon's, and finally that of John Hyrcanus I. In other words, Simon's death therefore implies not so much misfortune as the expectation of a continuation of the Hasmonean triumph. Thus, the final conclusion of the narrative includes Hyrcanus' successful escape from Ptolemy's plot and the author's statement about Hyrcanus' succession to high priesthood and ruler in Judea. The concept of Hasmonean succession is aptly stated in the words of Simon: '… And Simon called his two older sons, Judas and John, and said to them, "I and my brothers and the house of my father have fought the enemies of Israel from our youth until this very day, and we were successful in rescuing Israel by our hands many times. But now I have gotten old, but you mercifully are sufficient in years. *Become my replacement and my brother's*; then go out, and fight for our nation, and may the help from heaven be with you"' (1 Macc. 16.1-3). At one level, Simon is preparing his sons for the battle against Cendebeus, but at another level, Simon already prepares his end; it implies *transition* of leadership (see Dancy, *Maccabees*, 193, who rightly recalls Mattathias' deathbed blessing; Bartlett, *1 Maccabees*, 99, who comments the passage as 'dynastic continuation'; it has to be underlined, however, that the kind of hope for regathering scattered Israel is seen as fulfilled in 1 Maccabees. Major advocates of this view, such as Arenhoevel and Goldstein, rightly point out multiple passages relating to Jewish migration back to Judea (see below), and suggest that the Hasmoneans are the messianic Davidic heirs who acted on behalf of God in gathering all dispersed Israel, thereby bringing eschatological restoration of Israel.[35] However, does the text really indicate such a dramatic inauguration of a new, eschatological era? To put it differently, what do those multiple passages relating to the Hasmoneans' regathering of Judeans suggest?

It is in Judas' eulogy that the first reference to 'return from captivity' is found. The last phrase in the eulogy reads:

3.9b – And he gathered those who perished (Καὶ συνήγαγεν ἀπολλυμένους)

Prior to discussing the verse, however, there is a textual issue frequently noted by scholars. De Bruyne famously claimed that 3.9b, which resembles the immediately following verse, καὶ συνήγαγεν Ἀπολώνιος... ('and Apollonius gathered...'), is a sign of dittography.[36] All the manuscripts in Greek and Latin attest to the reading ἀπολλυμένους in 3.9b, with two minor exceptions, minuscule 340 and a later improvement of Venetus, which omit 3.9b.[37] And yet, De Bruyne claims that 3.9b is a later interpolation, because of (1) its apparent dittographic nature, (2) the context of the eulogy in which 3.9a, 'And he was renowned as far as to the end of the land', reads like the end of the eulogy, (3) and because ἀπολλυμένους 3.9b is an improper term, and the verse should instead read something like 'il a sauvé, il a rendu à la vie ceux qui périssaient' ('he has saved, he has restored to life those who perished').[38] De Bruyne's reading of 3.9b has been accepted by a few scholars.[39] Conversely, however, other

---

succession alluded to in this passage is not of high priesthood, but of military conduct [Grimm, *Maccabäer*, 230–1; Keil, *Makkabäer*, 249]). In this way, the passage serves a similar function to Mattathias' deathbed blessing (1 Macc. 2.49-70), i.e. an impartation of the family legacy to his children.

35. See §1.2.

36. Dom D. de Bruyne, 'Le texte grec des deux premiers livres des Machabées', *RB* 31 (1922): 31–54 (52).

37. Kappler, *Maccabaeorum*, 63.

38. De Bruyne, 'Machabées', 52.

39. E.g. Dancy, *Maccabees*, 88; Schunck, *Makkabäerbuch*, 308 (see on the same page a list of other scholars who follow De Bruyne on reading 3.9b as a dittograph and therefore secondary).

scholars noted, and rightly so in my opinion, that the idea of dittography is not necessary.[40] Most notably, Abel rightly points out the fact that ἀπολλυμένους is not an improper term with an example from Bar. 3.3,[41] and that the text still presents a good literary attire for rhythm, parallelism and continuation of ideas.[42] Indeed, Abel rightly points out that the reported suppression and massacre of the Jews in the regions of Gilead and Galilee in ch. 5, which is followed by Judas' (and Simon's) act of rescue and migration of those Jews to Jerusalem, could well be summarized in the eulogy.[43] In addition, in view of the Greek translator's aforementioned frequent wordplays within the eulogy, such as the contradictory use of ταράσσω / συνταράσσω (vv. 5, 6b) and the rhyme of ἐπίκρανε / εὔφρανε (v. 7), it may be an attractive inference that he deliberately chose the somewhat unnatural words in 3.9b to produce another wordplay: whilst Judas the Jewish hero gathered all those who were perishing, Apollonius the gentile antagonist gathered a massive army to attack the Jews (which of course failed, and he and his army were defeated by Judas).

Regarding scriptural sources behind 3.9b, Goldstein relates this phrase to Isa. 11.12 and claims that Judas is depicted as fulfilling the prophecy concerning gathering of the dispersed Israel.[44] The prophecy reads:

> He will raise a signal for the nations and *will assemble the banished of Israel* (נדחי ישראל ואסף; cf. in Greek, 'he will gather the lost ones of Israel' [συνάξει τοὺς ἀπολομένους Ισραηλ]), and gather the dispersed of Judah from the four corners of the earth.

While the precise meaning of the expression 'gathering those who perished' is less clear,[45] the second part of the prophecy more clearly

---

40. For example, Fairweather and Black (*Maccabees*, 89) refer ἀπολλυμένους to 'scattered Israelites'; Goldstein, *1 Maccabees*, 245; Tilly (*Makkabäer*, 113) rightly notes 5.23, 54 as potential references to the act of Judas in 3.9b.

41. We may add 2 Macc. 7.20, where the martyrdom of the seven sons is termed as ἀπολλυμένους.

42. Abel, *Maccabées*, 54–5.

43. I would add the similar verse in Simon's eulogy, καὶ συνήγαγεν αἰχμαλωσίαν πολλήν, although here the objective does not necessarily bear the same referent. See the next section for a more detailed discussion.

44. Goldstein, *Maccabees*, 245; 'Messianic Promises', 77. Doran ('Maccabees', 4:55) further adds Isa. 27.13.

45. The participle form of ἀπόλλυμι makes its meaning rather ambiguous because the Judeans who were in the state of 'perishing' do not necessarily refer to the Judean captives outside of Judea or geographically scattered people, but possibly those domestic victims of the aftermath of the Antiochan persecution in Judea. However,

expresses the geographical nature of the act of gathering. Likewise, the narrative of 1 Maccabees indicates a similar act on multiple occasions. Judas, when he received urgent requests from his kinsmen in the regions of Gilead and Galilee where they were persecuted,[46] went with Simon to bring vengeance for his people. And, upon his return to Judea, Simon brought with him 'all his kinsmen' from Galilee and Arbatta:

> And he took those from Galilee[47] and in Arbatta with the women and children and everything that was theirs and led them to Judea with great gladness. (1 Macc. 5.23)

The verse remarkably stresses that it was 'all the people, with their families and livestock' who migrated to Judea.[48] Likewise, a few verses later, Judas' vengeance of his people has a similar ending:

---

one could argue that συνάγω still retains a geographical sense of the act carried out, most likely referring to those Judean kinsmen who perished outside of the Judean territory.

46. 'Great gladness' (εὐφροσύνη μέγας) occurs as many as four times in 1 Maccabees to stress the state of the Judean restoration: the rededication of the Jerusalem Temple (4.58), Nicanor's death and the celebration of the victory (7.48), and Simon's eulogy (14.11).

47. The question of Jewish settlement in Galilee prior to the Hasmonean conquest (Josephus, *Ant.* 13.318-19) has been hotly debated and fostered interdisciplinary investigation which has not yet drawn any agreement amongst scholars. For a survey of scholarship in historical Jesus studies, see Roland Deines, 'Galilee and the Historical Jesus in Recent Research', in *Galilee: In the Late Second Temple and Mishnaic Periods: Vol. 1, Life, Culture, and Society*, ed. David A. Fiensy and James Riley Strange (Minneapolis: Fortress, 2014), 11–48. For a brief summary of scholarly opinions on the origin of Jewish settlement in Galilee in the Greco-Roman era, see Morten Hørning Jensen, 'The Political History in Galilee from the First Century BCE to the End of the Second Century CE', in the same volume, 51–77. The majority of scholars tend to be dubious about any major settlement in Galilee prior to the Hasmonean conquest that can be seen to be particularly 'Jewish'. There has been an influential archaeological survey of settlement in Galilee during the late Hellenistic and early Roman periods by Uzi Leibner, *Settlement and History in Hellenistic, Roman, and Byzantine Galilee: An Archaeological Survey of the Eastern Galilee*, TSAJ 127 (Tübingen: Mohr Siebeck, 2009). Leibner demonstrated that the settlement during the early Hellenistic period was relatively sparse, mostly found in hill-top areas indicating strategic purposes. Settlement became dramatically dense only from the Hasmonean period (John Hyrcanus I).

48. Goldstein (*1 Maccabees*, 300) regards the Hasmoneans' act as 'an attempt to follow biblical precedents and fulfill prophecies' (e.g. 2 Chron. 15.1-9; Jer. 31.6-12; Obad. 20-21; Zech. 10.6-8). Doran ('Maccabees', 4:78) likewise gives an analogy

> And Judas gathered together all of Israel who were in Gilead from the small to the great and their wives and their children and belongings, a very great company, to come to the land of Judea. (1 Macc. 5.45)

Repeatedly, the Hasmoneans' campaign to the Greek cities was concluded with migration of a large group of their kinsmen[49] which could indicate gathering of the diaspora as something of the Hasmonean ideology.[50]

Jonathan is of no exception. After defeating Bacchides and his army, Jonathan sent King Demetrius' ambassadors for a peace treaty, specifically requesting release of the Jewish captives:

> And Jonathan learned this, and he sent emissaries to him to conclude peace with him and to give back the captives (τὴν αἰχμαλωσίαν) to them... And he gave back to him the captives (τὴν αἰχμαλωσίαν) whom he had captured formerly from the land of Judea, and turning back he returned to his land and did not add to come again to their territory. (1 Macc. 9.70-72)[51]

With this agreement with the Seleucids, Jonathan further restores those captives in the Jerusalem citadel to their families (1 Macc 10.7-9).

Another reference that possibly refers to the same act of gathering the Jews is found in Simon's eulogy:

> And he gathered many captives... (καὶ συνήγαγεν αἰχμαλωσίαν πολλήν...) (1 Macc. 14.7a)

---

in Isaiah: 'the ransomed of the Lord are described as returning to Zion in the same way (51.11)'. In 5.54, Judas is said to offer 'whole burnt offerings' upon his arrival at Judea. Doran further notes that this imagery parallels 'the victory march of the Divine Warrior' (Exod. 15.1-17), and 'the in-gathering of the people' in Ps. 106.47; Isa. 35; 51.9-11. This ritual was, according to 2 Macc. 12.31, related to the festival of Pentecost during which Judas and the refugees arrived in Judea (Rappaport, 'Maccabees', 719).

49. Fairweather and Black (*Maccabees*, 121) rightly note that 'all people', however hyperbolical it may be, included 'all Israelites in the district who had adhered to the faith of their fathers'.

50. The statement of Fairweather and Black is noteworthy: 'The deportation to Judaea of all Jews resident in Gilead told advantageously in two directions. It secured them against further molestation on the part of the surrounding pagan population, while it also tended to strengthen the Jewish power at the centre' (*Maccabees*, 127).

51. Thus Abel (*Maccabées*, 178) notes αἰχμαλωσία as the Greek rendering of שבי in Num. 31.12; Isa. 20.4; Hab. 1.9.

Interpretation of this phrase is controversial since the 'many captives' could either refer to liberated Jews[52] or gentile war-captives.[53] Although in its immediate context Simon's conquest/control of Joppa, Gazara and Beith-sur (14.5-7) makes it possible to interpret the 'captives' as war prisoners, the use of αἰχμαλωσία, which probably goes back to שבי in the original Hebrew,[54] makes Jewish captives a more plausible candidate as the referent, as the word more clearly refers to the Jewish captives released by Jonathan in 9.70-72. In either case, the aforementioned references cumulatively suggest that the Hasmoneans consistently and almost systemically carried out Jewish migration, and the events were seen as part of the Judean restoration. To this list, we may add Cendebeus' capture and deportation of the Jews which was followed by John Hyrcanus' revenge and, allegedly, the captives' return (15.40; 16.9-10).

This systematic projection of gathering captives as part of restoration is further shaped with the contrasting, cataclysmic events that precede. For instance, the gentile persecution repeatedly ended up with deportation of Jewish captives. As well as ch. 5, Bacchides' release of Jewish captives to Jonathan in ch. 7 (and possibly Simon's eulogy too) indicates Jewish deportation in the first place. In fact, the Antiochan persecution in ch. 1 involved the following: 'they took the women and the children captive and took possession of the livestock' (1 Macc. 1.32). What is noteworthy is that this cataclysmic event is a result of the Jews' defilement of the divine covenant through making a covenant with the Seleucid king and following the Seleucid statutes and ways of life, which involved hiding the mark of circumcision (1.11-15), hence the author's comment that the Jews '*sold themselves to do evil*' (1.15). In other words, 1 Maccabees presents the full course of sin, exile, and return, following the Deuteronomic legacy (DCRB).[55]

In short, the term 'continuing exile' does not adequately represents 1 Maccabees' picture in which exile, or captivity, is emphatically seen as brought to an end by the Hasmonean triumph. The restoration scheme of

---

52. Abel, *Maccabées*, 251, emphatically rejecting the other interpretation; Fairweather and Black, *Maccabees*, 239; Dancy, *Maccabees*, 181; Goldstein, *1 Maccabees*, 303, with a suggestion of echoing Gen. 50.8-9 and Exod. 12.37, 42; Tilly, *Makkabäer*, 277.

53. Bartlett, *Books of the Maccabees*, 190; Doran, 'Maccabees', 4:159. Likewise, Schunck's translation (*Makkabäerbuch*, 356) renders αἰχμαλωσία as 'Kriegsgefangene zusammen' (prisoners of war).

54. Also, Abel, *Maccabées*, 178, 251.

55. See Chapter 4.

the heroic family systematically included gathering the dispersed, thus symbolically demonstrating Israel's restoration from the oppression of their enemy and their reconciliation with their covenant God. Despite a general sense of prophetic fulfilment, Goldstein's (and others') view of messianic, eschatological fulfilment of Israel's future cannot be fully accepted; there is no indication that an eschatological era has come from this set of passages relating to Jewish migration or the rest of 1 Maccabees.[56] The association of Judas' gathering of Jews with a messianic role is, again, not evident.

5.1.3. *Judas as the Davidic messiah?*

Through nearly all verses in his eulogy, Judas is depicted as a pious warrior who delivers salvation to his nation, and his deeds are identified with the fulfilment of Davidic messianic hope which is an underlining theme throughout. The following two verses in the eulogy, together with other references and allusions to David, the Davidic dynasty, or to a future Davidic heir that are found in 1 Maccabees, have often been incorporated into the argument for Hasmonean kingship propaganda. This section will discuss these two verses in detail.

> **3.4 – 'he was made like a lion in his deeds and like a whelp roaring in the hunt'** (ὡμοιώθη λέοντι ἐν τοῖς ἔργοις αὐτοῦ καὶ ὡς σκύμνος ἐρευγόμενος εἰς θήραν)

The image of Judas in the eulogy generally exhibits a warrior figure, and I have previously discussed the claims of Goldstein and van der Kooij, namely that the pro-Hasmonean author deliberately used materials relating to David, the Davidic kingship, or the future Davidic heir in the description of the Hasmoneans, with the conclusion that there is no clear case in 1 Maccabees which suggests a monarchical agenda. Van der Kooij, in his list of these biblical materials, included 3.4, arguing that the

---

56. Wright refers to Goldstein's argument to support his argument for the continuing exile (Wright, *Faithfulness*, 155 n. 317), but in my judgement, he misrepresents Goldstein's view. Wright is correct to observe that Goldstein claimed for the continuing age of wrath in view of 2 Maccabees (Wright, *Faithfulness*, 159, referring to Goldstein, 'Messianic Promises', 84). However, on the same page, Goldstein restates his argument that 1 Maccabees' case was *the opposite*, which was already made clear in the early part of his article, saying that 'the Hasmonean propagandist, on the contrary, wrote to prove that God's instrument for bringing permanent victory to the Jews was the Hasmonean dynasty' (Goldstein, 'Messianic Promises', 75).

combined image of 'lion' and 'whelp' in this verse is intended to echo the similar image in the description of the tribe of Judah in Jacob's blessing (Gen. 49.9):[57]

> [9] *Judah is a lion's whelp; from the prey, my son, you have gone up. He crouches down, he stretches out like a lion, like a lioness – who dares rouse him up?* [10] *The sceptre shall not depart from Judah, nor the ruler's staff from between his feet, until tribute comes to him; and the obedience of the peoples is his.* (Gen. 49.9-10)

Together with v. 10, v. 9 implies the rise of the Davidic dynasty.[58] Furthermore, the early Christian tradition called the Davidic heir 'a lion of the tribe of Judah' (Rev. 5.5). Van der Kooij argues that this passage generates an affinity with Judas' image in our eulogy, and adds Mic. 5.8, which also mentions the similar beast-like image and which is in the vicinity of a discourse on the Davidic hope (Mic. 5.2-6).[59]

However, the identification of Judas with the future Davidic heir obscures the fact that this beast-like image generates a broad range of application. It should be noted that most commentators on Jacob's blessing passage lack any particular interest in Judah's image in association with a Davidic heir.[60] The reasons have to do with the popularity of the lion image throughout the ancient Near East, as well as its occurrence over one hundred times in the Hebrew Bible, with the image applied in a variety of contexts.[61] The other reference to the lion/whelp image in Balaam's oracles (Num. 23.24) is close to the promise of a future Davidic heir, but it is 'people' that take up the beast metaphor.[62] Instead, the image is elsewhere attributed to different tribes, such as Gad and Dan (Deut. 33.20, 22). Similarly, Micah's prophecy does not refer to an individual messianic figure, but to a corporate, remnant Israel to be vindicated in the future, again stressing corporate identity rather than an individual sovereign

---

57. Van der Kooij, 'Maccabean Leadership', 45. Also, Doran, 'Maccabees', 4:54–5.

58. Gordon J. Wenham, *Genesis 16–50*, WBC 2 (Nashville: Thomas Nelson, 2000), 476–9.

59. Van der Kooij, 'Maccabean Leadership', 45.

60. However, Wenham (*Genesis*, 478) indicates a possibility of the association.

61. Wenham, *Genesis*, 478; Claus Westermann, *Genesis 37–50*, trans. John C. Scullion S.J. (Minneapolis: Augsburg; London: SPCK, 1986), 229.

62. See Westermann (*Genesis*, 229), who clusters the use of the lion/whelp (or, lion) image in the so-called tribal sayings – Judah (Gen. 49.9), the remnant people (Num. 23.24), Gad (Deut. 33.20), and Dan (Deut. 33.22) – and suggests their shared origin.

figure.⁶³ Moreover, the beast-like image is also attributed to Israel's enemy in numerous cases. The image enhances the terror and fear brought by gentile nations (e.g. Joel 1.6; Isa. 5.29; Jer. 28.38) or the mightiness of God who would judge the beast-like enemies (e.g. Isa. 31.4). Interesting is the Qumran sectarian group's use of a 'lion of wrath' image as a caricature of the Hasmonean king Alexander Jannaeus, who is often assumed as an enemy of the sectarian group.⁶⁴ In other words, the beast-like image in our eulogy seems to render a rather generic meaning of fierceness.⁶⁵

3.6c – 'salvation prospered in his hand' (καὶ εὐοδώθη σωτηρία ἐν χειρὶ αὐτοῦ)

This phrase is probably associated with the cardinal pro-Hasmonean statement 'they [priests Joseph and Azariah] were not of the seed of those men [the Hasmoneans] *to whom was given salvation to Israel by their hand*' (5.62), as well as another similar phrase, 'the work prospered in their hands' (2.47).⁶⁶ Again, in contrast to Goldstein's association of the phrase with the Davidic covenant in 2 Sam. 3.18, this should rather be associated with the similar references in Judges (6.36-37; 15.18),⁶⁷ that is, the kind of saving act that the Hasmoneans performed is most closely related to the similar saving acts carried out by the judges.

---

63. Commentators are of a view that the lion and whelp image produces a sense of fearsome power and illustrates a dichotomy between the vindicated Israel and judged gentile nations, e.g. James Luther Mays, *Micah*, OTL (London: SCM, 1976), 123.

64. For recent arguments for Alexander Jannaeus as the lion of wrath, see Hanan Eshel, *The Dead Sea Scrolls: And the Hasmonean State*, SDSSRL (Grand Rapids: Eerdmans, 2008), Chapter 6; Géza G. Xeravits, 'From the Forefathers to the "Angry Lion": Qumran and the Hasmoneans', in Xeravits and Zsengellér, eds., *The Books of the Maccabees*, 211–21. A contrasting view of Jannaeus regarding Josephus' account of his cruelty as legendary was made by Joseph Klausner, 'Judah Aristobulus and Jannaeus Alexander', in *The World History of the Jewish People: Vol. 6, The Hellenistic Age*, ed. Abraham Shalit (London: Allen, 1972), 222–41.

65. Also, Abel, *Maccabées*, 53. An interesting cross-reference to the lion-whelp image of Judas is offered by Oesterley ('Maccabees', 1:75) and Fairweather and Black (*Maccabees*, 89): 2 Macc. 11.11 describes Judas and his army as λεοντηδόν ('lionish'). This reference could suggest a widespread Jewish perception of Judas as a beastly, fierce figure to the enemy, without identifying him with Judah in Genesis or the Davidic heir.

66. For the same observation, see Abel, *Maccabées*, 54; Fairweather and Black, *Maccabees*, 89; Doran, 'Maccabees', 4:55.

67. For a detailed discussion, see Chapter 4.

To summarize, our analysis on the quasi-Davidic-messianic expressions in the eulogy leads us to a negative conclusion. It cannot be ascertained that the image of lion and whelp and the expression 'salvation prospering in his hand' bear any allusions to the Davidic messianic theme. The author's intention is limited to portraying a fierce, beast-like imagery unto Judas. Rather, he again incorporates the expressions characterizing biblical judges. Although our conclusion is negative about Hasmonean kingship propaganda as the authorial intention, we can freshly re-introduce the old view that 1 Maccabees portrays the Hasmoneans as national heroes who deliver the Judean nation from destruction, and who wait for the coming of the Davidic messiah. What is new in this re-introduction of the old view is the identification of the Deuteronomic covenantal framework as the streaming theme in the narrative of 1 Maccabees, and as the defining theme for the role of the Hasmoneans. In order to make this intention clear, the author incorporates the imagery of the judges and elaborates upon it to depict the Hasmoneans. The previous chapter already demonstrated the presence of this theme in the overview of use of Scripture in 1 Maccabees. We will continue to see the same pattern in Simon's eulogy.

5.1.4. *Summary*

Generally speaking, the eulogy evokes the biblical imagery of Israel's restoration. This is mainly achieved by allusion to scriptural themes and ideas rather than specific individual biblical materials. The comparison between Judas' and Simon's eulogies generates a noticeable degree of parallelism. And yet, there is a marked difference in which the vocabulary of Judas' eulogy seems deliberately less exaggerated and less impressive, and more ambiguous than Simon's. This difference means that whilst scriptural allusion regarding Israel's restoration is generally visible, the author takes notable care to differentiate Judas' career as the early stage of restoration which reaches climax under Simon's rule. Finally, the role of Judas is salvific, but little evidence is given for any Davidic-messianic designation.

5.2. *Simon's eulogy*

As observed from the comparison between the two eulogies, the consequences of Simon's leadership are exhibited on a greater scale than those of Judas. This difference may reflect the overall narrative development. By the time Simon was high priest and ruler in Judea, the nation was eventually liberated from the Seleucid overload with many duties such as taxation and tributes exempted, fortified both in and outside of it, and reformed/restored of its cultic system and religious values (13.41-53). The narrative reaches the final climax of the successes of the Hasmonean wars. We will see that many elements of Israel's future hope are seen as fulfilled in this eulogy. As Goldstein remarks, 'the abundant echoes of prophecies in the poem here are intended to suggest to the Jewish reader that the age of fulfilment of the prophecies of Israel's glory had begun in the years of Simon's rule'.[68] A similar viewpoint is expressed by Nickelsburg, who calls the eulogy a 'veritable pastiche of prophetic clichés strongly [suggesting] that the time of fulfilment of the prophecies of Israel's glory had begun in the years of Simon's rule'.[69] Note that he goes on to state, 'The covenantal blessings now rest on Israel, and the high priesthood and the title of "king" are legitimately the possession of the Hasmoneans',[70] a statement which will meet critical evaluation in due course.

5.2.1. *Restoration of Israel – covenantal blessing*
Just as in Judas' eulogy, on the whole, the depiction of Simon in the poem underlines the biblical theme of Israel's restoration. Simon's case is a relatively more explicit, morphologically identifiable allusion to the biblical theme. As such, we will see in this section the characteristics of the Deuteronomic covenantal blessing. In other words, the Judean restoration under Simon is depicted as Israel under covenantal blessing in accordance with the Deuteronomic covenant principles. It is in this eulogy that we will observe almost all the constituents of YHWH's promise of blessing upon his covenant people. In this regard, the following three verses, vv. 8, 9 and 12, are of particular interest.

> **14.8 – 'they were cultivating their land with peace and the land gave its produce and the trees in the plain their fruit'** (ἦσαν γεωργοῦντες τὴν γῆν αὐτῶν μετ' εἰρήνης, καὶ ἡ γῆ ἐδίδου τὰ γενήματα αὐτῆς καὶ τὰ ξύλα τῶν πεδίων τὸν καρπὸν αὐτῶν)

Scholars have unanimously made a link between this verse and Zech. 8.12. We will see that their syntactical arrangement is almost identical, and it is certainly possible that the original Hebrew version of this verse may have been identical with the Zecharianic passage. To this, Goldstein adds Lev. 26.4 and Ezek. 34.27,[71] which contain similar language. Indeed, all these references are plausible candidates as scriptural sources, and as

---

68. Goldstein, *1 Maccabees*, 490.
69. Nickelsburg, 'Eschatology', 589.
70. Nickelsburg, 'Eschatology', 589.
71. Also, Abel, *Maccabées*, 251; Doran, 'Maccabees', 4:159.

we shall see below, there are potentially more. A close look at each of these biblical references reveals a feature that is coherent and uniform, which in turn provides an important clue to understand our author's purpose of using Scripture.

Let us begin with Zechariah. The prophecy reads:

> For there shall be a sowing of peace. The vine shall give its fruit, and the ground shall give its produce, and the heavens shall give their dew. And I will cause the remnant of this people to possess all these things. (Zech. 8.12)

With the use of agricultural terminology, the Zecharianic reference bears great resemblance to 1 Maccabees. Cultivating the land in peace (γεωργοῦντες τὴν γῆν αὐτῶν μετ' εἰρήνης) in the eulogy recalls Zechariah's sowing (or seeds) of peace (זרע השלום), followed by productivity of the ground and fruitfulness of the tree (ἡ γῆ ἐδίδου τὰ γενήματα αὐτῆς καὶ τὰ ξύλα τῶν πεδίων τὸν καρπὸν αὐτῶν), recalling the same image in the prophecy (הגפן תתן פריה והארץ תתן את־יבולה). The Septuagint of Zechariah generally follows this syntactical arrangement, with the exception of the first part of the prophecy which reads, 'Rather, I will demonstrate peace' (ἀλλ' ἢ δείξω εἰρήνην), an alteration which reinforces divine initiative for the event.[72] Before turning to the semantic context of the prophecy, consider the prophecy in Ezekiel in which a similar picture of agricultural revitalization is promised:

> I will make with them a *covenant of peace* and banish wild beasts from the land, so that they may dwell securely in the wilderness and sleep in the woods...they shall be showers of blessing. *And the trees of the field shall yield their fruit, and the earth shall yield its increase*, and they shall be secure in their land. (Ezek. 34.25-27)

The covenant of peace (ברית שלום), which encompasses zoological as well as agricultural matters, entails the combined image of the productive land/fruitful tree. The Septuagint does not alter the syntax significantly except for replacing the people with David as the recipient of the covenant of peace.[73] Leviticus likewise reads:

---

72. That the eulogy follows the Hebrew version is in line with the suggestion that the Greek translator of 1 Maccabees was dependent on the Hebrew version of Scripture rather than the Septuagint. See §2.1.

73. Concerning the prominence of the future figure in the prophetic corpus, see below the discussion on scholarly claims about messianic depiction of Simon.

> If you walk in my statutes and observe my commandments and do them, then I will give you your rains in their season, and *the land shall yield its increase, and the trees of the field shall yield their fruit.* (Lev. 26.3-4)

Whilst the concept of peace is absent, the combined image of agricultural revival is retained. In fact, the divine act of bestowing peace on the land is addressed in v. 6 (also in the Septuagint). In that verse, the effect of the peace is security as much as fertility – revival of every aspect of life in the promised land. Such visions cohere with the prophets' aforementioned words, as well as the effect of Simon's achievements.

Crucial in these biblical references is their semantic inter-connection with one another. The Zecharianic prophecy concerning re-fertility lies within the prophet's overall vision of Israel's future restoration in ch. 8, comprising of the return of YHWH to Zion (vv. 2-3), the establishment of peace in Jerusalem (vv. 3-5), and the re-gathering of the dispersed (vv. 6-8). As Hinckley G. Mitchell and others have rightly commented, this vision strongly echoes the covenant language of Deuteronomy.[74] In particular, the prophecies of blessing are set as direct antitheses of the curses that fell upon Israel as the consequence of their covenantal defilement, strongly recalling the antithetical pair of covenantal blessing/curse set in Deuteronomy 29–30. Thus, the promise of re-fertility of the land is set directly opposite to its preceding verse (v. 10) which refers to the ruined and exilic state of the nation where there were 'no wages for men and animals' as 'insecurity' was present.

---

74. Hinckley G. T. Mitchell, John Merlin Powis Smith and Julius A. Bewer, *A Critical and Exegetical Commentary on Haggai, Zechariah, Malachi and Jonah*, 3rd imp., ICC (Edinburgh: T. & T. Clark, 1951), 206; David L. Peterson, *Haggai and Zechariah 1–8*, OTL (London: SCM, 1984), 306–7. Peterson is unconvincing when he comments, '[t]he situation [in Zechariah's vision of fertility] is different from that in the promises of Deut. 6.10ff., 8.7-10' (307). It is legitimate to differentiate the blessing in Deuteronomy 30 from the initial blessings stated in previous chapters, e.g. Deut. 6.10-12; 7.13; 8.7-10; 28.4, insofar as the blessing in ch. 30 is addressed specifically under the condition of Israel's repentance, and is characteristically about returning to the land and restoring the Israelite community. On the other hand, this set of texts – Deut. 30, previous chapters, and Zech. 8 – not only shares the same covenant terminology, but also uniformly stresses the agricultural revitalization as the reward of Israel's faithfulness to the covenant with YHWH, e.g. Deut. 7.13; 28.4, 11-12; 30.9. Thus, it is more precise to say that the Zecharianic vision of fertility is characteristically part of the Deuteronomic legacy concerning covenantal blessing.

The same is the case in Ezekiel. The whole of ch. 34 prophesies about restoration of Israel through the interweaving of judgement on false prophets and vindication/return of the remnant.[75] Striking is its explicit use of the covenant language which involves references to God's active initiative (for example, repeatedly claiming 'my sheep' in vv. 1-24, and 'my people' in vv. 25-31),[76] the expression 'I will make a covenant (of peace) with them' (v. 25, וכרתי להם ברית),[77] and the so-called Covenant Formula, 'I will be their God and they will be my people' (v. 30; also, 'I will be their God' in v. 24),[78] all of which are characteristically Deuteronomic.[79] Moreover, the promised act of 'banishing wild beasts' (v. 25) is an overturn of the punishment formerly made, that is, the covenantal blessing that overturns the curse formerly made in Deuteronomy 30.[80] The blessing bestowed on 'the hill' (referring to Jerusalem)[81] also resembles Zech. 8.13. The fertility and security in Ezekiel 34 (vv. 25-29) are compulsory elements in the Deuteronomic covenantal blessing. Thus, the two prophets uniformly exhibit the Deuteronomic covenant motif, and this type of connection is already evident in Leviticus.

In a way, the passage in Leviticus displays an even closer Deuteronomic connection. Set as a final remark of the so-called Holiness Code section (Lev. 17–26), ch. 26 sets out a juxtaposition of blessing and curse upon Israel in compliance with their covenantal relationship with YHWH.[82] It

---

75. Notable is an analogy between Zech. 1–8 and Ezek. 34–37 made by Stephen L. Cook, *Prophecy and Apocalypticism: The Postexilic Social Setting* (Minneapolis: Fortress, 1995), 148–53. The manifold similarities between the two suggest, says Cook, 'a dependence of the Zechariah group on the writings of the Ezekiel group' (149–50).

76. For the same comment, see Paul M. Joyce, *Ezekiel: A Commentary*, LHBOTS 482 (New York: T&T Clark, 2009), 196–7; Leslie C. Allen, *Ezekiel 20–48*, WBC 29 (Nashville: Thomas Dallas, 1990), 161–4.

77. Joyce (*Ezekiel*, 198) identifies this phrase with 'a covenant of peace…an everlasting covenant' in 37.26, the latter of which ('an everlasting covenant') also appears in 16.60.

78. E.g. 11.20; 14.11; 34.24; 36.28; 37.23, 27.

79. E.g. Deut. 29.13. For Deuteronomic phraseology (including covenantal terms), see Weinfeld, *Deuteronomic School*, 320–65.

80. Joyce, *Ezekiel*, 198.

81. See Joyce, *Ezekiel*, 199; Allen, *Ezekiel*, 158.

82. The holiness code's structure, in which the legal document ends with blessing/curse, is frequently found in the Hebrew Bible (e.g. Exod. 23.25-33; Deut. 28; Josh. 24.20), and is also a prominent feature in the ancient Near East. See Jacob Milgrom, *Leviticus 23–27*, AB 3B (New York: Doubleday, 2001), 2286.

has ample usage of covenant language such as direct references to making/breaking the covenant (vv. 9, 15, 25, 44), the covenant formula (v. 12), and references to the covenants of Abraham, Isaac, and Jacob (vv. 42, 45). Notably, unlike the two prophetic passages that parallel the former curse and the promised blessing, the chapter contains the three stages of Israel's fortune/misfortune, namely, the blessing of the promised land through territorial conquest (vv. 3-13), the curse that leads to devastation of, and exile from, the land (vv. 14-39), and the blessing of restoring their former fortune (vv. 40-45). This is precisely the Deuteronomic paradigm we have noted earlier.[83] In this scheme, the blessing of fertility (and security) in v. 4 not only blends the Deuteronomic sense of covenantal blessing but also interconnects itself with the aforementioned prophecies of Zechariah and Ezekiel. In fact, the phrase 'I will send down the rains in their season' (v. 4) is repeated in the Ezekielian prophecy we have discussed, as well as agricultural fertility that follows.[84] Therefore, the fertility themes in these texts are interconnected by the web of the covenant motif, most decisively expressed in Deuteronomy.

Indeed, the Deuteronomic covenantal framework and the fertility theme in particular reach out to a wider range of biblical texts. Hosea 2.21-23 renders a prophecy for an overturn of the cursed land into the fertile land.[85] Likewise, Jer. 31.27-28 again employs agricultural terms such as 'sowing the seed in Israel and Judah' and 'building and planting'. Jeremiah 23.3 also bears a strong resemblance to the Ezekielian prophecy with terms such as 'gathering the remnant', 'fruitfulness' and 'fertility'. In fact, the whole unit of Ezek. 34.25-30 has often been associated with Jer. 23.1-6 by commentators, noting the indictment of the rulers by using the same shepherd metaphor and the use of similar vocabulary throughout the passages.[86] Moreover, the quoted prophecy of Jeremiah is reminiscent

---

83. See Chapter 4. For the same comment, see Frank H. Gorman Jr., *Divine Presence and Community: A Commentary on the Book of Leviticus* (Grand Rapids: Eerdmans; Edinburgh: Handsels, 1997), 142. Unlike Deut. 30, Leviticus does not explicitly recapitulate the major components of blessing in the context of restoration (vv. 40-45). However, restored blessing should be understood as implicit when the text reads, 'But if they confess their iniquity…I will remember the covenant of their forefathers…' (Lev. 26.40, 42, 45).

84. See Arnold M. Hals, *Ezekiel*, FOTL 19 (Grand Rapids: Eerdmans, 1989), 252. Hals suggests Ezekiel's utilization of old traditions which include, in the case of Ezek. 34.25-30, Lev. 26.4-13.

85. Tilly (*Makkabäer*, 277) rightly adds Haggai to the list of relevant biblical materials to 1 Macc. 14.8.

86. E.g. Hals, *Ezekiel*, 251; Allen, *Ezekiel*, 160.

of Leviticus 26 (especially v. 9) which strongly resonates with the Deuteronomic theme of covenantal blessing.[87]

In short, the Deuteronomic covenantal framework, in which the conditional curse and blessing are dependent upon Israel's obedience to their covenant and the promise of 're-blessing' has the power to retract the harsh and devastated present reality, runs throughout the prophetic corpus and other biblical texts, such as Leviticus. The image of agricultural revitalization is one aspect of it. Let us consider another aspect in the next verse.

14.9 – 'Elders were sitting on the street, all talking about good things together, and young men clothed themselves with glory and war clothes'
(πρεσβύτεροι ἐν ταῖς πλατείαις ἐκάθηντο, πάντες περὶ ἀγαθῶν ἐκοινολογοῦντο, καὶ οἱ νεανίσκοι ἐνεδύσαντο δόξας καὶ στολὰς πολέμου)

This verse has often been linked with Zech. 8.4-5, the semantic context of which is again fundamentally covenantal and Deuteronomic.[88] The prophecy reads:

> Thus says the Lord of hosts: old men and old women shall again sit in the streets of Jerusalem, each with staff in hand because of great age. And the streets of the city shall be full of boys and girls playing in its streets. (Zech. 8.4-5)

The identification between the two texts may not be as apparent as the former case. On the one hand, certain words are correspondent: 'elders' in 1 Maccabees with 'old men and old women' in Zechariah; 'sitting in the streets' (of Jerusalem) in both texts; 'young men' with 'full of boys and girls'; and especially, the combined image of old and young generations peacefully dwelling in the city in both texts. The impression in both texts is peace and security for all generations of the community. On the other hand, the details lack similarities. The activities between the two elderly groups are somewhat different with peaceful conversation among the elderly in the eulogy missing in the Zecharianic vision. For the young generations, while the Zecharianic prophecy states 'boys and girls' (ילדים וילדות; παιδάριον καὶ κοράσιον in the Septuagint) playing in the street, 1 Maccabees has an image of young men of military careers.

---

87. Leslie C. Allen, *Jeremiah*, OTL (Louisville: Westminster John Knox, 2008), 258.
88. Cf. Goldstein (*Maccabees*, 491) relates Isa. 52.1 to the description of the youth putting on armour, but their relation is not clear.

Moreover, the polarity of the age groups of the society in Zechariah is less clear in 1 Maccabees, where the young male soldiers do not evoke the image of 'full of boys and girls'. If the two age groups in Zechariah collectively refer to the whole community on whom the blessing is bestowed,[89] its relation to the two age groups in 1 Maccabees is possible. If, on the other hand, the Zecharianic groups are intended to represent easily neglected, vulnerable groups of the society, thus indicating establishment of equality and justice,[90] such an image differs from that of 1 Maccabees in which the emphasis is on rejuvenation and re-vitality. Their differences thus prevent prophecy from being neatly identified with the verse in Simon's eulogy. Nevertheless, the combined image of the old and young peacefully dwelling in the street in both texts still tells of *a generic image of longevity*.[91]

The context of the peaceful, age-long inhabitancy of the old and young, which also takes a part in the Deuteronomic covenantal blessing, is significant, for example, 'And he will make you more prosperous and numerous than your fathers... The Lord your God will make you abundantly prosperous in all the work of your hand, in the fruit of your womb and in the fruit of your cattle and in the fruit of your ground. For the Lord will again take delight in prospering you, as he took delight in your fathers' (Deut. 30.5, 9). It is worth noting that the Zecharianic prophecy sits within the aforementioned semantic context of Zechariah 8, where the promise of fertility deeply resonates with the covenantal blessing in Deuteronomy. The peaceful inhabitancy is a direct effect of YHWH's return to Zion and Jerusalem (v. 3), and the land and everything in it will be blessed.

The overturning effect of blessing upon the previous, cursed state also recalls the same effect we have earlier discussed in Deuteronomy and other texts. As David L. Peterson rightly observes, the Zecharianic prophecy in 8.4-5 is a return to the depopulation of Jerusalem described in the preceding chapter (7.14, 'and I scattered them with a whirlwind among all the nations that they had not known. Thus the land they left was desolate, so that no one went to and fro, and the pleasant land was made desolate').[92] The 'streets' in 8.4, רחבות (πλατεῖαι), which Peterson trans-

---

89. E.g. Peterson, *Haggai and Zechariah*, 300.

90. Ralph L. Smith, *Micah–Malachi*, WBC 32 (Nashville: Thomas Nelson, 1984), 233.

91. Rex Mason, *The Books of Haggai, Zechariah and Malachi*, CBC (Cambridge: Cambridge University Press, 1977), 69.

92. Peterson, *Haggai and Zechariah*, 300, referring to a 'repopulation motif' coined by A. Petitjean. Peterson adds Jer. 30.18-21; 31.2-6, 23-30; 33.1-13.

lates as 'plazas', are the same place where death and devastation occurred. As he puts it, 'what was earlier a symbol for national degradation and defeat becomes a sign of hope'.[93] Likewise, 1 Maccabees presents a vivid contrast between curse and blessing in the πλατεῖαι. In ch. 1, the catastrophes in Judea are presented systematically, as well as theologically. The Judeans' making of a 'covenant' with the Seleucids results in 'defilement of their ancestral *covenant*' (1.15), followed by the horror of curse. It reads:

> [Antiochus IV Epiphanes] constructed an abomination of desolation on the altar, and in the cities around Judea they built altars and burned incense at the doors of the houses and in the city squares (πλατείαις)... And they were using their power on those who were found in Israel month by month in the cities... (1 Macc. 1.54-58)

The city squares, πλατεῖαι, were filled with, and contaminated by, gentile altars erected all around the Judean territory, and the people who observed their ancestral covenant were massacred on the streets. Such a picture is taken up in Mattathias' lament in the next chapter:

> Woe to me, why was I born to see this, the destruction of my people and the destruction of the holy city?... Her infants were killed in her city squares (πλατείαις), her young people by the sword of an enemy. (1 Macc. 2.7-9)

In fact, in this passage we find an image directly opposing longevity. Infants (νήπια) and young people (νεανίσκοι) died in their pre-blossoming age. These πλατεῖαι, described as a symbol of devastation and, indeed, curse in the introductory stage of the narrative of 1 Maccabees reappear in the climax of the narrative in Simon's eulogy, this time in a dramatic reverse fulfilment of the promise of covenantal blessing.

An essentially similar pattern of the old and young's longevity and peaceful inhabitancy in the restored land is recurrent in the prophetic literature. Consider Jeremiah:

> [10] Hear the word of the Lord, O nations... 'He who scattered Israel will gather him, and will keep him as a shepherd keeps his flock'... [12] They shall come and sing aloud on the height of Zion, and they shall be radiant over the goodness of the Lord, over the grain, the wine, and the oil, and over the young of the flock and the herd; their life shall be like a watered garden, and they shall languish no more. [13] Then shall the young women rejoice in the dance, and *the young men and the old shall be merry*... (Jer. 31.10-13)

---

93. Peterson, *Haggai and Zechariah*, 300–301.

Here in v. 13 a similar expression vis-à-vis peaceful inhabitancy and longevity is found. Despite its abbreviated form, the joyful image of the young and old men vividly recalls the same image in our eulogy. Strikingly, the preceding verse (v. 12) expresses a fertile image of the land very similar to the ones we have noted earlier, especially the promise of restoration in Hos. 2.21-23, reversing the former curse.[94] The multifaceted character of restoration – divine initiative uttered with the shepherd metaphor, the return of YHWH to Zion, fertility and security in the land, and peaceful inhabitancy with longevity – coheres with the image of covenantal blessing in Zechariah 8, as we have seen, and is indeed the same image depicted in the eulogy of Simon, except for the divine image, the absence of which is characteristic of 1 Maccabees. Like Zechariah 8, Deuteronomy 30, Simon's eulogy, and multiple other biblical texts, the gist of the rhetoric in this passage is the promise of reverting the curse; Leslie C. Allen regards Jeremiah 30–31 as 'a development of the sketch in chs. 26–29 of a positive future of God's people that would follow the period of exile'.[95] The overturning force is even self-evident in v. 13b, 'I will turn their mourning into joy; I will comfort them, give them gladness for sorrow'.

Consider another example from Isaiah:

> [17] For behold, I create new heavens and a new earth, and the former things shall not be remembered or come into mind. [18] But be glad and rejoice forever in that which I create; for behold, I create Jerusalem to be a joy, and her people to be a gladness. [19] I will rejoice in Jerusalem and be glad in my people; no more shall be heard in it the sound of weeping and the cry of distress. [20] *No more shall there be in it an infant who lives but a few days, or an old man who does not fill out his days*, for the young man shall die a hundred years old…they shall plant vineyards and eat their fruit. [22] They shall not build and another inhabit; they shall not plant and another eat; for like the days of a tree shall the days of my people be, and my chosen shall long enjoy the work of their hands… (Isa. 65.17-23)

Whilst the passage is more readily associated with the creation motif in Genesis 1–2, as evident from the exclusive use of the significant verb ברא 'to create' in vv. 17 and 18,[96] the covenant theme is also vividly manifest

---

94. Also, Hag. 1.10-11, which is reversed in Zech. 8.12.

95. Allen, *Jeremiah*, 333. Allen even titled the whole section of Jer. 30–31 as 'Covenant-Centred Hope' (330).

96. Many commentators do not mention the Deuteronomic language as a possible association with the Isaianic prophecy, but rather pay attention to the creation theme in Genesis. See Claus Westermann, *Isaiah 40–66*, trans. M. G. Stalker, OTL (London:

in this description of the paradisal state of inhabitancy in the promised land.[97] The multifaceted character of restoration, such as Jerusalem's refurbishment with peace and prosperity, agricultural revitalization, active divine initiative, and use of the covenantal term such as 'my people', should by now recall the aforementioned texts of Deuteronomy 30, Zechariah 8, Jeremiah 30, and Simon's eulogy. We may discuss one more verse in the eulogy before drawing a conclusion.

14.12 – 'each man sat on his vine and fig tree, and there was no-one who opposed them' (ἐκάθισεν ἕκαστος ὑπὸ τὴν ἄμπελον αὐτοῦ καὶ τὴν συκῆν αὐτοῦ, καὶ οὐκ ἦν ὁ ἐκφοβῶν αὐτούς)

Another strong biblical echo is found in the description of the secure state of the Judean community. Most commentators associate this verse with Mic. 4.4, Zech. 3.10 and 1 Kgs 5.5 (Heb. 4.25),[98] and we will discuss the first two texts and leave the last reference for later (see 'Simon as Davidic Messiah?'). While the syntax of the Zecharianic prophecy is not identical with that of Micah, the context of Zechariah's vision of restoration, as we have seen, is highly familiar to the author of 1 Maccabees, and the Zecharianic vision of secure inhabitancy certainly echoes in the eulogy. The crux in this verse of the eulogy, just as we have observed in the other verses, is its consistent and cumulative display of the Deuteronomic covenantal blessing as an underlining theme for the outcomes of Simon's achievements.

SCM, 1969), 408–11; John D. W. Watts, *Isaiah 34–66*, rev. edn, WBC 25 (Nashville: Thomas Nelson, 2000), 925–6. R. N. Whybray comments, 'what is promise here is a return to the legendary longevity of the age before the Flood recorded in Genesis'; see Whybray, *Isaiah 40–66*, paperback edn, NCB (London: Marshall, Morgan & Scott, 1981), 277.

97. It was Joseph Blenkinsopp who rightly notes the Deuteronomic covenant language in the prophecy. Thus, for instance, v. 20 is reminiscent of the blessing code in Exod. 23.26 ('no one shall have a miscarriage...') and vv. 21-22a of Deut. 28.30. See Blenkinsopp, *Isaiah 56–66*, AB 19 (New York: Doubleday, 2003), 287–90, especially 288.

98. An exception is Tilly (*Makkabäer*, 277), who adds Jer. 30.10. Although this passage is not included in the present discussion, the idea of secure inhabitancy in the land within the context of Deuteronomic covenantal blessing is certainly the underlying message in this passage, and provides another echo of the same theme as the other biblical materials. Also, Abel (*Maccabées*, 252) notes the last clause 'there was no-one who opposed him' and suggests some biblical materials on the clause, Deut. 28.26 and Neh. 2.11, as well as Mic. 4.4.

The syntax of Micah's prophecy is almost the same as that of the eulogy:

> but they shall sit every man under his vine and under his fig tree, and no one shall make them afraid, for the mouth of the Lord of hosts has spoken. (Mic. 4.4)[99]

The close verbal parallel between the two texts suggests that the Hebrew version of 1 Maccabees may well have used ישב ('to sit'), as does Micah (the deviation between καθίζω in 1 Maccabees and ἀναπαύω in the Septuagint of Micah is probably the result of 1 Maccabees' author's independent rendering of Greek in his translation).[100] The other difference between the two texts is an absence of divine reference in the eulogy which should probably be attributed to the characteristic of 1 Maccabees.[101] Consider the Zecharianic prophecy:

> In that day, declares the Lord of hosts, every one of you will invite his neighbour to come under his vine and under his fig tree. (Zech. 3.10)

---

99. Note that 1 Maccabees ὑπὸ τὴν ἄμπηλον αὐτοῦ καὶ τὴν συκῆν αὐτοῦ ('on/upon his vine and fig tree') contains only one ὑπό, whereas the Micean prophecy repeats it before 'fig tree' and uses a different word, ...תחת...ותחת in Hebrew and ὑποκάτω... καὶ ὑποκάτω... in Greek. The Lucianic group of 1 Maccabees agrees with Micah by using ὑποκάτω instead of ὑπό and repeating it for 'fig tree'. Even the Latin seems to follow the same pattern by inserting *sub* before *ficulnea*, 'upon fig tree' (La^L X (B) V). Should this mean that the Lucianic and Latin texts provide a better reading for 1 Macc. 14.12? It seems, however, that the Lucianic recension and the Latin were influenced by such stark similarities between 1 Macc. 14.12 and Mic. 4.4, and that scribes of 1 Maccabees smoothed out the verse by 'correcting' it with Micah^Gk, perhaps with an assumption that the Greek translator of 1 Maccabees consulted Micah^Gk. On the contrary, the main verb of the clause does not match between 1 Maccabees and Micah^Gk, καθίζω and ἀναπαύω respectively, and there is no textual variant of 1 Maccabees attesting to ἀναπαύω. In other words, there is no reason why 1 Maccabees should follow the pattern of repeating ὑποκάτω like the Lucianic and Latin readings. It seems more plausible that the scribes of 1 Maccabees later smoothed out the verse to look more Hebraic and to make 1 Maccabees' use of the Mican prophecy more deliberate.

100. See §2.1 for a more detailed discussion on the Greek vocabulary of 1 Maccabees in comparison to that of the Septuagint, which concludes that the author of 1 Maccabees was partly dependent upon, and partly independent from, the vocabulary of the Greek translation of biblical literature. Furthermore, one cannot easily determine the reason behind 1 Maccabees' deviation in certain cases, and it would be presumptive to impose the idea of intentional edition, as one might be tempted.

101. See a similar tendency found in 1 Macc. 14.8's echo of Zech. 8.12.

Here, again, despite the lack of syntactical resemblance, a secure state of inhabitancy as a future blessing is characterized by the symbolic image of dwelling under one's own vine and fig tree, which may well justify Goldstein's suggestion of this Zecharianic prophecy as another candidate.

The promise of secure inhabitancy is again an outcome of Israel's reversion to its former glory from a previous curse. In Micah, the unit in which the prophecy in question takes part (4.1-8) is preceded by the earlier unit (3.1-12) which delineates condemnation of unjust leaders of Jerusalem. The condemnation, which points out the leaders' injustice and bloodshed in their evil scheme of building up Zion (3.10), is climaxed by the last verse, 'Therefore because of you Zion shall be ploughed as a field; Jerusalem shall become a heap of ruins, and the mountain of the house a wooded height' (3.12). This cursed state is then dramatically interrupted by an eschatological-formulaic phrase, (והיה) באחרים הימים ('[it shall come to pass] in the latter days'), and is thematically extended to the unit in 4.1-8, which envisions God's involvement in the building project of Zion, replacing the unjust human leaders, and thereby inaugurating an eschatological era.[102] In this depiction, the Deuteronomic idea of covenantal blessing as a reversion of previous curse may not be apparent in the strict sense. Nevertheless, the pattern of reverting blessing upon a previous curse, enacted by divine initiative, is deeply resonant in the aforementioned prophecies concerning agricultural re-fertility and peaceful indwelling of the future community of God. Also resonant in the former prophecies is the theme of universal worship (Mic. 4.1-3), just as it was in the Zecharianic visions climaxing toward universal worship (Zech. 8.2-23). Zechariah 3.10 follows a similar pattern in which the previous curse is overtly turned to blessing in the days to come. Again, the theme of covenant is not spelled out in the text, and yet commentators recognize the vision of secure inhabitancy as an outcome of Israel's remission of their sins (in view of v. 9, 'I will remove the inequity of this land in a single

---

102. As Charles S. Shaw rightly observes, the two units (3.1-12 and 4.1-8) are 'united by theme and rhetorical situation'. That is, they are united by the theme of building up Zion, and the rhetorical situation that overtly envisages catastrophe in Jerusalem as a prerequisite for the restoration in 4.1-8 to take place; see Shaw, *Speeches of Micah: A Rhetorical-Historical Analysis*, JSOTSup 145 (Sheffield: Sheffield Academic, 1993), 101. Similarly, see D. R. Hillers, *A Commentary on the Book of the Prophet Micah*, Hermeneia (Philadelphia: Fortress, 1984), 50. Compare, in contrast, J. M. P. Smith, *A Critical and Exegetical Commentary on Micah*, ICC (Edinburgh, 1912), 84, and a general summary on the textual issue pertaining to these passages in Micah by William McKane, *The Book of Micah: Introduction and Commentary* (Edinburgh: T. & T. Clark, 1998), 117–27.

day', which belongs to the same unit as v. 10).¹⁰³ Michael R. Stead makes a succinct point when he observes the correlation between Zechariah 1–6 and 7–8 under the theme of covenant. Not only is it the latter chapters that further shape the former with 'a covenantal overtone... "They will be my people and I will be their God"', but also it is the former chapters in which the Deuteronomic theme of covenant is implicitly imbedded through echoes of the Deuteronomic covenantal idea, for example, the Deuteronomic dictum, '...if you diligently obey the voice of the Lord your God' (Deut. 28.1) being quoted in Zech. 6.15.¹⁰⁴ 'This intertext, which (in its wider context) links to all the blessings of the covenant', says Stead, 'reminds us that the return of Yahweh to dwell is because of his covenant promise to bless his people'.¹⁰⁵

The image of secure inhabitancy evoked by Micah and Zechariah thus complies with the other aforementioned prophecies in such a way that they uniformly generate the Deuteronomic theme of Israel's covenant with YHWH. Although their immediate contexts do not explicitly exhibit covenant terminology, their patterns of blessing reverting curse, divine initiative, and YHWH's universal lordship all take up the Deuteronomic covenant phraseology and motif. It can be said that the covenantal context is present at a grass-roots level of the prophets' vision for Israel's future.

In summary, the prophetic expressions in vv. 8, 9 and 12 of Simon's eulogy highlight the following themes: agricultural revitalization, social safety and longevity of life, and territorial security. What is more, these themes are the core characteristics of Israel's covenantal blessing in Deuteronomic terms. In turn, several conclusive points can be derived which largely echo our conclusions in the previous section (§2.5). First, Israel's welfare is determined by the mechanism of the Deuteronomic covenantal framework. The legitimation of covenantal obligation between God and Israel that was cemented in Deuteronomy 28–30 is consistently reaffirmed throughout prophetic literature. Second, this covenantal mechanism generated a default sequence of history such as covenantal defilement followed by covenantal curse which, provided that Israel returns to God, is then ultimately overturned by covenantal blessing – the covenantal DCRB paradigm.¹⁰⁶ Third, this covenantal DCRB paradigm

---

103. Smith, *Micah-Malachi*, 201; Mitchell et al., *Zechariah*, 157.
104. Michael R. Stead, *The Intertextuality of Zechariah 1–8*, LHBOTS 506 (New York: T&T Clark, 2009), 244. See Weinfeld, *Deuteronomic School*, 337, for the list of references to this phrase.
105. Stead, *Intertextuality*, 244.
106. For the rendering of the term in the present study, see Chapter 4.

shapes historical knowledge and, in turn, provides theological knowledge that God's providence for his covenantal people is everlasting. Fourth, as such, this covenantal mechanism, inasmuch as it maintains old tradition, continually fosters imagination for new hope in the midst of the present conditions and needs. This explains variations of future hope in the aforementioned prophecies. While there are differences in the prophetic visions of an ideal future (such as the trito-Isaianic future hope which is exceedingly cosmic and otherworldly compared to that of Zech. 8), it should be stressed that they uniformly promote the promise of covenantal blessing and the indispensability of covenantal obligation on Israel's part. Lastly, in those prophecies that do not render covenant terminology, the theme of covenant is still a premise upon which future hope is shaped.

5.2.2. *The Hasmoneans' territorial expansion and the biblical territorial theme*

One of the major Hasmonean achievements is undoubtedly territorial expansion. Although the expansion was mostly carried out under John Hyrcanus I,[107] 1 Maccabees readily introduces the early Hasmoneans' tendency of expanding the Judean territory as a result of their military campaigns against Seleucid cities.[108] Simon's eulogy directly deals with this extra-territorial aspect of his achievements in vv. 5-7. It states that he 'enlarged the border for his people and expanded the territory' (14.6), and mentions three cities in this regard, Joppa, Gazara and Baith-zur, all of which appear in the narrative with the depiction of the warfare between the Hasmoneans and their gentile enemies.[109] Scholars have disputed the connection between the Hasmonean military ideology and the biblical theme of conquering the promised land.[110] To what extent, if any, can we claim that the author of 1 Maccabees intends to draw a connection between the two?

---

107. E.g. Josephus, *Ant.* 13.254-258, 275-279.
108. 1 Macc. 5.21-22, 45, 66-68; 10.38; 11.28, 60-62; 12.32-34; 13.43-47.
109. For Baith-zur, 11.65-66; 14.33; for Gazara, 13.43-48; and Joppa, 12.33; 13.11; 14.34. Compare Josephus' statement that Simon conquered Gazara, Joppa and Jamnia. Goldstein (*1 Maccabees*, 491) suggests a scribal mistake of inserting 'Jamnia', which lies between Gazara and Joppa.
110. E.g. the Joshuan campaign and prophecies concerning the re-possession of the land (Deut. 12.20; 19.8-10). For Joppa, Goldstein (*1 Maccabees*, 490) adds Zeph. 2.5-7, prophecies against 'the inhabitants of the seacoast' (v. 5), perhaps due to Joppa's coastal location.

From the outset, it may seem that there is a surprising lack of evidence for a connection in the text, except for a discourse between Simon and Athenobius, the representative of Antiochus VII, in which Athenobius claims Joppa and Gazara. Simon replies as follows:

> Neither have we taken a foreign land, nor have we taken the property of foreigners, but the inheritance of our fathers, which was held unjustly by our enemies for a certain time. But we, seizing the occasion, are clinging to the inheritance of our fathers. But concerning Joppa and Gazara, which you claim, they were doing great harm to the people and our country, for these we will give one hundred talents. (1 Macc. 15.33-35)

Scholars often inferred from this passage that the Hasmonean ideology regarding conquest/expansion of the land is inspired by the biblical theme of conquering the promised land, imitating Joshua's military campaigns.[111] Goldstein even suggests that Joppa and Gazara were once parts of

---

111. Tcherikover (*Hellenistic Civilization*, 248–9) states that the Hasmoneans' Judaizing principles toward their subjects in the Greek cities they conquered were related to 'a broad nationalist outlook based on knowledge of Jewish history'. Bar-Kochva, *Judas Maccabaeus*, 154–5; Aryeh Kasher, 'The Changes in Manpower and Ethnic Composition of the Hasmonean Army (167–63BCE)', *JQR* 81 (1991): 325–52 (especially 344); Doran ('Maccabees', 4:55), in his comments on Judas' destruction of the ungodly in the Judean cities (3.8), refers to Josh. 10–11. Zeev Safrai makes a similar point, while distinguishing two different motives behind the Hasmonean conquest of the land: a 'holy war' of controlling the entire area of Jewish settlement and a regular war of expansion of the border (just as the distinction between Deut. 7.2 and 20.10-18 respectively), see Safrai, 'The Gentile Cities of Judea: Between the Hasmonean Occupation and the Roman Liberation', in *Studies in Historical Geography and Biblical Historiography Presented to Zecharia Kallai*, ed. G. Galil and M. Weinfeld, VTSup 81 (Leiden: Brill, 2000), 63–90 (especially 76–7). See also Rappaport ('Maccabees', 712), who observes in 1 Maccabees 'sentences reminiscent of Joshua's conquest of Canaan' (though examples are desired). It should be noted that some of these scholars make arguments that are less clear than those of others. Tcherikover, for instance, describes the Hasmoneans' acts as 'part of the political program of the Hasmoneans and not an ambition to engage in religious propaganda' (*Hellenistic Civilization*, 249). His cautious association of the territorial expansion to religious agendas reflects his overall argument that the Hasmoneans did not oppose the Hellenistic culture, and the gentile subjugation in the conquered cities was targeted at the Seleucid population rather than their culture. Bar-Kochva argues that the rationale behind the Hasmoneans' territorial expansion was a result of the following course of events: manpower growth in Judea, overpopulation, Jewish resettlement in conquered regions, and hiring and supplying foreign mercenaries to these regions. Thus he says, regarding 1 Macc. 15.33-35, that '[Simon's] declaration

Solomon's territory, now re-possessed by Simon, although his references to Ezek. 28.25 and Zeph. 2.5-7 as fulfilled prophecies concerning Joppa in 1 Macc. 14.5 are untenable.[112]

We have previously noted that Mendels rejects the idea, arguing that 1 Maccabees is deliberately ignorant of the biblical theme of territorial conquest.[113] More recently, Katell Berthelot put the same view forward in her articles, arguing that 'the notion of a 'greater Israel' based on the divine promise and the biblical texts seems to be considered a reality of the past, without programmatic effects on the present (i.e., on the period during which the authors lived)'.[114] She correctly observes that the biblical concept of the conquest of the land is not explicitly employed in 1 Maccabees. Whilst there is a reference to Joshua in the deathbed blessing (2.55), it lacks a bearing on the sense of the territorial conquest. Instead, she contends that it is the Deuteronomic ideology of 'faithfulness to the commandments of the Torah' that shaped 1 Maccabees.[115] Berthelot is also convincing when observing that the term 'the inheritance of our fathers' (τῆς κληρονομίας τῶν πατέρων ἡμῶν), which has often been taken as a reference to 'the promised land' in biblical texts by many scholars, is not to be understood as such, but rather a reference

---

is an apologia made to Athenobius…and cannot therefore reflect the original motives for the occupation [of those three gentile cities claimed by the Seleucids]'; see Bar-Kochva, 'Manpower, Economics, and Internal Strife in the Hasmonean State', in *Armée et fiscalité dans le monde antique* (Paris: Éditions du Centre National de la Recherche Scientifique, 1977), 167–94 (quotation, 175).

112. Goldstein, *1 Maccabees*, 490, 516. See also Tilly (*Maccabäer*, 277), who considers 1 Macc. 14.6 as fulfilment of biblical promises (such as Deut. 12.20; 19.8).

113. See §§1.2 and 2.5, as well as Mendels, 'Antiquity', 15. See also Mendels' monograph on the biblical concept of land conquest: *The Land of Israel as a Political Concept in Hasmonean Literature*. In that monograph, he concludes his analysis on 1 Maccabees as follows: 'the idea of the Land is not even found in the surprisingly few references to Israel's past: the rescue of the people of Israel, rather than the conquest of Palestine, seems to be their main theme' (51). Whilst Mendels' analyses on other Jewish books, which are considered as Hasmonean literature, led him to an opposite conclusion (e.g. 9–18, 57–88), in the case of 1 Maccabees (and 2 Maccabees for that matter) he seems to reject the presence of the biblical territorial theme.

114. Katell Berthelot, 'The Biblical Conquest of the Promised Land and the Hasmonean Wars According to 1 and 2 Maccabees', in Xeravits and Zsengellér, eds., *The Books of the Maccabees*, 45–60 (quotation from 46); 'Reclaiming the Land (1 Maccabees 15.28-36): Hasmonean Discourse between Biblical Tradition and Seleucid Rhetoric', *JBL* 133 (2014): 539–59.

115. Berthelot, 'Biblical Conquest', 46, 49–52.

to the Judean territory under Simon. The term shows, says Berthelot, the Hasmoneans' utilization of Hellenistic discourse, rather than anything distinctively biblical.[116]

However, although one could say that the evidence for the biblical territorial theme may not be decisive, it seems equally inadequate to entirely reject the presence of the theme in 1 Maccabees. For instance, Simon's Hellenistic, thus diplomatic, style of speech in his discourse with Athenobius was already observed by Goldstein. He aptly puts: 'Simon does not attempt to argue that Joppe [*sic*] and Gazara lay within the confines of the promised land or once belonged to Solomon... The Seleucid authorities might not have conceded the validity of the evidence. Simon claims the cities by right of conquest in just wars of retribution, a principle recognized in Greek international law.'[117] In other words, Simon could still have the biblical concept of the promised land in mind, and yet, in his diplomatic discourse with the Seleucids, he knows how to play the game. Let me elaborate on what it means to 'have the biblical concept of the promised land in mind'. It should thus far be explicit in the present study that 1 Maccabees contains ample resonances with the Deuteronomic covenant ideology (as Berthelot is also well aware), and that the covenant ideology is also the theme highlighted in the two eulogies. To this we should underline the fact that the territorial theme is a major aspect in the Deuteronomic covenant theme. Covenantal blessing is possession of the land, curse means the loss of it, and re-blessing (upon Israel's repentance) means re-possession of it. Thus, when the Hasmoneans highlighted again and again the paramount importance of the covenantal legacy as the motive of their fight,[118] and when territorial expansion was one of the key characteristics of the Hasmonean acts, it is difficult to conceive that the biblical territorial theme slipped their mind. When Simon speaks with Athenobius, it is not inconceivable that his words had two layers of meaning: displaying the manner well appreciated in Hellenistic civilization, and simultaneously bearing firm belief in the Jewish ancestral tradition. There is no need to separate one from the other.

Similarly, when Joshua is mentioned in the deathbed blessing, it reads, 'Joshua, by *fulfilling the word* (or commandment), became a judge

---

116. Berthelot, 'Seleucid Rhetoric', 539–9. Berthelot shows how expressions such as 'the land of our/my/his fathers', 'the kingdom of our/my fathers', and 'the throne of my fathers' are found in Seleucid documents sent to the Judeans (553–4).

117. Goldstein, *1 Maccabees*, 516.

118. See Chapter 4, where I have pointed out in 1 Maccabees a particular usage of the word διαθήκη, the associated idea of Israel's covenant with YHWH, and the narrative framework of what I call 'the covenantal DCRB'.

in Israel' (2.55). Despite the aforementioned scholars' claim for the reticence about the biblical concept of territorial conquest in this verse, the act of 'fulfilling the word' (πληρῶσαι λόγον) alludes to nothing but the conquest of the land.[119] Although this allusion is by no means explicit, neither is it an argument from silence. Consider Ben Sira's praise of Joshua (Sir. 46.1-8) which contains ample references to Joshua's battles against surrounding gentiles (e.g. v. 1, 'vengeance on enemies'; v. 3, 'led the wars of the Lord'; v. 5, 'rushed down upon a nation in battle', 'destroyed who resisted'), but again, there is not a single reference to 'conquest of the land' or 'the land' itself. The closest word to territorial terms is found in v. 2, 'how he was glorified when he lifted up his hands and when he *extended a sword against cities*' (v. 2). Some might see in Ben Sira's description of Joshua a clearer, lengthier indication of his conquest of the land, but some might also see the lack of pronouncement of the biblical conquest motive. And yet, this would not be considered as reticence about Joshua's conquest, as elsewhere Ben Sira clearly makes his stance on the matter known: 'Gather all the tribes of Jacob, and give them an inheritance, as from the beginning' (36.11).[120] Κληρονομία ('Inheritance'), in this verse, as well as in the praise of Joshua (46.8), is invariably associated with Israel's possession of the land. Note that this κληρονομία is attributed not only to Simon's discourse in 15.33-35 but also the reward of Caleb in Mattathias' deathbed blessing in 1 Maccabees ('Caleb, by bearing witness in the assembly, received an *inheritance* of land', 2.56).[121] Furthermore, one can observe that those statements in the eulogy highlighting the main characteristics of the Deuteronomic covenantal blessing, such as prosperity, safety, security, and joy in the land (14.8-14), are preceded by the statement that Simon has broadened the Judean territorial border (14.6), a sequence of events which implies the re-possession of the promised land first, followed by other blessings in the land, just as found in Deuteronomy 28 and 30. Therefore, despite the

---

119. Doran ('Maccabees', 4:50) suggests an alternative translation, 'completing the task', which might refer to Joshua being commissioned by Moses (Num. 27.18-23) and by God himself (Josh. 1.2-9). Also, Fairweather and Black, *Maccabees*, 85.

120. Thus, Mendels concludes his analysis on Ben Sira by stating that '[t]he concept of Israel and its Land is still traditional…[and] Ben Sira may have been using the traditional scheme of Jewish history, without altering it, in order to eventually create an antithesis to various aspects of his own reality' (*Land*, 15–17).

121. One can infer that the author's mention of the two symbolic biblical figures for Israel's conquest of the land (e.g. Josh. 14.5-10) in Mattathias' deathbed blessing highlights the biblical territorial theme. The 'inheritance' here refers to Hebron, where Caleb resided (Num. 14.24; Josh. 14.13-14).

lack of explicit evidence for the presence of the biblical territorial theme, there is, nevertheless, a strong impression that the theme is imbedded in 1 Maccabees, without needing to be pronounced.[122]

We should thus conclude that despite his general reticence about the biblical territorial theme, the author does not necessarily avoid, reject, or ignore the theme. It is possible that he lacked any need for associating the Hasmonean territorial expansion with the biblical tradition. That is, the significant amount of biblical allusions to the role of the Hasmoneans can be accounted for by the apparent need to legitimize the Hasmonean institution. On the other hand, the idea of territorial expansion was welcomed by the Judeans,[123] and it is possible that there was little need to convince anyone in Judea about it.

5.2.3. *Simon as the Davidic messiah?*

The advocates of Hasmonean kingship propaganda have readily claimed that Simon's eulogy provides evidence for the author's association of the role of the Hasmoneans with the Davidic messiah.[124] On the one hand, the passage collectively contains many of the attributes desired of the king by authors across the whole of biblical literature, as Goldstein argues. On the other hand, my contention throughout the present study has been that there is no single decisive evidence of Hasmonean kingship propaganda in the text.[125] The primary role of the Hasmoneans is essentially about biblical heroism which carries with it the Deuteronomic legacy in which the past, present, and future of the Judean nation irresistibly depend on

---

122. As Bartlett (*Books of the Maccabees*, 43) suggests, the fact that the two characters, Joshua and Caleb, appear as a pair, side by side, is itself formulaic in that the pair highlights nothing but Joshua's territorial campaign, just as the pair appears in Num. 14.5-10; Sir. 46.1-10.

123. As Bar-Kochva convincingly argues with rabbinic evidence ('Manpower', 175–6; also Kasher, 'Changes in Manpower', 347), the Pharisees welcomed the idea of territorial expansion. It should be recalled that the Pharisees were the main critics to the legitimacy of the Hasmonean institution (Josephus, *Ant.* 13.288-298, 372 par.). One can infer that if the Pharisees welcomed the idea, there probably was no one else in Judea.

124. For advocates of this view, see §1.2.

125. We have previously discussed, in contention with Goldstein's and van der Kooij's claims of the role of the Hasmoneans as Davidic kings, that there is no explicit indication in 1 Maccabees that the author promotes monarchical legitimation of the Hasmonean institution. Instead, the role of the Hasmoneans coheres to a greater extent with the biblical judges (see Chapter 4). Furthermore, our discussion of Judas' eulogy in the present chapter has also concluded that there is no decisively Davidic, nor messianic image, echoing biblical literature in his eulogy.

their ancestral covenant made with YHWH.[126] Therefore, as I will show below, despite the fact that some prophetic allusions in Simon's eulogy contain the Davidic theme, these cases are minor and rather abstract. In contrast, a majority of biblical sources behind the eulogy do not contain the theme at all. Instead, as a whole, they are more clearly associated with the Deuteronomic covenantal idea of Israel's restoration.

There are, for instance, expressions which appear in similar forms in Judas' eulogy depicting the image of Simon in a similar way as Judas. Simon 'sought for good things for his people and pleased them with his authority and his *glory* all his days' (v. 4b; cf. 3.3a), which might refer to the splendour of his court witnessed and reported by Athenobius (1 Macc. 15.32, 36),[127] but which does not echo any specific biblical material.[128] The phrase 'his glorious name was renowned as far as to the end of the earth' (v. 10; cf. 3.7c, 9a) is similarly found in Ben Sira's description of Solomon, which reads, 'To far-off islands did your name reach, and you were beloved in your peace' (Sir. 47.16). The phrase in Ben Sira lacks any considerable verbal parallel, and it is not found in Kings and Chronicles.[129] As a result of Simon' deeds, 'Israel rejoiced with great joy' (v. 11b; cf. 3.7b), and Abel points out that this Hebrew idiomatic phrase, εὐφράνθη (Ἰσραηλ) εὐφροσύνην μεγάλην (שמחה גדולה [ישראל] וישמח), is similarly found in the description of the peaceful state of Israel under Solomon (1 Kgs 1.40). However, I will contend below that this image of Solomon is in no way explicitly alluded to. Moreover, it is untenable to claim, as does Goldstein, that the allusion to Solomon's image is the pro-Hasmonean

---

126. As I have previously pointed out (see §2.5), the covenantal worldview is one of seven traits of the Jewish perception of the ancestral past in antiquity. Starting from Deut. 28–30, the covenantal framework continues to govern the shaping of the Jews' knowledge of history in the Former/Latter Prophets as well as Jewish literature of the Second Temple period, such as Jubilees, 1 Enoch and 2 Maccabees. My contention in the present study has been that this trait of the Jewish perception of the past is also one of key characteristics of the composition of 1 Maccabees.

127. The repeated term ἡ δόξα Σιμωνος ('the glory of Simon') in these verses may be a good indicator that these are alluded to in the eulogy. See also Fairweather and Black, *Maccabees*, 238.

128. No major commentators add biblical references to this verse. Goldstein (*1 Maccabees*, 490) suggests the 'glory', especially in 14.5, 'with *all his glory*, he took Joppa…', as a reference to political, military power, but his suggestions of Gen. 45.13 and Isa. 8.7 are of little help for understanding Simon's glory as ruler in Judea.

129. It should be noted that the image of Solomon tends to overlap with that of Simon to a certain extent, and some scholars' suggestion of the allusion to Solomon in Simon's eulogy is not to be ignored, a point to which we will return shortly.

author's intention.[130] Furthermore, the expression 'the kings were crushed in those days' (v. 13; cf. 3.7a) lacks any morphologically identifiable biblical parallels; it has only general thematic resemblance with the biblical judges, prophets or monarchs. Overall, these verses in the eulogy connect Simon with Judas, and create the general image of the Hasmoneans, but without bearing the image of the Davidic dynasty or the future Davidic heir.

The similarity between Solomon's heydays in 1 Kgs 4.25 (Heb. 5.5) and the description of secure inhabitancy in v. 12 of Simon's eulogy, which we discussed in connection with Mic. 4.4 and Zech. 3.10, is emphatically introduced by Goldstein, hence his emphasis on the allusion to Solomon's image in the eulogy.[131] The relevance of the description of Solomon's heydays in 1 Kgs 4.25, in Goldstein's judgement, is also stretched to the introductory remark of the eulogy in v. 4, 'And the land of Judea rested all the days of Simon'. On Simon's domestic act in v. 14, 'and he strengthened all the lowly of his people. He sought the law and removed away all the lawless and the evil', Goldstein connects this act with Ps. 72.4, a psalm that is attributed to Solomon, as well as Isa. 11.4. This combination of verses may create the impression that Solomon's image recurs in the eulogy, leading to the implication that the Hasmonean institution is comparable with the Davidic one.

However, these references to Solomon are not necessarily associated with the eulogy. Psalm 72.4 reads:

> May he defend the cause of the poor of the people,
> give deliverance to the children of the needy,
> and crush the oppressor!

Here, the similarity between this verse and 1 Macc. 14.14 is difficult to establish on morphological grounds. On thematic grounds, they still do not evoke the same image. In the psalm, the portrayal of the king is concerned with economic justice, such as dealing with the poor justly (vv. 2, 4; 'the poor' being עני/πτοχός and אביון/πενής), and delivering on prosperity for the people (v. 3), thus giving an impression of 'the oppressor' (v. 4) as the well-off (also, vv. 12-13). Ταπεινός in the eulogy, on the other hand, is more to do with religious cleansing and reform, emphasized with legalistic terms like 'seeking the law' or 'removing the lawless'. It is thus

---

130. Abel, *Maccabées*, 252.
131. Goldstein, *1 Maccabees*, 491.

preferable to translate the word as 'humble' rather than 'poor'.[132] Their difference, then, is between social welfare reinstated by the king in the psalm and religious reform carried out by Simon. Isaiah 11.4 is also more similar to the psalm than the eulogy:

> but with righteousness he shall judge the poor, and decide with equity for the meek of the earth; and he shall strike the earth with the rod of his mouth, and with the breath of his lips he shall kill the wicked.

The prophecy does not bear a sense of religious reform but rather administration with justice and righteousness so that the poor and the needy – the socio-economically oppressed – are protected. This is not to mention its syntactical dissociation from 1 Macc. 14.14. Likewise, the summative remark in the eulogy (14.4) is better associated with the judges rather than Solomon in 1 Kings. As we have seen in the previous chapter, the formulaic phrase 'ἡσυχάζω ἡ γῆ Ἰούδα + time' is a decisive indicator echoing Judges, and the cumulative similarities between 1 Maccabees and Judges support this association.[133]

Despite the aforementioned biblical references for vv. 8, 9 and 12 of the eulogy being associated with future hope for the restitution of the Davidic kingdom,[134] it should be underlined that the prophecies, on the whole, are merely conceptual about *who* is going to usher in the era of blessing upon Israel. Those aforementioned prophecies, other than the ones associated with a future Davidic heir, do not contain the Davidic theme.[135] For instance, the semantic context of Mic. 4.4 expressed a future hope that *divine* kingship will replace the wicked Jerusalem authorities and complete the building project of Zion. The promise of kingship in the following verses thus references a *divine* ruler of Israel: '…the Lord will reign over them [the remnant] in Mount Zion from this time forth and forevermore. And you, O tower of the flock, hill of the daughter of

---

132. Thus, the editors of *A Greek–English Lexicon of the Septuagint* (2nd edn) notes that ταπεινός is used 'often in a good sense of men and women favoured by the Lord' (paragraph 27273–79, accessed through Accordance).

133. See Chapter 4. See also Himmelfarb ('He Was Renowned', 81), who identifies the phrase with similar phrases in Judges.

134. E.g. Zech. 8.4, 12; Ezek. 34.25-27; Jer. 31.27-28; 31.10-14.

135. See, for instance, Paul L. Redditt, 'The King in Haggai–Zachariah 1–8 and the Book of the Twelve', in *Tradition in Transition: Haggai and Zechariah 1–8 in the Trajectory of Hebrew Theology*, ed. Mark J. Boda and Michael H. Floyd, LHBOTS 475 (New York: T&T Clark, 2008), 56–82.

Zion, to you shall it come, the former dominion shall come, kingship for the daughter of Jerusalem' (Mic. 4.7-8).[136] Thus, secure inhabitancy of the land in this case is established under divine kingship. When applied to Simon's eulogy, this prophetic vision does not allude to the idea of establishing human kingship, but to God's return to his dominion upon his covenant people. Likewise, the agricultural revitalization in Hos. 2.21-23 placed an emphasis on God's providence for his covenant people (again, without any association with human kingship). The idyllic description of Solomon's early days in 1 Kgs 4.25 is a part of a larger unit (1 Kgs 4.20-28) which highlights manifold aspects of the success of his reign. These highlights are, again, in compliance with the promise of covenantal blessing in Deuteronomy 28 and 30, implying its fulfilment. In other words, it could be argued that 1 Kgs 4.25 conforms to the Deuteronomic paradigm along with the aforementioned prophecies.

This series of prophecies, as well as other passages from Scripture, uniformly attests to the theme of the Deuteronomic covenant, and the expressions concerning the future Davidic heir operate under the rubric of that theme. Indeed, it should be noted that whether a Davidic king, non-Davidic messianic figures (such as priestly or otherworldly figures that frequently occur in apocalyptic literatures),[137] or God himself, the goal of a future salvific figure is essentially about blessing the people of God in every aspect of their life and establishment of an ideal relationship between the two covenantal parties. The description of a blissful, prosperous and triumphant state of Judea during Simon's days should therefore be seen in the paradigm of the Deuteronomic covenantal blessing, rather than specifically fulfilling the promise of a future Davidic king.

5.2.4. *Summary*

The eulogy on the whole contains a wealth of scriptural allusions at both morphological and thematic levels. Israel's restoration is highlighted by agricultural and social revitalization and rejuvenation in an expanded Judean territory. The scholarly claims for the author's rejection/ignorance

---

136. Among many, see Henry McKeating, *The Books of Amos, Hosea and Micah*, CBC (Cambridge: Cambridge University Press, 1971), 173–4; Shaw, *Speeches*, 109. A subtle difference in Shaw's argument is his overall claim for an early dating of the larger unit, 3.1–4.8. Thus, he observes none of the vocabulary in 4.8 to suggest a late, post-exilic dating, which is favoured by the majority of scholars.

137. See A. S. van der Woude and M. de Jonge, 'Messianic Ideas in Later Judaism', *TDNT* 9:509–27; Collins, 'Messianism', 97–109 (97–8); Nickelsburg, 'Eschatology', 2:579–94.

of the biblical territorial theme and his promotion of the idea of Davidic messianic fulfilment have been disputed, and alternative claims have been drawn. Just like that of Judas, Simon's eulogy demonstrates his role as bringing about the covenantal blessing promulgated in Deuteronomy.

5.2.5. Conclusion

It has emerged from the study of the Hasmonean eulogies that the Deuteronomic covenantal framework governs the author's account of the second-century BCE Jewish history and the role of the Hasmonean leadership. Within the theological understanding that the course of history is run in accordance with the Deuteronomic covenantal framework, that is, the cycle of defilement–curse–repentance–blessing, the two eulogies portray the Hasmoneans' achievements as having brought about covenantal blessing upon the Judean nation. The two eulogies contain some differences. Simon's achievements are depicted with clearer allusions to Scripture than those of Judas, and with more impressive vocabulary, which implies the spiral development of the covenantal blessing. This general difference of language between the two eulogies may reflect a kind of narrative development in which Simon's rule is also located in the climax of the book, or the political stance of the composition of the book which was carried out under the descendants of Simon.

Chapter 6

Final Conclusion

The scholarly interest in the use of earlier texts in later texts in Judeo-Christian tradition has rapidly grown in recent decades and witnessed the fact that this literary phenomenon reflects a much broader, interdisciplinary context. I have presented such a case in 1 Maccabees wherein study of this literary phenomenon opens up questions not only relating to the kind of textual variants that were available, and the scope of literature that was reflected, but also the kind of contemporary social and political dynamics prevailing at the time and location of composition, cultural and religious presuppositions governing the author's perspective towards tradition, all of which both shaped the use of Scripture and are themselves further shaped through a historian's investigation. As such, the present study engaged with historical questions as well as literary premises pertaining to study of 1 Maccabees and the Hasmonean family.

This interlocking web of contexts shaping the use of Scripture was explored in Chapter 2. First, through discussing textual issues arising from the loss of the original Hebrew version of 1 Maccabees and comparing the vocabulary of the Greek version of the text to that of the Septuagint (Chapter 2.1), I have concluded that the reconstruction of the original Hebrew wording through its Greek translation is generally reliable. This is because the translator extensively preserved Hebrew idioms, specific calendrical and topological nouns, and the Hebrew paratactical style of sentence. However, the reconstruction is partly limited due to the flexibility of the translator's incorporation of the Greek version of Scripture in which his vocabulary does not comply with that of the Septuagint. Examples include his preference of γίγας (3.3) over δυνατός or ἰσχυρός to describe a Jewish warrior, and his direct translation from the Hebrew version of Zech. 8.12 bypassing the Greek version. This acknowledgement allowed a critical evaluation of the philological parallels between anterior and posterior texts previously suggested by scholars (Chapter 3).

Second, I have sketched the political background that surrounded the composition of 1 Maccabees by determining the date of the composition. The currently available views are: (1) the early period of John Hyrcanus I, (2) his late period / the period shortly after his death, (3) Alexander Jannaeus' reign around 91/90 BCE. And my argument supported the second option, specifically during the last few years of Hyrcanus' reign. I argued that two passages – the author's comment concerning the Hasmonean tombs (13.27-30), 'this tomb…remains to this day', which necessitates a certain span of time, at least a gap of one generation from the beginning of Simon's rule, and the two ending verses of 1 Maccabees (16.23-24) which states John Hyrcanus I's regnal years – suggest that the dating should be at least during the late period of Hyrcanus' rule. In addition, the author's derogative view on kingship (8.14) predates the time of Alexander Jannaeus who turned his government into a kingdom at an early stage according to Josephus. Thus, the dating suggests that the author's pro-Hasmonean agenda reflects the time of John Hyrcanus in his last years, particularly the last few years of peace he enjoyed until his death in 104 BCE, and hence represents the Hasmoneans' pre-monarchical stance.

Third, now that we have determined the date of the composition, I moved on to a question regarding availability of scriptural texts, particularly focusing on the term 'the law and the prophets (and other writings)', which appears in Jewish texts of the surrounding era, such as Ben Sira[Gk], 4QMMT, and 2 Maccabees. Although we cannot be certain as to the precise nature of the corpora, I argued that this term implies a widespread awareness amongst Jews in the pre-Hasmonean period that most biblical books, including the Pentateuch and historical and prophetic writings, were already available. This conclusion has been further supported in Chapter 3, in which multiple occasions of scriptural evocation show considerable verbal parallels between anterior and posterior texts, suggesting the author's access to a broad range of written sources.

Fourth, we discussed the much-debated topic – the influence of Hellenism on Judaism – by exploring how Hellenistic traits appear in 1 Maccabees. There are indeed apparent Hellenistic concepts and ideas embedded both internally – the Greek ideas of heroism, titles and honours, and temple epiphanies appearing in the text – and externally – such as naming convention, burial style, and numismatic designs. However, the outlook of the narrative remains deliberately Jewish. The use of Ἕλλην is considerably rare in 1 Maccabees compared to other more neutral terms such as 'gentiles', 'others', 'foreigners', and 'nations'. Also, amidst the quintessentially Hellenistic features such as anchor, flower and wreath in Hasmonean coins, the image of human/deity is always omitted. The

Hasmonean culture therefore critically embraced the surrounding imperial culture, discerning what is acceptable and what is not in accord with their beliefs.

Fifth, we have extensively looked at seven characteristics of how Jews perceived their ancestral past. Here and there we saw how historical details were altered, re-shaped and silenced in early Jewish literature. These manipulations are often seen as a Jewish apologetic technique used to sustain the Jews' ethnic identity under the subversive imperial identity of the Hellenistic world. Instead, there was a collective attempt across Jewish communities to preserve a more-or-less shared understanding of their ancestral past. Such an understanding was structured around the 'core facts' running from Adam, through Abraham–Isaac–Jacob up to the Babylonian exile, which then forms a cyclic pattern within it. The selective criteria for choosing which bits of the past are to be remembered or silenced were often in accord with the Deuteronomic theme of covenant between God and his people. Coming to the Hellenistic period, Jews even endeavoured to construct both an accurate account of history aiming to explain quasi-discrepancies and historical inconsistencies, and a comprehensive history that interconnects their ancestral past to their present days and theirs to the surrounding imperial history. I have then demonstrated, briefly in Chapter 2.5.2 and more extensively throughout Chapters 3–5, that the use of Scripture in 1 Maccabees presents a similar tendency. Political manipulation is particularly prevailing when it comes to recording the recent past, i.e. the Maccabean revolt and the birth of the Hasmonean institution, and the pro-Hasmonean author effectively picks up what to be included and silences what to be ignored. When it comes to the ancestral past, on the other hand, the author almost assumes his audience to be aware of those core facts, the cyclic pattern and theological understanding of history shaped by the Deuteronomic covenantal theme.

In Chapter 3, I have analyzed philological parallels between Scripture and 1 Maccabees using Lange and Weigold's criteria-based search of anterior texts, as well as their list of biblical cross-references in 1 Maccabees. The analysis entailed a running critical dialogue of individual references informed by engagement with key commentaries over the last one and a half centuries. A critically selected list of philological parallels has been produced, which have been categorized into various types of scriptural expressions, using Dimant's terms such as explicit/implicit quotations, explicit/implicit allusions, and explicit mentions of person and circumstance. Thus our list of scriptural expressions in

1 Maccabees reflects a revised form of Lange and Weigold's list using Dimant's categorization, which both removes unrelated anterior texts and adds new materials.

The results in this chapter show that in the majority of cases of scriptural expression, the meaning of the expression within its original context in the anterior text is carried over to its new context in the posterior text, hence appearing in 1 Maccabees as a re-enactment of historical events or fulfilment of prophecies. In other cases of scriptural expressions, the author seems to use idiomatic Hebrew expressions, suggesting the clearly Hebraistic literary basis of 1 Maccabees, although occasionally there are expressions with unclear motives. In addition, the first five chapters of 1 Maccabees contain considerably more scriptural expressions than the remainder of the book, indicating that the author utilizes Scripture to effectively convey a theological significance of the Antiochan reform in Judea, the outbreak of the Maccabean revolt and the Hasmoneans' successful recapture of Judea and the Jerusalem temple. These recent past events are described as re-enactment of Israel's calamity/overcoming and fulfilment of particularly Mosaic law and prophecies as they appear in Pentateuch, Former and Latter Prophets, and even other writings such as Daniel and Psalms.

In Chapter 4, I have shown conceptual parallels between 1 Maccabees and two biblical books, Deuteronomy and Judges, arguing that 1 Maccabees' narrative scheme is based on, and alludes to, the Deuteronomic covenantal understanding of the course of history in which the covenantal fidelity/infidelity determines the destiny of the Judean nation. That is, the cyclic pattern of what I call the covenantal DCRB (Defilement–Curse–Repentance–Blessing) as it is stipulated in Deuteronomy 28–30 clearly shapes the course of the narrative development throughout 1 Maccabees, providing the Jewish audience a hermeneutic to apply to their understanding of the recent past events. Through an analysis of the term $\Delta\iota\alpha\theta\acute{\eta}\varkappa\eta$ in 1 Maccabees, I have also demonstrated that the author deliberately implies the Deuteronomic concept of the term and echoes the context of Israel's obedience and disobedience of the covenant between them and God.

Within this Deuteronomic framework, the role of the Hasmoneans is regarded as particularly analogous to that of biblical judges in Israel in the pre-monarchical era. The heroic motive of the book of Judges prevailed in the description of the deeds of the Maccabean brothers. Further, we have seen a considerable resemblance between Jephthah and the Hasmoneans and I have suggested that this remarkable resemblance, together with the apparent Judges motive, function as a way to legitimize the non-monarchical Hasmonean institution of John Hyrcanus I who, was, just like Jephthah, a mighty warrior but of dishonourable birth, whose leadership of Israel was sanctioned by the assembly of people, and whose family were post factum divine agents through whom the providence of the covenant God dwells amongst Jews.

In Chapter 5, the role of the Hasmoneans in 1 Maccabees has been discussed particularly through an analysis of scriptural expressions in the eulogies of Judas and Simon. In a nutshell, both eulogies express the mood that the hope for Israel's restoration was fulfilled through the Hasmoneans, with a consistent emphasis on the covenantal blessing in accordance with the Deuteronomic promulgation as it is set out in Deuteronomy 28–30. Notable in this regard is that, whilst several themes such as embittering gentile kings, gladdening the people through victory and receipt of glory and honour are displayed in both eulogies, Simon's achievement is depicted in a more climactic manner, lavished with fulfilment language of Hebrew prophecies concerning Israel's future restoration. I have also discussed the concept of the so-called continued exile coined by Wright and argued that the eulogies depicted the migration of Jews back to Judea as a 'return from exile', and implied yet another example of re-enactment of historical events and fulfilment of prophecies. Likewise, concerning the biblical territorial theme, I contended that it is implausible to deny the presence of the theme in 1 Maccabees. In my opinion, it is more reasonable to think that the author characterized the Hasmoneans' territorial expansion as an element of Deuteronomic covenantal blessing.

This theological significance of the role of the Hasmoneans, however, is characterized in a politically subtle way. That is, contrary to the often-made assumption that 1 Maccabees is a book representing the view of the Hasmonean usurpers who absorbed the future hope for a Davidic heir and made their rule a messianic embodiment, I have argued that the Davidic hope is rather upheld by this pro-Hasmonean author. In contrast to the observations made by Goldstein and van der Kooij, I have demonstrated that scriptural references and allusions to materials relating to David are in no way distinctive or proportionately large. The roles of the Hasmoneans in the eulogies of Judas and Simon, where such an attempt at associating the Hasmonean heroes with Davidic themes is expected, are clearly non-Davidic. Instead, the author seems to carefully designate the Hasmoneans as generically salvific heroes. This view is supported by the derogatory statement on kingship in 1 Macc. 8.14 as well as the Hasmoneans' resemblance with biblical judges. In other words, the author's portrayal of the Hasmonean family in 1 Maccabees points to divine agents who fought bravely for the Judean nation just like biblical heroes, and non-Davidic leadership whose legitimacy is disputed due to their dishonourable birth but who are nevertheless legitimated and sanctioned by people through their bravery and sacrifice.

The kind of Hasmonean propaganda as proposed by some experts of 1 Maccabees and Hasmonean studies, such as Goldstein, Rajak, and Mendels, namely that the Hasmoneans' political agendas subvert widely perceived traditions and religious beliefs, hence radically inventing new traditions to establish/justify their own rule over their Jewish subjects, does not seem to be the best description of 1 Maccabees' viewpoint. By all means, this Hasmonean literature is invariably *not apolitical*. However, the kind of subversive political propaganda, which especially involves Hasmoneans' usurpation of Jewish kingship, may fail to appreciate a more balanced stance between political agendas and preservation of traditions that I find in the book. What, then, is the purpose of 1 Maccabees? I suggest that a different question can be raised as a way of answering that question: what kind of target audience does the book attract? The book conspicuously eulogizes the Hasmonean leadership, but at the same time it condemns self-enthronement, along with self-ambition and self-aggrandization. It intersperses a vast amount of scriptural materials in various ways, and yet hardly makes a bold claim with quotation formulae that prophecies concerning Israel's restoration were actually fulfilled. It shows a keen interest in portraying the Hasmoneans as law-abiding Jews, upholding the law of Moses and the ancestral covenant with YHWH as their utmost values, but on a few occasions, such zeal is compromised.[1] In a way, 1 Maccabees presents quasi-contrasting interests simultaneously; the deliberately pro-Hasmonean writing, with obvious legitimizing aims

---

1. Examples include the Hasmoneans' profanation of the Sabbath by engaging in war (2.41-48; 9.43-53) and their failure to treat a gentile city Gazara and the citadel in Jerusalem in accord with the Mosaic laws on war (החרם תחרימם; 13.43-52; e.g. Deut. 20.17). For Seth Schwartz's similar comment on the inconsistency of 1 Maccabees' standpoint on observing the law; see his 'Nations Roundabout', 30–3 (his conclusion, 33–8, readdresses the issue). Schwartz concludes that such acts of the Hasmoneans contradict Deuteronomic values. However, I want to go further. On the one hand, the Hasmoneans did violate the laws regarding the Sabbath observation and treatment of gentile cities in war. On the other hand, it is notable that the author takes care in explaining, or better, justifying such acts in all these 'anomalous' (using Schwartz's term) occasions. And this is my point: because these anomalous examples are contradictory to Deuteronomic values, and because the author is not only aware of them but rather apologetic about them, one gets an impression about the implied audience.

for the Hasmonean institution, nevertheless emphatically presents and promotes religious values which would have attracted any conservative Jewish audience, whether that be the Pharisees, the enigmatic Hasidim, other forms of previous Hasmonean supporters, or even the Judean populace. If 1 Maccabees aims at claiming such traditionally acceptable viewpoints, in the end it is not surprising that they affirm the Davidic covenant (2.57), just as they affirm the Aaronite high priesthood (2.54) and the coming of a trustworthy prophet in the eschatological era, which the author, from his point of view, still awaits.

Bibliography

Abegg, Jr., Martin G. 'Exile and the Dead Sea Scrolls'. Pages 111–25 in *Exile: Old Testament, Jewish, and Christian Conceptions*, edited by James M. Scott. JSJSup 56. Leiden: Brill, 1997.

Abel, F.-M. *Les livres des Maccabées*. EB 38. Paris: Librairie Lecoffre, 1949.

Abingdon Press, ed. *The New Interpreter's Bible: General Articles & Introduction, Commentary, & Reflections for Each Book of the Bible, Including the Apocryphal/ Deuterocanonical Books*. Nashville: Abingdon Press, 1994–2004.

Ackroyd, Peter R. *Exile and Restoration: A Study of Hebrew thought of the Sixth Century BC*. London: SCM, 1968.

———. 'Criteria for the Maccabean Dating of Old Testament Literature'. *VT* 3 (1953): 113–32.

Aitken, James K. Review of *Judaism and Hellenism*, by Martin Hengel. *JBL* 123 (2004): 331–41.

Albertz, Rainer, and Jacob Wöhrle, eds. *Between Cooperation and Hostility: Multiple Identities in Ancient Judaism and the Interaction with Foreign Powers*. JAJSup 11. Göttingen: Vandenhoeck & Ruprecht, 2013.

Allen, Leslie C. *Ezekiel 20–48*. WBC 29. Nashville: Thomas Dallas, 1990.

———. *Jeremiah*. OTL. Louisville: Westminster John Knox, 2008.

Arenhoevel, Diego. *Die Theokratie nach dem 1. und 2. Makkabäerbuch*. WSAMA 3. Mainz: Matthias-Grünewald, 1967.

Assis, Ellie. *Self-Interest or Communal Interest: An Ideology of Leadership in the Gideon, Abimelech, and Jephthah Narratives (Judg. 6–12)*. VTSup 106. Leiden: Brill, 2005.

Attridge, H. 'Historiography'. Pages 157–84 in *Jewish Writings of the Second Temple Period*, ed. M. E. Stone. CRINT 2. Assen: van Gorcum; Philadelphia: Fortress, 1984.

Avigad, N. 'The Architecture of Jerusalem in the Second Temple Period'. Pages 14–20 in *Jerusalem Revealed: Archaeology in the Holy City, 1968–1974*, ed. Yigael Yadin. New Haven: Yale University Press, 1976.

Babota, Vasile. *The Institution of the Hasmonean High Priesthood*. JSJSup 165. Leiden: Brill, 2014.

Bakhos, Carol, ed. *Ancient Judaism in Its Hellenistic Context*. JSJSup 95. Leiden: Brill, 2005.

Bakhtin, Mikhail M. 'The Problem of Speech Genres'. Pages 60–102 in *Speech Genres and Other Late Essays*. Edited by Caryl Emerson and Michael Holquist. Translated by Vern W. McGee. Austin, TX: University of Texas, 1986.

———. 'The Problem of the Text in Linguistics, Philosophy, and the Human Sciences: An Experiment in Philosophical Analysis'. Pages 103–31 in *Speech Genres and Other Late Essays*. Edited by Caryl Emerson and Michael Holquist. Translated by Vern W. McGee. Austin, TX: University of Texas, 1986.

Baltes, Guido. 'The Use of Hebrew and Aramaic in Epigraphic Sources of the New Testament Era'. Pages 35–65 in *The Language Environment of First Century Judaea: Jerusalem Studies in the Synoptic Gospels, Vol. 2*, edited by Randall Buth and R. Steven Notley. JCPS 26. Leiden: Brill, 2014.

Barag, D. 'New Evidence on the Foreign Policy of John Hyrcanus I'. *INJ* 12 (1992/93): 1–12.

Bar-Kochva, Bezalel. *Judas Maccabaeus: The Jewish Struggle against the Seleucids*. Cambridge: Cambridge University Press, 1989.

———. 'Manpower, Economics, and Internal Strife in the Hasmonean State'. Pages 167–94 in *Armée et fiscalité dans le monde antique*. Paris: Éditions du Centre National de la Recherche Scientifique, 1977.

Barr, James. 'Hebrew, Aramaic and Greek in the Hellenistic Age'. *CHJ* 2:79–114.

Bartlett, John R. *1 Maccabees*. GAP. Sheffield: Sheffield Academic, 1998.

———. '1 Maccabees'. *ECB* 807–30.

———. '1 Maccabees'. *NOAB* 1555–98.

———. *The First and Second Books of the Maccabees*. CBC. Cambridge: Cambridge University Press, 1973.

———. Review of *The Structure of 1 Maccabees*, by D. S. Williams. *JTS* 52 (2001): 191–4.

Barton, John, and John Muddiman, eds. *The Oxford Bible Commentary*. Oxford, Oxford University Press, 2001.

Beckwith, R. T. *The Old Testament Canon of the New Testament Church and Its Background in Early Judaism*. London: SPCK, 1985.

Ben-Sasson, H. H., and S. Ettinger, eds. *Jewish Society through the Ages*. London: Vallentine & Mitchell, 1971.

Ben Zvi, Ehud. 'General Observations on Ancient Israelite Histories in Their Ancient Contexts'. Pages 21–39 in *Enquire of the Former Age: Ancient Historiography and Writing the History of Israel*, edited by Lester L. Grabbe. ESHM 9. LHBOTS 554. New York: Bloomsbury, 2013.

———. 'Shifting the Gaze: Historiographic Constraints in Chronicles and Their Implications'. Pages 38–60 in *The Land That I Will Show You: Essays on the History and Archaeology of the Ancient Near East in Honor of J. Maxwell Miller*, edited by J. Andrew Dearman and M. Patrick Graham. JSOTSup 343. Sheffield: Sheffield Academic, 2001.

Berlin, Andrea M. 'Jewish Life before the Revolt: The Archaeological Evidence'. *JSJ* 36 (2005): 417–70.

———. 'Power and Its Afterlife: Tombs in the Hellenistic Palestine'. *NEA* 65 (2002): 138–48.

Bernstein, Moshe J. 'The Employment and Interpretation of Scripture in 4QMMT: Preliminary Observations'. Pages 29–51 in *Reading 4QMMT: New Perspectives on Qumran Law and History*, edited by John Kampen and M. J. Bernstein. SBLSymS 2. Atlanta: Scholars Press, 1996.

———. 'Scriptures: Quotation and Use'. *EDDS* 2:839–42.

Bernstein, M. J., F. García Martínez, and J. Kampen, eds. *Legal Texts and Legal Issues. Proceedings of the Second Meeting of the International Organization for Qumran Studies, Cambridge, 1995: Published in Honour of Joseph M. Baumgarten*. STDJ 23. Leiden: Brill, 1997.

Berrin, Shani L. 'Pesharim'. *EDDS* 2:644–7.

Berthelot, Katell. 'The Biblical Conquest of the Promised Land and the Hasmonean Wars According to 1 and 2 Maccabees'. Pages 45–60 in *The Books of the Maccabees: History, Theology, Ideology: Papers of the Second International Conference on the Deuterocanonical Books, Pápa, Hungary, 9–11 June, 2005*, edited by Géza G. Xeravits and József Zsengellér. JSJSup 118. Boston: Brill, 2007.

———. 'Reclaiming the Land (1 Maccabees 15:28-36): Hasmonean Discourse between Biblical Tradition and Seleucid Rhetoric'. *JBL* 133 (2014): 539–59.

Bickerman, Elias J. *Der Gott der Makkabäer: Untersuchungen über Sinn und Ursprung der makkabäischen Erhebung*. Berlin: Schocken, 1937.

———. *The Jews in the Greek Age*. Cambridge, MA: Harvard University Press, 1988.

———. *Studies in Jewish and Christian History*. A New Edition in English Including *The God of the Maccabees*. AJEC 68/1. Leiden: Brill, 2007.

Bilde, Per, ed. *Aspects of Hellenistic Kingship*. Oakville: Aarhus University Press, 1996.

Blenkinsopp, Joseph. *Isaiah 56–66*. AB 19. New York: Doubleday, 2003.

Bockmuehl, Marcus, and James Carleton-Paget, eds. *Redemption and Resistance*. London: T&T Clark, 2007.

Boda, Mark J., and Michael H. Floyd, eds. *Bringing out the Treasure: Inner Biblical Allusion in Zechariah 9–14*. JSOTSup 370. Sheffield: Sheffield Academic, 2003.

——— eds. *Tradition in Transition: Haggai and Zechariah 1–8 in the Trajectory of Hebrew Theology*. LHBOTS 475. New York: T&T Clark, 2008.

Boling, R. G. *Judges: Introduction, Translation and Commentary*. AB 6A. New York: Doubleday, 1975.

Borchardt, Francis. *The Torah in 1 Maccabees: A Literary Critical Approach to the Text*. DCLS 19. Berlin: de Gruyter, 2014.

———. 'Concepts of Scripture in 1 Maccabees'. Pages 24–41 in *Early Christian Literature and Intertextuality: Vol. 1, Thematic Studies*, edited by Craig A. Evans and Daniel Zecharias. LNTS 391; SSEJC 14. London: Continuum, 2009.

———. 'Deuteronomic Legacy in 1 Maccabees'. Pages 297–319 in *Changes in Scripture: Rewriting and Interpreting Authoritative Traditions in the Second Temple Period*, edited by Marko Marttila, Juha Pakkala and Hanne von Weissenberg. BZAW 419. Berlin: de Gruyter, 2011.

———. 'Influence and Power: The Types of Authority in the Process of Scripturalization'. *SJOT* 29 (2015): 182–96.

Brooke, George J. 'The Explicit Presentation of Scripture in 4QMMT'. Pages 67–88 in *Legal Texts and Legal Issues: Proceedings of the Second Meeting of the International Organization for Qumran Studies, Cambridge, 1995: Published in Honour of Joseph M. Baumgarten*, edited by M. J. Bernstein, F. García Martínez and J. Kampen. STDJ 23. Leiden: Brill, 1997.

Brooke, George J., Daniel K. Falk, Eibert J. C. Tigchelaar, and Molly M. Zahn, eds. *The Scrolls and Biblical Traditions*. Proceedings of the Seventh Meeting of the IOQS in Helsinki. STDJ 103. Leiden: Brill, 2012.

Broughton, T. R. S. *The Magistrates of the Roman Republic*. New York: American Philological Association, 1951–52.

Bruyne, Dom Donatien de, with Dom Bonaventure Sodar. *Les anciennes traductions latines des Machabées*. AM 4. Maredsous: Abbaye de Maredsous, 1932.

———. 'Le texte grec des deux premiers livres des Machabées'. *RB* 31 (1922): 31–54.

Bryan, Steven M. *Jesus and Israel's Traditions of Judgment and Restoration*. SNTSMS 117. Cambridge: Cambridge University Press, 2002.

Burney, C. F. 'An Acrostic Poem in the Praise of Judas Maccabaeus'. *JTS* 21 (1920): 319–25.

Buth, Randall, and R. Steven Notley, eds. *The Language Environment of First Century Judaea: Jerusalem Studies in the Synoptic Gospels.* vol. 2. JCPS 26. Leiden: Brill, 2014.

Calduch-Benages, N., and J. Liesen, eds. *Deuterocanonical and Cognate Literature Yearbook 2006: How Israel's Later Authors viewed Its Earlier History.* Berlin: de Gruyter, 2006.

Campbell, Jonathan G. 'Josephus' Twenty-Two Book Canon and the Qumran Scrolls'. Pages 19–46 in *The Scrolls and Biblical Traditions: Proceedings of the Seventh Meeting of the IOQS in Helsinki*, edited by George J. Brooke, Daniel K. Falk, Eibert J. C. Tigchelaar and Molly M. Zahn. STDJ 103. Leiden: Brill, 2012.

Cancik, Hubert, and Helmuth Schneider, eds. *Brill's New Pauly: Encyclopedia of the Ancient World.* Leiden: Brill, 2002.

Carleton-Paget, James, and Joachim Schaper, eds. *The New Cambridge History of the Bible.* Vol. 2, *From the Beginnings to 600.* Cambridge: Cambridge University Press, 2013.

Carson, D. A. 'Summaries and Conclusions'. Pages 505–48 in *Justification and Variegated Nomism: Vol. 1, The Complexities of Second Temple Judaism*, edited by D. A. Carson, Peter T. O'Brien and Mark A. Seifrid. WUNT 2/140. Tübingen: Mohr Siebeck; Grand Rapids: Baker Academic, 2001.

Carson, D. A., Peter T. O'Brien, and Mark A. Seifrid, eds. *Justification and Variegated Nomism.* Vol. 1, *The Complexities of Second Temple Judaism.* WUNT 2/140. Tübingen: Mohr Siebeck; Grand Rapids: Baker Academic, 2001.

Chang, Dongshin Don. *Phinehas, The Sons of Zadok, and Melchizedek: Priestly Covenant in Late Second Temple Texts.* LSTS 90. London: T&T Clark, 2016.

Charles, R. H., ed. *The Apocrypha and Pseudepigrapha of the Old Testament in English: with Introductions and Critical and Explanatory Notes to the Several Books.* 2 vols. Oxford: Clarendon Press, 1913.

Charlesworth, James H., ed. *Old Testament Pseudepigrapha.* 2 vols. New York: Doubleday, 1983–85.

Chester, Andrew. *Future Hope and Present Reality: Vol. 1, Eschatology and Transformation in the Hebrew Bible.* WUNT 293. Tübingen: Mohr Siebeck, 2012.

———. *Messiah and Exaltation.* WUNT 207. Tübingen: Mohr Siebeck, 2007.

Clayton, Jay, and Eric Rothstein. 'Figures in the Corpus: Theories of Influence and Intertextuality'. Pages 3–36 in *Influence and Intertextuality in Literary Theory*, edited by Jay Clayton and Eric Rothstein. Madison: University of Wisconsin Press, 1991.

Clayton, Jay, and Eric Rothstein, eds. *Influence and Intertextuality in Literary Theory.* Madison: University of Wisconsin Press, 1991.

Cohen, Shaye J. D. *The Beginnings of Jewishness: Boundaries, Varieties, Uncertainties.* HCS 31. Berkeley: University of California Press, 1999.

Cohen, Shaye J. D., ed. *Studies in the Cult of Yahweh.* Vol. 1, *Historical Method, Ancient Israel, Ancient Judaism.* Leiden: Brill, 1996.

———. *Daniel, First Maccabees, Second Maccabees: With an Excursus on the Apocalyptic Genre.* 2nd pr. OTM 15. Wilmington, DE: Michael Glazier, 1989.

———. 'Artapanus'. *OTP* 2:889–903.

———. 'Messianism in the Maccabean Period'. Pages 97–109 in *Judaisms and Their Messiahs at the Turn of the Christian Era*, edited by Jacob Neusner, W. S. Green and E. S. Frerichs. Cambridge: Cambridge University Press, 1987.

———. 'The Epic of Theodotus and the Hellenism of the Hasmoneans'. *HTR* 73 (1980): 91–104.

Collins, John J., and Daniel C. Harlow, eds. *The Eerdmans Dictionary of Early Judaism*. Grand Rapids, MI: Eerdmans, 2010.
Collins, John J., and G. E. Sterling, eds. *Hellenism in the Land of Israel*. CJA 13. Notre Dame: University of Notre Dame Press, 2001.
Conybeare, F. C., and St. George Stock. *Grammar of Septuagint Greek*. Boston: Ginn & Co., 1905. Reprinted by Peabody, MA: Hendrickson, 1988.
Coogan, Michael David, Marc Zvi Brettler, Carol A. Newsom, and Pheme Perkins, eds. *The New Oxford Annotated Bible: New Revised Standard Version: with the Apocrypha: An Ecumenical Study Bible*. Oxford: Oxford University Press, 2010.
Cook, Stephen L. *Prophecy and Apocalypticism: The Postexilic Social Setting*. Minneapolis: Fortress, 1995.
Corley, Jeremy. 'The Review of History in Eleazar's Prayer in 1 Macc 6:1-15'. Pages 201–29 in *Deuterocanonical and Cognate Literature Yearbook 2006: How Israel's Later Authors viewed Its Earlier History*, edited by N. Calduch-Benages and J. Liesen. Berlin: de Gruyter, 2006.
———. 'Sirach 44:1-15 as Introduction to the Praise of the Ancestors'. Pages 151–81 in *Studies in the Book of Ben Sira: Papers of the Third International Conference on the Deuterocanonical Books, Shime'on Centre, Pápa, Hungary, 18–20 May, 2006*, edited by Géza G. Xeravits and József Zsengellér. JSJSup 127. Leiden: Brill, 2008.
Craigie, P. C. *The Book of Deuteronomy*. NICOT. Grand Rapids: Eerdmans, 1976.
Dahood, Mitchell. *Psalms III: 101–150*. AB 17A. Garden City, NY: Doubleday, 1984.
Dalman, Gustaf. *Die mit Berücksichtigung des nachkanonischen jüdischen Schrifttums und der aramäischen Sprache erörtert*. Leipzig: J. C. Hinrichs, 1898.
Dancy, J. C. *1 Maccabees*. Oxford: Blackwell, 1954.
Davila, James R. '(How) Can We Tell if a Greek Apocryphon or Pseudepigraphon has been Translated from Hebrew or Aramaic?' *JSP* 15 (2005): 3–61.
Davies, Philip R., and John M. Halligan, eds. *Second Temple Studies III: Studies in Politics, Class and Material Culture*. JSOTSup 340. London: Sheffield Academic, 2002.
Davies, Philip R., and Richard T. White, eds. *A Tribute to Geza Vermes: Essays on Jewish and Christian Literature and History*. JSOTSup 100. Sheffield: Sheffield Academic, 1990.
Davies, W. D., and Louis Finkelstein, eds. *The Cambridge History of Judaism*. Vol. 2. *The Hellenistic Age*. Cambridge: Cambridge University Press, 1990.
Dearman, J. Andrew, and M. Patrick Graham, eds. *In The Land That I Will Show You: Essays on the History and Archaeology of the Ancient Near East in Honor of J. Maxwell Miller*. JSOTSup 343. Sheffield: Sheffield Academic, 2001.
Deines, Roland. *Die Gerechtigkeit der Tora im Reich des Messias: Mt 5,13–20: als Schlüsseltext der matthäischen Theologie*. WUNT 177. Tübingen: Mohr Siebeck, 2004.
———. 'Did Matthew Know He was Writing Scripture? Part 2'. *EJT* 23 (2014): 3–12.
———. 'Galilee and the Historical Jesus in Recent Research'. Pages 11–48 in *Galilee: In the Late Second Temple and Mishnaic Periods: Vol. 1, Life, Culture, and Society*, edited by David A. Fiensy and James Riley Strange. Minneapolis: Fortress, 2014.
Destinon, J. *Die Quellen des Flavius Josephus in der Jüd. Arch. Buch XII–XVII=Jüd. Krieg Buch*. Kiel: Lipsius & Tischer, 1882.
Dimant, Devorah. 'Pesharim, Qumran'. *ABD* 5:244–51.
———. 'Qumran: Written Material'. *EDDS* 2:739–46.

———. 'Use and Interpretation of Mikra in the Apocrypha and Pseudepigrapha'. Pages 379–419 in *Mikra: Text, Translation, Reading and Interpretation of the Hebrew Bible in Ancient Judaism and Early Christianity*, edited by Martin Jan Mulder. CRINT 2/1. Assen: Van Gorcum; Philadelphia: Fortress, 1988.

Dines, Jennifer M. *The Septuagint*. London: T&T Clark, 2004.

Docherty, Susan E. *The Jewish Pseudepigrapha: An Introduction to the Literature of the Second Temple Period*. London: SPCK, 2014.

———. *The Use of the Old Testament in Hebrews*. WUNT 2/260. Tübingen: Mohr Siebeck, 2009.

Doran, Robert. 'The First Book of Maccabees'. *NIB* 4:3–178.

———. 'Pseudo-Eupolemus'. *OTP* 2:873–82.

———. *Temple Propaganda: The Purpose and Character of 2 Maccabees*. CBQMS 12. Washington, DC: The Catholic Biblical Association of America, 1981.

Draisma, S., ed. *Intertextuality in Biblical Writings: Essays in Honour of Bas van Iersel*. Kampen: Kok, 1989.

Dunn, James D. G., and J. W. Rogerson, eds. *Eerdmans Commentary on the Bible*. Grand Rapids, MI: Eerdmans, 2003.

Eckhardt, Benedikt, ed. *Jewish Identity and Politics between the Maccabees to Bar Kokhba: Groups, Normativity, and Rituals*. JSJSup 155. Leiden: Brill, 2011.

Eshel, Hanan. *The Dead Sea Scrolls: And the Hasmonean State*. SDSSRL. Grand Rapids; Cambridge: Eerdmans, 2008.

———. '4QMMT and the History of the Hasmonean Period'. Pages 53–65 in *Reading 4QMMT: New Perspectives on Qumran Law and History*, edited by John Kampen and M. J. Bernstein. SBLSymS 2. Atlanta: Scholars Press, 1996.

Ettelson, H. W. 'The Integrity of 1 Maccabees'. *TCAAS* 27 (1925): 249–384.

Evans, Craig A. 'Jesus and the Continuing Exile'. Pages 77–100 in *Jesus and the Restoration of Israel: A Critical Assessment on N. T. Wright's* Jesus and the Victory of God, edited by Carey C. Newman. Downers Grove: InterVarsity Press, 1999.

Evans, Craig A., and Daniel Zecharias, eds. *Early Christian Literature and Intertextuality*. Vol. 1, *Thematic Studies*. LNTS 391; SSEJC 14. London: Continuum, 2009.

Fairweather, W., and J. Sutherland Black, *The First Book of Maccabees*. CBSC. Cambridge: Cambridge University Press, 1908.

Fallon, F. 'Eupolemus'. *OTP* 2:861–72.

———. 'Theodotus'. *OTP* 2:785–93.

Feder, F., and M. Henze, eds. *Textual History of the Bible*. Leiden: Brill, 2019.

Feldman, Louis H. 'Hengel's *Judaism and Hellenism* in Retrospect'. *JBL* 96 (1977): 371–82.

———. 'How Much Hellenism in Jewish Palestine?' *HUCA* 57 (1986): 83–111.

———. 'Josephus' Portrayal of the Hasmoneans Compared with 1 Maccabees'. Pages 41–68 in *Josephus and the History of the Greco-Roman Period: Essays in Memory of Morton Smith*, edited by F. Parente and J. Sievers. SPB 41. Leiden: Brill, 1994.

———. 'The Concept of Exile in Josephus'. Pages 145–72 in *Exile: Old Testament, Jewish, and Christian Conceptions*, edited by James M. Scott. JSJSup 56. Leiden: Brill, 1997.

Feldman, Louis H., and Gohei Hata, eds. *Josephus, the Bible and History*. Leiden: Brill, 1989.

Fiensy, David A., and James Riley Strange, eds. *Galilee: In the Late Second Temple and Mishnaic Periods*. Vol. 1, *Life, Culture, and Society*. Minneapolis: Fortress, 2014.

Fine, Steven. *Art and Judaism in the Greco-Roman World: Toward a New Jewish Archaeology*. Cambridge: Cambridge University Press, 2005.

Finkielsztein, G. 'More Evidence on John Hyrcanus I's Conquests: Lead Weights and Rhodian Amphora Stamps'. *BAIAS* 16 (1998): 33–63.
Fischer, Thomas. *Seleukiden und Makkabäer*. Bochum: Brockmeyer, 1980.
———. 'Maccabees, Books of: First and Second Maccabees'. *ABD* 4:438–50.
Fishbane, Michael A. *Biblical Interpretation in Ancient Israel*. Oxford: Clarendon, 1985.
———. 'Types of Biblical Intertextuality'. Pages 39–44 in *Congress Volume: Oslo 1998*, edited by A. Lemaire and M. Sæbø. VTSup 80. Leiden: Brill, 2000.
Flavius Josephus. *Jewish Antiquities, Books 12–14*. Translated by Ralph Marcus, LCL. Cambridge, MA: Harvard University Press; London: William Heinemann, 1986.
Floyd, Michael H. 'Deutero-Zechariah and Types of Intertextuality'. Pages 225–44 in *Bringing out the Treasure: Inner Biblical Allusion in Zechariah 9–14*, edited by Mark J. Boda and Michael H. Floyd. JSOTSup 370. Sheffield: Sheffield Academic, 2003.
———. 'The Production of Prophetic Books in the Early Second Temple Period'. Pages 276–97 in *Prophets, Prophecy and Prophetic Texts in Second Temple Judaism*, edited by Michael H. Floyd and Robert D. Haak. LHBOTS 427. New York; London: T&T Clark, 2006.
Floyd, Michael H., and Robert D. Haak, eds. *Prophets, Prophecy and Prophetic Texts in Second Temple Judaism*. LHBOTS 427. New York; London: T&T Clark, 2006.
Fraser, P. M. *Ptolemaic Alexandria*. Oxford: Oxford University Press, 1972.
Frösén, Jaakko. 'Prolegomena to a Study of the Greek Language in the First Century A.D.: The Problem of Koiné and Atticism'. PhD diss., The University of Helsinki, 1974.
Fyfe, Theodore. *Hellenistic Architecture: An Introductory Study*. Cambridge: Cambridge University Press, 1936.
Gafni, Isaiah M. 'Josephus and 1 Maccabees'. Pages 116–31 in *Josephus, the Bible and History*, edited by Louis H. Feldman and Gohei Hata. Leiden: Brill, 1989.
Galil, G., and M. Weinfeld, eds. *Studies in Historical Geography and Biblical Historiography Presented to Zecharia Kallai*. VTSup 81. Leiden: Brill, 2000.
Gardner, Gregg G. 'Jewish Leadership and Hellenistic Civic Benefaction in the Second Century B.C.E'. *JBL* 126 (2007): 327–43.
Gardner, Gregg, and K. L. Osterloh, eds. *Antiquity in Antiquity: Jewish and Christian Pasts in the Greco-Roman World*. TSAJ 123. Tübingen: Mohr Siebeck, 2008.
Geiger, Abraham. *Lehr- und Lesebuch zur Sprache der Mischnah. Band 1: Lehrbuch zur Sprache der Mischnah*. Breslau: Leuckart, 1845.
Goldingay, John. *Psalms, Vol. 2: Psalms 42–89*. BCOTWP. Grand Rapids, MI: Baker Academic, 2007.
Goldstein, Jonathan A. *I Maccabees*. AB 41. Garden City, NY: Doubleday, 1976.
———. *2 Maccabees*. AB 41A. New York: Doubleday, 1983.
———. 'How the Authors of 1 and 2 Maccabees Treated the "Messianic Promises"'. Pages 69–96 in *Judaisms and Their Messiahs at the Turn of the Christian Era*, edited by Jacob Neusner, William S. Green, and Ernest Frerichs. Cambridge: Cambridge University Press, 1987.
———. 'The Dynasty of God's Resistors'. *HTR* 68 (1975): 53–8.
———. 'The Hasmonean Revolt and the Hasmonean Dynasty'. *CHJ* 2:292–351.
———. 'Jewish Acceptance and Rejection of Hellenism'. Pages 64–87, 318–26 in *Jewish and Christian Self-Definition*. Vol. 2, *Aspects of Judaism in the Greco-Roman Period*, edited by E. P. Sanders, A. I. Baumgarten, and A. Mendelson. London: SCM; Philadelphia: Fortress, 1981.
———. 'The Judaism of the Synagogues (Focusing on the Synagogue of Dura-Europos)'. Pages 109–57 in *Judaism in Late Antiquity. Part 2: Historical Syntheses*, edited by Jacob Neusner. HO 17. Leiden: Brill, 1995.

Gorman Jr., Frank H. *Divine Presence and Community: A Commentary on the Book of Leviticus*. Grand Rapids: Eerdmans; Edinburgh: Handsels, 1997.

Grabbe, Lester L. 'Did All Jews Think Alike? "Covenant" in Philo and Josephus in the Context of Second Temple Judaic Religion'. Pages 251–66 in *The Concept of the Covenant in the Second Temple Period*, edited by Stanley E. Porter and Jacqueline C. R. de Roo. JSJSup 71. Leiden; Boston: Brill, 2003.

———. 'The Law, the Prophets, and the Rest: The State of the Bible in Pre-Maccabean Times'. *DSD* 13 (2006): 319–38.

———. 'The Jews and Hellenization: Hengel and His Critics'. Pages 52–66 in *Second Temple Studies III: Studies in Politics, Class and Material Culture*, edited by Philip R. Davies and John M. Halligan. JSOTSup 340. London: Sheffield Academic, 2002.

Grabbe, Lester L., ed. *Did Moses Speak Attic? Jewish Historiography and Scripture in the Hellenistic Period*. JSOTSup 317. Sheffield: Sheffield Academic, 2001.

——— ed. *Enquire of the Former Age: Ancient Historiography and Writing the History of Israel*. ESHM 9; LHBOTS 554. New York: Bloomsbury, 2013.

Greenspoon, Leonard J. 'The Use and Abuse of the Term "LXX" and Related Terminology in Recent Scholarship'. *BIOSCS* 20 (1987): 21–9.

Grove, P. B., ed. *Webster's Third New International Dictionary of the English Language, Unabridged*. Springfield: Merriam, 1976.

Grimm, Carl L. W. *Das erste Buch der Maccabäer*. KEHAAT 3. Leipzig: Hirzel, 1853.

Gruen, Erich S. *Heritage and Hellenism: The Reinvention of Jewish Tradition*. HCS 30. Berkeley: University of California Press, 1998.

———. Review of *The Structure of 1 Maccabees*, by D. S. Williams. *CBQ* 62 (2000): 743–4.

Hague, W. V. 'Eschatology of the Apocryphal Scriptures, I, The Messianic Hope'. *JTS* 12 (1911): 57–98.

Hals, Arnold M. *Ezekiel*. FOTL 19. Grand Rapids: Eerdmans, 1989.

Hanson, J. 'Demetrius the Chronographer'. *OTP* 2:843–54.

Harrington, Daniel J. *The Maccabean Revolt: Anatomy of a Biblical Revolution*. OTS 1. Wilmington, DE: Michael Glazier, 1988.

Hendin, David. 'Current Viewpoints on Ancient Jewish Coinage: A Bibliographic Essay'. *CBR* 11 (2013): 246–301.

Hengel, Martin. *Judaism and Hellenism: Studies in Their Encounter in Palestine during the Early Hellenistic Period*. 2 vols. Translated by John Bowden. Philadelphia: Fortress, 1974.

———. 'Judaism and Hellenism Revisited'. Pages 6–37 in *Hellenism in the Land of Israel*, edited by John J. Collins and G. E. Sterling. CJA 13. Notre Dame: University of Notre Dame Press, 2001.

Henten, Jan Willem van. 'Royal Ideology: 1 and 2 Maccabees and Egypt'. Pages 265–82 in *Jewish Perspectives on Hellenistic Rulers*, edited by Tessa Rajak, Sarah Pearce, James Aitken and Jennifer Dines. HCS L. Berkeley, CA: University of California, 2007.

———. 'The Hasmonean Period'. Pages 15–28 in *Redemption and Resistance*, edited by Marcus Bockmuehl and James Carleton Paget. London: T&T Clark, 2007.

———. 'The Honorary Decree for Simon the Maccabee (1 Macc 14:25-49) in Its Hellenistic Context'. Pages 116–45 in *Hellenism in the Land of Israel*, edited by John J. Collins and G. E. Sterling. CJA 13. Notre Dame: University of Notre Dame Press, 2001.

Hieke, Thomas. 'The Role of "Scripture" in the Last Words of Mattathias (1 Macc. 2:49-70)'. Pages 61–74 in *The Books of the Maccabees: History, Theology, Ideology – Papers of the Second International Conference on the Deuterocanonical Books, Pápa, Hungary, 9–11 June 2005*, edited by Géza Xeravits and József Zsengellér. JSJSup 118. Boston: Brill, 2007.

Higbie, Carolyn. *The Lindian Chronicle and the Greek Creation of their Past*. Oxford: Oxford University Press, 2003.

Hillers, D. R. *A Commentary on the Book of the Prophet Micah*. Hermeneia. Philadelphia: Fortress, 1984.

Himmelfarb, Martha. '"He Was Renowned to the Ends of the Earth" (1 Maccabees 3:9): Judaism and Hellenism in 1 Maccabees'. Pages 77–97 in *Jewish Literatures and Cultures: Context and Intertext*, edited by Anita Norich and Yaron Z. Eliav. BJS 349. Providence, RI: Brown University Press, 2008.

Holladay, Carl R. ed. *Fragments from Hellenistic Jewish Authors*. Vol. 1, *Historians*. SBLTT 20; PS 10. Chico, CA: Scholars Press, 1983.

Horbury, William. *Jewish Messianism and the Cult of Christ*. London: SCM, 1998.

———. *Messianism among Jews and Christians*. London: T&T Clark, 2003.

Huizinga, J. 'A Definition of the Concept of History'. Pages 1–10 in *Philosophy and History: Essays Presented to Ernst Cassirer*, edited by R. Klibansky and H. J. Paton. Oxford: Clarendon, 1936.

Ilan, Tal. 'The Greek Names of the Hasmoneans'. *JQR* 78 (1987): 1–20.

Jacobson, David M. 'The Lily and the Rose: A Review on Some Hasmonean Coin Types'. *NEA* 76 (2013): 16–27.

Japhet, S. *The Ideology of the Book of Chronicles and Its Place in Biblical Thought*. 2nd Edition. BEATAJ 9. Bern: Peter Lang, 1997.

Jellicoe, Sidney. *The Septuagint and Modern Study*. Oxford: Clarendon, 1968.

———, ed. *Studies in the Septuagint: Origins, Recensions and Interpretations: Selected Essays with a Prolegomenon*. LBS. New York: Ktav, 1974.

Jensen, Morten Hørning. 'The Political History in Galilee from the First Century BCE to the End of the Second Century CE'. Pages 51–77 in *Galilee: In the Late Second Temple and Mishnaic Periods: Vol. 1, Life, Culture, and Society*, edited by David A. Fiensy and James Riley Strange. Minneapolis: Fortress, 2014.

Jobes, Karen H., and Moisés Silva. *Invitation to the Septuagint*. Grand Rapids, MI: Baker Academic, 2000.

Jonge, Marinus de. 'Messiah'. *ABD* 4:777–88.

Joosten, Jan. 'Varieties of Greek in the Septuagint and the New Testament'. Pages 22–45 in *The New Cambridge History of the Bible: From the Beginnings to 600*, edited by James Carleton-Paget and Joachim Schaper. Cambridge: Cambridge University Press, 2013.

Josephus. Translated by Henry St. J. Thackeray et al. 10 vols. LCL. Cambridge, MA: Harvard University Press, 1926–65.

Joyce, Paul M. *Ezekiel: A Commentary*. LHBOTS 482. New York; London: T&T Clark, 2009.

Kampen, John, and M. J. Bernstein, eds. *Reading 4QMMT: New Perspectives on Qumran Law and History*. SBLSymS 2. Atlanta: Scholars Press, 1996.

Kappler, Werner. *Maccabaeorum liber I*. 2nd edn. VTGASLG IX/1. Göttingen: Vandenhoeck & Ruprecht, 1967.

Kasher, Aryeh. 'The Changes in Manpower and Ethnic Composition of the Hasmonean Army (167–63BCE)'. *JQR* 81 (1991): 325–52.

Keil, Carl F. *Die Bücher der Makkabäer*. BCATSup. Leipzig: Döffling & Franke, 1875.
Kelle, Brad E., and Megan Bishop Moore, eds. *Israel's Prophets and Israel's Past: Essays on the Relationships of Prophet Texts and Israelite History in Honor of John H. Hayes*. LHBOTS 446. New York: T&T Clark, 2006.
Kilpatrick, G. D. 'I–III Maccabees (with Addendum)'. Pages 418–33 in *Studies in the Septuagint: Origins, Recensions and Interpretations: Selected Essays with a Prolegomenon*, edited by Sidney Jellicoe. LBS. New York: Ktav, 1974.
Kindler, Arie. 'The Hellenistic Influence on the Hasmonean Coins'. Pages 316–23 in *XII. Internationaler Numismatischer Kongress, Berlin 1997: Akten – Proceedings – Actes, Vol. I*, edited by Bernd Kluge and Bernhard Weisser. Berlin: Preußischer Kulturbesitz – Staatlichen Museen zu Berlin, 2000.
Kittel, Gerhard, G. W. Bromiley, and Gerhard Friedrich, eds. *Theological Dictionary of the New Testament*. 10 vols. Grand Rapids, Mich: Eerdmans, 1964–76.
Klausner, Joseph. 'Judah Aristobulus and Jannaeus Alexander'. Pages 222–41 in *The World History of the Jewish People: Vol. 6, The Hellenistic Age*, edited by Abraham Shalit. London: Allen, 1972.
Klibansky, R., and H. J. Paton, eds. *Philosophy and History: Essays Presented to Ernst Cassirer*. Oxford: Clarendon, 1936.
Kluge, Bernd, and Bernhard Weisser, eds. *XII. Internationaler Numismatischer Kongress, Berlin 1997: Akten – Proceedings – Actes*. Vol. 1. Berlin: Preußischer Kulturbesitz – Staatlichen Museen zu Berlin, 2000.
Kooij, Arie van der. 'The Canonization of Ancient Books Kept in the Temple of Jerusalem'. Pages 17–40 in *Canonization and Decanonization*, edited by Arie van der Kooij and K. van der Toorn. SHR 82. Leiden: Brill, 1998.
———. 'The Claim of Maccabean Leadership and the Use of Scripture'. Pages 29–49 in *Jewish Identity and Politics between the Maccabees to Bar Kokhba: Groups, Normativity, and Rituals*, edited by Benedikt Eckhardt. JSJSup 155. Leiden: Brill, 2011.
Kooij, Arie van der, and K. van der Toorn, eds. *Canonization and Decanonization*. SHR 82. Leiden: Brill, 1998.
Koole, J. L. 'Die Bibel des Ben-Sira'. *OTS* 14 (1965): 374–96.
Krentz, Edgar. 'The Honorary Decree for Simon the Maccabee'. Pages 146–53 in *Hellenism in the Land of Israel*, edited by John J. Collins and G. E. Sterling. CJA 13. Notre Dame: University of Notre Dame Press, 2001.
Kristeva, Julia. 'Word, Dialogue, and Novel'. Pages 64–91 in *Desire in Language: A Semiotic Approach to Literature and Art*. Edited by Leon S. Roudiez. Translated by Thomas Gora, Alice Jardine and Leon S. Roudiez. New York: Columbia University Press, 1980.
Kugel, James L. Review of *Biblical Interpretation*, by Michael Fishbane. *Prooftexts* 7 (1987): 269–305.
Laato, Antti. *A Star Is Rising: The Historical Development of the Old Testament Royal Ideology and the Rise of the Jewish Messianic Expectations*. ISFCJ. Atlanta: Scholars Press, 1998.
Lange, Armin. '2 Maccabees 2:13-15: Library or Canon?' Pages 155–67 in *The Books of the Maccabees: History, Theology, Ideology – Papers of the Second International Conference on the Deuterocanonical Books, Pápa, Hungary, 9–11 June 2005*, edited by Géza Xeravits and József Zsengellér. JSJSup 118. Boston: Brill, 2007.

———. 'Literary Prophecy and Oracle Collection: A Comparison between Judah and Greece in Persian Times'. Pages 248–75 in *Prophets, Prophecy and Prophetic Texts in Second Temple Judaism*, edited by Michael H. Floyd and Robert D. Haak. LHBOTS 427. New York; London: T&T Clark, 2006.
Lange, Armin, and Matthias Weigold. *Biblical Quotations and Allusions in Second Temple Jewish Literature*. JAJSup 5. Göttingen: Vandenhoeck & Ruprecht, 2011.
Lau, Andrew Y. *Manifest in Flesh: The Epiphany Christology of the Pastoral Epistles*. WUNT 2/86. Tübingen: Mohr Siebeck, 1996.
Leibner, Uzi. *Settlement and History in Hellenistic, Roman, and Byzantine Galilee: An Archaeological Survey of the Eastern Galilee*. TSAJ 127. Tübingen: Mohr Siebeck, 2009.
Leiman, Sid Z. *The Canonization of Hebrew Scripture: The Talmudic and Midrashic Evidence*. TCAAS 47. Hamden, CT: Archon, 1976.
Lemaire, A., and M. Sæbø, eds. *Congress Volume: Oslo 1998*. VTSup 80. Leiden: Brill, 2000.
Lemche, Niels Peter. 'Herodotus and the Persians'. *Transeuphratène* 23 (2002): 129–51.
———. 'The Old Testament – A Hellenistic Book?' *SJOT* 7 (1993): 163–93.
Levine, Lee I. *Jerusalem: Portrait of the City in the Second Temple Period (538 B.C.E.–70 C.E.)*. Philadelphia: The Jewish Publication Society in cooperation with the Jewish Theological Seminary of America, 2002.
———. *Judaism and Hellenism in Antiquity: Conflict or Confluence?* Seattle: University of Washington Press, 1998.
Levine, Lee I., and Daniel R. Schwartz, eds. *Jewish Identities in Antiquity: Studies in Memory of Menahem Stern*. TSAJ 130. Tübingen: Mohr Siebeck, 2009.
Lieu, Judith. 'Not Hellenes but Philistines? The Maccabees and Josephus Defining the "Other"'. *JJS* 53 (2002): 246–63.
Lim, Timothy H. 'The Alleged Reference to the Tripartite Division of the Hebrew Bible'. *RevQ* 20 (2001/2): 23–37.
———. 'Deuteronomy in the Judaism of the Second Temple Period'. Pages 6–26 in *Deuteronomy in the New Testament: The New Testament and the Scriptures of Israel*, edited by Maarten J. J. Menken and Steve Moyise. LNTS 358. London: T&T Clark, 2007.
Lindars, Barnabas. *Judges 1–5: A New Translation and Commentary*. Edinburgh: T. & T. Clark, 1995.
———. 'Some Septuagint Readings in Judges'. *JTS* 22 (1971): 1–14.
Lust, J., E. Eynikel, and K. Hauspie, eds. *A Greek–English Lexicon of the Septuagint*. 2nd edn. Collaborated with G. Chamberlain. Stuttgart: Deutsche Bibelgesellschaft, 2003.
Machiela, Daniel A. 'A Brief History of the Second Temple Period Name "Hyrcanus"'. *JJS* 61 (2010): 117–38.
Maier, J., and J. Schreiner, eds. *Literatur und Religion des Frühjudentums*. Würzburg: Echter, 1973.
Marcos, Natalio Fernández. *Septuagint in Context: Introduction to the Greek Version of the Bible*. Translated by Wilfred G. E. Watson. Leiden: Brill, 2000.
Martínez, García F., and E. Tigchelaar, eds. *The Dead Sea Scrolls Study Edition*. 2 vols. Leiden: Brill, 1997–99.
Martola, Nils. *Capture and Liberation: A Study in the Composition of the First Book of Maccabees*. AAA A 63/1. Åbo: Åbo Akademi, 1984.

Marttila, Marko, Juha Pakkala, and Hanne von Weissenberg, eds. *Changes in Scripture: Rewriting and Interpreting Authoritative Traditions in the Second Temple Period*. BZAW 419. Berlin: de Gruyter, 2011.
Mason, Rex. *The Books of Haggai, Zechariah and Malachi*. CBC. Cambridge: Cambridge University Press, 1977.
Mason, Steve. 'Jews, Judaeans, Judaizing, Judaism: Problems of Categorization in Ancient History'. *JSJ* 38 (2007): 457–512.
Maxwell-Stuart, P. G. '1 Maccabees VI 34 Again'. *VT* 25 (1975): 230–3.
Mays, James Luther. *Micah*. OTL. London: SCM, 1976.
McCarthy, S. J. *Treaty and Covenant*. 2nd edn. AB 21b. Rome: Pontifical Biblical Institute, 1981.
McKane, William. *The Book of Micah: Introduction and Commentary*. Edinburgh: T. & T. Clark, 1998.
McKeating, Henry. *The Books of Amos, Hosea and Micah*. CBC. Cambridge: Cambridge University Press, 1971.
Mendels, Doron. *Memory in Jewish, Pagan, and Christian Societies of the Greco-Roman World*. LSTS 45. London: T&T Clark, 2004.
———. *The Land of Israel as a Political Concept in Hasmonean Literature*. Tübingen: Mohr Siebeck, 1987.
———. *The Rise and Fall of Jewish Nationalism*. ABRL. New York: Doubleday, 1992.
———. *Why Did Paul Go West? Jewish Historical Narrative and Thought*. JCTCRS. London: Bloomsbury, 2014.
———. 'How Was Antiquity Treated in Societies with a Hellenistic Heritage? And Why Did the Rabbis Avoid Writing History?' Pages 131–51 in *Why Did Paul Go West? Jewish Historical Narrative and Thought*, 12–30. JCTCRS. London: Bloomsbury, 2014. Reprinted from *Antiquity in Antiquity: Jewish and Christian Pasts in the Greco-Roman World*, edited by Gregg Gardner and K. L. Osterloh. TSAJ 123. Tübingen: Mohr Siebeck, 2008.
———. 'Memory and Memories: The Attitude of 1–2 Maccabees toward Hellenization and Hellenism'. Pages 41–54 in *Jewish Identities in Antiquity: Studies in Memory of Menahem Stern*, edited by Lee I. Levine and Daniel R. Schwartz. TSAJ 130. Tübingen: Mohr Siebeck, 2009.
———. 'Phases of Inscribed Memory Concerning the Land of Israel in Palestinian Judaism of the Second Century BCE: The Case of 1 Maccabees'. Pages 78–93 in *Why Did Paul Go West? Jewish Historical Narrative and Thought*. JCTCRS. London: Bloomsbury, 2014. Reprinted from *TL* 138 (2013): 151–64.
Mendenhall, George E. 'Covenant Forms in Israelite Tradition'. *BA* 17 (1954): 50–76.
Menken, Maarten J. J., and Steve Moyise, eds. *Deuteronomy in the New Testament: The New Testament and the Scriptures of Israel*. LNTS 358. London: T&T Clark, 2007.
Meshorer, Y. *Ancient Jewish Coinage*, 2 vols. Dix Hill, NY: Amphora Books, 1982.
Metzger, Bruce M. 'The Lucianic Recension of the Greek Bible'. Pages 270–91 in *Studies in the Septuagint: Origins, Recensions and Interpretations: Selected Essays with a Prolegomenon*, edited by Sidney Jellicoe. LBS. New York: Ktav, 1974.
Milgrom, Jacob. *Leviticus 23–27*. AB 3B. New York: Doubleday, 2001.
Milik, J. T. *Ten Years of Discovery in the Wilderness of Judaea*. Translated by J. Strugnell. SBT 26. London: SCM, 1959.
Millar, Fergus. 'The Background of the Maccabean Revolution: Reflections on Martin Hengel's "Judaism and Hellenism"'. *JJS* 29 (1978): 1–21.
Miller, Geoffrey D. 'Intertextuality in Old Testament Research'. *CBR* 9 (2010): 283–309.

Mitchell, Hinckley G. T., John Merlin Powis Smith and Julius A. Bewer. *A Critical and Exegetical Commentary on Haggai, Zechariah, Malachi and Jonah*. 3rd impression. ICC. Edinburgh: T. & T. Clark, 1951.

Momigliano, Arnaldo. *Alien Wisdom: The Limits of Hellenization*. Cambridge: Cambridge University Press, 1975.

———. 'The Date of the First Book of the Maccabees'. Pages 561–6 in *Sesto contributo alla storia degli studi classici e del mondo antico, vol. 2*, edited by A. Momigliano. Rome: Storia e Letteratura, 1980.

Momigliano, A., ed. *Sesto contributo alla storia degli studi classici e del mondo antico*. Vol. 2. Rome: Storia e Letteratura, 1980.

Mulder, Martin Jan, ed. *Mikra: Text, Translation, Reading and Interpretation of the Hebrew Bible in Ancient Judaism and Early Christianity*. CRINT 2/1. Assen: Van Gorcum; Philadelphia: Fortress, 1988.

Neuhaus, Günter O. *Studien zu den poetischen Stücken im 1. Makkabäerbuch*. FB 12. Würzburg: Echter, 1974.

Neusner, Jacob, ed. *Judaism in Late Antiquity*. Part 2, *Historical Syntheses*. HO 17. Leiden: Brill, 1995.

Neusner, Jacob, W. S. Green and E. S. Frerichs, eds. *Judaisms and Their Messiahs at the Turn of the Christian Era*. Cambridge: Cambridge University Press, 1987.

Newman, Carey C., ed. *Jesus and the Restoration of Israel: A Critical Assessment on N. T. Wright's* Jesus and the Victory of God. Downers Grove: InterVarsity Press, 1999.

Newsom, Carol A. 'Rhyme and Reason: The Historical Résumé in Israelite and Early Jewish Thought'. Pages 293–310 in *Israel's Prophets and Israel's Past: Essays on the Relationships of Prophet Texts and Israelite History in Honor of John H. Hayes*, edited by Brad E. Kelle and Megan Bishop Moore. LHBOTS 446. New York: T&T Clark, 2006.

Nicholson, Ernest W. *God and His People: Covenant and Theology in the Old Testament*. Oxford: Clarendon, 2002.

Nickelsburg, George W. E. *Jewish Literature between the Bible and the Mishnah: A Historical and Literary Introduction*. Philadelphia: Fortress, 1987.

———. '1 & 2 Maccabees – Same Story, Different Meaning'. *CTM* 42 (1971): 515–26.

———. 'Eschatology (Early Jewish)'. *ABD* 2:579–94.

Niditch, S. *Judges*. Louisville: Westminster John Knox, 2008.

Niehoff, Maren R. *Jewish Exegesis and Homeric Scholarship in Alexandria*. Cambridge: Cambridge University Press, 2011.

Nongbri, Brent. 'The Motivations of the Maccabees and the Judean Rhetoric of Ancestral Tradition'. Pages 85–111 in *Ancient Judaism in Its Hellenistic Context*, edited by Carol Bakhos. JSJSup 95. Leiden: Brill, 2005.

Norich, Anita, and Yaron Z. Eliav, eds. *Jewish Literatures and Cultures: Context and Intertext*. BJS 349. Providence, RI: Brown University Press, 2008.

Oesterley, W. O. E. 'First Book of Maccabees'. *APOT* 1:59–124.

Orlinsky, Harry M. 'Some Terms in the Prologue to Ben Sira and the Hebrew Canon'. *JBL* 110 (1991): 483–90.

Palmer, Leonard R. *The Greek Language*. London: Faber, 1980.

Parente, F., and J. Sievers, eds. *Josephus and the History of the Greco-Roman Period: Essays in Memory of Morton Smith*. SPB 41. Leiden: Brill, 1994.

Peters, M. K. H. 'Septuagint'. *ABD* 5:1093–1104.

Peterson, David L. *Haggai and Zechariah 1–8*. OTL. London: SCM, 1984.

Pfeiffer, Robert H. *History of New Testament Times: With an Introduction to the Apocrypha*. London: Adam & Charles Black, 1949.

Philips, Anthony. *Deuteronomy*. CBC. Cambridge: Cambridge University Press, 1973.
Pietersma, Albert, and Benjamin G. Wright, eds. *A New English Translation of the Septuagint*. Oxford: Oxford University, 2007.
Pomykala, Kenneth E. *The Davidic Dynasty Tradition in Early Judaism: Its History and Significance for Messianism*. SBLEJL 7. Atlanta: SBL, 1995.
Porter, Stanley E., and Jacqueline C. R. de Roo, eds. *The Concept of the Covenant in the Second Temple Period*. JSJSup 71. Leiden: Brill, 2003.
Pritchett, Kendrick W. *The Greek State at War*. Part 3, *Religion*. Berkeley: University of California Press, 1979.
Qimron, Elisha, and John Strugnell, eds. *Qumran Cave 4.V: Miqsat Maʿaśê Ha-Torah*. DJD 10. Oxford: Clarendon, 1994.
Rad, G. von. *Deuteronomy*. OTL. London: SCM, 1966.
Rahmani, L. Y. 'Jason's Tomb'. *IEJ* 17 (1967): 61–100.
Rajak, Tessa. *Translation and Survival: The Greek Bible and The Ancient Jewish Diaspora*. Oxford: Oxford University Press, 2009.
———. 'Hasmonean Dynasty'. *ABD* 3:67–76.
———. 'Hasmonean Kingship and the Invention of Tradition'. Pages 69–96 in *The Jewish Dialogue with Greece and Rome: Studies in Cultural and Social Interaction*. Boston; Leiden: Brill, 2002. Reprinted from *Aspects of Hellenistic Kingship*, edited by Per Bilde, 99–115. Oakville: Aarhus University Press, 1996.
———. 'The Hasmoneans and the Uses of Hellenism'. Pages 261–80 in *A Tribute to Geza Vermes: Essays on Jewish and Christian Literature and History*, edited by Philip R. Davies and Richard T. White. JSOTSup 100. Sheffield: Sheffield Academic, 1990. Reprinted in *The Jewish Dialogue with Greece and Rome: Studies in Cultural and Social Interaction*, edited by Tessa Rajak, 61–80. Boston: Brill, 2002.
Rajak, Tessa, ed. *The Jewish Dialogue with Greece and Rome: Studies in Cultural and Social Interaction*. Boston: Brill, 2002.
Rajak, Tessa, Sarah Pearce, James Aitken, and Jennifer Dines, eds. *Jewish Perspectives on Hellenistic Rulers*. HCS L. Berkeley, CA: University of California, 2007.
Rappaport, Uriel. *The First book of Maccabees: Introduction, Hebrew Translations, and Commentary*. Jerusalem: Yad ben-Zvi, 2004 (Hebrew).
———. '1 Maccabees'. *OBC* 711–34.
———. 'The Birth of the Hasmonean State'. Pages 173–7 in *Recent Archaeology in the Land of Israel*, edited by Hershel Shanks and Benjamin Mazar. Translated by Aryeh Finklestein. Washington, DC: Biblical Archaeological Society; Jerusalem: Israel Exploration Society, 1984.
———. 'The Use of the Bible in 1 Maccabees'. Pages 175–9 in *Biblical Perspectives: Early Use and Interpretation of the Bible in Light of the Dead Sea Scrolls. Proceedings of the First International Symposium of the Orion Center, 12–14 May 1996*, edited by M. E. Stone and E. G. Chazon. Leiden: Brill, 1998.
Redditt, Paul L. 'The King in Haggai–Zachariah 1–8 and the Book of the Twelve'. Pages 56–82 in *Tradition in Transition: Haggai and Zechariah 1–8 in the Trajectory of Hebrew Theology*, edited by Mark J. Boda and Michael H. Floyd. LHBOTS 475. New York: T&T Clark, 2008.
Regev, Eyal. *The Hasmoneans: Ideology, Archaeology, Identity*. JAJSup 10. Göttingen: Vandenhoeck & Ruprecht, 2013.
Revell, E. J. 'Masoretic Text'. *ABD* 4:597–99.
Rey, Jean-Sébastien, and Jan Joosten, eds. *The Texts and Versions of the Book of Ben Sira: Transmission and Interpretation*. JSJSup 150. Leiden: Brill, 2011.

Ricoeur, Paul. *Time and Narrative*. Chicago: University of Chicago Press, 1984–88.

Romanoff, P. *Jewish Symbols on Ancient Jewish Coins*. Philadelphia: Dropsie College for Hebrew and Cognate Learning, 1944.

Safrai, Zeev. 'The Gentile Cities of Judea: Between the Hasmonean Occupation and the Roman Liberation'. Pages 63–90 in *Studies in Historical Geography and Biblical Historiography Presented to Zecharia Kallai*, edited by G. Galil and M. Weinfeld. VTSup 81. Leiden: Brill, 2000.

Sanders, E. P., A. I. Baumgarten, and A. Mendelson, eds. *Jewish and Christian Self-Definition*. Vol. 2, *Aspects of Judaism in the Greco-Roman Period*. London: SCM; Philadelphia: Fortress, 1981.

Satlow, Michael L. 'Beyond Influence: Toward a New Historiographical Paradigm'. Pages 37–53 in *Jewish Literatures and Cultures: Context and Intertext*, edited by Anita Norich and Yaron Z. Eliav. BJS 349. Providence, RI: Brown University Press, 2008.

Schiffman, Lawrence H. 'The Place of 4QMMT in the Corpus of Qumran Manuscripts'. Pages 81–98 in *Reading 4QMMT: New Perspectives on Qumran Law and History*, edited by John Kampen and M. J. Bernstein. SBLSymS 2. Atlanta: Scholars Press, 1996.

———, ed. *Archaeology and History in the Dead Sea Scrolls – The New York University Conference in Memory of Yigael Yadin*. JSPSup 8; JSOT/ASORMon 2. Sheffield: JSOT, 1990.

Schiffman, Lawrence H., and James C. VanderKam, eds. *Encyclopedia of the Dead Sea Scrolls*. New York: Oxford University Press, 2000.

Schniedewind, William M. 'Orality and Literacy in Ancient Israel'. *RSR* 26 (2000): 327–32.

Schorch, Stefan. 'The Libraries in 2 Macc 2:13-15, and the Torah as a Public Document in Second Century BC Judaism'. Pages 169–80 in *The Books of the Maccabees: History, Theology, Ideology. Papers of the Second International Conference on the Deuterocanonical Books, Pápa, Hungary, 9–11 June, 2005*, edited by Géza G. Zeravits and József Zsengellér. JSJSup 118. Leiden: Brill, 2007.

Klaus-Dietrich Schunck, *I. Makkabäerbuch*. JSHRZ. Gütersloh: Gerd Mohn, 1980.

Schürer, Emil. *The History of the Jewish People in the Age of Jesus Christ (175 B.C.–A.D. 135)*. 3 vols. A new English version revised and edited by G. Vermes, F. Millar, M. Black, and M. Goodman. Edinburgh: T&T Clark, 1973–87.

Schwartz, Daniel R. *2 Maccabees*. CEJL. Berlin: de Gruyter, 2008.

———. 'Judeans, Jews, and Their Neighbors: Jewish Identity in the Second Temple Period'. Pages 13–31 in *Between Cooperation and Hostility: Multiple Identities in Ancient Judaism and the Interaction with Foreign Powers*, edited by Rainer Albertz and Jacob Wöhrle. JAJSup 11. Göttingen; Bristol, CT: Vandenhoeck & Ruprecht, 2013.

———. 'On Pharisaic Opposition to the Hasmonean Monarchy'. Pages 44–56 in *Studies in the Jewish Background of Christianity*. WUNT 60. Tübingen: Mohr Siebeck, 1992.

———. Review of *1 Makkabäer*, by Michael Tilly. *JSJ* 47 (2016): 442–5.

———. *Studies in the Jewish Background of Christianity*. WUNT 60. Tübingen: Mohr Siebeck, 1992.

———. 'Textual History of 1 Maccabees'. Pages 113–7 in *Textual History of the Bible*, eds. F. Feder and M. Henze. Leiden: Brill, 2019.

Schwartz, Seth. 'Hebrew and Imperialism in Jewish Palestine'. Pages 53–85 in *Ancient Judaism in its Hellenistic Context*, edited by Carol Bakhos. JSJSup 95. Leiden: Brill, 2005.

———. 'Israel and the Nations Roundabout: I Maccabees and the Hasmonean Expansion'. *JJS* 42 (1991): 16–38.
Scott, James M. 'Exile and the Self-Understanding of Diaspora Jews in the Greco-Roman Period'. Pages 173–218 in *Exile: Old Testament, Jewish, and Christian Conceptions*, edited by James M. Scott. JSJSup 56. Leiden: Brill, 1997.
Scott, James M., ed. *Exile: Old Testament, Jewish, and Christian Conceptions*. JSJSup 56. Leiden: Brill, 1997.
Shalit, Abraham, ed. *The World History of the Jewish People*. Vol. 6, *The Hellenistic Age*. London: Allen, 1972.
Shanks, Hershel, and Benjamin Mazar, eds. *Recent Archaeology in the Land of Israel*. Translated by Aryeh Finklestein. Washington, DC: Biblical Archaeological Society; Jerusalem: Israel Exploration Society, 1984.
Shaw, Charles S. *Speeches of Micah: A Rhetorical-Historical Analysis*. JSOTSup 145. Sheffield: Sheffield Academic, 1993.
Sievers, Joseph. *The Hasmoneans and Their Supporters: From Mattathias to the Death of John Hyrcanus I*. SFSHJ 6. Atlanta: Scholars Press, 1990.
Simpson, J. A., and E. S. C. Weiner, eds. *The Oxford English Dictionary*. Oxford: Clarendon, 1989.
Skehan, Patrick W., and Alexander A. Di Lella. *The Wisdom of Ben Sira: A New Translation with Notes by Patrick W. Skehan; Introduction and Commentary by Alexander A. Di Lella*. AB 39. New York: Doubleday, 1987.
Smith, J. M. P. *A Critical and Exegetical Commentary on Micah*. ICC. Edinburgh, 1912.
Smith, Morton. 'What Is Implied by the Variety of Messianic Figures?' Pages 161–7 in *Studies in the Cult of Yahweh: Vol. 1, Historical Method, Ancient Israel, Ancient Judaism*. Edited by Shaye J. D. Cohen. Leiden: Brill, 1996.
Smith, Ralph L. *Micah–Malachi*. WBC 32. Nashville: Thomas Nelson, 1984.
Soggin, J. Alberto. *Judges*. Translated by John Bowden. 2nd edn. OTL. London: SCM, 1981.
Soisalon-Soininen, J. *Die Textformen der Septuaginta-Übersetzungen*. AASF 72. Helsinki: Suomalainen Tiedeakatemia, 1951.
Sommer, Benjamin D. *A Prophet Reads Scripture: Allusion in Isaiah 40–66*. CJOD. Stanford, CA: Stanford University, 1998.
Stead, Michael R. *The Intertextuality of Zechariah 1–8*. LHBOTS 506. New York: T&T Clark, 2009.
Stern, Menahem. *Studies in Jewish History: The Second Temple Period*. Jerusalem: Yad ben-Zvi, 1991 (Hebrew).
———. 'Die Urkunden'. Pages 181–99 in *Literatur und Religion des Frühjudentums*, edited by J. Maier and J. Schreiner. Würzburg: Echter, 1973.
———. 'The Hasmonean Revolt and Its Place in the History of Jewish Society and Religion'. Pages 91–106 in *Jewish Society through the Ages*, edited by H. H. Ben-Sasson and S. Ettinger. London: Vallentine & Mitchell, 1971.
Stone, M. E., ed. *Jewish Writings of the Second Temple Period*. CRINT 2. Assen: van Gorcum; Philadelphia: Fortress, 1984.
Stone, M. E., and E. G. Chazon, eds. *Biblical Perspectives: Early Use & Interpretation of the Bible in Light of the Dead Sea Scrolls*. Proceedings of the First International Symposium of the Orion Center, 12–14 May 1996. Leiden: Brill, 1998.
Swete, H. B. *The Old Testament in Greek according to the Septuagint, Vols. I–III*. Cambridge: Cambridge University, 1897–1912.

Tcherikover, Victor. *Hellenistic Civilization and the Jews*. Translated by S. Applebaum. New York: Atheneum, 1977.
Tilly, Michael. *1 Makkabäer*. HTKAT. Freiburg: Herder, 2015.
Tomes, Roger. 'Heroism in 1 and 2 Maccabees'. *BI* 15 (2007): 171–99.
Tov, Emanuel. *The Greek and Hebrew Bible: Collected Essays on the Septuagint*. VTSup 72. Leiden: Brill, 1999.
———. *The Text-Critical Use of the Septuagint in Biblical Research*. Jerusalem: Simor, 1997.
———. 'Theologically Motivated Exegesis Embedded in the Septuagint'. Pages 257–70 in *The Greek and Hebrew Bible: Collected Essays on the Septuagint*. VTSup 72. Leiden: Brill, 1999.
Ulrich, Eugene. 'The Non-Attestation of a Tripartite Canon in 4QMMT'. *CBQ* 65 (2002): 202–14.
Van Seters, John. *In Search of History: Historiography in the Ancient World and the Origins of Biblical History*. New Haven: Yale University, 1983.
VanderKam, James C. 'Exile in Jewish Apocalyptic Literature'. Pages 89–109 in *Exile: Old Testament, Jewish, and Christian Conceptions*, edited by James M. Scott. JSJSup 56. Leiden: Brill, 1997.
Vermeylen, Jacques. 'The Gracious God, Sinners and Foreigners: How Nehemiah 9 Interprets the History of Israel'. Pages 77–112 in *Deuterocanonical and Cognate Literature Yearbook 2006: How Israel's Later Authors viewed Its Earlier History*, edited by N. Calduch-Benages and J. Liesen. Berlin: de Gruyter, 2006.
Wacholder, Ben Zion. 'The Ancient Judaeo-Aramaic Literature (500–164 BCE): A Classification of Pre-Qumranic Texts'. Pages 257–81 in *Archaeology and History in the Dead Sea Scrolls – The New York University Conference in Memory of Yigael Yadin*, edited by Lawrence H. Schiffman. JSPSup 8. JSOT/ASORMon 2. Sheffield: JSOT, 1990.
———. 'The Letter from Judah Maccabee to Aristobulus: Is 2 Maccabees 1:10b–2:18 Authentic?' *HUCA* 49 (1978): 89–133.
———. 'Pseudo-Eupolemus' Two Greek Fragments on the Life of Abraham'. *HUCA* 34 (1963): 83–113.
Watts, John D. W. *Isaiah 34–66*. Revised edn. WBC 25. Nashville: Thomas Nelson, 2000.
Webb, Barry G. *The Book of the Judges: An Integrated Reading*. JSOTSup 46. Sheffield: Sheffield Academic, 1987.
Weinfeld, Moshe. *Deuteronomy and the Deuteronomic School*. Oxford: Clarendon, 1983.
Weiser, Artur. *The Psalms*. London: SCM, 1962.
Weitzman, Steve. 'Why Did the Qumran Community Write in Hebrew?' *JAOS* 119 (1999): 35–45.
Wenham, Gordon J. *Genesis 16–50*. WBC 2. Nashville: Thomas Nelson, 2000.
———. 'The Structure and Date of Deuteronomy'. PhD diss., University of London, 1969.
Werman, Cana. 'The Canonization of the Hebrew Bible in Light of Second Temple Literature'. Pages 337–65 in *From Author to Copyist: Essays on the Composition, Redaction, and Transmission of the Hebrew Bible in Honor of Zipi Talshir*, edited by Cana Werman. Winona Lake: Eisenbrauns, 2015.
———, ed. *From Author to Copyist: Essays on the Composition, Redaction, and Transmission of the Hebrew Bible in Honor of Zipi Talshir*. Winona Lake: Eisenbrauns, 2015.
Westermann, Claus. *Genesis 37–50*. Translated by John C. Scullion S.J. Minneapolis: Augsburg Publishing House; London: SPCK, 1986.

———. *Isaiah 40–66*. Translated by M. G. Stalker. OTL. London: SCM, 1969.
Wevers, J. W. 'Barthélemy and Proto-Septuagint Studies'. *BIOSCS* 18 (1985): 16–38.
Whybray, R. N. *Isaiah 40–66*. NCB. London: Marshall, Morgan & Scott, 1981.
Williams, D. S. *The Structure of 1 Maccabees*. Washington, DC: The Catholic Biblical Association of America, 1999.
———. 'Recent Research in 1 Maccabees'. *CurBS* 9 (2001): 169–84.
Wolde, Ellen van. 'Trendy Intertextuality?' Pages 43–9 in *Intertextuality in Biblical Writings: Essays in Honour of Bas van Iersel*, edited by S. Draisma. Kampen: Kok, 1989.
Woods, Edward J. *Deuteronomy*. TOTC 5. Downers Grove, IL; Nottingham, UK: InterVarsity, 2011.
Woude, A. S. van der, and M. de Jonge. 'Messianic Ideas in Later Judaism'. *TDNT* 9:509–27.
Wright, Benjamin G. 'Sirach: To the Reader'. Pages 715–19 in *A New English Translation of the Septuagint*, edited by Albert Pietersma and Benjamin G. Wright. Oxford: Oxford University Press, 2007.
———. 'Translation Greek in Sirach in Light of the Grandson's Prologue'. Pages 75–94 in *The Texts and Versions of the Book of Ben Sira: Transmission and Interpretation*, edited by Jean-Sébastien Rey and Jan Joosten. JSJSup 150. Leiden: Brill, 2011.
Wright, N. T. *Jesus and the Victory of God*. COQG 2. London: SPCK, 1996.
———. *New Testament and the People of God*. COQG 1. London: SPCK, 1992.
———. *Paul and the Faithfulness of God*. COQG 4. London: SPCK, 2013.
Xeravits, Géza G. 'From the Forefathers to the 'Angry Lion'. Qumran and the Hasmoneans'. Pages 211–21 in *The Books of the Maccabees: History, Theology and Ideology: Papers of the Second International Conferences on the Deuterocanonical Books, Pápa, Hungary, 9–11 June, 2005*, edited by Géza G. Xeravits and József Zsengellér. JSJSup 118. Boston: Brill, 2007.
Xeravits, Géza G., and József Zsengellér, eds. *The Books of the Maccabees: History, Theology, Ideology – Papers of the Second International Conference on the Deuterocanonical Books, Pápa, Hungary, 9–11 June 2005*. JSJSup 118. Boston: Brill, 2007.
———. *Studies in the Book of Ben Sira. Papers of the Third International Conference on the Deuterocanonical Books, Shime'on Centre, Pápa, Hungary, 18–20 May, 2006*. JSJSup 127. Leiden: Brill, 2008.
Yadin, Yigael, ed. *Jerusalem Revealed: Archaeology in the Holy City, 1968–1974*. New Haven: Yale University Press, 1976.
Zeitlin, Solomon. *The First Book of Maccabees*. Translated by Sidney Tedesche. JAL. New York: Harper & Brothers, 1950.
Zellentin, Holger M. 'The End of Jewish Egypt: Artapanus and the Second Exodus'. Pages 131–51 in *Antiquity in Antiquity: Jewish and Christian Pasts in the Greco-Roman World*, edited by Gregg Gardner and K. L. Osterloh. TSAJ 123. Tübingen: Mohr Siebeck, 2008.
Zervos, George T. '1 Makkabees'. Pages 478–502 in *A New English Translation of the Septuagint: And the Other Greek Translations Traditionally Included in That Title*, edited by Albert Pietersma and Benjamin G. Wright. Oxford: Oxford University Press, 2007.

Index of References

Hebrew Bible/ Old Testament		*Exodus*		29.38-42	128, 151, 153
Genesis		1.11	35	30.7-8	127
1–2	210	2.11-15	86	30.8	127, 151, 153
6.4	43	5.14	35		
10.8	43	12.11	119	34.2	120, 150, 153
12.10-20	86	12.37	196		
14	86	12.42	196	34.13-14	103, 104, 134, 149, 153
14.5	43	14	121		
14.16	86	14.5-31	150, 152		
15.6	105, 149, 152	14.8	36	34.13	104, 134, 151, 153
		14.13	123		
22.1-19	104, 149, 152	14.30	123	34.24	143, 144, 152, 153
		15.1-17	196		
22.1	104	16.20	185	35.21	175
25.17	71	18.13-15	117	40.4-5	126, 127, 151, 153
34	86	18.13	171		
34.24	86	18.21	116–18, 150, 152	40.33	128
35.29	71				
37.18-24	86	18.25	116–18, 150, 152	*Leviticus*	
37.34	166	19.5	120	11.43	99, 100, 149, 153
39.7-12	105, 106, 149, 152	20.25	125, 151, 152	14.40	124, 149
				14.45	124, 149
41.1	34	23.25-33	205	17–26	205
41.39-45	106, 149, 152	23.26	211	20.25	99, 100, 149, 153
		23.32	162		
44.34	34	25–27	126	21.4	99
45.13	221	25.2	175	24.5-9	127
49	92	25.30	127, 128, 151, 152	26	205, 207
49.9-10	199			26.3-13	206
49.9	199	26.1-10	127	26.3-4	204
49.10	199	26.31-35	127	26.4-13	206
49.16	171	26.33	127, 128, 151, 152	26.4	202, 206
49.33	71			26.9	206, 207
50.8-9	196	26.36	127		
		29–30	141		

Leviticus (cont.)		25.11-13	106, 107, 149, 153	12.20	215, 217
26.12	206			13	103, 162, 165, 166, 185
26.14-39	206	25.11	188		
26.15	206	26.6-15	56		
26.25	206	27.16-23	107, 108, 149, 153	13.2	162, 165
26.40-45	206			13.6	162, 165
26.40	206	27.18-23	219	13.7-12	160
26.42	206	28.3-7	128, 151, 153	13.9	93, 94
26.44	206			13.13	42, 162, 165
26.45	206	31.12	196	17.2	166
		31.14	117	17.10-11	163
Numbers		32.12	107, 149	17.14-20	14
6.1-21	115	35.24	103	18.15	71
6.13	115, 150, 153	35.33	42	19.8-10	215
				19.8	217
7.10	129	*Deuteronomy*		20	224
7.84	129	1.13	118, 150, 153	20.1-9	119
10.8-9	116, 124, 131, 150, 151, 153			20.2-4	119, 150, 154
		1.15	117, 118, 150, 153		
				20.3	138
13–14	109	1.28	43	20.5-8	117, 118, 150, 154, 160
13.30	109, 150, 153	2.26-30	132, 149		
		3.5	140, 143, 152, 153		
13.33	43			20.10-18	132, 216
14.5-10	220	4.10-14	158	20.17	231
14.6-9	109, 150, 153	5.2-4	158	23.12-14	125
		5.32-33	163	27.5-6	125, 126, 151, 154, 160
14.24	109, 150, 153, 219	6.10-12	204		
		6.21-22	121		
14.30	109, 150, 153	7.2	162, 165, 216	28–32	157
				28–30	78, 157, 158, 165, 167, 214, 221, 229, 230
16.40	170	7.5	103, 104, 134, 151, 154		
20.14-20	131, 132, 151, 153				
20.24	71	7.8	121	28	93, 157, 205, 219
20.26	71	7.13	204		
21.21-23	132, 151, 153	7.18-19	120, 121, 150, 154	28.1-14	158
				28.1	214
21.23	132	8.7-10	204	28.4	204
22.3	138, 152, 153	9.12	166	28.11-12	204
		9.16	166	28.15-68	158
23.24	199	11.3-4	121	28.26	211
25.4	188	11.16	165	28.30	211
25.6-15	102, 103, 149, 153	11.28	166	28.45-68	159
		12.2-3	104	28.61	136
25.7-8	93	12.3	104	28.68	165

29–30	204	14.15	169	5.2	174, 175		
29	93	18.9	135	5.9	174, 175		
29.1	158	20.7	41	5.31	169, 170		
29.2-15	158	21.32	41	6.2-6	173		
29.9-15	158	22.10 Gk	41	6.14	171, 173		
29.13	205	22.11 Gk	41	6.25-27	176		
30	159, 204, 219, 224	22.19 Gk	40	6.25	104		
		23	92	6.28	104		
30.1-10	158	23.16	166	6.30	104		
30.1-2	94, 159	24.6	121	6.34-35	116, 176		
30.1	166	24.20	205	6.36-37	171, 200		
30.2	159	24.25	108, 149, 154	7	118		
30.5	208			7.2	176		
30.6	159			7.3	118		
30.9	204, 208	*Judges*		7.9–8.28	176		
30.11-20	158	2	173	7.18-22	116		
31.7-23	16	2.2	104	7.19-25	176		
31.19	157	2.3	173	7.19-24	176		
31.29	166	2.6–3.6	173	7.19	176		
32.26	142, 152, 154	2.11-23	142, 173	7.20	176		
		2.11-20	173	7.22	176		
33	92	2.11-15	173	7.23-24	176		
33.20	199	2.11	173	7.23	176		
33.22	199	2.13	173	7.25	176		
		2.14-15	173	8.27	177		
Joshua		2.16	171, 173	8.28	169		
1.2-10	107, 108, 149, 154	2.17	166	8.32	176		
		2.18	171, 173	10.1	171, 173		
1.2-9	219	2.19	173	10.2	171		
1.6-9	16	2.20	166	10.3	171		
4.23	121	3.7-8	173	10.7-9	173		
6.24	184	3.8	173	11.1	178		
7.16	131	3.9-11	173	11.2	178		
8.31	126, 136, 151, 154	3.9-10	171	11.7-8	178		
		3.10	171	11.8-11	179		
8.32	135	3.11	169	11.12-27	132		
10–11	216	3.12	173	11.17	132		
11.23	169	3.15	171	11.19	132		
12.4	43	3.15-30	173	11.29-40	177		
12.23	41	3.27	116	11.29	177, 179		
13.2 GK	41	3.30	169–71	11.31	179		
13.12	43	4.2	173	11.34-40	179		
14.5-10	219	4.4	171	11.39	179		
14.13-14	219	4.49	184	12.7	171		
14.15-16	109, 150, 154	4.52	184	12.8	171		
		5	118, 174	12.11	171		

Index of References

Judges (cont.)
12.13	171
13.1	173
13.5	171, 173
15.18	123, 171, 200
15.20	171
16.31	171
18.7	169
20.10	117

Ruth
1.13 Gk	185
1.20 Gk	185

1 Samuel
1–4	85
1.1	34
2.12	42
4.18	171
4.30	178
5.12	130, 131, 151, 154
7.5-6	115, 150
8.5	14
8.12	117
10.17	115
11.11	131
11.13	123
12	92
12.20	166
12.21	165
13.3	116
14.1-23	123, 124, 148, 150, 154
14.23	122, 123, 150, 154
14.45	122, 123, 150, 154
17	123
17.1-58	123, 124, 148, 150, 154
17.4 GK	123
17.4 Gk	123
17.51	123
19.5	123
22.18	135
24.4-8	110
25.28	34
26.5-12	110

2 Samuel
2.7	119, 145, 150, 154
3.18	170, 200
3.31	166
7	48
7.1-17	110, 150, 154
7.8-17	14
7.16	56
7.17	110
13.23	34
13.28	119, 145
15.11	113
15.11 Gk	113
18.2-3	117
21.11	43
21.22	43
23.10	123

1 Kings
1.40	221
2	92
2.27	107
3.28	171
4.20-28	224
4.25	211. 222, 224
5.5 Heb.	211, 222
6.1	85
8	136
8.1-66	151, 154
8.29-30	136, 137, 149
8.29	137
8.30	137
8.38	137
8.43	136, 137
8.59	137
8.65-66	129
9.3	137
9.11	41
14.19	48
14.29	48
16.14	48
16.27	48
18.10-40	111
18.17	137
18.18	184
19.10	111, 150, 154
19.14	111, 150, 154
19.35	137
21.17-29	111
21.20	5, 34, 165
21.25	34, 165
22.27	5, 132, 133, 151, 154
22.40	48
22.43	166
49.54	137

2 Kings
1.9-16	117
1.10-12	111
1.18	48
2.1	111, 112, 150, 154
2.11	111, 112, 150, 154
4.20	103
10.34	48
11.4	117
11.14	103
11.18	104
11.20	169
13.5	123
15.29	41
17.2-6	90
17.7-18	98
17.15	98
17.16	98
17.17	5, 34, 98, 149, 154, 165
17.34	135
17.37	135

18.6	166	29.9	175	32.1-22	71, 137, 138
18.9	90	29.14	175	32.7	138
18.12	166	29.17	113, 175	33.8	77
18.17– 19.37	137, 138, 152, 154	29.17 GK	113	34.14	77
		29.22	85	35.6	77
				35.12	77
18.17– 19.36	71	*2 Chronicles*		36.11-20	77
		1.3	77	36.21	107
19.35	137, 138, 154	3.2	85		
		5.10	77	*Ezra*	
21.20	98	6.1-42	151, 155	3.5	175
22.11–23.3	125	6.20-21	137, 149	3.11	122
23.4	124	6.29	137	6.3	85
23.4-27	125	6.33	137, 149	6.15	34
23.6	124, 125, 151, 154	7	128	6.16-17	129
		7.9	128, 129, 151, 155	7.13	175
23.12	104, 124			7.15	175
23.15	104	7.10	129	7.16	175
23.17	104	8.13	77	7.23	102
25.23	115	11.11	143	10.14	188
31.1	104	12.12	188	14.27	34
33.3	104	13.19	34		
34.4	104	13.23 Heb.	169	*Nehemiah*	
34.7	104	14.1	169	2.11	211
		14.4	104	6.15	34
1 Chronicles		14.5 Heb.	169	8.18	103
1.10	43	14.6	140, 143, 149, 169	9	80
2.7	184			9.6-37	77
4.40	169	15.1-9	195	9.9-10	121
6.34	77	17.16	175	11.2	175
6.76	41	18.26	5, 133, 151, 155	16.14	34
9.1	77				
11.14	123	19.8	171	*Esther*	
11.15	43	20.15	138	9.17-19	133
14.9	43	23.18	77		
15.15	77	24.6	77	*Job*	
16.41	122	24.9	77	27.2 Gk	185
21.29	77	25.4	77		
22.13	16, 77	25.5	117	*Psalms*	
23.15	77	29.3-19	125	1	32
24.6	135	29.10	188	34.17	142
24.7-19	57	29.16	125, 151, 155	37.35-36	114
24.7-18	6			72.2	222
26.24	77	29.17-18	129	72.3	222
28.20	16	29.17	129	72.4	222
29.5	175	30.8	188	72.12-13	222
29.6	175	30.16	77		

Psalms (cont.)		Proverbs		65.17	210
76.2-3	5	10.7	187	65.18	210
76.9	169	15.4	111	65.20	211
78	77, 79	29.26	133	65.21-22	211
78.5	79			66.6	131
78.7	79	Ecclesiastes		66.15	184
78.10-11	79	10.4	111	66.19	34
78.17	79				
78.30-32	79	Isaiah		Jeremiah	
78.36-37	79	1.26	171	2.2	110
78.56-58	79	3.2	43	4.31	102
79.2-3	134, 147,	5.29	200	18.20	188
	151, 155	8.7	221	19.13-14	124
105-106	79	8.9	119	23.1-6	206
105	77	8.23	129, 130	23.11	34
105.1-5	79	8.23 Heb.	41	26–29	210
105.5-6	79	8.23 Gk	41	28.38	200
105.7-11	79	9.1	41	30–31	210
105.38	42	11.4	222, 223	30	211
106	77, 79, 80	11.12	194	30.10	169, 211
106.1	122	12.1	122	30.18-21	208
106.9	121	13.3	43	31.2-6	208
106.23	188	14.4-22	114	31.6-12	195
106.38 Eng.	42	14.7	169	31.10-14	223
106.44-48	80	14.9	43, 185	31.10-13	209
106.44-46	80	17.4	183	31.12	210
106.44	80	19.6	183	31.13	210
106.47	79, 80, 196	20.4	196	31.23-30	208
107.1	122	25	133	31.27-28	206, 223
109.15	142	27.13	194	32.32	185
112.6	187	31.4	200	33.1-13	208
118.1	121, 150,	32.6	42	33.9	185
	155	35	196	33.11	122
118.29	121, 150,	35.10	133	36.27	135
	155	36–37	71	37.15	185
131	111	36.2	138	46.27	169
131.1 Gk	111	36.2–37.38	137, 152,	49.26	149
135	77, 80		154	49.29	101
135.9	121	37.36	137, 138,	50.30	101, 149
136	77		152, 154		
136.1	122	51.9-11	196	Lamentations	
136.15	121	51.11	133, 196	1	102
145.4 Gk	114	51.12-13	114	1.4	102
146.4	114, 150,	52.1	207	1.4 Gk	185
	155	52.11-12	133	1.10	102
		57.1-2	81	2.11	101, 102,
		65.17-23	210		149, 155

2.18	102	3.24 Gk	112	*Micah*	
2.21	101, 102, 149, 155	3.88 Gk	112	3.1–4.8	224
		3.95	113	3.1-12	213
4.7-10	102	6.17-24	113, 150, 155	3.10	213
5.1	102			3.12	213
5.15-18	99, 149, 155	6.22	113	4.1-8	213
5.15	99	7–12	100	4.1-3	213
5.16	102	9.16	188, 189	4.4	6, 43, 144, 152, 155, 211, 212, 222, 223
		9.27	100, 149, 155		
Ezekiel		11.9	114		
10.14	188	11.20	35	4.7-8	224
11.20	205	11.31	100, 149, 155	4.8	224
14.11	205			5.2-6	199
20.4-44	77	12.11	100, 101, 149, 155	5.8	199
28.25	217				
34–37	205			*Habakkuk*	
34	205	*Hosea*		1.9	196
34.1-24	205	2.21-23	206, 210, 224		
34.24	205			*Zephaniah*	
34.25-31	205	6.4	110	2.5-7	215, 217
34.25-30	206	6.6	110	2.5	215
34.25-29	205	14.4	188		
34.25-27	203, 223			*Haggai*	
34.25	205	*Joel*		1.10-11	210
34.27	202	1.6	200		
34.30	205	1.16	133	*Zechariah*	
36.28	205	3.4	40	1–8	205
37.23	205	3.4 Eng.	129	1–6	214
37.27	205	3.4 Gk	41	1.2	188
38.11	169	3.17 Eng.	141	1.7	34, 144–6, 152, 155
39.18	43	4.4	129, 130, 151, 154		
39.20	43			1.11	169
47.8 Gk	41	4.4 Gk	41	3.9	213
		4.4 Heb Gk	40	3.10	211–14, 222
Daniel		4.17	140, 141, 149	6.15	214
1.6-7	112, 113, 150, 155			7–8	214
1.7	112	*Amos*		7.1	34
1.11	112	8.10	98, 99, 139, 140, 149, 152, 154, 155	7.14	208
1.19	112			7.43	34
2.17	112			7.49	34
2.49	112			8	204, 208, 210, 211, 215
3	112	*Obadiah*			
3.1-30	112, 113, 150, 155	20–21	195	8.2-23	213
3.12-30	112			8.2-3	204
3.24	112			8.3-5	204

Zechariah (cont.)		11.29	121	46.2	219
8.4-5	6, 144, 152, 155, 207, 208	11.33-34	112	46.3	219
				46.5	219
		James		46.8	219
8.4	208, 223	2.21-24	105	46.11-12	187
8.6-8	204	2.23	105	47.16	221
8.10	204	5.10-11	77	48.21	71
8.12	6, 43, 144, 152, 155, 202, 203, 210, 212, 223, 226			49.9	59
		Revelation		50	81, 187
		5.5	199	50.5-21	81
				50.23	81
		APOCRYPHA			
8.13	205	*Tobit*		*Susanna*	
9.8	35	2.6	99	63 OG	113
10.4	35				
10.6-8	195	*Judith*		*Baruch*	
		5.5-21	77	3.3	194
Malachi		5.13	121		
3.23-24 Heb.	60, 71	5.25-26	104	*1 Maccabees*	
				1–13	30
4.5-6	71	*Wisdom of Solomon*		1–7	24
		1.1	113	1–2	102, 160
NEW TESTAMENT		10.1–12.27	77	1	42, 93, 188, 196, 209
Luke		10.18	121		
12.35	119	19.7	121	1.1–6.17	24
				1.1-10	53, 186
Acts		*Ecclesiasticus*		1.3	169
7.2-53	77	10.17	142	1.11-15	32, 172, 196
21.23	115	36.11	219	1.11	34, 42, 93, 161, 162, 164, 165
21.26	115	36.28	111		
		40–41	187		
Romans		41.12-13	187	1.12-15	165
4.3	105	44–50	69, 81, 93	1.15	5, 34, 93, 98, 149, 154, 161, 162, 165, 196, 209
		44–49	57, 59, 81, 187		
Galatians					
3.6	105	44.1-15	81, 187		
		44.8-15	81		
Ephesians		44.9	81	1.16-64	172
6.18	137	44.13-14	187	1.21-23	42
		44.20	93, 104	1.21	40
Philippians		45.5	93	1.24	42
4.6	137	45.17	93	1.25-28	4, 181
		45.26	81	1.26	181
Hebrews		46.1-10	220	1.28	35
11.2-39	77	46.1-8	219	1.29	34, 35
11.17	105	46.1	219	1.32	196

1.36-40	181	2.25	40, 103, 104	2.63	114, 150,
1.36	35	2.26	102, 103,		155
1.38-40	4		149, 153	2.66	178
1.38-39	102	2.27	93, 94, 162,	3–16	172
1.39-40	98		163, 166	3.1–9.27	181
1.39	99, 139, 149,	2.30	150	3.3-9	4, 181
	154, 155,	2.32-48	46	3.3-8	181
	181	2.37	113	3.3	35, 42, 184,
1.40	99	2.41-48	231		221, 226
1.43	160	2.42	178	3.4	197
1.47	40, 160	2.44	181	3.5-6	185
1.48	99, 100, 149,	2.45-48	68	3.5	184, 185
	153	2.45	40, 103, 104	3.6	184, 185,
1.51-64	68	2.47	34, 200		200
1.54-58	209	2.49-70	16, 92, 193	3.7	185–7, 221,
1.54	34, 40, 100,	2.49-68	4, 181		222
	101, 149,	2.49-60	77, 92	3.8	188, 216
	155, 160	2.49-51	93	3.9	35, 193, 194,
1.56-57	49	2.50	93, 94, 162–		221
1.56	160		4, 166, 174	3.12	51
1.57	93, 161	2.51-60	53	3.14	186
1.59	40, 100	2.52-60	46	3.15	35
1.63	161	2.52	104, 105,	3.18-22	4, 176
2	162, 172,		149, 152	3.27	185
	181	2.53	105, 106,	3.35	142
2.1	6, 57		149, 152,	3.41	35, 41
2.7-13	4, 102, 166,		160, 163	3.43-44	7
	181	2.54	8, 35, 106,	3.43	127
2.7-9	209		107, 149,	3.44	110
2.8	35		153, 162,	3.45-46	181
2.9	99, 101, 102,		232	3.45	181
	149, 155	2.55	107, 108,	3.46	115, 150,
2.11	102		149, 153,		154
2.12	102		154, 217,	3.47	127
2.14	166		219	3.48	49, 160
2.15-27	68	2.56	109, 150,	3.49	115, 127,
2.20	94, 162, 164,		153, 154,		150, 153
	166		219	3.50-53	4, 181
2.22	160, 163	2.57	11, 14, 110,	3.51	102
2.23	40		150, 154,	3.54	116, 124,
2.24-26	102		232		131, 150,
2.24	40, 102, 103,	2.58	46, 111, 150,		153, 176
	122, 149,		163	3.55-60	119
	153, 160	2.59	112, 113,	3.55	116–18, 150,
2.25-26	103, 134,		150, 155		152, 153
	149, 153	2.60	113, 155		

Index of References

1 Maccabees (cont.)

Ref	Pages
3.56	117, 118, 122, 150, 154
3.58	34, 119, 120, 145, 150, 153, 154
3.59	46
4.8-11	4
4.8-9	120, 121, 150, 152, 154
4.9	35
4.10-11	163
4.12	41
4.14	176
4.19	35
4.22	41
4.24	35, 121, 122, 150, 155, 181
4.25	122, 123, 150, 154
4.26	41
4.30-33	181
4.30	41, 123, 124, 148, 150, 154
4.36-58	176
4.38	40, 181
4.40	116, 124, 151, 153, 176
4.43	124-26, 149, 151, 154, 155
4.44	40
4.45	40
4.47	40, 122, 125, 126, 151, 152, 154, 160
4.49	40, 126, 151, 153
4.50	40, 127, 151, 153
4.51	127, 128, 151, 152
4.52	34
4.53	40, 128, 151, 153
4.56	40, 128, 151, 155
4.58	195
4.59	7, 34, 40, 194, 196
5	40
5.1	40
5.5	194
5.6	194
5.7	194
5.15	40, 41, 129, 130, 151, 154
5.16	7
5.21-22	215
5.23	6, 12, 194, 195
5.30-33	35
5.31	130, 131, 151, 154, 176
5.32	131
5.33	116, 131, 151, 153, 176
5.34	131
5.45	6, 12, 196, 215
5.48	131, 132, 149, 151, 153
5.53-54	6, 12
5.54	5, 132, 133, 151, 155, 194, 196
5.56	51, 69
5.62	8, 170, 200
5.66-68	215
5.66	30, 41
5.68	40, 41, 103, 104, 134, 151, 153, 154
6.7	40, 160
6.10-13	4
6.11-13	185
6.13	34
6.18–14.15	24
6.21	35
6.28	185
6.31	69
6.34-35	116
6.34	35
6.37	36
6.59-62	28
6.63–7.2	28
7	196
7.1	185
7.4	53
7.5-50	8
7.16-17	5, 147
7.17	134, 151, 155, 181
7.26-50	7
7.33	35
7.36	40
7.37	136, 137, 149, 151, 154, 155, 160
7.41	137, 138, 152, 154
7.42	171
7.45-50	176
7.45-48	7
7.45	176
7.46	176
7.47	176
7.48-49	7
7.48	195
7.50	168, 169
8	19, 24, 25, 32
8.1-16	19, 47, 49, 52, 55
8.1	164
8.2	51, 52
8.4	53
8.5	53

8.6	52, 53	9.57	168, 169	12.38	143
8.7	164	9.70-72	196	12.39	53
8.8	52	9.70	12, 164	12.53	142, 152, 154, 172
8.9-10	52	9.72	10, 12		
8.11-13	53	9.73	142, 169, 171	13.1–16.17	181
8.11	53			13.1-6	179
8.12	53	10–11	19	13.2-6	174
8.13	53	10.15	51, 69	13.3-6	53
8.14	48, 49, 53, 55, 227, 230	10.19	178	13.3	8
		10.25-45	140	13.11	215
8.17-20	85	10.26	164	13.25-26	192
8.17	164	10.31	140, 141, 149	13.27-30	50, 53, 55, 227
8.20	164				
8.26	164	10.33	12	13.30	48
8.28	164	10.38	141, 215	13.32	53
8.29	36, 164	10.47	51	13.33	140, 143, 149, 152, 153
8.31-32	25	10.52-53	53		
9–11	24	10.54	164		
9	25	10.65	69	13.38	164
9.1	25	10.72	35	13.41-53	202
9.6	138, 152, 153	10.84	104	13.43-52	231
		11	186	13.43-48	215
9.8	138	11.9	164	13.43-47	215
9.9-10	46	11.13	53	14–16	25
9.10	4, 69	11.28	215	14.4-15	3, 181
9.12	116	11.33	164, 171	14.4	51, 168–70, 221, 223
9.19	176	11.34	34		
9.21	181	11.38	168, 169	14.5-7	196, 215
9.22	51, 69	11.49	34	14.5	221
9.23-27	172	11.52	53, 168, 169	14.6	143–5, 152, 153, 215, 217, 219
9.23	172	11.54	53		
9.24	35, 172	11.59	69		
9.27	192	11.60-62	215	14.7	12, 185, 196
9.28–12.53	181	11.65-66	215	14.8-15	4
9.28	172, 179	11.66	143	14.8-14	219
9.36	139	11.68	41	14.8	6, 43, 143, 144, 152, 155, 202, 206, 212, 214, 223
9.41	99, 139, 140, 152, 155, 181	11.74	41		
		12.1-23	24, 32		
		12.1	164		
9.43-53	231	12.6-7	19		
9.43-49	46	12.9	49	14.9	6, 143, 144, 152, 155, 202, 207, 214, 223
9.44	35	12.16	73		
9.50	140, 143, 152, 153	12.24–14.15	24		
		12.32-34	215		
9.52	143	12.33	215	14.10	221
9.54-56	70	12.35	143	14.11	186, 195, 221

1 Maccabees (cont.)		16.23-24	9, 46, 50, 53, 54, 227	30	86	
14.12	6, 43, 143, 144, 152, 155, 202, 211, 212, 214, 223	16.23	48, 51	39.6-7	106	
		26–26	103	39.6	106	
				Letter of Aristeas		
		2 Maccabees		Frag. 3	37	
14.13	222	1.10–2.18	49, 62			
14.14	185, 222, 223	2.13-15	49, 62	*Liber Antiquitatum Biblicarum*		
		2.14	49			
14.16– 16.24	24–6	4.1-2	69	6	105	
		4.11	85			
14.18	164	5.24	35	*Psalms of Solomon*		
14.24	164	6.2	101	2.13	103	
14.25-49	69	7.20	194	17	48	
14.25-47	10	8.16-20	120			
14.26	8	8.19	71, 137	*Testament of Levi*		
14.27-28	179	8.21-22	116	6.3	87	
14.28	7	10.2	103, 104	6.6-7	87	
14.29	6, 71, 174	11.11	200	6.8	87	
14.30	71	12.2	35			
14.31	71	12.31	196	*Testament of Moses*		
14.33-34	143	15.22-24	71	2	157	
14.33	215	15.22	137	3.1-4	157	
14.34	215			3.5–4.4	157	
14.36	71	PSEUDEPIGRAPHA		4.5-6	157	
14.41-45	48	*3 Maccabees*		5.1-6	157	
14.41	10, 71	3.21	113	8	157	
15.1-14	25	5.2	36	9	157	
15.25– 16.24	25	5.10	36	10	157	
		5.45	36			
15.27	164	6	80	DEAD SEA SCROLLS		
15.32	221	6.5	71	*1QM*		
15.33-35	216, 219	6.6	112	2.15–3.11	116	
15.36	221	16.21	112	2.15-17	117	
15.38	69	18.12	112	10.7-8	116	
15.40	196			11.1-3	123	
16.1-3	192	*Jubilees*		11.9-10	121	
16.2-3	53, 174	1	157	15.7	119, 145	
16.2	8	17.17-18	105			
16.3	36	23.16-32	157	*1QS*		
16.8	116	23.16-21	157	2.19-22		
16.9-10	196	23.16	163	2.21-22	117	
16.11-17	12, 48	23.22-25	157			
16.14	144, 152, 155	23.26	157	*4Q397*		
		23.27-31	157	Frag. 14-20		
16.16-17	192	23.32	157	col. 10	61	
16.18-22	12					

Philo
De vita Mosis
2.25-44	37
2.292	87

Josephus
Against Apion
1.38-40	58
1.40	59
1.218	85

Jewish Antiquities
12–14	30
12.4	72
12.5–13.7	26
12.6-11	72
12.186-236	72
12.261	69
12.353	30
12.415	85
13.3	73
13.11	73
13.249-81	48
13.254-258	215
13.275-279	215
13.288-298	220
13.318-19	195
13.318	73
13.372	220
14.149-155	69
20.95	74

Jewish War
1.57-66	48
2.577-78	117
5.375-93	77
5.388	71

Mishnah
'Abot
5.3	105

Megillah
1.10-11	115

Soṭah
8.1	123

Babylonian Talmud
Shabbat
19a	46

Yoma
85b	46

Tosefta
'Erubin
3.7	46

Classical and Ancient Christian Literature
Artapanus
Frags. 1–3	83
Frag. 2 par 23.4	83
Frag. 3 par 23-25	83

Augustine
City of God
18.42	37

Clement
Stromata
1.141.1-2	87, 89
1.141.4	84, 91
1.22.148	37
1.23.154.2-3	83

Demetrius
Frags. 1–5	87
Frag. 2	90
Frag. 6	87, 88

Diodorus
10.6	69
11.5	69
17.6.2	69

Eupolemus
Frags. 1–4	84
Frag. 2 par 33	85
Frag. 5	84, 85

Eusebius
Demonstratio evangelica
10.1.12	135

Historia ecclesiastica
6.25	32

Praeparatio evangelica
9	82
9.17.2-4	84
9.17.4-9	86
9.17.4-5	86
9.17.8-9	84
9.18.1	83
9.19.4	87
9.21.1-19	87
9.21.3-5	88
9.21.13	88
9.21.18	90
9.22.4-6	86
9.22.7	86
9.22.9	86
9.23.1-4	83
9.23.2	83
9.26.1	84
9.27.1-37	83
9.27.3-6	84
9.29.1-3	87
9.29.15	87
9.29.16	87, 88
9.30.1-34.18	84
9.30.8	85
9.34.4	85
9.34.20	84
9.39.2-5	84
10	82
13	82
13.12.1-2	37

Herodotus
History
6.80	184
8.35-39	70

Irenaeus
Against Heresies
3.21.3	37
4.32.2	105

Isocrates
Philippus
134-135   69

Pausanius
History
10.23.1-10   70

Plato
Republic
427D-435A 69

Polybius
1.31.8   69

Prologus Galeatus
28.593-604 33

Tertullian
Apology
18   37

Theodotus
Frag. 4   86

INSCRIPTIONS
Cathedral Library
B IV 6 fol. 169   28

Index of Authors

Abegg Jr., M. G. 191
Abel, F.-M. 3, 50, 92, 96, 101, 103, 106, 107, 110–15, 117, 119, 121, 125, 126, 129, 135, 137, 143, 162, 165, 168, 183, 184, 186–8, 194, 196, 197, 200, 202, 211, 222
Ackroyd, P. R. 57, 189, 190
Aitken, J. K. 65
Allen, L. C. 205–7, 210
Arenhoevel, D. 11, 12
Assis, E. 177
Attridge, H. 47, 82
Avigad, N. 74

Babota, V. 47, 48
Bakhtin, M. M. 23
Baltes, G. 45
Bar-Kochva, B. 36, 40, 47, 117, 216, 217, 220
Barag, D. 48
Barr, J. 45
Bartlett, J. R. 3, 6–8, 15, 19, 25, 28–30, 33, 40, 45, 51, 92, 93, 96, 97, 102, 105, 106, 110, 112, 114, 115, 121, 126–30, 143, 163, 176, 182, 183, 192, 197, 220
Beckwith, R. T. 59, 63
Ben Zvi, E. 20, 77
Berlin, A. M. 73
Bernstein, M. J. 60, 61
Berrin, S. L. 61
Berthelot, K. 217, 218
Bewer, J. A. 204
Bickerman, E. J. 14, 18, 47, 70
Black, J. S. 4, 19, 48, 50, 51, 93, 96, 103, 104, 107, 109, 110, 113, 117, 119, 121, 122, 127, 129, 130, 133, 135, 142, 162, 168, 183, 184, 187, 188, 194, 196, 197, 200, 219

Blenkinsopp, J. 211
Boling, R. G. 168, 173, 177
Borchardt, F. 24, 26, 55, 56, 160, 163, 166
Brooke, G. J. 61
Broughton, T. R. S. 25
Bruyne, D. D. 29, 131, 136, 193
Bryan, S. M. 190
Burney, C. F. 183

Campbell, J. G. 63
Cancik, H. 71
Carson, D. A. 190
Chang, D. D. 161
Charlesworth, J. H. 82
Chester, A. 11
Choi, D. 52
Clayton, J. 22, 23
Cohen, S. J. D. 26
Collins, J. J. 10, 11, 66, 73, 83, 96, 110, 117, 126, 173, 224
Conybeare, F. C. 34
Cook, S. L. 205
Corley, J. 80, 81
Craigie, P. C. 159

Dahood, M. 80
Dalman, G. 44, 45
Dancy, J. R. 6, 19, 45, 46, 96, 101, 103, 104, 107, 110, 115, 125, 129, 132, 135, 141, 143, 182, 183, 192, 193, 197
Davila, J. R. 40
Deines, R. 10, 63, 176, 195
Destinon, J. 25, 26
Di Lella, A. A. 58–60, 81
Dimant, D. 61, 97, 146–8
Dines, J. M. 28, 29, 31, 37–9
Docherty, S. E. 37–9, 157

Doran, R. 4, 8, 10, 16, 33, 48, 53, 70, 84, 96, 99, 105–12, 115, 119, 121, 124, 126, 129, 130, 132, 139, 162, 163, 165, 168, 170, 173, 184, 186, 188, 192, 194, 195, 197, 199, 200, 202, 216, 219

Eshel, H. 62, 200
Ettelson, H. W. 26, 33, 35, 42

Fairweather, W. 4, 19, 48, 50, 51, 93, 96, 103, 104, 107, 109, 110, 113, 117, 119, 121, 122, 127, 129, 130, 133, 135, 142, 162, 168, 183, 184, 187, 188, 194, 196, 197, 200, 219
Fallon, F. 85, 86, 91
Feldman, L. H. 30, 65, 191
Fine, S. 73–5
Finkielsztein, G. 48
Fischer, T. 6, 12, 47
Fishbane, M. A. 146
Floyd, M. H. 22, 59
Fraser, P. M. 89
Frösén, J. 31
Fyfe, T. 73

Gafni, I. M. 30
Gardner, G. 10, 68–71
Geiger, A. 44
Goldingay, J. 79
Goldstein, J. A. 13, 14, 25, 29, 30, 33, 34, 40, 41, 49–52, 62, 67, 68, 70, 92, 96–9, 103, 107–12, 114, 119, 121, 122, 130–3, 135, 138, 141, 168, 170, 171, 183, 184, 187, 191, 194, 197, 198, 202, 207, 215, 217, 218, 221, 222
Gorman Jr., F. H. 206
Grabbe, L. L. 57–9, 65, 161
Greenspoon, L. J. 38
Grimm, C. L. W. 3, 30, 48, 50, 96, 100, 103, 107, 109, 110, 112, 116, 117, 121, 126, 130, 141, 142, 193
Grove, P. B. 26
Gruen, E. S. 25, 66

Hague, W. V. 11
Hals, A. M. 206
Hanson, J. 87, 88, 90
Harrington, D. J. 3
Hendin, D. 74
Hengel, M. 65

Henten, J. W. van 8, 10, 70, 171
Hieke, T. 56, 97
Higbie, C. 70
Hillers, D. R. 213
Himmelfarb, M. 55, 67–9, 72, 97, 170, 183, 223
Holladay, C. R. 82–5, 88, 89
Horbury, W. 11
Huizinga, J. 18

Ilan, T. 72

Jacobson, D. M. 75
Japhet, S. 77
Jellicoe, S. 29, 38, 39, 168
Jensen, M. H. 195
Jobes, K. H. 28, 31, 38
Jonge, M. de 11, 224
Joosten, J. 43, 44
Joyce, P. M. 205

Kappler, W. 28, 34, 193
Kasher, A. 216
Keil, C. F. 4, 19, 96, 103, 106, 107, 109, 110, 112, 116, 121, 128, 130, 142, 193
Kilpatrick, G. D. 28, 31–3
Kindler, A. 74, 75
Klausner, J. 200
Kooij, A. van der 49, 59, 62, 63, 97, 199
Koole, J. L. 59
Krentz, E. 70
Kristeva, J. 21–3
Kugel, J. L. 146

Laato, A. 11
Lange, A. 59, 63, 64, 96, 97, 146–8
Lau, A. Y. 71
Leibner, U. 195
Leiman, S. Z. 63
Lemche, N. P. 57
Levine, L. I. 65, 73
Lieu, J. 68
Lim, T. H. 61, 63, 158
Lindars, B. 168, 173, 175

Machiela, D. A. 72
Marcos, N. F. 38, 39
Marcus, J. 141
Martola, N. 24, 25, 181
Mason, R. 208

Mason, S. 26
Maxwell-Stuart, P. G. 36
Mays, J. L. 200
McCarthy, S. J. 158
McKane, W. 213
McKeating, H. 224
Mendels, D. 16–18, 53, 65–8, 72, 217, 219
Mendenhall, G. E. 158
Meshorer, Y. 74, 75
Metzger, B. M. 28
Milgrom, J. 205
Milik, J. T. 45
Millar, F. 65, 68
Miller, G. D. 22
Mitchell, H. G. T. 204, 214
Momigliano, A. 47, 52, 53, 65

Neuhaus, G. O. 3, 12, 181
Newsom, C. A. 77, 78
Nicholson, E. W. 157
Nickelsburg, G. W. E. 3, 157, 160, 202, 224
Niditch, S. 175, 177
Niehoff, M. R. 88
Nongbri, B. 160

O'Connell, K. G. 65
Oesterley, W. O. E. 5, 34, 45–7, 51, 93, 96, 103, 109, 111, 112, 125, 130, 141, 142, 183, 200
Orlinksy, H. M. 59

Palmer, L. R. 31
Peters, M. K. H. 168
Peterson, D. L. 204, 208, 209
Pfeiffer, R. H. 6, 7, 33, 34, 40, 42, 44, 46, 97, 171, 192
Philips, A. 158
Pomykala, K. E. 11
Porter, S. E. 157
Pritchett, K. W. 70

Qimron, E. 62

Rad, G. von 158
Rahmani, L. Y. 74
Rajak, T. 14, 37, 67–9, 75

Rappaport, U. 3, 7, 8, 10, 19, 25, 46–8, 53, 96, 118, 129, 130, 143, 165, 171, 182, 196, 216
Redditt, P. L. 223
Regev, E. 15, 47, 74, 75
Revell, E. J. 167
Ricoeur, P. 78
Romanoff, P. 75
Roo, J. C. R. de 157
Rothstein, E. 22, 23

Safrai, Z. 216
Satlow, M. L. 66
Schiffman, L. H. 62
Schneider, H. 71
Schniedewind, W. M. 17
Schorch, S. 63
Schunck, K.-D. 171, 183, 193
Schürer, E. 3, 19, 33, 49, 50, 73, 82
Schwartz, D. R. 10, 19, 26, 29–31, 33–6, 42, 62, 63, 71
Schwartz, S. 45, 47, 192, 231
Scott, J. M. 190, 191
Shaw, C. S. 213, 224
Sievers, J. 10, 48
Silva, M. 28, 31, 38
Simpson, J. A. 26
Skehan, P. W. 58–60, 81
Smith, J. M. P. 204, 213, 214
Smith, M. 11
Smith, R. L. 208
Soggin, J. A. 167, 173, 177
Soisalon-Soininen, J. 168
Sommer, B. D. 22
Stead, M. R. 214
Stern, M. 9, 25, 48
Stock, St. G. 34
Strugnell, J. 62
Swete, H. B. 29

Tcherikover, V. 65–7, 69, 73, 216
Tilly, M. 8, 9, 96, 102–104, 107, 109–12, 115, 122, 125, 128–30, 139, 143, 163, 194, 197, 206, 211, 217
Tomes, R. 69, 183
Tov, E. 39, 40

Ulrich, E. 61

Van Seters, J. 18
VanderKam, J. C. 191
Vermeylen, J. 80

Wacholder, B. Z. 45, 62, 84
Watts, J. D. W. 211
Webb, B. G. 177
Weigold, M. 96, 97, 146–8
Weiner, E. S. C. 26
Weinfeld, M. 163, 165, 173, 205, 214
Weiser, A. 79
Weitzman, S. 45
Wenham, G. J. 158, 199
Werman, C. 61, 62
Westermann, C. 199, 210, 211

Wevers, J. W. 39
Whybray, R. N. 211
Williams, D. S. 24, 25, 30
Wolde, E. van 22
Woods, E. J. 158, 159
Woude, A. S. van der 224
Wright, B. G. 58–60
Wright, N. T. 76, 189–92, 198

Xeravits, G. G. 200

Zeitlin, S. 4, 46, 96, 110, 115, 119, 129, 130
Zellentin, H. M. 83
Zervos, G. T. 34

Printed in the USA
CPSIA information can be obtained
at www.ICGtesting.com
LVHW021520140624
783255LV00001B/105